SANCTITY AND MOTHERHOOD

GARLAND MEDIEVAL CASEBOOKS
VOLUME 14
GARLAND REFERENCE LIBRARY OF THE HUMANITIES
VOLUME 1767

GARLAND MEDIEVAL CASEBOOKS

JOYCE E. SALISBURY AND CHRISTOPHER KLEINHENZ
Series Editors

SEX IN THE MIDDLE AGES
A Book of Essays
edited by Joyce E. Salisbury

MARGERY KEMPE
A Book of Essays
edited by Sandra J. McEntire

THE MEDIEVAL WORLD OF NATURE
A Book of Essays
edited by Joyce E. Salisbury

SAINT AUGUSTINE THE BISHOP
A Book of Essays
edited by Fannie LeMoine
and Christopher Kleinhenz

SOVEREIGN LADY
*Essays on Women in
Middle English Literature*
edited by Muriel Whitaker

THE CHESTER MYSTERY CYCLE
A Casebook
edited by Kevin J. Harty

MEDIEVAL NUMEROLOGY
A Casebook
edited by Robert L. Surles

MANUSCRIPT SOURCES
OF MEDIEVAL MEDICINE
A Book of Essays
edited by Margaret R. Schleissner

FOOD IN THE MIDDLE AGES
A Book of Essays
edited by Melitta Weiss Adamson

SANCTITY AND MOTHERHOOD
*Essays on Holy Mothers
in the Middle Ages*
edited by Anneke B. Mulder-Bakker

Sanctity and Motherhood
Essays on Holy Mothers in the Middle Ages

Edited by
Anneke B. Mulder-Bakker

Garland Publishing, Inc.
New York and London
1995

Library of Congress Cataloging-in-Publication Data

Sanctity and motherhood : essays on holy mothers in the Middle Ages / edited
by Anneke B. Mulder-Bakker.
      p.   cm. — (Garland reference library of the humanities ; v. 1767.
Garland medieval casebooks ; v. 14)
    Includes bibliographical references (p.   ).
    ISBN 0-8153-1425-6 (alk. paper)
    1. Christian women Europe—History. 2. Mothers—Europe—His-
tory. 3. Christian saints—Europe—History. 4. Motherhood—Religious
aspects—Christianity—History of doctrines—Middle Ages, 600–1500.
5. Europe—Church history—600–1500. I. Mulder-Bakker, Anneke B.
II. Series: Garland reference library of the humanities ; vol. 1767. III. Series: Garland reference library of the humanities. Garland medieval casebooks ; vol. 14.
BX4656.S32   1995
274'.0085'2—dc20   95-13824
                                                    CIP

Cover Illustration: Holy Kinship of Saint Anne. Southern Netherlands, 15th c.
Courtesy of Museum voor Schone Kunsten, Ghent

Printed on acid-free, 250-year-life paper
Manufactured in the United States of America

CONTENTS

Acknowledgments

This book began with Mother Saint Anne benignly smiling at us from dozens of late medieval paintings, with all her Kinship around her, and from statues with her daughter and grandson on her lap. She stayed with us full term from the very conception of the book until its completion.

An exhibition in 1992, devoted to her cult and initiated by the Anne-expert Ton Brandenbarg, induced us to organize a symposium on Holy Mothers and led us to discover how intriguing and rewarding the history of sanctity and motherhood, the study of Holy Mothers, is. We looked for an opportunity to more comprehensively study these themes for Northern Europe in the Middle Ages. We are grateful that Garland Publishing enabled us to do so.

We, the Dutch équipe, received much material and immaterial support both in The Netherlands and in the United States. The Royal Dutch Academy of Sciences (KNAW), endowed the translation costs of contributions by senior researchers, the Rijksuniversiteit Groningen—both the EEVA-Commissie and the Werkgroep Vrouwenstudies Letteren—subsidized the junior female authors. Anja Petrakopoulos, Van der Wilden-Fall and Kofod translated the Introduction and chapters 2, 5 and 7 respectively.

We experienced it as a great compliment that Clarissa W. Atkinson, author of *The Oldest Vocation: Christian Motherhood in the Middle Ages* (1991) accepted the invitation to write an epilogue. Joyce Salisbury, as editor of the Medieval Casebooks series was a great support. Mary Prindiville probably does not realize how her careful reading of the texts and her final editing brought reassurance and peace of mind to the Dutch editor.

Anneke B. Mulder-Bakker
Groningen
Saint Anne's Day, 1994

Landgravina Saint Elizabeth breastfeeding one of her two little children, bids her husband Landgrave Louis farewell. Panel 15 of the Elizabeth cycle in the Heiligen-Geist-Hospital in Lübeck (Germany) (Heiligen-Geist-Hospital)

PART I
INTRODUCTION

Figure 1.1. Saint Regina and her ten virgin daughters. Engraving in Heribert Rosweyde, Generale Legende *(Antwerp, 1649)*. *(U.B. Groningen)*

1. INTRODUCTION

Anneke B. Mulder-Bakker
in collaboration with
Mireille Madou (iconography)

In his *Legends of the Saints (Generale Legenden der Heiligen)*, the founder of modern hagiographical research Heribert Rosweyde (1569–1629) described the life of Saint Regina. Published in 1619, Rosweyde's *Vita* is the first known account of her life. According to this, Regina, a noble Saxon woman, wife of Count Adalbert of Oostervant, was the epitome of a saintly mother (fig. 1.1). She gave birth to ten daughters, who, carefully nurtured in religion by the saint, all became consecrated virgins of God. They entered the monastery their mother founded for them in Denain, part of Adalbert's territory in what is now Northern France. Her daughter Ragenfreda was its first abbess and Regina herself was buried there.[1]

We could cynically remark that Regina as a married woman practiced what the Church Father Jerome preached: the only merit a wife could aim for was to bring forth pious virgins. In the *Generale Legende*, however, Saint Regina has more to her credit than childbearing alone. The name Regina was fit for this saint, so writes Rosweyde, for she was not only royal by birth, but also in character. Furthermore, she had devoted herself to Mary, the Queen of Heaven. She behaved as a woman of rank and quality should: she was an obedient daughter, a submissive wife, and a good mother. Together with her husband, she lived a pious life and did many works of charity. For her, marital love and love for God were parts of one whole.[2] In reward, God bestowed upon Regina the blessing of wealth in goods and property and an offspring of ten virgin daughters. Regina seems to outdo Saint Anne, who in the course of the Middle Ages became (only) thrice a mother, as Brandenbarg explains in the first study in this collection.

From the eleventh century on, a modest-sized local cult of Saint Regina can be traced, whereby *lectiones* were read in the monastery of Denain on her feast day, the first of July. Rosweyde based his epitomy on these readings. In historical sources, however, there is neither trace of Regina, nor of her husband Count Adalbert. The only documented personage is Ragenfreda, who appears in a charter of 877 as foundress and first abbess of the Denain monastery. Regina appears to be a fiction, a legend which provided abbess Ragenfreda with holy antecedents.[3]

Such a phantasm is intriguing for our purposes. A figure like Saint Regina represents all that clerical authors such as Rosweyde believed an ideal mother to be: she is a stereotype of the mother saint. Like Saint Anne, who also received a *curriculum vitae* of her own in the transition from the medieval to the early modern period, Regina was a model saintly mother. Her *Life* encapsulates the ideology of sanctified motherhood in the late Middle Ages and early modern period.

It is significant that to introduce *Sanctity and Motherhood* I must resort to a fiction like Saint Regina. The usual corpus of "sacred biographies"[4] contains almost no mother saints, that is, saints whose sanctity is based on motherhood. One may cite the overwhelming popular Virgin Mother Mary and her mother Saint Anne, along with the complete Holy Kinship, but the life stories of these mother saints are also essentially phantasms. Beyond Mary and Anne, both sanctified for their role of mother to key figures in salvation history, what examples of mother saints do we have? There were, of course, saints who were mothers, but they were honored at the altar despite rather than because of their children. There are moreover very few of these.

Delooz, in his sociological studies of saints, found but sixteen married among canonized saints, of whom five were parents, three women and two men. Weinstein and Bell came up with the same number in their well-known study: indeed, they drew their sample of saints from Delooz's corpus and studied them in more detail. In the later Middle Ages it appears that more women, and among them more married women and mothers, were canonized. Vauchez, who studied all the canonization trials of the thirteenth to sixteenth centuries came up with 25% or even 28% in the thirteenth and fourteenth centuries[5]—Elizabeth of Thuringia is the first, Birgitta of Sweden the most famous of these late medieval saints, both studied in this volume. Why are there so few? And what is more, can we really compare these few to the mother saints Mary and Anne? Are we, in other words, justified to term them *mother saints*, as defined in this volume? As I will argue below, it seems more apt to term them *holy mothers*, that is holy women whose public role in society was based on their status as spouse and mother; it was this status of motherhood that gave them entrance to the public sphere (in a similar way as entering the job-market does now) and this opened for them the road to sanctitude.

The articles here presented offer some new food for thought. Firstly, we have the studies of Ida of Boulogne, Ivetta of Huy, Elizabeth of Thuringia, and Birgitta of Sweden. Ivetta of Huy, an early thirteenth-century patrician widow, whom I have studied in this volume, appears to have continued an intense contact with her family after she became a recluse. Indeed, after the ritual of enclosure Ivetta was seen as a mouthpiece of God; she became a *sapientissima mater* for community, clergy, *and* kin. In her study of Elizabeth of Thuringia, Petrakopoulos notes that there is a discrepancy between the role marriage and motherhood played in the life of Elizabeth and their role in the later symbolization of the saint. Marriage and motherhood did not hinder Elizabeth from attaining holy charisma in her lifetime, but in hagiography these aspects are not portrayed as an integral part of her sanctity. Petrakopoulos can ascertain this because of the nature of the sources about Elizabeth: in her case we do not have to rely on polished images presented by learned Church clergy. This is something to remember. Nieuwland shows how Birgitta of Sweden imparts to her readers her personal ideas and conceptions, her worries and doubts. She shows us how Birgitta spontaneously uses maternal imagery to describe the concept of God, and she also shows how Birgitta finds succour in the Holy Mother Mary during labor and how she learns from Anna to depend on saints who themselves have been mothers. In the lives of Ivetta, Elizabeth and Birgitta, the links between holiness and motherhood are apparent, in their *Vitae*, much less so. Ida of Boulogne, studied by Nip, is the only woman who owed her sainthood to her sons, the famous leaders of the First Crusade and the first Kings of Jerusalem. She is rightly called a mother saint. To distinguish her from the others, I allot the term holy mothers to the latter.

Secondly, in late medieval sources religious phenomena are described which had until then no recorded history, religious phenomena which concern sanctity and motherhood. The studies of Brandenbarg and Tilmans show that late medieval people, even learned humanists, honored Mary and Anne in an immensely popular cult. These mother saints somehow answered the devotional needs of medieval people, and their cults induce us to reconsider the link between sanctity and motherhood.

We need to take a critical look at the nature of the sources. Medieval history is a history made up of several layers. At the bottom we have the chaotic and dispersed traces of life: artifacts like a kitchen spoon or a child's shoe, which have survived by accident and were not meant to tell a story. There are also layers made up for the needs of the moment, texts to inform, to instruct, to recreate; or for the short term memory, such as city accounts. Hagiography and historiography on the other hand were intended to preserve events of the past for the long term, and often enough the writers explain they are writing these events down because they should not be forgotten. These sources also serve the needs of the moment, but in a different way. Asking just how they did, what they selected for preservation and what they chose to omit, in other words, a critical assessment of these sources, is a crucial part of our work.

Our sources, however, have not only undergone processes of omission and selection during their creation. There is also the process of transmission, which can be happenstance, casual, or, and for hagiography this is of vital importance, a conscious, concerted, group effort to collect and preserve. As we will see, the *Acta Sanctorum*, a source on which medievalists rely, is in fact a collection of saints' lives of the seventeenth and later centuries. Thus Counter-Reformational choices also color our view of medieval history, and in the present case, of the relation between sanctity and motherhood. Another factor contributing to the selective view sources can give us is that different groups in medieval society reached different levels of literacy and subsequently have left different degrees of documentation. In the early Middle Ages especially, the pen was wielded by clergy and monks. Only that which pertained to them was set down on parchment. Other sectors of society—and this applies as well for the later Middle Ages—were predominantly oral; they left hardly any written records. Studies in the field of institutional history show that it is especially new developments which are documented, new developments in which the top ranks, men in other words, played an important role. Areas which were ruled by tradition, precisely those areas in which women played an important and accepted role as wives and mothers of future generations, have much less resonance in written sources. Why record a tradition? It is, after all, common knowledge. At the very best we find these female roles in chivalric epic or pedagogical tracts.[6] However, the yield of sources from the late Middle Ages is much richer: there are more of them, and they originate from broader segments of society. On the basis of what they tell us, we can do some guesswork for earlier periods.

In this introduction I will pursue some of the topics which present themselves in the above: a) a second inventory of the sources which we have, this time the iconography of saintly mothers, which will help us set the geographic boundaries for the studies in this volume, b) the nature of the hagiographical selection included in the *Acta Sanctorum*, c) characteristics of the saints' lives which have been handed down to us and the discrepancies between holy persons and saints, and d) the cultural force of the laity.

This introduction does not allow for an exhaustive treatment of these topics. Rather it will serve as a preliminary survey of the terrain, in which various problems are charted. Clarissa Atkinson will in her conclusion analyze and comment on the broader trends and developments which come to the fore in the articles in this collection.

A SECOND SURVEY: THE ICONOGRAPHIC DOSSIER

Next to hagiography, iconographic sources can give us a perspective on the medieval history of sanctity and motherhood. Mireille Madou,[7] the art historian who made an inventory of the visual material about saintly mothers for this volume, confirms that every search for mother saints in the visual arts inevitably leads to the countless portrayals of Mary with her child Jesus. Almost as inevitably the search leads to Saint Anne, often surrounded by the Holy Kinship. The iconography of these saints succinctly reveals the essence of their sanctity: they are mothers of the key figures in salvation history; their attributes are these children. No other saints are iconographically distinguished by their children as mother saints in the way Mary and Anne are.

During the times of the persecutions in the early Church, many married women and mothers were martyred. Only four of them, however, and then only from the twelfth century onwards, were occasionally depicted with their children. The other mother martyrs were celebrated in the liturgy, represented in frescoes and altarpieces, sculpted in wood or stone, but without their children. De Nie, in her contribution, calls to attention Perpetua, the mother of a young child, who was thrown into prison with her pregnant slave Felicitas. There Felicitas bore her child. In 203 they suffered a gruesome martyrdom. Neither saint is depicted with child. It is again among the legendary martyrs that we find iconographic links between sanctity and motherhood, saints such as Julita and her three-year-old son Quiricius, who supposedly suffered under Diocletian, or Felicitas and her seven sons, and Symphorosa, also with her sevensome. The historical trustworthiness of their lives is with reason subject to doubt. Their *Passios* show a remarkable similarity to the seven brethren and their mother of 2 Macc. 7. Saint Sophia and her daughters Fides, Spes, and Caritas are all martyrs who belong to the world of allegory. Precisely these saints are shown with children: Julita, Felicitas and Symphorosa with their seven sons, Sophia with her three daughters (fig. 1.2). Aside from one sixth-century image of Felicitas and her children in Maximus's catacomb in Rome, the earliest iconographic representations of these saints as mother saints date from the twelfth century. In a Salzburg codex, Felicitas appears, holding a platter bearing the seven heads of her sons. In a *Martyrologium* from Zwiefalten, she embraces her seven children. A Catalan antependium, also dating from the twelfth century, shows

Figure 1.2. Saint Symphorosa and Saint Felicitas both with their seven sons. Altarpiece, Cologne. (Photo Madou)

Julita, enthroned, surrounded by a mandorla, with her son Quiricius on her lap. Her bare feet, her child's lack of a halo and cross, as well as inscriptions, distinguish her from the usual *Sedes Sapientiae* images of Mary and Child.[8]

Other icons of mother-martyrs date from the late Middle Ages and almost all originate in the Germanic World. Felicitas, Sophia and Symphorosa are depicted in paint as well as statuary. Regina was depicted in an etching in the *Generale Legende*. The mothers are surrounded by their children, or hold them on their lap. Only with Felicitas does the artist depart from tradition when she is shown with seven sons' heads held on a platter.

In this volume we also meet with saints from the fourth century, after the persecutions ended, who were mothers: Helena, empress and mother of Constantine; Monica, mother of Augustine of Hippo; and Paula. Helena, as empress-mother, fulfilled a public role. She helped spread the Christian faith, she built churches and found the (presumed) Cross of Christ. It is not clear whether her motherhood was an influential factor in her religious life. Monica, on the other hand, is the paragon of a devout and dedicated mother. She was a model of patience and meekness. Once widowed, her only concern was the conversion of her son Augustine, for whom she suffered and prayed. Paula was, as we shall see in De Nie's study, a devoted mother of five. As a widow she dedicated herself to the care of the poor and the sick. She left her two youngest children, and in the company of her daughter Eustochium, went with Jerome to the Holy Land where she founded a women's monastery in Bethlehem. Jerome, who maintained close ties with Paula, said of her, "No mother loves her children more than she . . ." Nevertheless, she renounced them. It may be that Monica and Paula experienced a religious dimension in their maternal roles, and indeed even saw motherhood as sanctifying, though in the sense of renunciation and suffering. In iconography, however, neither have children as an attribute.

The same applies for mothers in later periods. Again, there is no saint whose iconography shows her to be a mother saint; in other words, no saint is distinguished by children as attribute. One exception is Saint Notburga (ninth century), who was according to her *Vita*, a Scottisch duchess. In 820 she was, again according to her *Vita*, driven from the dukedom after the murder of her consort. Notburga fled to Bühl (Württemberg, Germany), where she gave birth to nonaplets. Her iconographic attributes signify this: she is usually shown with her children on her lap (fig. 1.3). Again, her *Vita* has a preeminently legendary character.

Historical saints who were mothers—in the early Church and in later times—are depicted in their function as abbess, nun, or sovereign. To commemorate their church or monastery foundations they are often shown with the model of a church in hand; to commemorate their charity they are shown with a beggar, or a basket of bread, or a pitcher of wine. From the iconography, one could never guess they had been mothers. The same principle applies for the iconography of male saints: their identifying attributes refer to their function in the Church, for instance, a cardinal's hat or bishop's staff, or to a significant event in their *Vitae*, like Saint Martin's cloak.

In total, Madou traced just five mother saints in iconography: four of them are martyrs; the fifth, Notburga, is the only medieval saint; Regina pops up only during the Counter Reformation. With the possible exception

*Figure 1.3. Saint Notburga with her nonaplets. Schwaben, c. 1420
(Photo Madou)*

of Julita, all seem to be fictitious saints, phantasms whose very name indicates their allegorical nature. It is striking that all the images of mother saints originate in Germany and surrounding areas. This gives us one reason to demarcate the geographical boundaries for this volume.

The cycles of saints' lives, series of images which portray the events in the life of a saint, form a different iconographic category than the isolated images of saints discussed above. In these cycles sporadic images of saints with their children are found. Iduberga is shown with her daughter Gertrude; Elizabeth of Thuringia with her children; Berswinde with her daughter Odilia.[9] A cycle is by definition a narrative and the saint is shown with others in various phases of life. When the cycle concerns a saint who was a mother, the events of motherhood will usually show up somewhere in a cycle.

The one find in the search for saintly mothers is a miniature in a Flemish Book of Hours.[10] Saint Monica, in widow's weeds, a book open on her knee, sits in a garden, under a canopy. She is together with her son Augustine, a schoolboy with his bag slung over his shoulder. This original illustration is a significant iconographic document, in which the meaning of the mother-child relationship is effectively portrayed. As the mother of the future Church Father Monica is one of the few saints whose maternity gained a sanctified character. This miniature is late medieval (fig. 1.4). Brandenbarg's study shows that the cult of Saint Anne reached its greatest popularity in the same period. Anne is also depicted in that period as *magistra*, teaching Mary from an open book in hand.[11] The pedagogical function of saintly mothers is illustrated in both cases; both derive from the Low Countries, in consequence a region to focus on in this volume. It remains unanswered, as yet, whether the iconography of pedagogical mother saints testifies to a new development, part of the rising cult of Saint Anne, or whether it reveals something with a longer history, previously undocumented, due to the nature of written and material sources. With this, we return to our initial question and the geographical focus of this study.

THE OUTLINE OF THE BOOK

The iconographical and hagiographical representations of sanctified motherhood suggest that in Northern Europe—the Low Countries, the Rhineland and environs, Northern France, the Anglo-Saxon areas and Scandinavia, in short the old Germanic world as demarcated by Samplonius in his contribution—"something happened" with respect to sanctity and motherhood. Secondly, both surveys indicate that our research must extend beyond mother saints, whose motherhood constituted their sanctity, to include holy moth-

Figure 1.4. Saint Monica and her son Augustine. Miniature in a Flemish Book of Hours, Munich, CLM 28346, fol. 223v

ers, whose public role was based on their social positions as wives and mothers. If we limit ourselves to Anne and Mary and the Holy Kinship, we will miss many essentials of the complex and intriguing history of religious motherhood in the Middle Ages. We have formulated our questions to allow for a wider scope: our interest will go out to different links between sanctity and motherhood. Instead of concentrating on notions of Christian motherhood in Church doctrine and theology, which has already been done in Clarissa Atkinson's admirable study, we will focus on the religious experience of holy mothers and saints and how they were perceived by their communities and their biographers. Thirdly, the cult of Saint Anne reached simultaneously its climax and its conclusion around 1500, a date which provides us with a *terminus ad quem*. Her cult provides the motivation for delving deeper into the history of sanctity and motherhood. On the one hand, she is a legendary saint from distant times, a magnificent figure of divine grandeur removed from the confines of historical actuality. On the other hand, she is homey and familiar, a saint who appealed to so many precisely because of her proximity and relevance to everyday matters of life in the family. This symbolization is profoundly late medieval. What happened in the in-between? How did the Christian mothers to whom she spoke experience motherhood? Were there precedents to her cult in earlier times? Focussing on representative saintly women and mothers in Northern Europe "before" Saint Anne, we investigate the development of ideas concerning 1) female sanctity and virginity, 2) marriage and sexuality, 3) childbirth and motherhood, the relationship between mother and children before as well as after renunciation of the world, and 4) ideas of a holy family, even of holy dynasty.

THE PREPONDERANT *ACTA SANCTORUM*

Modern hagiographical research is still based on the work of the Bollandists. These Jesuits of the southern Netherlands were in the seventeenth century entrusted with the mission of saving the saints of the Church. The saints, ridiculed by Protestants, were to be disassociated from folktale and fiction; to do this the Bollandists had to find the most historically reliable *vitae* and present these to believers as venerable and educative models. To this end they published Greek and Latin *vitae* in the *Acta Sanctorum*. The first volume was published in 1643; in 1925 the 66th and last volume to this date appeared with the saints of November 9 and 10. When Delooz researched saints in the sixties he perforce relied on this dossier. He counted 1190 saints and beati to 1600. Very few were canonized by papal procedure, officially "listed" so to say (125); most were simply accepted as saints because they enjoyed spontaneous veneration (1065), with or without the approval of a bishop.[12] German scholars have spoken in this regard of "Volkskanonization."[13] Only in the time of the Counter Reformation did sanctification become the sole preserve of the papal office, with clear and inflexible criteria and procedure. In 1625 Pope Urban VIII recognized (in a sort of general amnesty) all saints who had enjoyed a cult in the past and determined that in the future no public cult was allowable without papal canonization. It was then that the Bollandists began their painstaking labor.

Tales were told about the old, spontaneously venerated saints, but these were not usually put down in writing. The number of saints and cults about which we know nothing more than that they did exist is terribly high.[14] There are furthermore many saints, and among them female saints and holy mothers, who have escaped study and their place in surveys because they were—for whatever reason—left out of the corpus of the *Acta Sanctorum*. If we compare the *Oxford Dictionary of Saints*[15] to the *Acta Sanctorum* the results are telling. Take for example the entries in the *Oxford Dictionary* under the letter B. For the period to 1500 there are 67 names, of which 40 refer to English saints. Among these 40 there are well-known historical figures like Bede and Queen Bathild, along with legendary saints like Brandan and Bridget of Kildare. For these *Vitae* have been handed down, just as for some of the local saints. For only seven of them, however, were *Lives* included in the *Acta Sanctorum*, that is, one in six. About most of the remaining 33 almost nothing is known: the name Breage is known because this nun accompanied missionaries to Cornwall, the name of Blida because she was the mother of a saint, and Buryan because she was the titulary of a church. Brychan was the father of twelve or, in other traditions, sixty-three saints: he is shown with them in a stained glass window in Cornwall. These saints are not included in Delooz's or Weinstein and Bell's studies because they are not included in the *Acta Sanctorum*. In total, there are eleven holy mothers among the local saints of England. None of them appear in the *Acta Sanctorum*, although five were queen or abbess and more or less extensively documented in other sources like Bede.

Even the *Oxford Dictionary of Saints*, however, cannot be relied on for a total survey of the cult of saints in medieval England. Saint Thenew, for instance, cannot be found in the entries. She was the unmarried mother of Saint Kentigern (or: "Mungo"), patron saint of Glasgow.[16] How many other holy mothers, legendary or historical, have been left out? Saint Thenew refused to marry the suitor whom her father had found for her and was raped by him thereafter. She was venerated in Glasgow, where a chapel, a gateway and a square are named after her. Thus she cannot justly be ignored. And this is not to mention the holy mothers in folk legends, like the one about the anonymous saint from Britten, who fed her hungry child by ripping off her breast and nursing it on her heart's blood.[17]

In conclusion, then, the Latin corpus of the *Acta Sanctorum* renders only a small portion of our research potential, much smaller than is generally recognized. Moreover, when the Bollandists sought out the most reliable *vitae* in the seventeenth century, they did their best, but of course they didn't find everything. Delooz observed that there seemed to be an overdose of Belgian saints and wondered whether this might be attributed to the fact that the Bollandists, busily searching for what had survived the Reformation, simply found more close to home than far away.[18] It is also feasible that the small number of Dutch saints is due to the thoroughness of the iconoclasm and Prostestantization in the northern Low Countries. The Bollandists, Jesuits as they were, did not simply publish everything they came across. In principle they limited themselves to saints who received public veneration, but every now and then they bent their own rules to include simple religious who in their opinion led an exemplary life and would therefore be useful for Christian education. One of my own favorite saints, crippled Margaret, a very opinionated woman and the opposite of the languid lilies of the Counter Reformation, for whom no less than thirteen lives have survived, did not make it through the Bollandist selection: she was known to them, but is mentioned only under the *praetermissi*.[19] Did the Bollandists choose to relegate her to oblivion for safety's sake? Bollandist ideals also seem apparent in their treatment of Godelieve of Gistel, as Renée Nip's study shows. Not the oldest *Vita* was taken up, but a later version, which highlights the saint's virginity. Coincidence?

Latin *vitae*, such as contained in the *Acta Sanctorum*, were produced when needed for a specific purpose, e.g., when a religious establishment desired liturgical celebration or a public cult; when clergy wished to direct veneration for their own ends or when papal canonization was the goal. In those cases the saint in question was often a person of high rank, or somehow the case of sanctity related to legitimation of property or privileges. It could also be that the Church intended the *vitae* for religious instruction. In the Low Countries many *Lives* were written with this purpose in mind in the thirteenth century, the period of the inner conversion of the individual. *Vitae* are, in other words, written with a clear purpose, and shaped by that purpose. The life stories are (re)constructed and reflect the ideals and purposes of the group for which they were produced. It is striking in the studies done for this collection that in the hagiography for canonization trials there is always somebody saying they remember the saint would have preferred a virgin life: Elizabeth of Thuringia expressed her regrets to Conrad of Marburg, Birgitta's daughter testified that her mother had not wanted to marry. Did these women internalize the ideals of the Church? Or were the witnesses brought to say this because they thought it advantageous for a successful canonization?

Some *vitae* suppress or leave out details of maternity and familial ties. Van't Spijker shows that in the *Life of Waldetrude*, the saint's daughters are absent. Indeed, the same types of omissions occur in male saints' lives.[20] In other cases, later versions of saints' lives will delete the themes of motherhood and family originally included in the previous versions, due to changing ideals in the Church.[21] In these cases we can note omissions through comparison with the earlier *Lives*, but how often is it so that these other sources simply do not exist, have not survived, or have not yet been researched?

The problematic nature of the sources, as described above, is understandable. The authors were almost always men who were imbued with Church tradition. They learned that virginity and martyrdom were the highest roads a religious could travel, especially a religious woman. These ideals influenced their selections, whether they were aware of it or not. Usually a hagiographer who had personally known a saint and was impressed by her personality tends to stick closer to the historical reality than later writers. He would also tend to record matters which did not accord with Church ideals, but were important to the saint. The strong personality of Ivetta of Huy colors the hagiography written by Hugh. He could not, perhaps did not even want to, muffle away her nurturing role as a mother to her children and the close bonds she had with her kin. These bonds of motherhood and family are integral to her ideal of sanctity, and in Hugh's hagiography they remain integral. To what extent does the same apply to other holy mothers, whose lives were either written later or styled by real Church politicians, as in the case of Mary of Oignies. James of Vitry rigorously and capably made her *Life* conform to the Church's conception of a female mystic.[22] In Petrakopoulos' study of Elizabeth of Thuringia we see her contemporary Caesarius of Heisterbach wrestling to get the facts of marital happiness and motherhood into the traditional Church definition of female sanctity. Two generations later Dietrich of Apolda provides a polished portrait.

I wonder whether the relationship between saint and hagiographer is more influential for the content of a *vita* than prevailing ideals of sanctity. That might explain why in the later Middle Ages, when more contemporaneous hagiography and historical sources were produced, we find more holy mothers. They might have existed in earlier ages as well.

SANCTITY AND THE HOLY: THE QUICK AND THE DEAD

Historians and ethnologists have long pondered the question of why some people were perceived to be holy and others not.[23] In the case of religious mothers, we are led to ask: why were some mothers perceived to have supernatural powers and charismatic authority, and not others? Why was one woman perceived to be a divine mediatrix during her life on earth, only to be forgotten once she had joined the realm of the dead, while another was perceived to be a potent intercessor and miracle worker only after she had joined heaven's communion of saints? Sainthood is not an absolute category; it changes continuously, dependent on differences in time and place, and the particulars of the group selected for research. Usually scholars research sanctity from the point of view of the Church, thus the Church's categories of sainthood determine the disposition of their research. They study apostles, martyrs, confessors, and virgins, the types defined in liturgy and canon law. Holy mothers and mother saints are thus absent from the research horizon. But research into historical reality and the experience of medieval communities suggest another categorization. Researching the views of the medieval faithful and the manifestations of sanctity and supernatural power in historical actuality leads us to distinguish different types of sanctity. In the case of holy women I see at least two types. The first consists of women who were perceived as holy during their earthly lives; the second of women who gained sainthood and were perceived to have miraculous and intercessory power only in their afterlife. Among the holy, the categories of the quick and the dead apply.[24] The holy in the first category were seen as God's special representatives in the community; they often died in the odor of sanctity but it didn't always follow that they were honored at the altar. No cult developed around the *mulieres sanctae* of the Low Countries, not even for someone like Ivetta of Huy. I suggest, however, that this group cannot be excluded from the category of saints if we define sanctity on the basis of the religious experience of medieval communities. The second category, the holy dead, achieved their status by virtue of their cult. They were the holy the Church reckoned saints, and for them *Vitae* were written. About these holy we know the most. Let us start with them.

Virgin Saint

The world of the New Testament knew no individual saints. Sanctity was a collective concept, found in the *communio sanctorum*, the community of the saints. Only in the second and third century did Christians, in deep admiration and respect for the martyrs who suffered brutal torture and violent death for their faith, begin to distinguish these faithful as saints, separate from the rest. They began to visit their graves and honor their memory. They called upon them to intercede with God, and they saw them as holy, a quality conferred upon them not for their exemplary lives but for their exemplary deaths.[25] It was their *Passio* which was recorded in writing. Christians treated these martyrs like heroes. Delooz explains this behavior as fitting with the pattern of expectations of the Late Antique individual. In Antiquity Greeks and Romans honored their heroes as half-gods and cults of heroes developed. The Late Antique individual was, as it were, programmed to perceive heroic qualities. When this occurred in a Christian context, the same honor was given to the heroes of Christianity and cults developed around martyrs just as they had around heroes.[26] Delooz's thesis is interesting and I think we can see the influence of expectations in other times and places as well. Church history knows more periods in which human suffering made a deep impression and formed the impulse to honor the sufferer as a saint: see for instance the "rois souffrants" in the Germanic world and the *Life of Godelieve* in this volume. Christians were convinced that the victims of injustice and violence were received in the circle around the throne of God and there could intercede on their behalf. For poor sinners this was a great comfort.

As shown by the iconographic survey, martyrs were people of all kinds, men and women, young and old, married and unmarried. As the cults of saints developed, however, virgin-martyrs gained a dominant role. Seen as dependable miracle workers, they became a separate liturgical category and were invoked in the litany. A spectacular career was ahead of them once the Christian religion penetrated the Germanic world. There, in Northern Europe, were countless sacred places, linked to a holy person, about whom, as we have seen, hardly anything was known. This was not only the case with holy places in medieval England, but on the continent as well. About Oda, whose sarcophagus was discovered in Brabant meadows, almost nothing was known.[27] When the scholaster of Oda's minster had to compose a Latin life for her in the thirteenth century, the time of interior conversion, he added an *Epistola Apologetica* in which he reacted to critics and defended his view that Oda had been a virgin. Just like martyrdom, he holds, virginity was incontestable proof of sanctity. With wives and widows one must wait for the judgment of God; pious virgins, however, one can entrust with one's soul and salvation without reserve, virginity is sure proof of sanctity: "Happy are the barren, the wombs that never bore a child, the breasts that never fed one" (Lk. 23:29). Powerful virgins were seen to be potent intercessors and patrons. In Duffy's words: "[T]he dynamic of such prayers was not designed primarily to present the chastity of the saint as a model, but as providing the basis of their intercessory power."[28]

Since Jerome, as De Nie's study indicates, virginity was the dominant ideal of the Church. But was it also the favorite image of lay society? Of course, lay communities drew on the powerful resource of virgin intercessors, but did they also turn to these heroic maidens for their needs of solace and spiritual nourishment? The villagers of Sint-Oedenrode were skeptical about the scholaster's attribution of virginity to Oda. They thought it as likely that Oda had been a widow, somewhat like Oda of Amay, another sarcophagus saint. At about the same time, this Oda of Amay had also received a fabulous *curriculum vitae*, so good that the scholaster of Sint-Oedenrode drew on it for his own Oda. Oda of Amay's biographer, however, had made her a different type of saint: she seems to be an other Elizabeth of Thuringia. As a spouse, and even more so as a widow, she lived an exemplary religious life. She distributed her riches, visited the poor and cared for the sick and needy. In times of famine she distributed food. As a young widow she left the regency over her son to others and devoted herself to founding hospitals and nursing the sick. Her life reflects the ideals of Beguines and thirteenth-century religious women. Her *Vita* focusses, therefore, on her role in this life. She was modeled into an exemplary wife and mother, to which status she owed her social position and property. She used her fortune for the benefit of the needy: it was the basis for her intercessory power. She is not a distant force in heaven, like Oda of Sint-Oedenrode. The Amay biographer chose to shape her according to a fundamentally different, even opposite type of female sanctity. It seems this ideal suited his audience. This brings us to the second type, the category of the "quick."

The Holy Woman

The second category of female sanctity fits in the pattern of social and economic development in Northern Europe in the later Middle Ages. In this period the Low Countries and environs experienced intense change. New techniques in agriculture, the development of a cloth industry, long distance trade and the rise of towns, brought prosperity and cultural renewal. New social groups appeared, among them many women, especially in the new cities. As spouses, and even more as widows, they appear to have had a great range of activities. In family circles they were valued as wise grandmothers, in guilds and cities they built careers as businesswomen, in the parish they were religious mothers.

Concurrent with these developments, the Christian religion entered the sphere of daily life in lay society. While before lay people were satisfied with ritual, they now wanted to understand the tenets of faith and live a spiritual life. Peter Damian had already expressed Church concerns about the will of laypeople to come to their own terms with the faith: peasants and fools, he complained, discuss the Holy Scripture with old women.[29] In the course of the centuries they became ever more interested. These people wanted religious practices to appeal to their hearts and emotions; an affective spirituality rather than intellectual deliberations in theology. *Caritas* was worth more to them than *castitas*; a religious life in the world was valued above a life of monastic seclusion. Walter Hilton advised not to "wholly give themselves to contemplative life. . . . For charity, as you know well, lies both in love of God and of your fellow-Christians."[30]

Women, especially of the upper classes, took part in this development. They were often literate, able to read and write, wealthy enough to purchase books and prints for religious education.[31] Judith Oliger traced a whole series of prayerbooks and Books of Hours which belonged to thirteenth-century women in the Low Countries.[32] Donovan claims a female owner for the magnificent Book of Hours from Oxford (13th c.).[33] These women shared their cultural assets with their husbands, and especially with their children. The mystics, whose writings still have the power to touch our hearts, were often well-educated women, acquainted with literary convention and able to innovate their own literary language. In short, in the later Middle Ages there were literate laypeople, and among them many women, who were imbued with serious-minded piety and formed "a rising cultural force."[34]

In his prologue to the *Life of Mary of Oignies*, James of Vitry wrote that in the Southern Low Countries not only the religious fervor of holy virgins and widows was attracting attention, but also "holy women serving the Lord devoutly in marriage, . . . women teaching their sons in the fear of the Lord, keeping honourable nuptials and 'an undefiled wedding bed' (Heb. 13:4), 'giving themselves to prayer for a time and returning afterwards together again . . .'"[35] These women successfully combined marriage and motherhood with a religious life, and functioned as holy mothers for and in their communities. These were women who, according to their *vitae* written by friars—*vitae* which did not lead to canonization—cared for lepers and the sick, comforted their fellows in need, boosted the self-confidence of inexperienced priests, and stood in manifest contact with the divine each time they experienced mystical ecstasy. According to Vauchez, women were especially active in works of charity in the thirteenth century—see for instance Ivetta of Huy and Elizabeth of Thuringia in this volume—but in the fourteenth and fifteenth century it was more by mystical experience and visions that they played a public role, as for example in the case of Birgitta of Sweden: "Ainsi, par l'expérience mystique, la femme parvint, à la fin du Moyen Age, à rompre le lien de dépendance qui la rattachait à l'homme et à l'inverser à son profit. Exclue jusque la du ministère de la Parole, elle devint alors l'organe dont l'Esptit se servait pour s'adresser directement au peuple chrétien."[36] It strikes me that these late medieval women lived a life suspiciously similar to the lives ascribed to legendary female saints of the distant past, holy mothers like

Oda of Amay or, more significantly, like late medieval Saint Anne. Were these written to provide an illustrious history for these new types of female religiosity, an educative model for the holy mothers of late medieval reality?

So we arrive at the second type of female sanctity, the holy woman, a type that also has a long history which goes back to the early Church, although there is less to find about it in the predominantly clerical sources.

Once the persecutions ended, a new type of martyr was honored by Christians: bloodless martyrs, ascetics, hermits, missionaries; men and women who removed themselves from their communities, tangibly in contact with the divine, and authoritative mediators of God's Word. They practiced extreme asceticism and renunciation, especially sexual renunciation, often living far from the inhabited world, though never losing contact with it. They saw into the hearts of others, they worked wonders and prophesized. They were, as Burrows said of Pachomius, founder of cenobitic monasticism, "the new focal point, . . . the mediating locus by which the distant God of the desert hermit journeys to the proximity of the village."[37] In Burrows's view it was not on the ground of moral example and virtuous life that a man became a holy man, nor was it the wisdom of his words. Indeed, Vauchez shows that virtue and an exemplaric life became central to sanctity only during the papal canonization trials of the late Middle Ages.[38] Rather, it is through his presence that the holy man proves his bond to God and his mediating power. He is a vehicle of salvation. That is why Pachomius refused clerical ordination: it would detract from the immediacy of his identity as a man of God. The holy man is almost literally a living symbol (symbolein = converge), in him heaven and earth converge, he lives, in Burrows's words, "at the juncture of heaven and earth." To this he owes his power and on this is founded his powerful authority.

I think the same applies for the holy woman. Brown, to whom we owe the discovery of the holy man, is of the opinion that women never attained this status, but he is mistaken.[39] Angenendt is correct when he, following Muschiol, maintains that ascetic women could function in the same way as these ascetic men. To quote his own words: "Neben dem 'vir Dei' steht in gleicher Weise die 'famula dei,' die Gottesdienerin. Wenn es den Gottesmenschen ausmacht, asketisch zu leben und die Gotteskraft erbitten zu können, diese angesammelt in sich verspüren und wunderbar anzuwenden, so trifft das genauso auf asketische Frauen zu."[40] In my opinion women had excellent chances of becoming holy women once Christianity entered the Germanic world. In Northern Europe, as described by Samplonius, there was a long tradition of female prophets, married or unmarried. These women were the gateway and mouthpiece of the gods, similar to kings but possibly also queens, they played an intermediary role with (fertility) gods. If we reason with Delooz's concept of the pattern of expectations, the Germans, once Christianized, might have transferred these roles to Christian saints. Indeed, in the judgement of many scholars, the Anglo-Saxon and Ottonian rulers exhibit many characteristics of saints.[41] German scholars have spoken in this respect of "Adelsheilige" and "Königsheil," the noble saint and the kingly charisma. Rulers guaranteed their people's well-being and prosperity, a good harvest, fertility, and victory in battle.[42] After the conversion to Christianity, the "Königsheil" was translated into Christian ceremonies of anointment and crowning and stood in service of the Christian God. In Latin sources it was now described as *fortuna atque mores*, as we see in Widukind of Corvey.[43]

How does this relate to holy mothers? I think we should keep in mind that the queen, always married and usually a mother, was also anointed. She was the *consors regni*, the sharer of royal power,[44] and thus, I would argue, the sharer of "Königsheil." Barely any historical research has been conducted on this aspect of the queen's function. Even Robert Folz, who devoted a study to *Les Saintes Reines*, does not mention it.[45] Nevertheless it appears to be significant. It strikes me that historical sources show a certain division of responsibility between the king and queen. In my reading of Widukind of Corvey, it seems that the king's duty was to provide *fortuna*, the queen's, or the queen-mother's, was to see to the *mores*, which included maintaining contacts with the Church. Otto the Great, for instance, conquered the Magyars; Mathilda his mother showed honor to God for this victory. Widukind describes her as a prudent woman. Due to her intervention, *de monitu et intercessione sanctae matris*, peace and unity were restored, churches were built, and a great blessing of children was bestowed on the family. After the death of her consort, she learned to read and taught her children and household; she was a support and comfort to all.[46] We read this in Widukind, who was a historian, not a hagiographer. Much the same thing would be written about Adelheid, Otto's widow. Here in historical sources we see the contours of the holy mother, the *sancta mater* according to Widukind: she is the queen, indeed, the only woman whose role was documented in this period; about other women we are simply not well informed.[47]

In her holy motherhood the queen was held jointly responsible for the *fortuna atque mores* of her subjects; marriage and maternity, the nurture of future generations as well as saintly virtue are thus inextricably bound to the queen's exercise of royal power. As the queen consort she was entitled to intercede with the king for the people's well-being and happiness, as is documented in numerous interventions in charters. The queen was *mediatrix*, but her intermediary power depended on the function of the sovereign and was by definition implemented during her earthly life. It is not surprising that scholars such as Corbet and Folz have found very few lasting cults of these saint-queens[48]—just as it is not surprising that very few cults developed around the late medieval *mulieres sanctae*. These women were simply not recognized as saints. Only when they were distinguished by the characteristics of Church-defined female sanctity, such as childlessness (due to a presumably chaste life), or unjust suffering, or a violent death, were they honored by the Church, and only then did they exercise intercessory power after death. Adelheid is a modest, Elizabeth of Thuringia a spectacular example of this.

This reminds us of what Gianarelli has established as the role of the wise old mother in Late Antiquity, as well as the role of the early-Christian grandmother who oversaw the religious instruction of children and participated in a broad variety of social activities.[49] This wise old mother can, in my opinion, be seen as the predecessor of the *sancta mater* in the Ottonion period, the *mulier sancta* in the thirteenth century, and, as we will see presently, the *vetula* and Saint Anne in the late Middle Ages.

In the thirteenth century, the period for which there are many more lay sources, entire genealogies of royal and princely lines were constructed around these holy mothers.[50] This might indicate that the type of holy mother was more popular in lay society than the clerical sources reveal. Indeed, in the same thirteenth century, the sources reveal that the ideal of holy mother was taken up and transformed by the urban classes—as I indicated above.

In the late Middle Ages we meet with the bourgeois version of the holy mother in theological and scientific treatises.[51] She is then among the devout women scornfully termed *vetulae* by the leading intellectuals of the time. They formed a mixed devout company, from wise grandmothers to herbalists and witches. They were simple folk, who believed they received their knowledge from God, the Virgin or the saints. The Parisian scholaster Jean Gerson, who also expressed his reservations about the revelations of Birgitta of Sweden, announced a scathing judgement on the *mulieres sanctae*, because they "dogmatize in secret, they teach, preach and affirm," they pretend to have mystic visions and prophesy, "they even climb onto the pulpit, preach and teach as *magistri*."[52] Lay members of society, however, welcomed these women as they had done with the holy mothers of previous times, they accepted them as mouthpieces of God and vehicles of salvation. The rational arguments of intellectuals meant nothing to them; the Church, too, with its emphasis on *sacerdotium* and the sacraments, barely touched them. The holy mother, on the other hand, did: "Efficace, persuasive, délicate . . . , telle apparaît l'influence pédagogique de la *vetula*, veuve ou nonne, qui circule librement d'une maison à l'autre et dans l'intimité de chaque foyer, dans les villes comme dans les campagnes. . . ."[53]

The Cultural Force of the Laity

In my view the "cultural force" of the laity, which we see at work here, should not be underestimated. Current studies of the process of Christianization and the interiorization of religion generally concentrate on institutional Church history, often as not combined with the genesis of the early-modern State. In this context, methods of Church regulation and discipline of lay believers are studied and scholars are wont to speak of "Socialdisziplinierung und Konfessionalisierung."[54] They describe how Church and State regulated, or at any rate tried to regulate, the religious practices of lay believers with injunctions and prohibitions. They research the rules and neglect more or less what actually happened. It seems to me time to come to terms with the cultural force of the laity self. What were the religious perspective and contributions of Christians who were not ordained and who did not belong to any particular Order?

We do not know much about the spiritual world of the common faithful: only in the late Middle Ages, as we have seen, is there such a wealth of sources that we can form some impressions. And only recently have scholars begun to explore this fascinating material. Eamon Duffy's admirable book, *The Stripping of the Altars*, is one of the first fruits of this new trend.[55] But we can catch a few glimpses in earlier periods. I assemble some of the observations as made by the contributors to this volume.

In "Consciousness Fecund through God," De Nie shows how the Late Antique Church tended towards an otherworldly, ascetic conception of saintly life, one that devalorized or excluded earthly marriage and motherhood, and exalted their spiritual equivalents. Ordinary lay people were encouraged to admire such saints from afar, not to take them to heart as models for their lives. They were to accept their more mundane lifeway as second-best. Currently this view has been adjusted with respect to actual religious practice.[56] There are signs that the religious input of married men and women was valued; indeed that marriage itself was esteemed. It seems that the common faithful had their own brand of spirituality, their own religious world.

Especially interesting is that the Church program for the instruction of the laity does not seem to be a one-way process, with the Church directing the masses. Lay members of society appear to have a profound and manifest influence on Church ideals. To give one example, now from the later Middle Ages, James of Voragine confined himself to mostly saints of the early

Church in his *Legenda Aurea* (c. 1270).[57] He included twenty-one women, almost half of whom are *not* virgins: this is a departure from tradition and seems to comply with the wishes of lay society. We know, for instance, something about the wishes of Cecily, Duchess of York, who daily read religious tracts and bits of hagiography. She chose the *Lives* of Mathilde of Scotland, Catherine of Siena and Birgitta of Sweden, thus evincing a marked preference for religious women in the world and mothers.[58] When James of Voragine compiled the *Legenda Aurea*, he shortened the older *Lives*, selected anecdotes and familiar situations to appeal to his audience. Again, his choices are telling. Many anecdotes concern the situations of marriage and parenthood. As Petrakopoulos observed, the apostle Peter is a caring father in the *Legenda Aurea*. She also points out that the fifteenth-century cycle of Saint Elizabeth's life in Lübeck shows mainly the events of her marriage and life in the world, rather than her years of renunciation in religious habit. Well-known stories about saints were invested with new meaning (cf. fig. 1.5).

It is with this audience that the cult of Saint Anne enjoyed such popularity. To quote Duffy once more: "At a time when much in the cult of the saints militated against a positive valuation of human sexuality and the realities of marriage and childbearing, the cult of Anne provided an image of female fruitfulness which was maternal rather than virginal, and her thricemarried state, rivalling the career of the Wife of Bath, was an unequivocal assertion of the compatibility of sanctity and married life . . ."[59] It is remarkable that even the learned humanists Tilmans studied in her contribution do not succeed in separating Anne from her motherly cares and homey concerns.

In conclusion, in all times examples can be found of more or less happily married wives and mothers, who lived a more or less holy life: Paula, Rictrudis, Ida of Boulogne, Elizabeth of Thuringia, Birgitta of Sweden. Only for the last two do the sources allow us to research how they experienced motherhood and marriage in their own lives and the reactions of lay people and clergy.

Up to now, the history of sanctity and motherhood has been studied mainly from the perspective of the Church and from that perspective the combination of sanctity and motherhood was not a very happy one. Holy mothers are scarce and motherhood all too often an exercise in traumatic renunciation. In recent years scholars have undertaken new approaches to sources and have in addition begun to exploit different sources. In the above I have surveyed some of their finds. In this collection we hope to make a contribution to this new trend in scholarship. Moving back in time from the cult of the archmother Saint Anne to discover the history of holy mothers,

Figure 1.5. A Holy Father with his children, the saint and martyr Vitalis.
Engraving in Heribert Rosweyde, Generale Legende *(Antwerp, 1649)*
(U.B. Groningen)

we have studied older lives of holy mothers: Perpetua and Felicitas, Paula, Waldetrudis and Rictrudis, Ida of Boulogne, Ivetta of Huy, Elizabeth of Thuringia and Birgitta of Sweden. We hope that in the future others will pick up the trail where we left off, encouraged and made curious by our small finds. When that happens, we will consider our research a success.

NOTES

　　　1. Heribert Rosweyde, *Generale Legenden der Heiligen* (2 vols.) (Antwerp, 1619), based on the French *Fleur de Saints* by Pedro de Ribadeneyra. I used the fourth edition *Generale Legende der Heylighen vergadert wt de H. Schrifture, Oude Vaders, ende Registers der heylighe Kercke door Petrus Ribadineira ende Heribertus Rosweydus* (2 vols.) (Antwerp: Verdussen, 1649), 2–3.

2. Rosweyde, *Generale Legende*, 2.2: "Zij zijn voor d'eerste by malcanderen inde vereenighe der liefden met God vereenicht ende hebben door Godt oock malkanderen te believen."

3. See the *Bibliotheca Sanctorum* (Roma: Citta Nuova, 1961–1987), vol. 11, 1–3 sub voce "Ragenfreda." The *lectiones* on which Rosweyde based his account are edited in *De Sancta Regina, Ostravandiae Comite* in the *Acta Sanctorum*, 1 Julii, (3d ed. Paris-Rome, 1867), vol. 28, 237–241.

4. A term shaped by Thomas Heffernan, *Sacred Biographies: Saints and Their Biographers in the Middle Ages* (New York [etc.]: Oxford University Press, 1988).

5. Pierre Delooz, *Sociologie et Canonisations* (The Hague: Nijhoff, 1969), 330–333; cf. his "Towards a Sociological Study of Canonized Sainthood in the Catholic Church," in *Saints and Their Cults: Studies in Religious Sociology, Folklore and History*, ed. Stephen Wilson (Cambridge: Cambridge University Press, 1985), 189–216; Donald Weinstein and Rudolph M. Bell, *Saints and Society. The Two Worlds of Western Christendom, 1000–1700* (Chicago: University of Chicago Press, 1982); André Vauchez, *La sainteté en Occident aux derniers siècles du Moyen Age: d'après les procès de canonisations et les documents hagiographiques* (Bibliothèque des Ecoles françaises d'Athènes et de Rome, 241) (Rome: Ecole française, 1981), 315–318.

6. Cf. Sharon Farmer, "Persuasive Voices: Clerical Images of Medieval Wives," *Speculum*, 61 (1986), 517–543 or Lee Patterson, "For the Wyves of Bathe: Feminine Rhetoric and Poetic Resolution in the *Roman de la Rose* and the *Canterbury Tales*," *Speculum*, 58 (1983), 656–695.

7. Mireille Madou started to write a contribution to this volume. Her iconographic research, however, yielded too little to justify a full-fledged article. That is why we chose to include her results in the Introduction.

8. For the images see: Felicitas in the codex *Tutonis opusculum de praeconiis sanctae Felicitatis*, in the Stiftsbibliothek of Admont and the twelfth-century *Martyrologium* from Zwiefalten, now in the Landesbibliothek of Stuttgart; Julita on a painting of about 1100 from the Ermita de Sant Quirze, Durro, Lerida, now in the Museo de Arte de Cataluña, Barcelona, inv. 15.809.

9. See e.g. the (copy of the) Saint Gertrudis shrine in Nivelles, Belgium, dating from 1272–98; the stained-glass windows in the Saint Gertrudis church in Gars am Kamp in Austria (c. 1350); the Saint Elisabeth panels in the Heiligen Geisthospital of Lübeck, dating from about 1420 (see the illustrations to the contribution of Petrakopoulos in this volume) or the tapestry with the life of Saint Odilia, 1470–80, in the Musée de l'Oeuvre Notre Dame in Strassbourg.

10. Bayerische Staatsbibliothek, Munich, CLM. 28346, fol. 223v.

11. Pamela Sheingorn, "'The Wise Mother': The Image of St. Anne Teaching the Virgin Mary," *Gesta*, 32 (1993), 69–80.

12. Delooz, *Sainteté et Canonisations*, 131v, 440–446. He based himself on *Butler's Lives of the Saints* and the *Les Petits Bollandistes: Vies de Saints . . .* (17 vols.) (Paris, 1874), both encyclopedic works meant to popularize the saints of the *Acta Sanctorum*.

13. Nikolaus Kyll, "Volkskanonisation im Raum des alten Trierer Bistums," *Rheinisches Jahrbuch für Volkskunde*, 11 (1960) 7–61, here 7; and the other studies in this *Jahrbuch*.

14. See the admirable study of Julia M.H. Smith, "Oral and Written: Saints Miracles and Relics in Brittany, c. 850–1250," *Speculum*, 65 (1990), 309–345.

15. David H. Farmer, *The Oxford Dictionary of Saints* (1978; 3d ed. Oxford: Oxford University Press, 1992).

16. I owe this information to Alasdair A. Macdonald, who told me her story. Kentigern, Thenew's son, is included in the *Oxford Dictionary*.

17. Kyll, "Volkskanonization," 29.

18. Delooz, *Sainteté et Canonisations*, 182.

19. See my "The Reclusorium as an Informal Centre of Learning," (forthcoming).

20. In the *Life of Gobert of Aspremont* the sons of the saintly knight and father Gobert of Aspremont were called "nephews of his brother," see *Vita Goberti Confessoris*, in *Acta Sanctorum*, 20 Augustii (3d ed. Paris-Rome, 1867), vol. 38, 370–395.

21. Robert Bartlett, "Rewriting Saints' Lives: The Case of Gerald of Wales," *Speculum*, 58 (1983), 598–613.

22. Michel Lauwers, "Entre Béguinisme et Mysticisme: La Vie de Marie d'Oignies (d. 1213) de Jacques de Vitry ou la définition d'une sainteté féminine," *Ons Geestelijk Erf*, 66 (1992), 46–69.

23. A good general introduction to sainthood is Richard Kieckhefer, "Imitators of Christ: Sainthood in the Christian Tradition," in *Sainthood: Its Manifestations in World Religions*, ed. Richard Kieckhefer et al. (Berkeley [etc.]: University of California Press, 1988), 1–42.

24. Cf. J.M. Petersen, "Dead or Alive? The Holy Man as Healer in East and West in the Late 6th Century," *Journal of Medieval History*, 9 (1983), 91, who holds that the living holy man was more important in the East and the dead wonder-worker in the West. This may apply if we only take into consideration canonized saints in the West, but it remains open to question whether living "saints" in the West were unimportant—in the East no procedure of an ecclesiastical canonization existed.

25. Charles Pietri, "L'Evolution du culte des saints aux premiers siècles chrétiens: du temoin à l'intercesseur," in *Les Fonctions des Saints dans le monde occidentale (iiie–xiiie s.)* (Rome: Ecole française de Rome, 1991), 16–36.

26. Delooz, *Sainteté et Canonisations*, 179.

27. Anneke B. Mulder-Bakker, "Woudvrouwen: Ierse prinsessen als kluizenaressen in de Nederlanden," *Tijdschrift voor Sociale Geschiedenis*, 20 (1994), 1–23; also for the following.

28. Eamon Duffy, *The Stripping of the Altars: Traditional Religion in England 1400–1580* (New Haven [etc.]: Yale University Press, 1992), 175.

29. Quoted by Karl Bosl, "Laienfrömmigkeit und religiöse Bewegung in der Spannung zwischen Orthodoxie und Häresie im europäischen 12. Jahrhundert," in his *Historia Magistra: Die geschichtliche Dimension der Bildung*, ed. H. Freilinger (Munich: Beck, 1988), 90.

30. "Walter Hilton's Advice on Which Men May Undertake the 'Mixed Life,'" partly edited in *English Historical Documents*, ed. David C. Douglas, vol 4: *English Historical Documents 1327–1485*, ed. A.R. Myers (London: Eyre & Spottiswoode, 1969), 818, nr. 488.

31. C.A.J. Armstrong, "The Piety of Cicely, Duchess of York: A Study in Late Medieval Culture," in his *England, France and Burgundy in the Fifteenth Century* (London: Hambledon Press, 1983), 135–156, gives a telling example.

32. Judith Oliger, *Gothic Manuscript Illumination in the Diocese of Liège (c. 1250–c. 1330)* (Louvain, 1988); see also her "'Gothic' Women and Merovingian Desert Mothers," *Gesta*, 32 (1993), 124–134 and R.S. Wieck, *The Book of Hours in Medieval Art and Life* (London, 1988).

33. Claire Donovan, *The de Brailes Hours: Shaping the Book of Hours in Thirteenth-Century Oxford* (London: British Library, 1991).

34. Richard Kieckhefer, "A Church Reformed Though Not Deformed? . . ." *Journal of Religion*, 74 (1992), 243 and Hilary M. Carey, "Devout Literate Laypeople and the Pursuit of the Mixed Life in Later Medieval England," *Journal of Religious History*, 14 (1986–7), 361–381.

35. Jacobus de Vitriaco, *Vita Mariae Oigniacensis* in *Acta Sanctorum*, 23 Junii (3d ed. Paris-Rome, 1867), vol. 25, 542–581; trans. Margot H. King, *The Life of Marie d'Oignies by Jacques de Vitry* (Saskatoon: Peregrina, 1986), here 4.

36. André Vauchez, "La sainteté mystique en Occident au temps des papes d'Avignon et du Grand Schisme," in *Genèse et Débuts du Grand Schisme d'Occident* (Colloques Internationaux du CNRS, 586) (Paris, 1980), 362.

37. Mark S. Burrows, "On the Visibility of God in the Holy Man: A Reconsideration of the Role of the Apa in the Pachomian Vitae," *Vigiliae Christianae*, 41 (1987), 11–13, where he holds: "Pachomius' *praesentia* is the constitutive gesture of *potentia* in the emerging communities."

38. André Vauchez, "Saints admirables et saints imitables: les fonctions de l'hagiographie ont-elles changé aux derniers siècles du Moyen Age?" in *Fonctions des Saints*, 161–171. See also Dieter von der Nahmer, *Die lateinische Heiligenvita: Eine Einführung in die lateinische Hagiographie* (Darmstadt: Wissenschaftliche Buchgesellschaft, 1994), 46–56.

39. Peter Brown, "The Rise and Function of the Holy Man in Late Antiquity," in his *Society and the Holy in Late Antiquity* (London: Faber and Faber, 1982), 151, quoted by Angenendt: see hereafter.

40. Arnold Angenendt, *Heilige und Reliquien: Die Geschichte ihres Kultes vom frühen Christentum bis zur Gegenwart* (Münich: Beck, 1994), 71f, where he refers to Gisela Muschiol, "*Famula Dei*: Zur Liturgie in merowingischen Frauenklöstern," (1994), which was not yet available to me. See also *Sainted Women of the Dark Ages*, ed. and trans. Jo Ann McNamara et al. (Durham: Duke University Press, 1992) for examples of such holy women, especially 51–53.

41. André Vauchez, "Heilige" in: *Lexikon des Mittelalters* 4 (Munich: Artemis, 1989), 2015: "Die während des gesamten Frühmittelalter verehrten 'Göttesmänner' können zwar nicht als Nachfolger der antikheidnischen Götter angesehen werden, galten aber beim einzelnen Gläubigen wie in Gemeinschaften, die sich einem heiligen Schutzpatron unterstellt hatten, als wirksame Helfer und Vermittler gegenüber Gott. Ihren Reliquien wurde übernatürliche (Wunder-) Kraft (virtus) zugeschrieben; die Sanktuarien zahlreicher Heiliger wurden zu Ausgangspunkten der Wallfahrt. In ihrer grossen Mehrzahl waren es Mitglieder der Führungsschicht, die als Heilige verehrt wurden, und es setzte eine Verschmelzung zwischen der Idee der Heiliger, hoher, aristokratischer Herkunft und Ausübung der Macht ein (Adelsheiliger). . . .

Seit ottonischer Zeit rühmte der Klerus die Gestalt des heiligen Königs oder der heiligen Königin, die ihr Volk gemäss den Vorschriften der Kirche regierten. . . . Diese Bewegung erlebte ihren Höhepunkt in den Ländern an der Peripherie des christlichen Europa in denen die Herrscher, die dort das Christentum eingeführt hatten, als Heilige verehrt wurden."

42. Alcuin wrote to King Aethelred of Northumbria: "regis bonitas est gentis prosperitas, victoria exercitus, aris temperies, terrae habundantia, filiorum benedictio, sanitas plebis," in *Monumenta Germaniae Historica. Epistolarum 4: Epistolae Karolini Aevi 2*, 51, letter 18.

43. *Widukindi Res Gestae Saxonicae*, 1.25, ed. and trans. Albert Bauer et al. in *Quellen zur Geschichte der Sächsischen Kaiserzeit* (Ausgewählte Quellen zur deutschen Geschichte des Mittelalters, 8) (Darmstadt: Wissenschaftliche Buchgesellschaft, 1977), 56.

44. Jean Chélini, *L'Aube du Moyen Age: Naissance de la Chrétienté occidentale. La Vie religieuse des laïcs dans l'Europe carolingienne (750–900)* (Paris: Picard, 1991), 218.

45. Robert Folz, *Les Saintes Reines du Moyen Age en Occident (vi–xiiie s.)* (Subsidia Hagiographica, 76) (Brussels: Sociétée des Bolandistes, 1992). See further the collection of studies *La Royauté sacrée dans le monde chrétien*, ed. Alain Boureau et al. (Paris: Ecole des Hautes Etudes, 1992).

46. *Widukindi Res Gestae Saxonicae*, 2.36, ed. Bauer, 116–118; 3.49.158; 3.74.178.

47. Patrick Corbet, *Les Saints Ottoniens: Sainteté dynastique, sainteté royale et sainteté féminine autour de l'an Mil* (Sigmaringen: Thorbecke, 1986) studied the *vitae* of these saintly women. See further the outstanding historical introduction to this period and to the role of women in K.J. Leyser, *Rule and Conflict in an Early Medieval Society: Ottonian Saxony* (London: Arnold, 1979), esp. 49–74.

48. Folz, *Les Saintes Reines*, 66 and Patrick Corbet, *Les Saints Ottoniens*, passim.

49. Elena Gianarelli, *La tipologia femminile nella biografia e nell'autobiografia cristiana del iv secolo* (Rome, 1980).

50. To give one example: Gilles d'Orval, *Nomina quorundam sanctorum et sanctarum prosapie illustrissimorum ducum Lotharingie et Brabantie* in *Monumenta Germaniae Historica. Scriptores*, vol. 25, 391–399.

51. See the seminal article by Jole Agrimi and Chiara Cristiani, "Savoir médical et anthropologie religieuse: les représentations et les fonctions de la *vetula* (xiiie–xve s.)," *Annales.Economies. Sociétés.Civilisations*, 48 (1993), 1281–1308; also for the following.

52. Quoted by Agrimi, "Savoir médical," 1297.

53. Agrimi, "Savoir médical," 1295.

54. Michael Prinz, "Sozialdisziplinierung und Konfessionalisierung: Neuere Fragestellungen in der Sozialgeschichte der frühen Neuzeit," *Westfälische Forschungen*, 42 (1992), 1–25.

55. see n. 27.

56. Elizabeth A. Clark, "Heresy, Asceticism, Adam, and Eve," in her *Ascetic Piety and Women's Faith: Essays on Late Ancient Christianity* (Lewiston: Mellen, 1986), 353–385 and David G. Hunter, "On the Sin of Adam and Eve: A little-known Defense of Marriage and Childbearing by Ambrosiaster," *Harvard Theological Review*, 83 (1989), 283–299.

57. *Jacobi a Voragine Legenda Aurea vulgo historia Lombardica dicta*, ed. Th. Graesse (1890, rpt. Osnabrück: Zeller, 1969); or *Die Legenda Aurea des Jacobus de Voragine*, trans.Richard Benz (rpt. Cologne, 1969).

58. "A Pious Lady's Household: Cecily Duchess of York, c. 1485," edited in *English Historical Documents*, vol. 4, 837, nr. 498; see also Armstrong, "The Piety of Cicely."

59. Duffy, *Stripping of the Altars*, 181.

2. SAINT ANNE

A HOLY GRANDMOTHER AND HER CHILDREN

Ton Brandenbarg

In 1495 the Antwerp printer Govert Back published a prayer book entitled *Der Kerstenen Salicheyt (On the Christian's Salvation).*[1] The booklet is remarkable for the attention paid to the kinship of Christ, containing as it does not only prayers to Mary and her mother Anne, but also to a large group of relatives, including Anne's parents, who in this edition bear the names Emerentiana and Stollanus. Step by step a family tree is constructed, with the most important members portrayed in simple woodcuts: the marriage ceremonies of all the family members, followed by an illustration of the family with the parents and their children (figs. 2.2, 2.3, 2.4). The story of Jesus' life up to and including his crucifixion and resurrection completes the family portrayal.

This prayer book is but one proof of the strong veneration of Saint Anne in northwest Europe around 1500. Churches, chapels and altars were dedicated to her, brotherhoods, chambers of rhetoric and guilds took her as their patroness, more and more women bore her name, places of pilgrimage proclaimed her miracles and cities vied with one another to acquire costly relics. In the visual arts representations of the Saint Anne Trinity, the three generations, in which Anne was depicted together with Mary and Jesus, were especially popular. At the same time there were impressive pictures of the holy Kinship with Anne as the ancestress and central figure of an influential family. Her facts of life were derived from the numerous *vitae*, which began to circulate at the end of the fifteenth century, especially in the Low Countries and Germany.[2] These *Lives* begin with the story of her parents and of her sister Hysmeria or Esmeria, of Anne's wondrous birth, and continue with the already longer known history of her marriage to Joachim and the birth of Mary. Then follows the legend of Anne's three marriages. After Joachim's death she is said to have married twice more, first to Cleophas, according to some the brother of Joseph, and after his death to Salome. Two

Figure 2.1. Holy Kinship of Saint Anne. Engraving of Lucas Cranach the Elder, c. 1510

daughters were born of these two later marriages, Mary Cleophas and Mary Salome. They became the mothers of important apostles. Finally the story of Mary's marriage to Joseph and the birth of Christ is told. The *Lives* conclude with miracle stories and prayers. The legends derived from the Bible and the *Apocrypha* naturally had a pre-eminent function in the propagation of Christian doctrine. They visualized the Incarnation of Christ, but at the same time they referred to recognizable situations in the realm of marriage, household, and family life in earthly reality.

In this article I want to investigate the polysemous imagery in the cult of Saint Anne by analyzing the growth, distribution, and appreciation of the writings of theologians and pastors in relation to views on virginity, sexuality, marriage, and family life. The emphasis is on the "boom period" from about 1480 to 1550. My research is restricted to Northern Europe, the geographical framework of this volume. In these areas there is a demonstrable connection between Anne's visual representation in, for example, altar-pieces of the important brotherhoods of Saint Anne and the description of Anne and her family as given in the texts.[3]

Anne's Popularity: A Characteristic Example

The *Lives* depict Anne as an influential grandmother, who on account of her closeness to Mary and Jesus, was second to none in pleading for her worshippers. Her power seemed almost boundless: Anne could see to prosperity and success on earth and guaranteed safe arrival in Heaven, change poverty into riches and disgrace into honor. She promoted fertility and took especial care of marital and family life. Of the some forty miracles which are intended to illustrate her power, the story of Emmericus of Hungary is the most widely known.[4] In rapid succession he loses all his worldly goods, but through Anne's intervention his setbacks are turned into prosperity and success. Since the miracle story provides particulars of the devotion and the expectations of the faithful, I give it here in more detail.

After all the disasters which have befallen him, Emmericus decides to make a pilgrimage to the grave of James, his patron saint, in Santiago de Compostella. On the way James appears to him as a pilgrim. He explains that he is a grandson of Mother Anne. She has great power, because she is not only his "old mother" (grandmother), but also the grandmother of Christ. Anne is able to change poverty into riches and can see to it that her worshippers acquire social prestige. The young man, who has never heard of this Anne, asks who she is and how she is depicted. James thereupon describes the picture of Saint Anne Trinity, an "honorable woman, having with her Mary her daughter with Jesus her son." (fig. 2.5) Emmericus is then given the task: "Make such an effigy of her, for it is God's will that people through-out the world shall venerate her."[5] James then points out that the best day to practice the devotion is on Tuesdays, since Anne was born and died on that day, the day she also gave birth to Mary. On that day "three Paternos-ters and three Hail Maries" should be said and a lighted candle placed be-fore her effigy. It is even better if candles are offered not only for Anne, but also for Mary and Jesus. From that day onwards Emmericus becomes a fer-vent venerator of Anne.

After some time Emmericus is given the task of painting a mural of Anne on the west face of the highest tower in the town, so that everybody will be inspired to worship Anne on seeing the picture. The town and the faithful will then be assured of riches and prosperity. Emmericus diligently sets to work and paints the Saint Anne Trinity with Anne, Mary, and Jesus. Above the mural he writes: " Help us Saint Anne with you three." How-ever, at the moment at which he has completed his work, a gust of wind causes him to lose his balance and he falls from the lofty scaffolding. Anne immediately comes to his aid by handing him her cloak. The painter reaches the ground unharmed. The king is so impressed by this miracle that he re-wards Emmericus with a large sum of money. Thus Anne indeed changes poverty into riches and setbacks into success. Emmericus is appointed mayor of the town and counsellor to the king. At his request the king promotes Anne's cult by ordering the production of a large number of effigies of her and by instituting her feast day.

At the end of his life Mary comes to Emmericus in person to ask how her "brother" is. Emmericus replies that he has no "sister," but Mary ex-plains that Anne has also become *his* "mother" and that she and Emmericus are therefore brother and sister. Thus, as venerator of Anne, Jesus has be-come his nephew: "As Saint Anne is your mother, so am I your sister and my son Jesus your nephew."[6] Thereupon Anne, Mary, and Jesus accompany him through death into Heaven. The story concludes with concrete hints for the cult: "Thus Anne helps her servants to attain felicity and blessing for body and soul. Therefore every man shall worship Saint Anne, namely with candles or alms every day, and by saying three Paternosters and three Hail Marys before her effigy. And if that cannot be done or if one has no effigy then fervently pray to her with his heart."[7]

In the format of an exciting story the miracle clearly illustrates who Anne is, why she is worth venerating and how to practice her cult. The most remarkable aspect is that the devotion is presented as an unknown phenomenon. Before Emmericus met with the apostle James, he is said to have known nothing about Anne and her family. This corresponds exactly with historical reality. In a sermon of 1538 Martin Luther designated the devotion as new and fashionable: "When I was a boy of 15" (thus in 1498), "nobody knew who Saint Anne was."[8] Nevertheless, the feast of Saint Anne had been known for centuries in the western world. The only thing that was new was the response it now evoked amongst broad strata of the population.

The storyteller goes to great pains to elucidate the powerful position which Anne occupies as mother and grandmother. She derived her power from her motherhood, as can be understood from the representations of the

Figure 2.2 (above). The Story of Emerentiana: the vision of the tree. Woodcut in Der Kerstenen Salicheyt *(Antwerp, 1485). (Rijksmuseum Meermanno-Westreenianum, The Hague) Figure 2.3 (top right). The suitors of Emerentiana. Idem. Figure 2.4 (bottom right). Emerentiana with her husband and two daughters Anne and Esmeria. Idem.*

Saint Anne Trinity and the Holy Kinship. Of equal importance is that instructions are given for the practical devotion. The Tuesday, the third day of the week, is presented as Anne's special day.[9] Sunday was generally devoted to Christ and Saturday to Mary. Thus Anne acquires a comparable place to both Mary and Jesus. The instruction to propagate the cult with the help of the Saint Anne Trinity fits in with the devotional reality of this period, when numerous representations of Anne were produced. Finally a recurring theme is that the worshippers of Anne themselves form part of the Holy Kinship. They thus become the next of kin of Mary and Christ! This is not solely a literary motif. The members of brotherhoods and chambers of rhetoric, who had chosen Anne as their patron saint, called themselves Anne's children.[10]

MARY'S CONCEPTION

These pictures of the protective mother and powerful saint on behalf of her devotees have probably contributed more to the success of Anne's cult than the heated discussions of the theologians, as has been assumed by modern scholarship.[11] Theologians disputed at this time as to whether Mary as the mother of the Savior was still tainted by original sin or whether she had already been purified by God's special grace before her conception or in the womb. For a long time the meeting between Joachim and Anne at the Golden Gate in Jerusalem represented the moment at which the conception of Mary—in a chaste embrace—was supposed to have taken place.[12]

The feast of Mary's Conception was introduced from the East in the ninth century and was at first only celebrated in Italy. It quickly spread northward and found especial response in England, from where it spread throughout Europe. From the twelfth century onwards discussions over Mary's conception flared up in all intensity and in the thirteenth century the learned Dominican Thomas Aquinas (1225–74) summarized the arguments as follows: if Mary had been free of original sin at her conception, then Christ would not have died for her. This idea was unacceptable to the Dominicans. However, the Franciscan Duns Scotus (c. 1266–1308) suggested a solution by arguing that Mary's being free of original sin from her conception was of a prevenient nature and could only take place with a view to the Salvation of mankind through the Cross. At the creation of the world Christ would have obtained complete purity for his mother. His future death on the Cross also provided for the salvation of his mother.[13]

During the Council of Basle in 1439 an attempt was made to terminate the dispute between the protagonists and antagonists of the Immaculate Conception, the Maculists and Immaculists. After long internal discus-

*Figure 2.5. Saint Anne Trinity. Northern Netherlands, c. 1500
(Rijksmuseum Het Catharijneconvent, Utrecht)*

sions the Council finally pronounced itself in favor of the Immaculate Conception. Because the judgment was given after the Pope had withdrawn in 1437 and the Council had consequently become schismatic, the Dominicans did not accept the decision.[14] According to them Mary was not sanctified until after her conception in the mother's womb.

About thirty-five years later the dispute flared up again and more violently than ever before. In 1475 the Dominican Vincent Bandelli, the future general of the Dominican order in Paris, published his now notorious tract against the Immaculate Conception *Libellus Recollectorius Auctoritatum de Veritate Conceptionis B. Virginis Gloriosae*. His argument caused general commotion amongst scholars. Protagonists and antagonists disputed with a degree of vehemence which we can scarcely credit.[15]

In such an atmosphere increasing attention was paid to the ancestry of Mary. If she had been conceived without original sin, to what extent were her parents involved in that extraordinary grace? The facts of life of Saint Anne and her mother Emerentiana were now collected by the learned theologians and propagated in a wider circle. The evidence was further used by the propagandists attempting to reform the religious and the faithful. They "translated" the information in attractive formats and inspiring, exciting *Histories of Saint Anne*.

Although the discussions over the Immaculate Conception perhaps led to scholars becoming more interested in the cult of Saint Anne and propagating it, this does not explain the success amongst broad strata of society. It is striking, indeed, that in most of the *Lives* the discussions over the Immaculate Conception do not play a prominent role. Most of the faithful were simply seeking a sense of security and paid little heed to the theological background. The discussions mostly concentrated on subjects such as marriage, sexuality, fertility or conception, and the position of Anne as mother and grandmother within the family structure.

It is characteristic of Saint Anne's cult that so many and widely differing social groups were involved. Men and women in the towns and at court, in the country and in the convents, amongst the educated and the uneducated, rich and poor allowed themselves to be swept along in the euphoria over Saint Anne. In the late medieval town Anne embodied the bourgeois ideals of public welfare, moderation, and success. Old Christian values of chastity and modesty fitted in well with the burgher's profit economy society, demanding order and stability, in which self-control, reliability, diligence, profit making and achievement were important values. Regulation of sexual intercourse within a legally concluded marriage, harmonious family life, in which men and women kept to their appointed place, and a growing awareness of belonging to an eminent and influential dynasty go with this framework.[16]

In this climate Anne could have a special attraction. Was she not the ancestor of a powerful line, was she not an exemplary wife and dedicated mother, was she not the chaste widow who assumed a helpful and modest role? Did she not promote prosperity and success? Such characteristics appealed to the burgher and represented his fundamental values. But Anne was also an appealing model for other groups. In the peasant society she was reminiscent of the old grandmother who from time past occupied a central position and advised and assisted the community, especially in matters of life and death. The nobility and the clergy were willingly inspired by Anne: the first group admired her for her descent and dynastic power as a progenetrix amidst a "royal family" and the clergy valued her pious and chaste conduct in close proximity to Mary and Christ. The ideal of Anne's Kinship was just as recognizable in the monastic family as in the outside world. The social relationships within the monastery were after all expressed in family terms such as father, mother, brother, and sister. Anne as mother, her three daughters as sisters, and Jesus and the apostles as nephews inspired the devotees of Anne to mystic meditation.

In the circles of the reform movements within the Church the popular devotion to Saint Anne was used as a means of supporting their goals. Finally the humanists used the literature on Anne not only to elaborate on theological questions, but also as a literary motif in composing poems after classic example.[17] It will be clear that no unequivocal explanation can be given for Anne's success in the transition from the fifteenth to the sixteenth century. The cult is too complex to make this possible.

Before I go more deeply into the imagery as reflected in the text corpus at the end of the fifteenth century, I shall give a broad survey of the genesis of Anne's life story.

GROWTH OF THE TEXT CORPUS
The Oldest Sources

The birth and youth of Mary, particulars about her marriage to Joseph and the childhood of Jesus, were given scanty attention in the canonical Gospels. There is no trace whatsoever in the Bible of Anne, the mother of Mary and grandmother of Christ. When in the second century interest began to grow in Christ's family, stories appeared about the parents of Mary. In the *Protevangelium of James*, which originated at that time and was devoted to the life of Mary, her parents' names are mentioned for the first time.[18] Anne and Joachim remained childless for more than twenty years, despite their pious way of life. When they felt humiliated on this account among family and friends—not to have any offspring was a great disgrace for the Jews—and Joachim had withdrawn to his shepherds from shame, God changed their destiny. Anne became a mother after all in her old age. From this account it appears that Mary was the fruit of prayer. It is thus not surprising that Anne was invoked in both East and West for having children.

The history of Anne and Joachim links up with traditions in the Old and New Testament. Anne belongs to a group of initially barren women who still have a child at an advanced age, such as Sarah, Rachel, the mother of Sampson, the mother of Samuel in the Old Testament; and Elizabeth, the mother of John the Baptist, in the New Testament. These children often mark an important era in Jewish history. In particular the life of Hannah, the mother of Samuel, bears near resemblance to that of Anne (I Sam. 1–2). Not only the name, but also the circumstances surrounding the birth and the further course of the child's life, are comparable. Hannah is distressed on account of her infertility and feels humiliated. When as a last resort she prays to God for a child, she promises, just as the mother of Mary did, to dedicate to God the child he has given. After the birth of respectively Samuel and Mary, both Annes sing a magnificat to God.

The Gospels on Mary and her parents also spread to the West. In the Carolingian Empire in the eighth and ninth century and the Ottonian Empire in the tenth, the number of texts increased considerably. Mary is predominantly described as the Queen of Heaven together with God the Father and Christ his Son, who form a unity as King and Judge. This imagery was in keeping with the ideas of the Carolingians over family relationships in earthly reality.[19]

The *Liber de Ortu Beatae Mariae et Infantia Salvatoris*, also known as the *Pseudo-Matthew*, because it was assumed that the apostle Matthew was the author, was of great influence. It was prefaced by a prologue which was erroneously ascribed to Jerome (345–420), the Church Father and Bible translator. It was probably composed about 800 as a compilation of the *Protevangelium* and the *Gospel of Thomas*. In the tenth century the literarily gifted nun Hroswitha of Gandersheim used it for her famous Latin Marian poem, which was for a great part devoted to Anne.[20] Not long after the *Pseudo-Matthew* a version appeared entitled *De Nativitate Sanctae Mariae*, also called *The Gospel of the Birth of Mary*.[21] This second work is generally ascribed to Paschasius Radbertus, a scholar at the court of Charles the Great. It is more compact than the *Pseudo-Matthew* and maintains that the family tree of Christ should not be reconstructed via Joseph, as was done in the canonical Gospels, but via Mary. It is then explained that Mary was descended from the priestly line of Levy and thus not from the royal line of David. This story circulated widely throughout Western Europe, as in the thirteenth century it had been included in its entirety in the famous collection of legends by James of Voragine, known as the *Legenda Aurea* (*Golden Legend*) or as the *Passionael* in vernacular versions.[22]

The story of Anne's three marriages and her three daughters and seven grandchildren was also included in the *Legenda Aurea*. However, the first traces of this legend are already to be found in the western world in the Carolingian period. Haymo of Auxerre (ninth century) recorded them in the *Historiae Sacrae Epitome*, but the legend only began to spread about 1100 from Anglo-norman regions.[23] Up to the twelfth century the references are few and far between. In the *Legenda Aurea* Anne's family tree has in the meantime been linked with the history of Servatius, the Bishop of Tongres-Maastricht, who was said to be descended from Esmeria. He too is thus related to Christ.

Family Trees in Visual Art

In the visual arts we see an interesting parallel with the imagery in the text material. Initially the family tree of Mary and Christ was shown in the Tree of Jesse. The origins of Christ were schematized via the male line, thus in accordance with the genealogy in the Gospels of Matthew and Luke, in which the Old and New Testament were linked with one another. The trunk grows from the father of David, Jesse, who is usually depicted in a recumbent posture.[24] In all sorts of variations the branches grow out of this trunk into a mighty tree of prophets, kings and patriarchs, finally ending in the crown with Mary and Jesus. The motif was already known in the fourth and fifth century at the time of the Syrian popes, but only developed in the visual arts in the West in the twelfth century. The Holy Kinship of Saint Anne, on the other hand, only deals with Christ's immediate family in three or four generations; it indicates the more horizontal (cognate) family relationships and focuses on the origins in the female line. The principal place is not occupied by the far (agnate) forefather Jesse or David, but by Anne or her mother Emerentiana. Hence it is often referred to as the *Arbor Annae*, and usually associated with fertility, as is so fittingly expressed in the hymns about Anne: "*Arbor Anna Fructuosa.*" Occasionally Joachim and Anne are situated in the center of the representation, shown with intertwined branches growing from their breast, but usually Anne is seated on a throne alone. In her immediate vicinity are her daughter Mary and her grandson Jesus, the Saint Anne Trinity. Grouped round them are her other two husbands, her daughters from these marriages, Mary Cleophas and Mary Salome, and their

Figure 2.6. Holy Kinship of Saint Anne. Southern Netherlands, 15th c. (Museum voor Schone Kunsten, Ghent)

respective husbands with their children—the six apostles. About 1500 the portrayal of the Holy Kinship was at its zenith (fig. 2.6). Royal houses, the nobility, the clergy and rich burghers gave numerous commissions for the painting of this type of picture.[25]

High Middle Ages

The question as to why people began to embellish Anne's life with such systems of family relationships, is difficult to answer. We can establish that the *trinubium* appeared at a time when the feudal society was showing interest in its own ancestry. It thus coincided with the upcoming dynasties and the changing family structure after about the year 1000.[26] Although the horizontal clan structure maintained its place, the vertical dynasty, in which the right of inheritance was determined via the agnate line, was becoming steadily more dominant. As a result of this "Houses" began to develop. The family was now centered round the master of the House and the family property passed from father to son. The family acquired its own name, which was connected with the House. This new structure also brought new symbolism in its train. Heraldry and genealogy supported the vertical line of descent. The extent to which people were keen to enhance their own status is evident from the way in which they tried to link earthly and heavenly dynasties.[27]

On the other hand, the legend which placed Anne in the midst of her family and made her into the ancestress of an important line fitted in with the changing religious views in the Ottonian period. In his study *Les saints Ottoniens* Patrick Corbet pointed out that according to text material round the year 1000, married women and widows from the prominent Ottonian dynasty were fulfilling an important role in religious and social life.[28] Apart from Queen Matilda (895–968), who was married to Henry I, and Edith (d. 946), the wife of Otto I, he mentions Oda of Gandersheim (d. 912), who was married to Ludolph of Saxony and became the mother of nine children. As well as the stereotype picture of the saint who embodied an ascetic, monial ideal and spent his or her life in seclusion, the hagiographers of these Ottonian female saints left the possibility open of a connection with a worldly life in harmony with the Christian values. Family relationships, marital life and motherhood had a clear role in this context. As exemplary wives and mothers these female saints, according to Corbet a sort of "sainteté dynastique," embodied the ideals of spouse, mother and ancestress. The Merovingians and Carolingians had placed less emphasis on these dynastic aspects in their hagiography. Later on, in the thirteenth century, this imagery found a sequel in Central Europe in the holy life of married sovereigns, such as Saint Hedwig of Silesia (1174–1243) and Saint Elizabeth of Thuringia (1207–1231). In the fourteenth century comparable developments can be observed in the North in the life of Saint Birgitta of Sweden (1302–1372). Birgitta in particular is closely connected with the veneration of Anne, since in her revelations she saw a vision of the family life of Mary and her parents.[29]

Late Medieval Lives: The Carmelite Tradition

At the end of the fifteenth century there was an evident change in the text tradition. From the time of the *Protevangelium* onwards Anne's life story had always been part of the history of Mary's birth, to which the legend of the three marriages was added later on. At the end of the fifteenth century it not only grew into a *Life* in its own right, supplemented with miracles and prayers, but was also considerably expanded with details about her parents and her sister Esmeria. In this prehistory the choice which Anne's mother Emerentiana has to make between virginity or marriage and motherhood forms the principal theme. At the same time a defensive attitude regarding the three marriages of Anne is to be traced in the texts. For centuries people had scarcely, if at all, worried about the legend of the three marriages, but now it seems as though people were beginning to feel uncomfortable about the idea that the mother of Mary and grandmother of Christ had been married three times. There are indications that Anne's *trinubium* was regarded as a sign of unbridled lust, which drove her to keep taking another husband at a ripe age.[30] The propagandists felt obliged to fiercely oppose any accusation that Anne had married for unseemly motives. In their defence more attention than ever was paid to questions connected with marriage law, sexual morals and holy motherhood. Only in the course of the sixteenth century, thus after the appearance of the *Histories of Anne*, did the image of Anne as the ancestress become subjected to increasing pressure. Scholars not only doubted the authenticity of the legend, but began to object to the idea that the mother of the Immaculate Virgin should have given birth to two other daughters. In the sixteenth century the *trinubium* and the related representation of the Holy Kinship retreated into the background.

The history of Emerentiana emerged in the last quarter of the fifteenth century. The Church Father, Cyril of Alexandria, who after the Council of Ephesus was said to have drawn up a letter in which he recorded the lineage of Anne, was the supposed author.[31] He is introduced as one of the monks of Mount Carmel, followers of the prophets Elijah and Elisha, who would have been in close confidential contact with Mary, Anne, and her mother Emerentiana in the days before the birth of Christ. When

Emerentiana was to be married off by her parents (or guardians), she is said to have consulted the brothers of Mount Carmel. In a vision of a tree with many branches, one of which bore fine and precious fruit, it was revealed to her that she was "the root of Jesse," out of whom the Savior would be born. She then entered into marriage with Stollanus from divine love and not from carnal desire. Emerentiana is represented as the ancestress, from whom sprang both the branch of Anne with the three Maries, Jesus and the six apostles, as well as that of her sister Esmeria with John the Baptist and Bishop Servatius. Thus in the *Histories of Saint Anne* the accent is on the prehistory of Mary: the life of her mother Anne and her grandmother Emerentiana, who chose marriage and bore children.

Given the connection with the monks of Mount Carmel it is obvious that the source of this story can be found in the Carmelite literature, such as in the works of the Ghent Carmelite, Arnold Bostius, in 1479.[32] Being an ardent advocate of the cult of Anne and her husband Joachim, he defended the doctrine of the Immaculate Conception of Mary. From Ghent he maintained close contact with a group of humanist scholars throughout Europe, including the Benedictine abbot of Sponheim, Johannes Trithemius, Robert Gaguin from Paris and Sebastian Brant in Strasbourg. He was, moreover, involved in the Brotherhood of Saint Anne, which met in the Carmelite monastery in Frankfurt. An international group of merchants, including some from the Low Countries, were prominent members.[33]

The Humanistic Tradition

The abbot of Sponheim, Johannes Trithemius, was undoubtedly one of the best known protagonists of Saint Anne's cult. He was much more to the fore than Bostius. For a long time it was assumed that the explosive growth of the veneration was due to him. From the foregoing it will have become sufficiently evident that there had already been widespread devotion earlier on, which, however, now received new impulses through the activities of the reformist clergy and their sympathizers, such as Trithemius.[34] In 1494 Trithemius published *De Laudibus Sanctissimae Matris Annae*, which had originally been written for the Brotherhood of Saint Anne in Frankfurt. In contrast to the *Lives of Anne* in the Low Countries, which were written as narratives, the *De Laudibus* was more of a treatise for a learned public. In a letter which prefaced the actual tract, Trithemius informed his readers that he did not intend to describe Anne's miracles, so as not to frighten off his (learned) readers in advance. He argued that the devotion had old roots; her relics were proof of centuries' long devotion. In that connection he mentioned the relics in the Benedictine monastery in Lyon. It is therefore not surprising to learn that in 1493 the Frankfurt Brotherhood gained possession of a costly relic of Anne from this monastery, thanks to the intermediary of merchants from the Low Countries and the humanist and printer Judocus Badius, a friend of both Bostius and Trithemius.[35] In his tract Trithemius summarizes the evidence in Christian literature up to then that Anne formed an essential link in the ultimate salvation of mankind. In his opinion Anne was holy when she conceived Mary, and he cites important Church Fathers, such as Augustine, Epiphanius, Jerome, and Cyril of Alexandria to confirm his statements.

The learned friends around Trithemius and Bostius waited impatiently for his work to appear. They were curious to learn how he would defend the Immaculate Conception of Mary. Trithemius had assured himself of their support in advance by collecting poems by his friends in which they took their stand beside him. The poems were printed as an appendix to the *De Laudibus*. Apart from the contributions of famous humanists such as Konrad Celtis, Dietrich Gresemund, Adam Werner von Themar, Rudolf Langen and the Parisian printer Jodocus Badius, we also find a poem by Rudolf Agricola, studied by Tilmans in her contribution to this volume.

The *De Laudibus* can be regarded as a reaction to the increasing intellectualism, which could block the path to innerly experienced piety. Nobody, however learned, need be ashamed of invoking and worshipping Anne. Great attention is paid to the *educatio*, so highly valued by the humanists, which found expression in practical piety and morals. According to Trithemius, Anne's way of life can serve as a guideline for clergy and laity. Anne contemplated God's commandments day and night; she had a strong faith and holy love. Her life was characterized by good works, and she was prudent in her contact with others and humble before God.

Although the tract was intended for (learned) men, it was emphasized that Anne was above all an example for women and mothers. She was never seen gossiping in the street or with the neighbors. She never danced or went to the theater. From her youth onwards she had learned to stay at home and work with her hands. Once a mother she taught her daughters to flee the worldly clamor and stay at home. In support of this Trithemius points to the Annunciation: the archangel did not find Mary in the street, but at home occupied with reading and prayer. Anne is represented as the prototype of the virtuous woman, the exact opposite of the bossy and voluptuous woman, the negative type that more than once appears in this period in religious and profane literature and art.[36] Anne exemplifies the view that only parents who are themselves pious and chaste can expect their children to follow their example.

Although Trithemius did not include any miracles, he did refer to occasions on which Anne was able to bring help. It is not difficult to recognize the well-known miracles of Anne therein. Anne was a patron saint against sickness in general and the plague in particular. She had power over death and could change poverty into wealth. She came to the assistance of women during pregnancy and confinement. Moreover, according to Trithemius, Anne was a support to both clergy and laity when the lusts of the flesh threatened to gain the upper hand. She quenched the carnal desire and dispelled melancholy.

Trithemius's tract with its attention to *educatio* and the growing interest in themes connected with marriage and the family fitted in with the needs of a lay public, which was trying to chart the course of a changing society. In 1490 the Brotherhood of Saint Anne, for whom Trithemius wrote his tract, commissioned an imposing retable, whose sixteen panels reproduced the history of Emerentiana and her daughter Anne, including some of the miracles. The principal themes found visual expression here. Considerable attention was paid to the Carmelites and their close ties with Emerentiana and Stollanus (or Anne and Joachim). One panel was entirely devoted to the doctrine of the Immaculate Conception. The painting is one of the highlights of the many Anne retables from this period.[38]

Anne's cult was not propagated exclusively by the Carmelites. As a matter of fact the production of *Lives of Anne* in the last decade of the fifteenth century was so overwhelming, that at least ten different versions have been traced, in Latin or the vernacular. Many of the titles are so similar that they are scarcely to be distinguished from one another. Moreover, the contents correspond closely, since the authors drew on the same sources and borrowed supplementary information from each other. Sometimes the details of the story are subtly altered to proclaim a particular point of view. Amongst the most important authors are the secular priest Jan van Denemarken, the Carthusians Pieter Dorlant (or Petrus Dorlandus), Wouter Bor, and an anonymous Franciscan. A number of these *Lives* are closely connected with the propaganda activities of the Dominicans in Cologne. In this text corpus the authors elucidate the familiar themes of marriage, motherhood, family and lineage mainly from the perspective of the doctrine of Redemption, but at the same time offer material to comment on the significance of marriage and motherhood in earthly reality. A case in point is given below.

JAN VAN DENEMARKEN AND THE COMMON FAITHFUL

The secular priest Jan van Denemarken, who probably worked in the diocese of Utrecht, belongs, with his *Die Historie, die Ghetiden ende die*

Exempelen van der Heyligher Vrouwen Sint Annen, which he claims to have written in 1486, to the earliest authors of *Lives of Anne* in northwest Europe (fig. 2.7). In the period from about 1490 to 1497 this *History of Anne* was printed at least five times in Antwerp. After that the market was taken over by other editions.[39] In his version Anne, as a married woman, mother, grandmother and widow, is given an exemplary function in social reality. Apart from the *History* mentioned above, he probably wrote a second *Life* ten years later, as well as a *Leven van Joachim* and a *Historie van Jozef*. Moreover, a processional play by him about Mary and Joseph's marriage has been handed down. He spread the idea that Joseph was not much older than his bride Mary and that Jesus was brought up by them both.[40]

In the *Vita* Van Denemarken restricts himself specifically to Anne's life course; he adds to this separate miracle stories and prayers for the practical devotion. Reinforcing the impression which the miracle of Emmericus created, Van Denemarken shows the unfamiliarity of the devotion to Saint Anne up to then. By means of his writings he wants to propagate the cult, because he believes that Anne deserves just as much worship as her daughter: "He who venerates the daughter, should also venerate her parents."[41] This is strengthened again in one of the seven miracles, in which Van Denemarken describes Anne's appearance to Birgitta of Sweden. Anne comforts her and reiterates that she gives married people special assistance and makes them fertile in body and soul. She teaches Birgitta a prayer, which was not only directed to Christ and his mother Mary, but also to Joachim and Anne, since whoever venerated the daughter should also include the parents.

Van Denemarken's *History* illustrates the time-honored viewpoint that virginity is to be preferred to the married state, but at the same time that marriage is legitimized if the union is aimed at begetting children to the glory of God; he even holds that it is possible to live a chaste life within marriage. The description of Emerentiana's marriage seems strongly influenced by the story of Tobias, who began his marriage with praying together with his bride and refraining from sexual contact. In the story of Emerentiana the first six suitors all die because they desired her for the wrong reasons, such as her beauty, descent or wealth. Jerome, and with him other theologians, emphasize that the Fall of mankind was caused by lust.[42] After Adam and Eve had eaten of the tree of knowledge, they discovered sexuality. Their eyes were opened and God therefore covered not their mouth nor their hands, which had caused the evil, but their genitals. In his view original sin was transmitted to the next generation through sexual desire, passion or lust during the coitus. Since Jesus did not descend from Heaven, but was born of a woman,

Figure 2.7. Jan van Denemarken, Die Historie, die Ghetiden ende die Exempelen van der Heyligher Vrouwen Sint Annen *(Antwerp, 1496) (Royal Library, The Hague)*

it was of fundamental importance that his conception should take place in an undefiled womb. Seen from this angle the emphasis on the virginity of Mary and the chastity of her ancestors is quite understandable. Through Emerentiana, who was without lust, and the pious and chaste Anne the way was paved for the Incarnation of Christ. Thus the matrilineal descent and the question to what extent Mary and possibly also Anne remained free from original sin by special grace in anticipation of the Incarnation of Christ play an important part. That also explains why sexual desire had to be absent in the marital relations of Mary's and Jesus' ancestors. Sometimes the continence is attributed to the advanced age of the couple, elsewhere it is emphasized that they are able to exercise superhuman self-control. The notion that the conception of Mary took place through the kiss of Anne and Joachim at the Golden Gate is based on this point of view.[43]

These views are not solely developed within a purely theological framework. Van Denemarken, who as a secular priest lived amongst the ordinary believers, used the history of Emerentiana and Anne to go explicitly into marital and sexual morality. In that respect his work exhibits a similarity with the practical moral approach of Trithemius.

THE POSITIVE VALUES OF MARRIED LIFE

In comparison with other *Lives of Anne*, Van Denemarken is only modestly elaborating on the history of Emerentiana. He pays more attention to the marriage of Anne and Joachim, explicitly emphasizing the solid and loving bond between man and wife. Elsewhere he praises Anne's obedience to her husband, whilst Joachim is outstanding for his caring behavior. The two developed into an exemplary married couple in a recognizable context for the lay public. Van Denemarken goes in depth into the question as to why Joachim and Anne remained childless for twenty years, though leading a pious and modest life. Commenting on this he brings in the two later marriages and makes it clear that Anne was not barren on account of her advanced years. Thus, according to him, Anne is not to be compared with other women from the Old Testament, who "above the course of nature's time" still conceived children through the will of God. He calculates that it was perfectly possible for her still to have children in her second and third marriage. She married, according to the law of Moses, at the age of fifteen. After twenty years Mary was born, five years later followed by Joachim's death. Within ten years Anne twice remarried and had a child by each husband. Her third child was born when she was about fifty years old. Thus in Van Denemarken's view there is no question of a supernatural passive conception by old and barren parents. He also produced proof of Anne's natural fertility from the reality of society: "It still happens daily that there are women who bring forth fruit up to their fiftieth year."[44]

Van Denemarken ascribes a positive value to marriage as a religious form of life; that is why he propagates marriage. He is the only author who explicitly goes into natural fertility as the condition for a lawful marriage and who emphasizes having children as the sole aim of a marriage. He thus once again underlines the marriage law of the Church. His description of Joseph explicits further his views on the family and the relationship between husband and wife. Mainly due to the realistic preaching technique of the Friars Minor, Joseph had in the Middle Ages been turned into a ridiculous, naive old man, who could not be considered capable of fathering a child. In this way any idea of active conception was purposely removed. In about 1400 Jean Gerson (1363–1429), chancellor of the University of Paris, defended the view that Joseph was a worthy husband who deserved respect and veneration. He contested the notion that Joseph was an old man. According to the Parisian scholar, Joseph could not have been more than 36 years old, for otherwise he would never have been able to protect his young wife Mary and the infant Jesus on the flight into Egypt. This line of argument returns in the work of Van Denemarken. He emphasizes that Joseph and Mary were about the same age. According to him it was all the more remarkable that Joseph was able to control himself. Thus Joseph increasingly acquires the features of the exemplary chaste husband and loving father in the Christian family: he becomes a man who commands respect.[45]

If so much emphasis is placed on conjugal morality and an exemplary family life, the *trinubium* calls for extra explanation. Van Denemarken defends Anne by pointing out that she did not enter into marriage on her own initiative, but from obedience. God had revealed to her that she would receive three fruits. He seeks an explanation in the holy number three, which fulfils a fundamental role in Anne's cult. Anne was accustomed, he explains, to do everything in threes, because God himself is threefold. Therefore God ordained that there should be not one or two, but three husbands, even though that was distasteful to Anne![46]

This defensive attitude is also apparent from the sequence of the miracles. Van Denemarken devotes the first two miracles to the three marriages of Anne. The first tells the story of a pious woman, Colette of Corbie (1381–1447), reformer of the Order of Poor Clares in the Netherlands, who at first refused to venerate Anne, because of her three marriages, until a vision made her change her mind (fig. 2.8).[47] The next example shows what happens to slanderers. An English bishop wanted to forbid Anne's cult and circulated wicked rumors about her. He spread the story that Anne was a woman "won by impurity." Punishment was not long coming: when the bishop tried to block the way to the church against the venerators of Anne, his horse stumbled and he fell off and broke his neck! Both examples act as an effective counterattack on anyone who wants to associate Saint Anne's "eagerness to marry" with sensuality.

The author goes extensively into the pedagogic function of Anne. From the two later marriages Mary Cleophas and Mary Salome were born, who act as models of a virtuous and pious upbringing: they were obedient to their parents and remembered their lessons. According to the author, that is how children should behave. Parents should instil into their children good manners, chastity, honesty and morals. Moreover, they should instruct them in spiritual matters, so that they know how to serve and honor God, how to avoid evil and do good, just as that was to be seen in the life of Mary and her parents.

Van Denemarken is reserved when it comes to discussing marriage as the normal way of life, certainly as far as remarriage is concerned. He emphasizes that Anne with her three husbands occupied an exceptional position, since she had provided the best fruits since the Creation. Only good trees, God-fearing mothers such as Emerentiana and Anne who did not marry from sexual desire, could bring forth good fruit. If the example of these dedicated mothers and chaste wives were followed and Christian conjugal morality were adhered to, there would be no obstacle to entering into marriage.

In particular in the discussion of Anne's life as a widow, Van Denemarken's admonitory tone is to be observed. After her third husband's death Anne did not want to marry again. She had offered God three fruits and knew that she was no longer fertile. That fact provides the author with the opportunity of repeating his point of view on conjugal morality. "Therefore it is not fitting nor honorable nor godly that she should again enter into marriage."[48] Thus Anne knows her place as an older woman in the Christian community. Van Denemarken sharply criticizes (older) women who still marry, even though they are no longer fertile. Marriage has then lost its real objective and is only directed towards sexual satisfaction. But, says the author severely, they will sorely rue that unchaste behavior in the life to come. He once more explains in detail that Anne was no ordinary woman, in spite of her worldly traits. Nobody else was worthy of bringing forth the tabernacle of the Holy Trinity, he says, and her other two marriages must be judged in the light of that sacred calling.

Van Denemarken then sums up all the qualities of Anne as an exemplary widow: she was virtuous, honest, unpretentious, charitable, tender, peace-loving and above all chaste. Even the devils in hell had to admit that from the beginning of mankind no woman had been as perfect as this exemplary mother. Now, says the author, she is one of the mightiest advocates in heaven, and he already alludes to the examples which show her power. The Christian virtues are summarized in the form of the customary *topoi*,

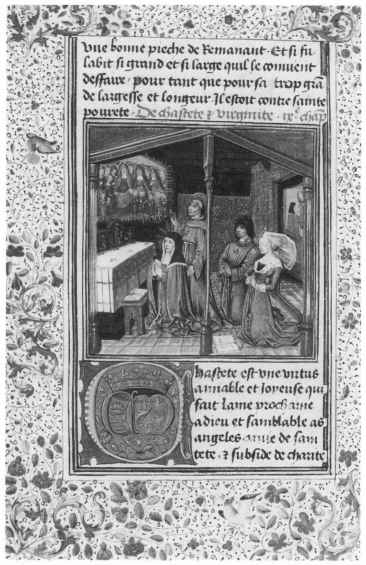

Figure 2.8. Coletta's vision of Saint Anne and the Holy Kinship. Miniature in Vita Sanctae Coletae, Arme Klaren Convent, Ghent, MS 8

just as Trithemius was to do some years later. Anne remained unpretentious in spite of her prosperity and never felt herself superior, even though many people looked up to her, even though she was descended from a powerful and prominent family. She gave her wealth away to the poor and the Church, the sin of "Lucifer with all his companions" (i.e. pride) never had a chance with her, since she submitted to God's commandments.

In other *Lives of Anne*, too, special emphasis is placed on the cardinal sins of pride and unchastity. In the legend which was published in 1496 in Louvain and had originally been written by an anonymous Franciscan, we read that Anne guarantees a good name, that she protects her worshippers from shame and knows how to prevent men and women getting entangled in the temptations of lust, especially outside marriage. She could in particular give special assistance to priests and adulterers if lechery got the better of them.[49]

The preoccupation with unchastity and the power of evil apparently forms a main theme at this time. The notorious *Malleus Maleficarum*, dating from this same period, warns of the danger of witches. Insatiable lust was seen as one of the principal characteristics of a witch, whereby they did not even shrink from sexual intercourse with the devil. In their diabolic conspiracy the witches endangered the divine order.[50] In this context Mary, but more especially Anne, could acquire the function of a positive counterpart. She is the symbol of the chaste marriage and of divinely controlled fertility and has proved to be impervious to the temptations of affluence and lust. Notwithstanding her *trinubium* she had only desired a man at God's command in order to bring forth offspring. She shunned merry company, in contrast to many people who pursued a licentious life. She engaged in good works and was moderate in the consumption of food and drink, so that she was able to keep her body under control. She could thus play a beneficial role in God's kingdom.[51]

Anne as the Patron Saint of Married Couples and of Motherhood in The Miracle Stories

Broadly speaking it is difficult to discover for whom the *Lives of Anne* were intended. The miracle stories can provide more insight.[52] Almost forty miracles of Anne have been handed down to us. The majority are concerned with the daily life of a lay public in an urban society. Anne comes to people's aid in adversity and brings her venerators wealth and success. She takes especial care of married couples, promotes fertility, assists women in pregnancy and confinement and is the patron saint of the family and of widows on their own. The prayer which Anne taught Birgitta, quoted by many propagandists of Anne, is characteristic: "Ego sum Anna, domina omnium coniugatorum. . . ."[53]

Most of the miracles testify to Anne's function as patron saint of marriage and the family. In fact her role in miracle stories would be worth a separate study. I shall therefore limit myself to a few examples derived from the widely distributed *Life of Anne* by Wouter Bor.[54]

In his miracle story "Two People Who Were Married" we make the acquaintance of a married couple who want to follow the pious example of Anne and Joachim by dividing their possessions into three. In answer to the couple's fervent prayer, Anne sees to it that the initially barren woman gives birth to a healthy triplet. Shortly after, when all the family and neighbors are out harvesting in the fields, fire breaks out. Everyone is convinced that the mother and the triplet have died in the childbed, but it appears that Anne, together with Mary and Jesus, has saved her worshipper by protecting her and her children under her cloak. This miracle exemplifies Anne's role as patron saint of childbearing and the Christian family.

A second miracle concerning a married couple shows how Anne can alter a hopeless situation and bring prosperity and success. A desperate man, trying to drown himself, is restrained in the water by the apostle John, a cousin of Christ, who advises him to venerate Anne.[55] From that moment onwards the man's fortunes take a turn for the better. He becomes wealthy and after twenty-eight years he and his wife have triplets, to whom they give the names of Anne's three husbands: Joachim, Cleophas and Salome. However, the mother dies shortly afterwards. The father is so desperate that he leaves his children beside the life-sized effigy of Anne on the altar. Anne thereupon restores the mother to life. The miracle makes such an impression that the lord of the manor has a picture of Anne included in his coat of arms. In this miracle the imagery surrounding Anne as a woman who became pregnant at a more advanced age forms an important motif. It is also once more apparent that the *trinubium* does not arouse opposition and that the accent is on Anne's role as a protective mother.

How great Anne's power is, appears from the story of the well-to-do lady from Lorraine, who is at first unable to bear children.[56] When, on the advice of a woman who was poor, but blessed with many children, the lady starts to venerate Anne, she almost immediately becomes pregnant. From gratitude her husband has a chapel built, dedicated to Saint Anne, where he goes for daily prayer. His wife however becomes negligent in her prayers with all the consequences: after the ninth month the child is stillborn. When the woman has confessed her guilt, Anne brings the child to life in answer to the prayers of the bystanders. It is given the name Anne. Thus Anne has power over life and death, over fertility and barrenness. But she expects absolute loyalty from her venerators and does not hesitate to punish negligence. There is no question here of "witch-like" behavior, as Wirth still maintained.[57] The punishment had a pedagogic function, even though the measures seem to us out of proportion.

To conclude this short selection it is worth telling the widely known miracle of Procopius of Prague, who is pursued by disaster after he has forsaken his calling to marry the beautiful daughter of a rich lord (fig. 2.9). The young bride dies and when he marries her sister, she too dies shortly afterwards. At his wits' end Procopius withdraws from society to live as a hermit until he comes into contact with a pilgrim who tells him about the power of Anne. From the moment that he starts to venerate her, good fortune smiles on him once more. When digging a well he comes across gold, which he gives to the king on condition that he will have medallions struck from it bearing the likeness of the Saint Anne Trinity. One day when the heavily pregnant queen has gone out riding alone, she is caught unawares by labor pains. She kisses the medallion, calls on Anne and the birth takes place without any problems for mother and child. The king honors Procopius by creating him archbishop of the whole kingdom and by promoting the cult of Anne. In this story the most important motifs have been incorporated: Anne's preoccupation with marriage or continence, her power to change misfortune into prosperity, her influence on fertility and growth and her protective power for women in pregnancy and childbirth. At the same time there is an indication of the way in which the veneration of Anne can be propagated.

It is striking that Anne's power over fertility not only plays a part in miracle stories, but also in the devotional practice. Thus in Düren, a place of pilgrimage near Aachen, women had an Anne girdle put round their waist to protect the unborn child or to promote pregnancy.[58] In other places women were said to pray for a child before an altar with an effigy of the Saint Anne Trinity or to pin a picture of Anne on their beds. Bor also describes miracles which show that Anne offers special protection to widows who have been put under great pressure or threatened to be forced into marriage again.[59]

The Life of Anne as an Example for Family Life?

To what extent the notions about marriage, the family, and the position of husband and wife therein are visible outside these devotional texts can partly be gathered from the visual arts. Elsewhere I have discussed the relation between texts and representations of Anne in more detail. I shall limit myself here to the work of Lucas Cranach the Elder.[60]

Cranach produced two paintings and a woodcut of the Holy Kinship. Since 1505 he had been a court painter in the service of the Elector of Saxony in Wittenberg. In his commission he painted the triptych of the Saint Anne altar in the church of Saint Mary in Torgau. In his composition the Holy

Kinship changes from a solemn family portrait into a jovial family scene. The three generations are depicted in the center of the middle panel, the family of Alpheus and Mary Cleophas and of Zebedee and Mary Salome occupy a prominent place within the greater family context on the wings. Mary Cleophas is breast feeding her youngest child, while Mary Salome is doing

Figure 2.9. The Miracle of Procopius. Panel of the retable of the Brotherhood of Saint Anne in Frankfurt, c. 1500 (Historisches Museum, Frankfurt am Main)

the hair of one of her children. The husbands regard this exemplary motherly care indulgently from a distance. This representation fitted in with the painting by Bernard Strigel of 1515, in which the imperial family was portrayed as a Holy Kinship.

Cranach painted a second Holy Kinship in 1510–12 on the occasion of his own marriage to Barbara Brengbier. In the figures we can recognize in Alpheus and Mary Cleophas the painter and his wife and in Zebedee and Mary Salome his father- and mother-in-law. In this picture the theme of the father, who is involved in the upbringing, has been given a more prominent place. Zebedee is instructing his son (John). Mary Cleophas is again breast feeding one of the four children while Alpheus looks on at this homely scene.[61]

One of the best-known portrayals of the Holy Kinship is Lucas Cranach's woodcut. This piece of work is exceptional in several respects. In the first place the composition is remarkable: the Kinship is shown in a number of scenes with Anne, Mary, and Jesus in the center. Joseph stands rather doltishly to one side and the three husbands of Anne are talking to one another on the other side of the Saint Anne Trinity. At lower left we observe Alpheus's family and lower right Zebedee's. Also in this picture Mary Cleophas is giving the youngest child the breast and Mary Salome is playing with one of the children. But the fathers are placed much closer to the family now than in the paintings and they take an important task upon themselves in the upbringing. Alpheus (instead of Zebedee in the painting) is instructing his two eldest sons with the severity of a schoolmaster, the rod in his hand. Zebedee places a fatherly hand on the shoulder of his son, John the Evangelist, who is holding a closed book in his hand. In this representation the fathers incorporate both severity and affection. They take the upbringing of the children in hand. The mothers represent the loving care. The ideal division of tasks and roles between husband and wife within the family is depicted here in an exemplary manner, as it was propagated in word and picture, above all in the town, at the end of the Middle Ages.[62]

CONCLUSION

From the earliest times the devotion to Anne has always been indissolubly bound up with the veneration of her daughter Mary. Not until the Late Middle Ages did Anne receive more attention in the West, but always in her role as mother of Mary, grandmother of Christ and as ancestress of a Holy Family. About 1500 this mother and kinship cult reaches its zenith and the details already known for centuries are expatiated on with new historical information about her lineage. The increasing interest in Anne in the fifteenth century is undoubtedly connected with the highly impassioned discussions on the possible Immaculate Conception of Mary. Notwithstanding this are the theological questions of minor importance in the narrative text corpus.

Here, in the narratives as well as in the prayers and the miracles, the accent is on her power as a protective mother. Her influence on both fertility and growth as well as on death and destruction sometimes gives her the traits of the Great Mother of the pre-Christian era. At the same time the imagery is closely connected with the doctrine of Redemption. According to her propagandists Anne forms an important link in the completion of the work of Salvation. That is why Anne's lineage and her closeness to Mary and Jesus is described in such detail. In the Saint Anne Trinity the Incarnation of Christ via the female line is visualized. In this light it is also understandable that the veneration of Anne in word and picture was often connected with the ultimate work of Salvation. It is illustrative that many of the *Lives of Anne* end with the Gregorian Mass and the devotion to Christ's five wounds. Baldung Grien's well-known woodcut with the representation of the Saint Anne Trinity, in which Anne makes a scissor movement beside Christ's genitals, also has significance in this context. It refers to the circumcision, in which Christ's blood flowed for the first time, portending his ultimate death on the Cross. The convergent symbolism of the vine confirms this interpretation.[63]

However, it is striking that around 1500 the descriptions of Anne and her relatives are used not only to spread the views on chastity and virginity, but also the value of marriage, the characteristics of the Christian family and the place of husband and wife within that family. In most of the *Lives of Anne* around 1500 the tension over the legend of the *trinubium* can be strongly felt. Saintliness and remarriage, certainly if the woman is no longer fertile, are increasingly seen as incompatible. On the one hand the change in imagery is the result of the emphasis on Anne's position as mother of the immaculate Virgin, but on the other hand elements of the imagery link up with the preoccupation with marriage and the family, as is evident, for example, in Jan van Denemarken's *History of Anne* and in the work of Lucas Cranach.

In the course of the sixteenth and seventeenth centuries the nature of the devotion changes, partly caused by developments in the Church doctrine and partly through the changing needs of the common faithful. After the rejection of the *trinubium*, the picture of Anne as the ancestress in the Holy Kinship recedes into the background and the more powerful position of Anne as grandmother of Christ and mother of Mary, who can act as intercessor, is toned down in the representation of the Saint Anne Trinity. Instead she now acquires a more modest role as the upbringer of Mary. Anne is represented as the mother of the young girl Mary. Usually they are shown reading a book together.

The shift in the imagery fits in with the changing views on marriage and the Christian family, as they are developed in particular in later centuries. In the sixteenth century Catholics and Protestants formulated a new conjugal and family morality, which had already emerged in the previous century and which was to be further elaborated in the seventeenth century. The description of Anne as faithful spouse, dedicated mother and grandmother, and as chaste widow can acquire an exemplary function in a society where marriage is increasingly highly valued. In the stories at the end of the fifteenth century which describe the life of Anne and her family and in the representations of the Holy Kinship, we see the first traces of these developments.

NOTES

I am very grateful to Anneke Mulder-Bakker for her comments on previous versions of this article.

1. A copy of this book is kept in Rijksmuseum Meermanno-Westreenianum/ Museum van het Boek, The Hague, 1 F 30.

2. Standard work on the veneration of Saint Anne: Beda P. Kleinschmidt, *Die heilige Anna: Ihre Verehrung in Geschichte, Kunst und Volkstum* (Düsseldorf: Schwann, 1930). On the Saint Anne Trinity see the contribution of Willemien Deeleman-van Tyen, in Ton Brandenbarg et al., *Heilige Anna, Grote Moeder: De cultus van de Heilige Moeder Anna en haar familie in de Nederlanden en aangrenzende streken* (Nijmegen: SUN, 1992), 99–165, and Sigfried Gohr, "Anna Selbtritt," in *Die Gottesmutter: Marienbild in Rheinland und in Westfalen*, vol. 1, ed. Leonard Küppers (Recklinghausen: Bongers, 1974), 243–254. On the Holy Kinship: Werner Esser, *Die heilige Sippe: Studien zu einem spätmittelalterlichen Bildthema in Deutschland und den Niederländen* (Bonn: Rheinische Friedrich-Wilhelms-Universität, 1986). Surveys of the literature on Saint Anne round 1500: Albert Ampe, "Philips van Meron en Jan van Denemarken," *Ons Geestelijk Erf*, 50 (1976), 10–37, 148–203, 260–308, 353–377; 51 (1977), 169–197, 367–390; 52 (1978), 397–427; 53 (1979), 240–303; 54 (1980), 113–157; Ton Brandenbarg, "Jan van Denemarken en Pieter Dorlant over de maagschap van Sint-Anna: Een vergelijkende studie," *Ons Geestelijk Erf*, 63 (1989), 201-244; Ton Brandenbarg, *Heilig familieleven: Verspreiding en waardering van de Historie van Sint-Anna in de stedelijke cultuur in de Nederlanden en het Rijnland aan het begin van de moderne tijd (15de/16de eeuw)* (Nijmegen: SUN, 1990); Angelika Dörfler-Dierken, *Die Verehrung der Heiligen Anna in Spätmittelalter und früher Neuzeit* (Göttingen: Vandenhoeck & Ruprecht, 1992). See also Kathleen Ashley and Pamela Sheingorn, eds., *Interpreting Cultural Symbols: Saint Anne in Late Medieval Society* (Athens [etc.]: University of Georgia Press, 1990).

3. On the relation between texts and representations in the visual arts in the former Carmelite monastery in Frankfurt, the Sint-Salvator church in Bruges, Sint-Goedele in Brussels: Ton Brandenbarg, "St. Anne and her family: The veneration of St Anne in connection with concepts of marriage and the family in the early modern period," in *Saints and She-devils: Images of Women in the 15th and 16th Centuries*, ed. Lène Dresen-Coenders (London: Rubicon Press, 1987), 101–127. For the relation between texts and the retable in the former Franciscan abbey church (now St Peter's

church) in Dortmund, see Ton Brandenbarg, *Heilige Anna, Grote Moeder*, 64–67. See also: O. Stein, "Die flämischen Altäre Westfalens mit besonderer Berücksichtigung des Altars in der Petrikirche zu Dortmund," *Beiträge zur Geschichte Dortmunds und der Grafschaft Mark*, 22 (1913), 286–310.

4. The miracle is already to be found in the first known print of a Latin Life of Saint Anne in the Netherlands, *Legenda seu Vita Beatissime Anne*, included as the second work in *Speculum Rosariorum Jhesu et Mariae* (Antwerp: Geraert Leeu, 1489), the pages are not numbered. The author is often given as Reginaldus, chaplain to King Stephen of Hungary, who is said to have recorded the miracle in 1018. The name Emmericus is reminiscent of Saint Emerius, son of Saint Stephen of Hungary (975–1038). I quote from the extended version in Wouter Bor, *Die Historie van die Heilige Moeder Santa Anna* . . . (Zwolle: Petrus van Os van Breda, 1499), fols. 147r–155r. See also n. 54.

5. Bor, *Die Historie*, fols. 150r–150v, "Sinte Jacob seide hoer fyguere wert ghemaelt in ghedaente eender eerbaere vrouwe hebbende by hoer dochter jonffer maria met jhesum haren soen. Maect haer alsulcken figure ende want die wyl godes is datmen haer over al die werelt aenbeden sal."

6. Bor, *Die Historie*, fol. 152r, "Maria seide Is sant anna u moeder so bin ic u suster ende jhesus mijn soen is u neve."

7. Bor, *Die Historie*, fol. 155r, "Hierom sal een yeghelic mensche die heylige vrouwe sant anna met haren gheslachte gerne eren ende dienen namelic met de kersen dagelicx of met die aelmissen ende drie pater nosters ende drye ave maria te lesen voer hoer beelde ist datmen dat so bi brengen kan of heeftmen beelde niet datmen dan metter harten daer voer si met ynnicheit ende goeden betrouwen ter eren gods die daer regneert in ewicheit Amen."

8. Martin Luther, *D. Martin Luthers Werke: Kritische Gesamtausgabe*, 47 (Weimar: Böhlau, 1883–1948; rpt. 1969–), 383.

9. Tuesday, the third day of the week has traditionally been connected with fertility and growth. In the Jewish-Christian story of the Creation God made the separation between land and sea on the third day and bestowed on the earth fertility and growth.

10. According to *Dysz ist eyn seltzemme und gute Legende von Sant Annan und von irem gantzen Geslecht*, (Strasbourg: Krysteler, 1501), fol. 53r, an altar and an effigy of Saint Anne were placed in the Commandery of Saint John in Strasbourg in 1501. For the occasion Anne was symbolically invited by her children, grandchildren and relatives to keep them company in the church. The members of the chamber of rhetoric of Veere in Zeeland (circa 1500) had also chosen Anne as their patron saint and called themselves "Saint Anne's children."

11. E. de Bachelet, "Immaculée Conception," in *Dictionnaire de Théologie Catholique*, 7 (Paris, 1927), col. 845–1218; Jean de Dieu, "Sainte Anne et l'Immaculée Conception," *Etudes franciscaines*, 46 (1934), 15–39; Jean Gallot, "L'Immaculée Conception," in *Marie: Etudes sur la Sainte Vierge*, vol. 7, ed. Hubert de Manoir (Paris: 1964), 11–116. Important art historical studies: Bruno Borchert, "L'Immaculée dans l'iconographie du Carmel," *Carmelus*, 2 (1955), 85–131; Mirella Levi d'Ancona, *The Iconography of the Immaculate Conception in the Middle Ages and Early Renaissance* (New York: College Art Association of America, 1957); Marina Warner, *Alone of All Her Sex: The Myth and Cult of the Virgin Mary* (London: Weidenfeld and Nicolson, 1976), 236–254; compare also Karin Tilmans' contribution, "Sancta Mater versus Sanctus Doctus" in this volume.

12. The doctrine of the Immaculate Conception should not be confused with the Virgin Birth, the doctrine that Mary had borne Christ as a virgin.

13. Brandenbarg, *Heilig familieleven*, 86–93; Dörfler-Dierken, *Die Verehrung*, 45–66 (in particular the role of Pope Sixtus IV); Levi d'Ancona, *Iconography*. For the discussions in the thirteenth century see De Bachelet, "Immaculée Conception," 1073–1078.

14. Gallot, "L'Immaculée Conception," 71–77.

15. Paul Oskar Kristeller, *Le Thomisme et la pensée italienne de la Renaissance* (Montreal: Institut d'Etudes médiévales [etc.], 1967) 52, 104–123. See the copy in the Herzog August Bibliothek, Wolfenbüttel, 35.13 Th. (2); cf. *Gesamtkatalog der Wiegendrucke* (Leipzig: Hiersemann, 1925), 3237.

16. Erich Maschke, *Die Familie in der deutschen Stadt des späten Mittelalters* in *Sitzungsberichte der Heidelberger Akademie der Wissenschaften. Philosophisch-historische Klasse* 1980:4; Natalie Zemon Davis, *Society and Culture in Early Modern France: Eight Essays* (Stanford: Stanford University Press, 1975); *Die Stadt des Mittelalters*, vol. 3, ed. Carl Haase (Darmstadt: Wissenschaftliche Buchgesellschaft, 1973); Martha C. Howell, *Women, Production, and Patriarchy in Late Medieval Cities* (Chicago: University of Chicago Press, 1986).

17. See Karin Tilman's contribution, "Sancta Mater versus Sanctus Doctus" in this volume.

18. Oscar Cullman, "The Protevangelium of James," in *New Testament Apocrypha*, vol. 1, *Gospels and Related Writings*, ed. Edgar Hennecke et al. (Philadelphia: Westminster, 1963), 370–388. See also the excerpt in Ashley and Sheingorn, *Interpreting Cultural Symbols*, 53–57.

19. Cf. Leo Scheffczyk, *Das Mariengeheimnis in Frömmigkeit und Lehre der Karolingerszeit* (Leipzig: St. Benno-Verlag, 1963).

20. Jan Gijsel, "Die unmittelbare Textüberlieferung des sogenannte Pseudo-Mattheus," *Verhandelingen van de Koninklijke Academie voor Wetenschappen, Letteren en Schone Kunsten van Belgie, Klasse der Letteren*, 43 (1981), nr 96; Jacqueline Lafontaine-Dosogne, *Iconographie de l'enfance de la Vièrge dans l'Empire byzantin et en Occident*, vol. 2 (Brussels: Academie Royale de Belgique, 1964–1965), 13–17; see also Dörfler-Dierken, *Die Verehrung*, 120–124. For Hrosvitha, see *Roswitha von Gandersheim, Werke*, vol. 1, trans. Hélène Homeyer (Paderborn: Schöningh, 1936), 41–80.

21. Dörfler-Dierken, *Die Verehrung*, 123f.

22. *Jacobi a Voragine Legenda Aurea vulgo Historia Lombardica dicta*, ed. Th. Graesse (1890, rpt Osnabrück: Zeller, 1969), 585–597; see also *Die Legenda Aurea des Jacobus de Voragine*, trans. Richard Benz (rpt Cologne, 1969), 676–688.

23. On the *trinubium*: Max Förster, "Die Legende vom Trinubium der Hl. Anna," in *Probleme der englischen Sprache und Kultur: Festschrift Johannes Hoops zum 60. Geburtstag*, ed. Wolfgang Keller (Germanissche Bibliothek, 2d ser. 20) (Heidelberg: Winter, 1925), 105–130; Brandenbarg, *Heilig familieleven*, 23f, 55f, 62–66, 167–180, 204f; Dörfler-Dierken, *Die Verehrung*, 125–145.

24. Arthur Watson, *The Early Iconography of the Tree of Jesse* (London: Oxford University Press, 1934), 3, 46.

25. Esser, *Die heilige Sippe*, 52f.

26. Frances and Joseph Gies, *Marriage and the Family in the Middle Ages* (New York: Harper & Row, 1989), 121–145. See also Georges Duby, *The Knight, the Lady and the Priest: the Making of Modern Marriage in Medieval France*, trans. Barbara Bray (London: Lane, 1984).

27. André Vauchéz, "Beata stirps: Sainteté et lignage en Occident aux xiiie et xive siècles," in *Famille et parenté dans l'Occident mediéval*, ed. Georges Duby and Jacques Le Goff (Rome: Ecole française de Rome, 1977), 404, holds: "De plus, comme le premier ancestre attribué au Christ par le Nouveau Testament est le roi David, il paraissait normal que cette efflorence de sainteté se soit manifestée spécialement dans certaines familles royales. Fréderique II lui même avait insisté sur ce point en soulignant les liens familiaux qui l'attachaient à sa parente St. Elisabeth de Hongrie, à la fois pour exalter le dignité impériale et pour renforcer le prestige de sa dynastie, alors en butte aux attaques de la papauté;" see also Leopold Génicot, *Les généalogies* (Typologie des sources du Moyen Age occidental, 15) (Turnhout: Brepols, 1975), in which he discusses this mingling of family trees in England in the ninth century and Bertold Hinz, "Studien

zur Geschichte des Ehepaarbildnisses," *Marburger Jahrbuch für Kunstwissenschaft*, 19 (1974), 139–218.

28. Patrick Corbet, *Les saints Ottoniens: Sainteté dynastique, sainteté royale et sainteté féminine autour de l'an Mil* (Beihefte der Francia, 15) (Sigmaringen: Thorbecke 1987); see also Ortrud Reber, *Die Gestaltung des Kultus weiblicher Heiliger im Spätmittelalter: die Verehrung der heiligen Elisabeth, Klara, Hedwig und Birgitta* (Hersbruck, 1963).

29. Clarissa W. Atkinson, *The Oldest Vocation: Christian Motherhood in the Middle Ages* (Ithaca: Cornell University Press, 1991), 170–184, esp. 173. See also Jeanette Nieuwland's study "Motherhood and Sanctity in the Life of Saint Birgitta of Sweden: An Insoluble Conflict?" in this volume.

30. See for instance: Petrus Dorlandus, *Historie van Sint-Anna* (Antwerp: Govert Back, 1501), ch. 3.2 (the pages are not numbered): "hi (plach) mit valscher tonghen te blasphemeren seggende dat si verwonnen was met oncuysheyt om dat si drye mans gehadt heeft."

31. The earliest indication is to be found in Arnold Bostius, *De Patronatu et Patrocinio Beatissimae Virginis Mariae in dicatum sibi Carmeli Ordinem* (1479) in Daniel de BVM, *Speculum Carmelitanum*, 1 (Antwerp, 1680), col. 375–431.

32. See Brandenbarg, *Heilig familieleven*, 118–124; P. Demaerel, *Arnold Bostius O. Carm. (1446–1499): Vita et Epistola*, (Licentiaats thesis Louvain: University of Louvain, 1983); Christine Jackson-Holzberg, *Zwei Literaturgeschichten des Karmelitenordens: Untersuchungen und kritische Edition* (Erlangen: Palm und Enke, 1981).

33. See Brandenbarg, *Heilig familieleven*, 129–135; for the circle of humanists round Trithemius see B. Zimmerman, "Les carmes humanistes 1465–1525," *Etudes Carmelitaines*, 20 (1935), 19–93; Johannes Trithemius, *De Laudibus Sanctissimae Annae* (Mainz: Friedberg, 1494) and Klaus Arnold, *Johannes Trithemius (1465–1516)* (Würzburg: Schöningh, 1971).

34. Cf. Noell L. Brann, *The abbot Trithemius (1462–1516): The Renaissance of Monastic Humanism* (Leiden: Brill, 1981).

35. See H.H. Koch, *Das Karmelitenkloster zu Frankfurt am Main (13. bis 16. Jahrhundert)* (Frankfurt am Main, 1912), 80–90.

36. See Renée Pigeaud, "Women as Temptress: Urban Morality in the Fifteenth Century," in *Saints and She-devils*, ed. Dresen-Coenders, 39–58.

37. Brandenbarg, *Heilig Familieleven*, 132–135; see also the "Introduction" of Ashley and Sheingorn in *Interpreting cultural symbols*, 2–68, especially 27–43.

38. Recent literature surveys in Brandenbarg, *Heilig familieleven*, and Dörfler-Dierken, *Die Verehrung*. Brandenbarg restricts himself to the description of a connected text corpus and points to two propaganda centres: a. the circle of scholars round Arnold Bostius in Ghent, who wanted to spread the doctrine of the Immaculate Conception and the devotion to Joachim and Anne; b. the Dominicans in Cologne, with Dominicus van Gelre, who used the devotion to Saint Anne for their reformatory activities within the Church and monastic life. They linked the veneration of Saint Anne with the Rosary devotion and the Eucharist. Dörfler attempts to give a more or less complete survey of the literature on Saint Anne in the Late Middle Ages.

39. The first two editions of Van Denemarken were published anonymously in about 1490/91 and 1493 in Antwerp by Geraert Leeu; the other three editions were published in 1496 and 1497 (2x) by Van Liesveldt. I use the (complete) edition of 1496 (*Gesamtkatalog* 1498). Albert Ampe, "Petrus Dorlandus O. Carth. en Dominicus van Gelre O.P.," in *Hellinga Festschrift/Feestbundel/Mélanges: forty-three studies in bibliography presented to Prof. dr. Wytze Hellinga* (Amsterdam: Israel, 1980), 5–46, ascribed this *Life of Saint Anne* to an anonymous Dominican. Dörfler-Dierken, *Die Verehrung*, 155, 268 assumes, without proof, that this text was written by an anonymous Carmelite. For Jan van Denemarken, see Brandenbarg, *Heilig familieleven*, 41–80.

40. Jan van Denemarken, *Een scoon genuchlike Historie vanden heilighen Joseph*, printed by Van Elzen in Nijmegen, c. 1547, of which a copy is kept in the Royal Library of Copenhagen. This print contains also *Leven van Joachim (Life of Joachim)* and the processional play about Mary and Joseph's marriage, see Albert Ampe, "Philips van Meron en Jan van Denemarken," (1977), 169–197 and "Jan van Denemarken's processiespel," *Handelingen der Koninklijke Zuidnederlandse Maatschappij van Taal- en Letterkunde en Geschiedenis*, 32 (1978), 5–19.

41. Jan van Denemarken, *Die Historie*, 2v.

42. See Peter Brown, *The Body and Society: Men, Women and Sexual Renunciation in Early Christianity* (New York: Columbia University Press, 1988), 303–334.

43. In the sixteenth century this vision was abjected. See J. Molanus and J.H. Paquot, *De historias ss. Imaginum et Picturarum, pro vero earum Usu contra Abusum Libri Quattuor* (Louvain, 1570, 2d ed. 1771), 395.

44. Jan van Denemarken, *Die Historie*, 22v.

45. See Marjory Bolger Foster, *The Iconography of St. Joseph in Netherlandish Art (1400–1550)* (Ann Arbor: University of Michigan Press, 1979); see also Joseph Seitz, *Die Verehrung des Hl. Joseph in ihrer geschichtlichen Entwicklung bis zum Konzil von Trient dargestelt* (Freiburg im Breisgau, 1908); P. Glorieux, "St. Joseph dans l'oeuvre de Gerson," *Cahiers de Joséphologie*, 19 (1971), 414–428. For the changing tradition of imagery, see Herman Pleij, "Jozef als pantoffelheld," *Symposium*, 3 (1981), 66–81; David Herlihy, "The Family and Religious Ideologies in Medieval Europe," *Journal of Family History*, 12 (1987), 3–17; see also Atkinson, *The Oldest Vocation*, 159–162.

46. Jan van Denemarken, *Die Historie*, 30v.

47. Colette saw a distinguished lady amidst a great throng who all treated her with respect. However, the lady ignored Colette and walked past her with her noble company. When Colette asked who the lady was, she was told that it was Saint Anne. She was the most eminent in the great multitude of saints, because through her three marriages she was not only the mother of Mary and grandmother of Christ, but also of a great number of apostles. She had thus gained great esteem in heaven. Colette thereupon begged forgiveness and became a faithful venerator of Anne and her kinship, see *Vita sanctae Coletae (1381–1447)*, intr. Charles van Corstanje et al. (Tielt: Lannoo, 1982), 218, from a manuscript in the Arme Klaren Convent, Ghent, MS 8, fol. 40v.

48. Jan van Denemarken, *Die Historie*, 32v, 35r.

49. *Dysz ist eyn seltzemme und gute legende von Sant Annan und von irem gantzen geslecht*, a German translation of the *Legenda sanctae Annae* (Louvain: Joh. de Westfalia, 1496), fol. 43v: "that all excesses and lechery of the wanton flesh be wiped away through the intercession of Saint Anne."

50. Brian P. Levack, *The Witch-hunt in Early Modern Europe* (London: Longman, 1987), 41–85; see also Lène Dresen-Coenders, "Witches as Devils' Concubines: On the Origin of Fear of Witches and Protection against Witchcraft," in *Saints and She-devils*, ed. Dresen-Coenders, 59–82.

51. Ton Brandenbarg, "St Anne and Her Family: The Veneration of St Anne in Connection with Concepts of Marriage and the Family in the Early-modern Period," in *Saints and She-devils*, ed. Dresen-Coenders, 121f.

52. A survey of the miracles of Saint Anne in: Albert Ampe, "Philips van Meron en Jan van Denemarken," (1980), 113–157. See further Dörfler-Dierken, *Die Verehrung*, 327–328.

53. Sancta Birgitta, *Revelaciones Liber VI*, ed. Birger Bergh (Samlingar utgivna av Svenska Fornskriftsällskapet, ser. 2. Latinska skrifter 7:6) (Stockholm: Almqvist & Wiksell International, 1991)], 266.

54. Wouter Bor, *Die Historie van die Heilige Moeder Santa Anna ende van haer olders daer si van geboren is ende van horen leven ende hoer penitenci ende mirakelen mitten exempelen* (Zwolle: Petrus van Os van Breda, 1499); miracle in cap.

55. This translation by Bor was circulated up into the twentieth century; early translations were made into German and French. Ampe, "Philips van Meron en Jan van Denemarken," (1979 and 1980) ascribed the original Latin *Life of Saint Anne*, which Wouter Bor translated, to Jan van Denemarken. However, compare my comments on Ampe's hypothesis in Brandenbarg, "Jan van Denemarken en Pieter Dorlant," 104–112 and Brandenbarg, *Heilig familieleven*, 307–309.

55. Bor, *Die Historie*, cap. 57.

56. Ibid., cap. 63.

57. Jean Wirth, "Sainte Anne est une sorcière," *Bibliothèque de l'Humanisme et de la Renaissance*, 40 (1978), 449–480.

58. See Erwin Gatz, *St.Anna in Düren* (Mönchengladbach: Külen Verlag, 1972), 117f. See also Jacques Gélis, *L'Arbre et le fruit: La naissance dans l'Occident Moderne (XVIe–XIXe siècle)* (Paris: Fayard, 1984).

59. Brandenbarg, *Heilig familieleven*, 157–165; Dörfler-Dierken, *Die Verehrung*, 227–252.

60. Brandenbarg, *Heilig Familieleven*, 144–153; Werner Schade, *Die Malerfamilie Cranach* (Dresden: VEB Verlag der Kunst, 1974).

61. Christiane D. Andersson, "Religiöse Bilder Cranachs im Dienste der Reformation," in *Humanismus und Reformation als kulturelle Kräfte in der deutschen Geschichte*, ed. Lewis W. Spitz (Berlin [etc.]: De Gruyter, 1981), 43–80; see also Pamela Sheingorn, "Appropriating the Holy Kinship: Gender and Family History," in Ashley and Sheingorn, *Interpreting Cultural Symbols*, 187–194.

62. Steven Ozment, *When Fathers Ruled: Family Life in Reformation Europe* (Cambridge, Mass.: Harvard University Press, 1983); Pamela Sheingorn, "'The Wise Mother': The Image of St. Anne Teaching the Virgin Mary," in *Gesta* 32 (1993), 69–80.

63. Brandenbarg, *Heilig familieleven*, 153–157, responding to Wirth, "Sainte Anne est une sorcière." Striking is the growing attention to Anne's cult in relation to the Eucharist. The many *Histories of Saint Anne*, especially those from the sphere of influence of the Dominicans in Cologne, were provided with indulgences in connection with the Gregorian Mass and "The Five Wounds of Christ." In the visual arts the relation between Anne's cult and the Eucharist is strongly expressed in the so-called "Golden miracle of Dortmund," a retable by Antwerp masters, 1521, from the former Franciscan monastery (now the church of St Peter).

For the Gregorian Mass see Uwe Westfehling, *Die Messe Gregors des Grossen: Vision, Kunst, Realität. Katalog und Führer zu einer Ausstellung im Schnütgen-Museum.* (Cologne: Schnütgen-Museum, 1982).

PART II
THE ANCIENT WORLD
TRANSFORMED

Figure 3.1. Scene on stone from Altuna, Uppland, Sweden
(Photo Samplonius)

3. FROM VELEDA TO THE *VÖLVA*

ASPECTS OF FEMALE DIVINATION IN GERMANIC EUROPE

Kees Samplonius

According to Bynum, male suspicion of female visionary power was alerted by the increasing numbers of women saints in the later Middle Ages, and articulated in a series of influential works on the testing of spirits.[1] The observation, if correct, assumes the presence, outside the Church, of an inherent female capacity for divination. Indeed, female visionaries were by no means confined to the Christian world. Female visionary power manifested itself in Antiquity, where it culminated in the oracling sibyls, as well as in those parts of Europe that were only integrated in the Christian world at a later stage, like Germanic Europe, for instance.

Divination may seem a surprising theme in a book about sanctity and motherhood, but its choice as *leitmotiv* is not accidental. It is an element that was present in both Christian and Old Germanic culture. In the Christian Middle Ages prophecy, revelation and divination could be important features in the manifestation of female saints. In the Germania, the gift of prophesying appears to have been one of the few qualities that gave women an air of holiness. It is a quality, therefore, that provides us with something of a Germanic equivalent of Christian women saints. There is also a practical reason for it: seeresses are one of the few categories of Germanic women about whom we are slightly better informed. Finally, there are signs that female divination and oracling were practiced in connection with cults of fertility, for instance those of the mother goddesses or *matres*.

Interest in the lives of women in the Germanic and Viking world is nothing new—Weinhold's book on Germanic women appeared more than a century ago[2]—but in recent times, inspired probably by the feminist movements of the sixties, scholarly attention has truly intensified.[3] This research has led to rather different pictures, varying from women as strong heroines, to drudges, domestic slave laborers subjected by their macho men. So interpretations vary, not least because of the preconceived approaches of some of the authors. On some points, however, consensus has been reached. It is generally accepted that married women had a better social position than their unmarried sisters, especially if they had given birth to an heir. The many stipulations in early Germanic laws are probably responsible for the fact that a lot of research has been carried out on the legal status of women. As a result we are relatively well informed about their rights to divorce, or inherit, and all procedures involved. Research on divination and Germanic seeresses, on the other hand, has been limited. It is this white spot on our map this study will try to fill in. Point of departure is the Germanic seeress as a person of flesh and blood, but for reasons that will become obvious Germanic religion and mythology will also be drawn upon.

I will first define the area of our investigation, then look at the sources that are at our disposal, and evaluate the value of any information that can be extracted. Next I will survey belief in the predictive power of women, and look into its characteristics, such as the equipment the seeress used. After that I will discuss her place in society, look into the relation between the Germanic seeress and religion, and find out what changes took place over the centuries. Subsequently an explanation will be offered for the apparent decline of her status in the later Germanic period. Finally the possibility that some of her functions, or paraphernalia, were taken over by Christian women saints will be discussed in a short section.

GERMANIC CULTURE AND ITS SOURCES
Definitions and Terminology

This study will focus on the way in which female visionary power manifested itself in the Germanic world, *Germanic* being used conventionally, to refer primarily to societies that are both pre-Christian and of Germanic tongue. The definition is simple, but necessitates a historical sketch. In the first century A.D. Tacitus located most of the Germanic tribes in an area bordered to the west by the Rhine, to the south by the Main and to the east by the Oder. Their homesteads remained mainly outside the Roman Empire, though in the Lower Rhineland some overlapping occurred. In the Migration Period the area expanded over most of Western Europe, but these new territories soon lost their Germanic character as they became Romanized and Christianized. Around A.D. 800, after Saxony had been violently incorporated in the Carolingian Empire, only the Scandinavian homelands remained Germanic in the sense of our definition. The area then expanded again, until it comprised Iceland, Greenland, the Faeroes, Shetland, the Orkneys, the Hebrides and the Isle of Man. In England the area around York was reckoned to belong to the Old Norse Commonwealth, as were parts of Ireland.

In this last period of expansion organized Viking traders even attacked Byzantium and concluded treaties with its emperor. In these regions Germanic institutions and religion lived on until they, too, gave way to Christianity. The Scandinavian homelands held out longest, but before the end of the eleventh century, this last area had been converted, too. In the following the term *Old Germanic* will be restricted to the period before A.D. 700.

Sources

As Germanic culture was essentially oral, it left us no written documents. Records like *vitae*, and charters, such as we possess for the Christian world, can be problematic at times, but they do at least represent autochthonous records from the culture that is studied. In our case we have to rely on secondary sources, varying from classical fascination to clerical outrage, to Arab travelogues, iconographical peculiarities and, as in Iceland, later vernacular writing. They all contribute their own specific bits of information, which may or may not shed some light on the issue. The secondary nature of these data confronts us with the difficult question of interpretation. Even when we find indications of a characteristic female divination practice, its significance is a matter for dispute. Is it certain that they reflect an underlying Old Germanic belief?

There is certainly reason for caution here. First of all, similarities that are spotted may have to be regarded as the universal features of common mantic practice and thus represent genetically unrelated phenomena. Secondly, the long span of time and the huge geographical area allocated to the epithet *Germanic* make it unavoidable that customs and habits were subject to change, and it is conceivable that originally related phenomena are no longer recognized as such. Thirdly, the sources themselves pose no less of a problem. Scholars have become aware that a writer like Tacitus occasionally merely reverted to the ethnographical conventions (*topoi*) of his time.[4] As for later retrospective writing, such as Saxo Grammaticus's *History of the Danes* (*Gesta Danorum*), written around 1200, and the Icelandic sagas, Sawyer has argued that we must allow for a large element of fiction projected back in time for specific purposes.[5] In her view many of the motifs and stories describing women of the past actually represent the writer's concern with issues of his own Christian time, rather than a reliable tradition about pagan times. It is too early to say whether, as Sawyer suggests, we also have to allow for this kind of influence in the Icelandic family sagas, but the possibility cannot be rejected outright.

Questions of this kind, crucial as they may be, should not keep us from trying to reconstruct the way female divination manifested itself in the

Germania. The information that can be extracted from our sources may be meagre, but at least a kind of prototype may emerge. When we realize that our data: a) are from independent sources without any interconnections; b) stem from very different places—which means that we have to envisage the possibility of local variance; c) cover a thousand years, a period during which all kinds of change could, and probably did, occur; then it will be clear that any correspondence found between, for instance, Roman historiographers from the first centuries A.D. and Old Icelandic sagas written down in the early thirteenth century is of the greatest interest. They are the prerequisites for any attempt to establish the beliefs and customs of the interluding Germanic period.[6]

GERMANIC SEERESSES

The Old Germanic period

A quick glance at the sources suffices to see that, in marked contrast to the suspicion that visionary women were often met with in Christian theology, Germanic seeresses were held in high esteem in the first centuries A.D. Few words of Tacitus have been quoted more often than his comment on the Germanic belief in the predictive power of women: "Yes, they even ascribe to them a sacred and prophetic quality."[7] The importance of this passage may have been exaggerated in the past,[8] but there is no reason to deny its validity altogether. The existence of prophesying Germanic women is amply evidenced by writers like Strabo, Plutarch, Cassius Dio, and Caesar.[9] According to Suetonius, writing at the turn of the first century A.D., the emperor Vitellius relied upon the words of a Chattian seeress (*vaticans Chatta mulier*) as an oracle (*oraculum*).[10] Tacitus describes the Bructerian seeress Veleda, who lived in a tower (*turris*) by the river Lippe in Westphalia, as a person of great influence. A seeress Ganna, said to have succeeded Veleda in her office, was honored by Domitian.[11] A Germanic seeress Waluburg (*Baloubourg*) is mentioned in a Greek inscription on a second century ostracon from the Egyptian island Elephantine.[12] In later centuries the belief in the prophesying power of women is attested in glossaries.[13] Among the Goths, who migrated southeast towards the Black Sea area, its existence can be deduced from a note in Jordanes' *Getica*, discussed below.

Later Germanic Tradition

When we turn to the North, a similar picture emerges. Quite elaborate descriptions of prophesying women can be found in Old Icelandic literature. Here both men and women were thought capable of possessing mantic power, but there is a clear difference in objectives. Women are far less often involved in black magic, and their performances suggest a remote connection with fertility cults.[14] Of special interest is the figure of the *völva* (plural: *völur*), a kind of shamanistic sibyl, who was able to see what was hidden and to predict the future. The Icelandic sagas, written in the thirteenth century but dealing with events of the late tenth century, exploit her prophetic role to the full, though conspicuously little takes place in Iceland itself. The lengthiest report of a seance is found in chapter four of the *Eirik's Saga* (*Eiríks saga rauda*) where a *völva* called Thorbjorg[15] is introduced as a person of bone and flesh:

> At that time there was severe famine in Greenland. Those who had gone out on hunting expeditions had had little success, and some had never come back.
>
> There was a woman in the settlement who was called Thorbjorg; she was a prophetess [*völva*], and was known as the Little Sibyl. She had had nine sisters, and they all had been prophetesses, but she was the only one left alive. It was her custom in winter to attend feasts; she was always invited, in particular, by those who were most curious about their own fortunes or the season's prospects. Since Thorkel of Herjolfsness was the chief farmer in the district, it was thought to be his responsibility to find out when the current hardships would come to an end.
>
> Thorkel invited the prophetess to his house and prepared a good reception for her, as was the custom when such women were being received. A high-seat was made ready for her with a cushion on it, which had to be stuffed with hens' feathers.
>
> She arrived in the evening with the man who had been sent to escort her. She was dressed like this: she wore a blue mantle fastened with straps and adorned with stones all the way down to the hem. She had a necklace of glass beads. On her head she wore a black lambskin hood lined with white cat's fur. She carried a staff with a brassbound knob studded with stones. She wore a belt made of touchwood, from which hung a large pouch, and in this she kept the charms she needed for her witchcraft. On her feet were hairy calfskin shoes with long thick laces which had large tin buttons on the ends. She wore catskin gloves, with the white fur inside.
>
> When she entered the room everyone felt obliged to proffer respectful greetings, to which she responded according to her opinion of each person. Thorkel took her by the hand and led her to the seat which had been prepared for her. He asked her to cast her eyes over

his home and household and herds; she had little to say about anything.

Later that evening the tables were set up; and this is what the prophetess had for her meal: she was given a gruel made from goat's milk, and a main dish of hearts from the various kinds of animals that were available there. She used a brass spoon, and a knife with a walrus-tusk handle bound with two rings of copper; the blade had a broken point.

When the tables had been removed, Thorkel went over to Thorbjorg and asked her how she liked his home and people's behavior there, and how soon she would know the answer to his question which everyone wanted to learn. She replied that she would not give any answer until the following morning, when she had slept there overnight first.

Late the next day she was supplied with the preparations she required for performing the witchcraft. She asked for the assistance of women who knew the spells needed for performing the witchcraft, known as Warlock-songs; but there were no such women available. So inquiries were then made amongst all the people on the farm, to see if anyone knew the songs.

Then Gudrid said, "I am neither a sorceress nor a witch, but when I was in Iceland my foster-mother Halldis taught me spells which she called Warlock-songs."

Thorbjorg said, "Then your knowledge is timely."

"This is the sort of knowledge and ceremony that I want nothing to do with," said Gudrid, "for I am a Christian."

"It may well be," said Thorbjorg, "that you could be of help to others over this, and not be any the worse a woman for that. But I shall leave it to Thorkel to provide whatever is required."

So Thorkel now brought pressure on Gudrid, and she consented to do as he wished. The women formed a circle round the ritual platform on which Thorbjorg seated herself. Then Gudrid sang the songs so well and beautifully that those present were sure they had never heard lovelier singing. The prophetess thanked her for the song.

"Many spirits are now present," she said, "which were charmed to hear the singing, and which previously had tried to shun us and would grant us no obedience. And now many things stand revealed to me which before were hidden both from me and from others.

"I can now say that this famine will not last much longer, and that conditions will improve with the spring; and the epidemic which has persisted for so long will abate sooner than expected.

"And as for you, Gudrid, I shall reward you at once for the help you have given us, for I can see your whole destiny with clarity now. You will make a most distinguished marriage here in Greenland, but it will not last for long, for your paths all lead to Iceland; there you will start a great and eminent family line, and over your progeny there shall shine a bright light, but it is beyond my power to see it sharply. And now farewell, my daughter."

Then everyone went over to the prophetess, each asking her whatever he was most curious to know. She answered them readily, and there were few things that did not turn out as she had prophesied.

After this a messager arrived for her from a neighboring farm and she went there with him. Then Thorbjorn was sent for; he had refused to remain in the house while such pagan practices were being performed.[16]

The session, which had been organized to find out for how much longer a severe famine was going to last, takes place on a farmstead in eleventh century Greenland. The description betrays a familiarity with shamanistic customs that can hardly stem from learned speculation. We are told that Thorbjorg is the last survivor of ten sisters, each of which had been a *völva*.[17] The detail is remarkable, given the fact that elsewhere, for instance among some Siberian tribes, shamanism was reportedly hereditary in some families.[18] Other features that could echo shamanistic practice are the bird feathers inside the cushion on which the *völva* sits, and the animal hearts she has for a meal.[19] The most striking parallel, however, is the helping spirits employed by Thorbjorg to travel to, or communicate with, the underworld of the dead.

Details like these make it difficult to regard Thorbjorg's performance entirely as a piece of literary fiction. The saga in which the description is embedded cannot have been compiled before 1264, though.[20] It probably represents a deliberate revision of the older *Grænlendinga Saga*, in which the *völva* scene is not found, and it follows that the passage must have been incorporated by the revisor. The compiler of *Eirik's Saga* was certainly a learned man, who used written sources, and who was acquainted with encyclopedic medieval geography. Most scholars are of the opinion that the narrative of Thorbjorg's session was written by the compiler himself.[21] Some even argue that the author must have been familiar with such sessions, which would imply that *völur* were still active in Iceland in the second half of the thirteenth century.[22] I sincerely doubt that this was the case. All that can be said is that the episode appears to draw upon genuine tradition. It may well have circulated separately before it became incorporated in our saga. In the Icelandic family sagas the *völva* occurs only sporadically, but when she does, she is often treated with respect. Sometimes, as in *Eirik's Saga*, she is even led to the seat of honor by the host himself. All the same, the saga writers seem ambivalent about her. They make no attempt to deny the esteem in which she was reportedly held—which makes it tempting to conclude that they took her status as a fact—but at the same time they seem eager to express Christian disapproval. Why was she not condemned outright, when, after all, the acts of her male counterpart, the *seidmadr*, were portrayed as devilish? It is worth noting that the author of *Eirik's Saga* uses the prophecy to make the *völva* more or less allude to the coming of a new faith—Christianity—even though she is still unable to identify it.[23] The Greenland setting is depicted as religiously backward, and reminiscently heathen: none of the inhabitants object to the performance of the *völva*; the Icelanders, on the other hand, all do. Details like these don't fail to leave the impression of a highly un-Christian, and even pagan environment,[24] but as the saga makes clear, it is paganism in decline, where people have the greatest difficulty in fulfilling its rituals.[25] Thorbjorg is, indeed, introduced as the last of her kind, a remnant of the heathen past: "She had had nine sisters, and they all had been prophetesses, but she was the only one left alive." As such her depiction matches that of Vergil's Cumaean Sibyl, who according to Augustine's interpretation hailed the coming of Christianity.[26] In my view a similar construct is present in the Eddic poem *Sibyl's Vision* (*Völuspá*), where it largely constitutes the poem's framework. This *Sibyl's Vision* is older than the sagas—though probably not as old as is generally thought[27]—and the influence of the poem may account for the respectful attitude towards the *völva* in some of the family sagas. It would explain the ambivalent attitude on the part of the saga authors, and the esteem that we are told the *völva* was held in would be no more than a literary convention deriving from the influence of *Sibyl's Vision*.[28]

In the mythological lays of the Edda, the *völva* is elevated into the worlds of the gods.[29] In *Sibyl's Vision* the *völva*, after having recalled the Old Norse myths of creation, is asked by Odin to disclose the destiny of the gods. The connection between the underworld and mantic power is evident in a related mythological poem, *Balder's Dreams* (*Baldrs draumar*), where Odin, the most important of the heathen gods, and the one who deals with magic and hidden wisdom, rides to the dead *völva*'s grave and evokes her by his spells. She is loath to answer, but is won over in the end, perhaps with precious gifts like in *Sibyl's Vision*. She reveals that Balder will be slain by his own brother. In an attempt to negate this ominous prediction Odin, in the style of some of the later sagas, denounces her prophetic power and calls her "a mother of three giants." The sibyl has the last word, however: she simply alludes to his own forthcoming fate, when he will be torn apart by the monster Fenrir.

Balder's Dreams is often considered to be of a late date—not older than the twelfth century[30]—but its theme must have been well known. It has a counterpart in *Sibyl's Vision* (stanza 28), where the *völva* recalls how she was sitting "alone out in the night (listening for, conjuring, spirits)." The expression "sitting out," *sitja úti* used here signifies more than location alone, it is the technical expression for the witches' and sorcerers' communing with spirits, out of doors at night.[31] Its semantic spectrum comprised the evoking of all kinds of spirits through certain rituals.[32] The Old Norwegian laws, for example, strictly banned all "sitting out at night for the sake of evoking spirits," *útiseta at vekja troll upp*[33], or *útisetumenn er troll vekja*, "people that sit out at night in order to evoke spirits."[34] The reason why people behaved like this is made explicit by an Icelandic episcopal ordinance of 1178 condemning people who "sit out at night for the sake of gaining knowledge," *sitja úti til fródleiks*.[35] It is the performance of this practice by the seeress that is referred to in stanza 28 of *Sibyl's Vision*. It is not the only reference in the poem, for, as Dronke points out, a similar practice is alluded to in stanza 22: *vitti hon ganda*, "by her magic power she summoned, or controlled, spirits." As Dronke puts it: "Like the medium and the shaman, the *völva* was believed to converse with spirits, especially the spirits of the dead, and to communicate to her living audience what they—'he' or 'she'—told her."[36]

The idea advocated above, that the figure of the *völva*, as portrayed in some of the Icelandic family sagas, was largely a literary convention, finds support in the fact that no *völva* in Old Norse literature has any fixed abode. They have no ancestry and no progeny; they are shadowy figures, mostly with stereotypical names, who travel from farmstead to farmstead, turning up when the narrative needs them and disappearing when they are no longer necessary. There is little in Old Norse literature to suggest a firmer base in reality. One possible exception is found in the *Book of Settlements* (*Landnámabók*)[37] where it is stated that: "the *völva* Thurid the Sound-Filler and her son Stein went from Halogaland to Iceland . . . . She was called 'the Sound-Filler' because during a famine in Halogaland she filled every sound with fish by means of magic, *seid*. She also fixed the Kvíar fishing ground in the open sea in front of Isafjord Bay, and took a hornless ewe in return from every farmer in Isafjord."[38] She must have been an impressive person, since her son Stein, the skald, was named after her, and not after his father, as was usual.

Of the *völur* mentioned in Old Icelandic literature Thurid may be the one historical figure; all the other descriptions must be highly literary. However, even if the historical existence of most *völur* described in the sagas must be doubted, there is no reason to reject categorically the details that emerge from the descriptions. Stereotyped as they may appear, they do reflect the way later generations remembered them, and as such they may contain a kernel of truth.

Modern historians who study later traditions about past events have grown skeptical of the possibility to discern historical truth from later accretions. Some even maintain that the portrayal of people and things in these traditions tell us more about the way the writer looked upon such matters in his own time than about the events he claimed to describe. Recently Birgit Sawyer put forward the view that the belligerent figure of the Nordic pagan shield-maiden, anxious to defend her state of chastity, and eager to live independently, was in fact created by Saxo in order to express his disapproval of wealthy women who in his days chose to live independent of men by embracing a religious life. As nuns or pious widows these women often donated gifts to the church, which regularly led to the alienation of land from family property. This development was felt as a threat by wealthy land-owning families, and by criticizing the chaste maidens of the past Saxo was able to address the issues of the day, and voice his disapproval.[39]

Sawyer's conclusion is a welcome reminder of the caution needed in the use of later historiography, but it has little bearing on the tradition about the *völva* embedded in Icelandic saga-writing. If the tradition about the *völva* were a learned fabrication, where do all the details stem from? Saxo may have used the shield-maiden for his own purpose, perhaps inspired by the Amazon warrior of Antiquity, but it is unlikely that he, as Sawyer claims, introduced the Nordic shield-maiden into Scandinavian pagan history. The figure seems to have existed in Nordic tradition well before the days of Saxo, and she may even have had some basis in reality.[40] A similar state of affairs surrounds our Nordic *völva*, the characteristics of whom are not found in any prototype from classical tradition. She, too, may have been revived for some particular purpose, for instance, as suggested earlier, in order to predict the coming of a new religious world order, but the very fact that this role is bestowed on her indicates that people must have been familiar with her. Or to reverse the matter: would there be any point in putting this prediction in the mouth of a prophesying woman if the audience were totally unfamiliar with seeresses? The answer can only be negative, and consequently the figure of the *völva* must have roots in genuine tradition. It means that in the late tenth and early eleventh century the figure of the *völva* must have played some role in Nordic society, but as pointed out above, it can only have been marginal: a travelling figure without any real power. In no way can her stature be comparable to that of a Veleda or a Ganna.

Lexical Evidence

Compared with the rich Old Norse tradition, the Old High German and Old English evidence about seeresses is meagre, and its information not very specific. The compound gloss *hliodarsaza* shows that the practice of spirit-listening was known in Old High German.[41] The last part of the gloss, -*saza*, is derived from the same stem as Old Norse *(úti)seta*, its first part corresponds to Old English *hleodor*, "hearing." De Boor paraphrased the gloss as "to sit down in order to listen attentively for something."[42] Burial sites (graves, grave mounds and graveyards) were considered favorable locations for contacting spirits, and it is conceivable that the practice was regarded as necromancy—and condemned accordingly—if performed in their vicinity. Wesche suggested that apart from *helliruna*, "necromancy," there may have been a homonymous agent noun from the same stem in Old High German (OHG), with the meaning "female necromancer, sorceress."[43] The OHG evidence for this is rather thin, but the idea finds some support in other branches of Old Germanic. A weak derivative from an Old Germanic compound similar to the OHG one is attested in Old English *hellerune*, glossing Latin *pythonissa*, "sorceress."[44] A similar derivative appears to be present in Gothic **haljaruna*. The word is not extant in the form quoted, but can be deduced from Jordanes' *haliurunnas*, with Latin plural ending.[45] Again knowledge is thought to have been obtained from the other world with the help of spirits. Word form and context show that the performers in the Old English and Gothic cases must have been women, but the OHG gloss shows that it was not an exclusively female practice. This is confirmed by Charlemagne's capitulary concerning Saxony, which stipulates that: "We have decided to hand over the diviners (*divini*) and sooth-sayers (*sortilegi*) to the churches and the clergy."[46] Whether or not the Old High German and Old English evidence has ancient roots, it contains little to help outline the characteristics of a Germanic seeress. The Gothic tradition is meagre, too, but it does at least provide a useful context (see below).

THE SEERESSES'S ATTRIBUTES

It should now be clear that the only substantial information on divination is found in writings from Antiquity, and in Old Icelandic literature. Different as these sources are, it is possible to mark out a few common features that may, or may not, be characteristic. Veleda, we are told, received gifts for her prophecies, just as the *völva* was used to getting presents. This is probably universal and as such only of minor importance. The same holds true for the presence of a person, or persons, serving as intermediary, or interlocutor, between the entranced women and the outside human world. In *Sibyl's Vision* and *Balder's Dreams* Odin questions the *völva* about the future. In the description of the Greenland *völva* a ring of women gathers around the platform on which she is seated. About Veleda we learn that people were not allowed to approach her and address her directly; instead: "one of her kinsmen, selected for the purpose, carried to her the questions and brought back her answers."[47] This, too, is possibly part of the universals of mantic sessions, though it might simultaneously signal the respect she was regarded with.

The Platform

Of greater significance could be the ritual platform mounted by the *völva* Thorbjorg. The word used is *hjallr*, meaning a raised platform, a framework of timber.[48] If we are to believe the sagas—some of which are rather fantastic—up to four people could be seated on this dais. It was here that the *völva* held her sessions. It is tempting, as Meyer and Kiil propose,[49] to connect this elevated platform, described in one saga as being supported by four poles, with the *turris* the seeress Veleda was reported to have resided on: "*ipsa edita in turre.*"[50] The phrase is sometimes rendered as "She herself lived in a high tower," but this translation represents merely one possibility: no finite form corresponding to "lived" can be found in the Latin text, and the word *turris* can denote any timber construction on posts, from dovecotes to movable wooden towers.[51] In Caesar's *Gallic War* it is used for timber constructions built on ship decks to board enemy vessels.[52] Tacitus's *turris* must refer to a raised timber construction, since building in stone was unknown among the Germanic tribes at that time. If we accept Kiil's interpretation the correspondence with the *völva*'s raised platform is remarkable. The fact that the use of a platform finds some parallel in Siberian shamanism could lend further support to this assumption, although it weakens the argument at the same time.[53] All that was involved may have been a sort of barrier to prevent profane interference, but it may also have symbolized the communing with the other world. Kiil[54] has compared the platform with an episode in the *The War of the Irish with the Foreigners* (*Cogadh Geadhel re Gallaibh*), where Ota, the wife of a Viking king in early ninth century Ireland, is said to have chanted heathen spells and oracles at the high altar of the sacred church of

Clonmacnois.[55] It is possible that the high altar here was a substitute for a platform, but other considerations may have played a role as well,[56] and the reliability of the work is not beyond doubt.[57]

A woman using a timber structure to commune with the other world has been described, early in the tenth century, by the Arab traveller Ibn Fadlan, who had the opportunity of observing a funeral ceremony of a chief of the *Rus*, the Scandinavian settlers and traders living on the Lower Volga. He claims to be describing what he saw himself, putting questions to an interpreter, and reporting the answers. His eyewitness account contains the following episode, in which a girl who had volunteered to die, ritually symbolizes her journey to the world of the dead which is to follow shortly:

> They brought her to something they had made, which resembled the frame of a door. She put her feet on the palms of the men there, and looked over the frame. She said what she had to say, and they lowered her. Then they lifted her up a second time; she did the same and they lowered her. They lifted her up a third time, and she did the same again, after which they gave her a hen, and she cut off its head and threw it into the boat [i.e., the ship prepared for the pyre]. I asked the interpreter what she was doing, and he replied: "This first time she said, 'Behold, I see my father and mother.' The second time she said, 'Behold, I see my master seated in Paradise, and Paradise is green and fair, and with him are men and servants. He is calling me. Send me to him.'"[58]

The woman, a servant girl, acts in a state of ecstasy that is brought about by sex and drugs, and we are hardly entitled to call her a *völva*. What interests us above all here is the technique of the ritual that enables the girl to view the other world. It is tempting to compare the timber structure described by Ibn Fadlan, with the *hjallr*, the platform used by the Old Norse *völva*. It is even possible that a structure of this kind is illustrated on the Altuna Stone from Uppland, Sweden[59] (fig. 3.1). On its picture side we find Thor fishing for the world serpent, but above this there is a scene that until recently defied all attempts to give a convincing explanation.[60] A man, or woman, is looking over what appears to be a timber structure. A bird is depicted as well, it resembles a raven rather than a hen or cock.

More uncertain is whether the scene depicted on a sixth century bracteate should be drawn into the discussion[61] (fig. 3.2). The structure on which the person stands could be interpreted as a kind of dais or platform. Since it has been demonstrated that the iconography of bracteates often draws upon shamanistic concepts, the idea is certainly attractive.[62] If it holds true, then there can be no doubt that a kind of platform, or elevated structure, was in some cases part of the equipment. It must be stressed, however, that to judge from the iconography the shaman of the bracteates appears to be male rather than female. On the Beresina bracteate the figure on the platform seems to represent a woman, but on the other five specimens belonging to this small group of bracteates, it appears to be a man.

The Bird

The possible significance of the feathers Thorbjorg is sitting on has already been mentioned. In Ibn Fadlan's account the bird is probably killed to provide a helping spirit for the journey. The motif is also found in the First Book of Saxo's *History of the Danes*, where a woman mysteriously appears out of the floor and takes a young hero, Hadingus, on a trip to the underworld.[63] She shows him sunny green fields in the midst of winter as well as the abodes of resurrected warriors. Confronted with an unsurpassable barrier, she pulls off the head of a cock and flings it over the wall, where it comes to life and starts crowing.[64] Here the account breaks off. The motif shows a remarkable resemblance to the so-called cock miracle, Swedish *tuppundret*, found in the legendary story of Staffan the stable lad, and popular in Swedish early medieval iconography.[65] This miracle of the dead cock that comes to life again is depicted as early as the middle of the twelfth century, i.e. considerably earlier than Saxo. Its popularity may be due to the fact that the motif already existed in Sweden, but if so, its original context can only be guessed at. Even if we assume a link with pagan traditions the Staffan story offers no clues to an older meaning of the cock miracle.

The Rod

Finally, a detail of uncertain meaning is the stick the *völva* is carrying, possibly the wand of modern witches.[66] It is only recorded in Northern sources, but its importance is evident from the etymology of the word *völva*, generally regarded as a derivate from *völr*, "stick" (Gothic *walus*). The etymon occurs also as the first part of the compound name *Waluburg*, the Germanic sibyl mentioned on an ostracon from the island Elephantine. The use of a rod may be further indicated by the name of the wise *Gambara* (discussed below) explained by some as "stick-carrier." The figure on the Beresina bracteate is also holding a kind of stick, but here the iconographical analysis is too uncertain to allow any conclusion.

All in all our survey of the Germanic corpus is not very encouraging. No clear-cut picture emerges of what could be called a prototype of the Ger-

Figure 3.2. Bracteate from Beresina. After Ikonographischer Katalog *(reproduced with kind permission of K. Hauck)*

manic seeress. There are bits of evidence, but features like the receiving of gifts or special songs that are sung are not sufficient to establish a genetic relationship. It is in fact only the recurrent mention of a platform, or dais, that may confirm the idea that we are dealing with scattered reflexes of an underlying Old Germanic practice. Much depends on Kiil's identification of Veleda's *turris* as a raised platform, and the same holds true for our interpretation of the Beresina bracteate. If we accept them, the occurrence of a platform constitutes the only characteristic feature so far.

DIVINE HIGH WOMEN AND THEIR CULTS

There is no reason to doubt the words of the writers of Antiquity that Germanic seeresses had great influence, at times even politically. Tacitus writes that the intermediary who passed on Veleda's answers was almost regarded as "a messenger of a god."[67] The remark leaves no doubt that Veleda and her collegues were regarded as vehicles of divine knowledge. It brings to mind the question of the relation between oracles and cult. Oracles have a special relation with the other world: they give voice to the divine powers.[68] So if the Germans in the first centuries A.D. revered seeresses, we may assume their prominent status to be reflections of practiced cults.

Tacitus mentions several goddesses: *Nerthus*, whom he calls a *terra mater*, and the cult of Isis among the Suebi.[69] An apparently popular cult of female goddesses is evidenced by the so-called *Matron* votive altars that appear in the Lower Rhine Region from the second half of the second century A.D.; the dedication of these altars to the *Matres/Matronae* was a Roman fashion, but the dedicants themselves no doubt represented an indigenous layer of the population.[70] It is likely that these divinities were also worshipped in other parts of Germanic Europe, but as the custom of votive altars did not spread there, we cannot be certain. On these relief picture stones, presented by grateful dedicants, the goddesses are addressed as *Deae Matronae*, "Divine High Women," or *Deae Matres*, "Divine High Mothers," among whom the *Aufaniae* hold a prominent place. As a rule the *Matres/Matronae* appear in groups of three, but this probably represents a later development. Often, though not always, the title *Matres/Matronae* is combined with an epithet relating them to a specific area or group. This limited field of action makes them comparable to the *civitatum genii* of Antiquity, or the Roman Catholic patron saints.[71] No dedication can be dated later than A.D. 260, but it is likely that the cult continued for some period after that.

One aspect of the *Matronae* or *Matres* is their connection with fertility of soil, as is made clear by the iconography.[72] The baskets with fruits they are holding, and the cornucopiae that are occasionally depicted on the sides, are evidently symbols of prosperity and affluence.[73] The concern with prosperity lies at the bottom of names like *Afliae*, "bestowers of growth," *Gabiae*, "endowers," *Vapthiae*, "caretakers," et cetera.[74] The representations of snakes (often in trees), or dogs, have been regarded as symbols of the underworld and the regenerating chtonic power that springs from it. The combination is not surprising: death and fertility are intimately related; like *yin* and *yang* they represent the ever-recurring cycle of vegetation. This dual character relates the *Matres* to the archetypical Great Mother, whose ambivalent nature likewise houses such oppositions as birth–death, growth–decay, create–destroy.[75] It is a not uncommon belief that motherhood represents an intimate link with the other world.[76] This close relation with the other world the *Matres* had in common with the psychopomp *Mercurius*, and it is no coincidence that they have been found worshipped in the same sanctuary.[77]

Isabella Horn has pointed out that the frequent formula *ex imperio ipsarum*, "at their command," indicates that the sanctuaries of the *Matres* served oracular purposes.[78] Archeological excavations suggest that at an early stage the *Matres*, probably before their triplification, and before the dedication of votive altars became fashionable, were worshipped in a tree-cult,[79] which, together with this oracular practice, brings to mind the idea of the navel of the earth. Just like the world tree *Yggdrasill* in Old Norse mythology, these trees had a mediating function between upperworld and underworld, and consequently, it is probably no coincidence that secret knowledge was obtained from there.[80]

In the Germania the cult of the *Matres* is mainly found in the Lower Rhine region between Maas and Rhine. More to the North over a hundred votive altars have come to light of a goddess *Nehalennia*, worshipped in two sanctuaries in the present East Scheldt area (Netherlands). Whether she is Celtic, or Germanic, as advocated by the majority of earlier scholars, or *vor-keltogermanisch*, as favored by modern scholarship, is uncertain.[81] The close links of her cult with that of the *Matres* is best shown by a votive altar from Domburg on which she appears as a triad.[82] The iconography shows approximately the same symbols of abundance and prosperity as the altars of the Rhineland *Matres*. Of interest is the occurrence of pomegranates, traditionally taken to represent a connection with fertility and afterlife.[83] Especially prominent is the presence of a dog in many representations of the goddess. Early scholarship linked it with the underworld, too, but more recently scholars have argued against this: they stress its peaceful appearance, point to the faithful way it is looking up to its mistress, and claim that the little bell it is occasionally carrying makes it a domesticated dog, a symbol of watchfulness and loyalty, rather than a Cerberus.[84] These arguments don't prove much. The dog's appearance may be a secondary development, just as Cybele's lions acquired a peaceful appearance, whereas the dog itself may well echo an ancient relation of the goddess with the underworld. Her name, if derived from the Indo-European root **nek*, "to kill," could point in the same direction,[85] but other explanations have also been suggested.[86] On the Lower Rhine we find indications that the cult of the goddess was connected with oracular practice: three times we meet the formula *ex iussu* and once *ex imp(erio) ips(ius)*, "at her command."[87]

The existence of a dozen or more other Germanic goddesses in the Roman period is evidenced by scattered finds of isolated votive altars, dedicated to deities like *Vagdavercustis, Hludana, Vihansa, Garmangabis*.[88] Little is known about them, but their cults are proved by the altars.

These votive altars and stones indicate that in this early Germanic period female deities had an important place in local cult life, and that their sanctuaries were used as oracles. This finding accords well with the reports of Antiquity about the esteem seeresses enjoyed in the Germanic world.

Goddesses in the High Middle Ages

If we move on to the High Middle Ages and to the period of the Old Norse literature, reflecting the last stage of Germanic Europe, things appear to have changed. We still find both gods and goddesses, but the position of the latter has become less prominent. Poetry from the ninth and tenth century indicates the existence of a variety of goddesses, but their myths are few, and no traces of cults can be detected. Yet they were not invented by the poets: the Germanic background of the Old Norse goddess *Fulla*, for example, is shown by the occurrence of her name (spelled *Volla*) in the Old High German Merseburg Charms, where her powers prove insufficient to heal a broken horse leg, so *Uuodan* (Odin) has to do the job.[89] She and her colleagues, it seems, have just faded into the background. In the Eddic poems the male gods dominate heavily; it is mostly they who appear as actors and creators, while the female divinities have only subservient roles.[90] Of some importance is *Freyja*, a goddess not only of fertility but also of war and death. This dual nature relates her to the Rhineland *Matres* and *Nehalennia*, but her position differs markedly in that she has to share the dominion of fertility with two male gods: her brother Frey (*Freyr*) and her father Njord. Nothing illustrates the change better than this god Njord (*Njördr*). Etymologically his name corresponds exactly with *Nerthus*, the Old Germanic goddess Tacitus describes. In the Old Norse pantheon she has been reshaped, it seems, into a male god.[91] A better example of the patriarchal tendency will be hard to find.

As regards the Old Germanic period we already established a link between mother goddesses, *matres*, and oracling practices. We will now return to our *völur*, the Germanic seeresses of the Scandinavian North, and try to define the relation between their ability to predict the future and the cults of fertility and procreation. In Eirik's Saga and elsewhere in Old Norse literature the activity of the *völva* is called *seid* (*seidr*). In the first chapters of his *History of the Norse Kings* (*Heimskringla*), written around 1230, the Icelandic historian and mythographer Snorri Sturluson shows us where this practice originated. As he explains, the *Æsir*, progenitors of the clan and celestial battle gods, made war on the *Vanir* (the collective name of the deities of fertility), who resisted stoutly, and both devastated the lands of the others. When they wearied of this, they concluded peace, giving each other hostages. The *Vanir* gave their most outstanding men, Njord the Wealthy and his son Frey. Odin appointed them to be priests for the sacrificial offerings, with Freyja, Njord's daughter, as priestess. It was she who first taught the *Æsir seid*, magic skill to obtain knowledge of things, as was practiced among the *Vanir*. In a later chapter Snorri alludes once again to this origin of *seid* by informing us that this kind of sorcery was attended by such wickedness that manly men considered it shameful to practice it, and so it was taught to priestesses. Odin himself, however, not hampered by moral objections, learnt it and made good use of it. As Snorri tells us, Odin had the skill which gives great power and which he practiced himself. It is called *seid*, and by means of it he could know the fate of men and predict events that had not yet come to pass. At times he shifted his appearance. When he did so his body would lie there as if he were asleep or dead, but he himself, in an instant, in the shape of a bird or animal, a fish or a serpent, went to distant countries on his or other men's errands. A reflex of this theriomorphic shift is found in the two ravens to whom Odin had bestowed the gift of speech. They flew far and wide over the lands and told him many tidings.[92]

Snorri's account teaches us a number of things: a) there was a clash between two divine communities, b) the skill of *seid*, the activity of the *völva*, came from the *Vanir*, patrons of fecundity and riches, c) after the clash Odin took over this skill, and became the great master of it.

The *Sibyl's Vision* also commemorates a war between two divine communities, probably the same as related by Snorri, but in a wording that almost defies interpretation. It appears from stanza 23 that the dispute that preceded the battle focused on the question "if the gods should all (*godin öll*) have [separate] offerings, and [as a consequence] the *Æsir* endure losses." The difficult lines may, or may not, have some connection with a passage in Saxo's *History of the Danes*, where a usurper of divine power ordained that the gods should not be prayed to as a group, i.e. collectively, but that separate offerings be made to each deity.[93] Evidently there was a conflict about tribute, but whether the struggle belonged to myth or reflected an actual clash of interests remains unclear. The war between the Æsir and the Vanir is not the only story. A similar tale is found in the seventh century *Origo Gentis Langobardorum* and again, a century later, in a slightly different version, in Paul the Deacon's *History of the Langobards* (*Historia Langobardorum*): the Langobards, then called *Winnili*, were said to have come from Scandinavia under the leadership of two brothers, Ibor and Agio. When the Vandals demanded tribute of them, they were persuaded by their mother, Gambara, to take up arms. Before joining battle, the Vandals called on Wotan (Odin) to award them victory. Gambara, in her turn, invoked Frea (Frigg), Wotan's wife. She tells them how to trick Wotan, and to secure victory: the women were to spread their hair over their faces, and all should assemble in view of a window, from which Wotan used to look on the earth. The outcome is that the embarrassed Wotan calls them "Longbeards" (*longibarbi*), and, having become their godfather, bestows victory upon them.[94]

Scholars have long ago interpreted this *ridicula fabula*, as Paul calls it, as a change of cult: a tribe that worshipped the goddess Frea as their main deity went over to the cult of Wotan. They point out that Gambara and her two sons seemed to have ruled over the Winnili. It is explicitly stated that the Winnili valued her insight and trusted her wise counsels in times of need.[95] Gambara is called *phitonissa*, "priestess, sorceress," in the Chronicon Gothanum also *sibylla*, "seeress."[96] As said, *Gambara* may mean "stick-carrier," which would relate her to the Old Norse *völva*, but other etymologies are also conceivable. *Ibor* means "boar," the animal sacred to Frey, the main god of the Vanir, and a symbol of fertility. *Agio* is explained by Plassmann as "snake," the animal connected with death, as well as with rebirth.[97] Finally the "window" (*fenestra*) through which Wotan looks out over the world, brings to mind the Old Norse *hliðskjálf*, discussed below.

It is possible that king Filimer's action against the *haliurunnas*, mentioned above, should be included here. Jordanes tells us only that king Filimer, the fifth ruler of the Goths after they left Scandinavia, drove into exile certain "wise women called *haliurunnas* in the native tongue."[98] The short note suggests that the women must have enjoyed some influence before Filimer chased them away. His action may have been a move against their growing power in political affairs, but it may also have had a religious background. The links of the Gothic royal dynasty with Odin cannot be doubted, and Filimer's action may have resulted in the strong position of Gothic kingship recorded by the ethnographers of Antiquity. Simultaneously we may consider greed as a possible incitement. If these women had been prophesying on a regular basis, receiving gifts in return, their sanctuaries must have prospered. It must have been tempting for a monarch to grab their riches, just as the treasures of Delphi were plundered on occasion. The explanation has historical parallels in Gustav Wasa's conversion to Lutheranism, which cost the Catholic Church overnight all it possessed in Sweden, and, even more strikingly, in the premeditated suppression of the religious Order of the Templars by the French king Philip IV, who confiscated their vast possessions. Unfortunately Jordanes' short note leaves all this open.

The takeover of supreme mantic skill by Odin, resulting from the confrontation between the Æsir and the Vanir, manifested itself in small changes, such as attributes that shifted hands. Earlier I compared the timber construction of Ibn Fadlan's report with a scene depicted on the Altuna Stone. The person on the stairs is not marked as a woman, and it is conceivable, even likely, that the scene represents Odin on *hlidskjálf*, literally "gate-shelf," a mythological seat that enabled the god to look out over all the worlds.[99] The difference is not very important: the two concepts are clearly related.[100] The timber structure that allowed one to travel through space, guided by helping bird-spirits, or animated as a bird, seems to have given rise to two mythological concepts. On the one hand the *hlidskjálf*, whence Odin views all that happens; on the other his two ravens that fly to and fro to tell him what goes on. As the scene on the Altuna Stone has a little of both, the timber structure plus the raven depicted beside the head, it presumably represents an early intermediary stage.

WHY THE GODDESSES AND THE SEERESSES LOST GROUND

It will be clear that the changes were not so dramatic that in the first centuries A.D. there were mostly goddesses, whereas in the last stages of Germanic Europe there were hardly any left. Tacitus even states that, of the gods, the Germanic tribes pay highest honors to Mercurius. Yet the tendency is undeniable, the most conspicuous change being the transformation of Tacitus's *terra mater Nerthus* into the male god Njord of the Old Norse period.[101] So a shift of focus is there, and needs to be explained. A remarkable solution has been proposed by Jochens, who explains all that is positive with regard to women and female qualities in Germanic societies as erratic remnants of an older, pre-Germanic culture in which:

> perhaps during some distant period, a full-fledged mother goddess reigned supreme. Reflecting a society that hailed maternity as the only life-giving principle, this female figure may also be at the root of the deference with which the Germanic tribes treated prophetesses. In due course the invading, patriarchal Indo-Europeans swept this religion away and absorbed only a few traces. A more simple solution would suggest that Scandinavian mythology arrived in its entirety with the Indo-Europeans. In this case, the elements of older female deities and cult practices can be seen as fragments of an ancient, more primitive Indo-European religion and society, or they are vestiges—embedded into the later tripartite division—from peoples absorbed by the Indo-Europeans.[102]

My solution approaches along different lines. As I see it the causes lay in the changes that took place in the social structures of the Germanic communities themselves. The same period that saw a weakening of female divination in cult and religion also witnessed an unprecedented growth of royal power. Kingship was traditionally known among the Germanic tribes, but it was not hereditary, and its power was limited, as Tacitus explicitly states.[103] The noble families from whom the kings were chosen by the assembly of the free men also brought forth the leader (*princeps*) of the *comitatus*: a chieftain followed by a band of warrior companions that he provided for and who followed them to war. The rights of this leader were not self-imposed, but bestowed by the assembly. In times of peace he and his followers (*comites*) may have acted as keepers of law. In combat they served as a battle unit of fighters grouped around its leader, with military codes and duties. Often the *comites*, unmarried young men full of energy and eager to distinguish themselves, associated themselves with a successful leader (often from a different tribe), seeking riches and prestige. Their undertakings were strictly organized, in that each *comes* was bound by a holy oath to defend and protect the leader.[104] If the *comitatus* had a religious basis, as could be suggested by the oath, the god venerated must have been Woden (Odin), the god of human sacrifice and supreme tactics. The Germans knew the custom of the *ver sacrum*, which obliged all the young men of one generation to go abroad and seek their fortune by force of arms.[105] The confrontation with the Roman Empire offered golden opportunities for the bold and daring. The risks were considerable, but so were the stakes, and when the young men returned home loaded with booty, their prestige was greatly enhanced. The leader of a successful expedition was a man of influence and power. Intertribal undertakings like these must have contributed greatly to the restructuring of many of the Germanic tribes attested by the later ethnographers of Antiquity. The tribal units that Tacitus and Pliny mention, which were based more on communities of traditional cult than on political convenience, broke up, and new, larger confederations of a more military nature came into being from the end of the second century onwards. The structure of these new formations was influenced, apparently, by the military organization of the *comitatus*, although increased acquaintance with the totalitarian Roman way of exercising power must have left its mark, too. It is from these restructured new tribes, like Saxons, Francs, and Alamans, that powerful Germanic royal families emerged in the fourth and fifth century. The enormous treasures collected by Frankish kings enabled them to maintain a large force of supporters.[106] What interests us here is that most of the royal families of which genealogies are preserved traced their descent from Woden.[107] Similarly the Goths traced their kings back to *Gaut, one of the many names of Odin in Old Norse mythology. The ancestors of this royal dynasty, Jordanes tells us, were regarded not as ordinary people (*puri homines*), but as demigods or *Ansis*.[108] There can be no doubt that *ansis* is cognate with Old Norse *Æsir*, the warrior-gods who, led by Odin, confronted the *Vanir*, patrons of fecundity.

In my opinion it is the unprecedented growth of power of Germanic kingship during the fourth and fifth century A.D. that lies at the bottom of the prominent position of Woden/Odin, the royal progenitor, in later mythology. This career of Odin and the *Æsir* affected the structure of Germanic religion; the new status was won at the expense of the cults of older deities. It gives us a possible explanation for the disappearance, or the fading away, of the goddesses of fertility and their cults, at the end of the Germanic period.

Conclusion

In the early Germanic Europe of Tacitus's time an important place was occupied by oracling seeresses, possibly connected with amply attested cults of goddesses ruling fertility and death. The power of kings was limited.

The military restructuring of tribal organizations in the third century A.D. led to a new type of Germanic kingship, probably influenced by, or arising out of Tacitus's *princeps comitatus*. At the start of the Middle Ages Germanic kingship had evolved into a hereditary office of power, and its rise contributed greatly to the prominent place its divine progenitor Woden (Odin), patron-god of kingship, held in religious ideology at the end of the Germanic period. It was achieved at the expense of the more matriarchally oriented cult of goddesses ruling fertility and death of which Tacitus and archeology give us a glimpse. The fertility cult did not stop, but its status was reduced. It lost its matriarchal character, two of its three divine representatives, Frey and Njord, were male gods now, and at least some of the sacrificial ceremonies were performed by the king.[109] As for the Germanic seeress, valued so highly by Antiquity, her vast initial stature was probably lost at an early stage, conceivably in connection with this shift of religious concepts. Things may have been different in those areas where fertility cults maintained a prominent place, like in Sweden—the region that the Scandinavian traders on the Volga must have come from—but we cannot be certain. In Old Norse literature the Germanic seeress has developed into the *völva*, a seemingly independent literary figure, whose ancient ties with a fertility cult have almost faded.

All this is, of course, a simplification. Dealing with problems of this nature one soon becomes involved in a tangle of conjectures, where the temptation to be overingenious is always present. However, a shift towards a male-oriented religious ideology, probably helped or even caused by the strengthening of Germanic kingship, seems plausible; also that it was achieved at the expense of ancient religious concepts, viz. goddesses ruling fertility (prosperity) and death, in whose cult oracular practice was a prominent feature.

The Coming of Christianity

The question whether these archaic concepts, or some of them, continued to be present, and even influenced the attitudes displayed towards women in the following periods, I must leave to others. It seems hard to believe that it could all disappear overnight without a single trace.

Scholars have indeed found that the lives and cults of some of the female saints have overtones of earlier fertility cults, and the idea that the cult of the *Matres* continued, at least iconographically, as the veneration of triad female saints, such as Fides, Spes and Caritas, has ardent supporters.[110]

It has been argued that the procession of Saint Gertrud, whose statue was driven around annually, to bring fertility to the people, is reminiscent of the celebration of Nerthus, who, seated in her chariot, was drawn around in jubilee every year.[111]

The place Mater in Flandres, situated at the well of the little river *Sint-Amalbergabeek*—named after Saint Amalberga—was called *Materna* in the ninth century, a hydronyme deriving from Indo-European **mâter*, "mother." The placename originally denoted the very same little river, and Gysseling has remarked that Saint Amalberga apparently succeeded the *matres* here.[112]

Bynum has pointed out that the the symbol of ears of corn with which Saint Walburga (d. 779) is depicted "seems to have been borrowed, along with other detail, from an earlier fertility cult, that of Walborg or Walpurg, the earth goddess."[113] Of particular interest is a miracle recorded in the earliest *Life of Walburga*, written some hundred years after her death by the priest Wolfhard: An ill man named Irchinbald hears a voice telling him to go to a place where some of Walburga's relics were kept, to pray to the Saint and to drink from the chalice that would be offered to him by three nuns. As soon as the man drinks he is cured. The story brings to mind the formula *ex imperio* used by some dedicants of the *Matres* votive altars.

It is difficult to assess the validity of such alleged parallels. We are on slippery soil here. Similarities may have a common origin, and indicate some continuity of cult-habits, but they can also be universal, coincidental or archetypical, and thus be unconnected. In each case the spotted parallel needs careful further study by scholars specialized in divination, sanctity, and motherhood of the Christian Middle Ages.

1. Caroline Walker Bynum, *Holy Feast and Holy Fast: The Religious Significance of Food to Medieval Women* (Berkeley [etc.]: University of California Press, 1987), 241.

2. Karl Weinhold, *Die deutschen Frauen in dem Mittelalter* (3d ed. Vienna: Carl Gerold's Sohn, 1897). The first edition was published 1851 in Vienna.

3. Judith Jesch, *Women in the Viking Age* (Woolbridge: Boydell Press, 1991); Birgit Sawyer, "Women and the conversion of Scandinavia," in *Frauen in Spätantike und Frühmittelalter: Lebensbedingungen, Lebensnormen, Lebensformen. Beiträge zu einer internationalen Tagung an den Freien Universität Berlin*, ed. Werner Affeldt (Sigmaringen: Thorbecke, 1990), 263–281. It is no use trying to list all that has been published on the subject.

4. Gerold Walser, *Rom, das Reich und die fremden Völker in der Geschichtsschreibung der frühen Kaiserzeit* (Baden-Baden: Verlag für Kunst und Wissenschaft, 1951), passim. Recently scholars have started to question the validity of this view, e.g. Klaus Bringmann, "Topoi in der taciteischen Germania," in *Beiträge zum Verständnis der Germania des Tacitus*, ed. Herbert Jankuhn and D. Timpe (Bericht über die Kolloquien der Kommission für die Altertumskunde Nord- and Mitteleuropas im Jahr 1986) (Göttingen: Vandenhoeck & Ruprecht, 1989), 59–78.

5. Sawyer, "Women," passim, esp. 265, 281. The idea of retrospective historiography reflecting contemporary interests is not new, but Sawyer's view that the alienation of land by women was a cause for concern to early post-conversion writers has not been advocated before. It may hold true for Saxo but as regards the Icelandic sagas, it still needs to be proved.

6. The difficulty of interpreting later sources, especially as regards paganism, is the subject of a recent article by Rudi Künzel, "Paganisme, syncrétisme et culture religieuse populaire au Haut Moyen Age: Reflexions de méthode," *Annales Économies Sociétés Civilisations*, 47 (1992), 1057–1071.

7. Tacitus, *Germania*, 8.2, ed. Eugen Fehrle (5th ed. Richard Hünnerkopf) (Heidelberg: Carl Winter, 1959), 24: "inesse quin etiam sanctum aliquid et providum putant."

8. Reinhold Bruder, *Die germanische Frau im Lichte der Runeninschriften und der antiken Historiographie* (Berlin: Walter de Gruyter, 1974), 152.

9. Gunnar Rudberg, *Zum antiken Bild der Germanen: Studien zur ältesten Germanenliteratur* (Avhandlinger utgitt av Det Norske Videnskaps-Akademi i Oslo, 2: Historisk-Filosofisk Klasse 1933, 5) (Oslo: Jacob Dybwad, 1933), 57ff.

10. Suetonius, *Vitellius*, 14.5, ed. Franz Rolf Schröder, *Quellenbuch zur germanischen Religionsgeschichte* (Berlin: Walter de Gruyter, 1933), 136; trans. R. Graves, *The Twelve Caesars* (Harmondsworth: Penguin, 1984), 275.

11. Cassius Dio, *Roman history (Historia romana)*, 67.5.3, ed. H.E. Cary (Loeb Classical Library) (London: Heineman, 1955), 346.

12. Ludwig Schmidt, *Geschichte der deutschen Stämme bis zum Ausgang der Völkerwanderung: Die Westgermanen* (Zweite, völlig neubearbeitete Auflage Munich: Beck, 1940), 67.

13. See Richard Jente, *Die mythologischen Ausdrücke im altenglischen Wortschatz* (Anglistische Forschungen, 56) (Heidelberg: Carl Winter, 1921), 330.

14. Folke Ström, *Diser, Nornor, Valkyrjor: Fruktbarhetskult och sakralt kungadöme i Norden* (Kungl. Vitterhets, Historie och Antikvitets Akademiens handlingar) (Stockholm: Almqvist & Wiksell, 1954), 59.

15. Most Old Norse proper names have been anglicized.

16. *Eiríks saga rauda*, ed. Einar Ólafur Sveinsson (Íslenzk fornrit, 4) (Reykjavik: Hid Íslenzka Fornritafélag, 1935), 206–209, trans. Magnus Magnusson and Hermann Palsson, *The Vinland Sagas* (New York: New York University Press, 1966), 81–83, here used with some alterations of my own.

17. So AM 544 qv. (Hauksbók), dating from the early fourteenth century. The detail is, however, missing in the fifteenth century manuscript AM 557 qv. and influence of medieval encyclopedic learning can not be ruled out here. Cf Isidor of Seville (d. 636), *Etymologiae*, 8.8, ed. Lindsay (Oxford: Oxford University Press, 1911), 3 "Decem autem Sibyllae a doctissimis auctoribus traduntur."

18. Mircea Eliade, *Schamanismus und archaische Ekstasetechnik* (Zürich: Rascher Verlag, 1954), 24ff.

19. Hilda R. Ellis Davidson, *The Viking Road to Byzantium* (London: Allan & Unwin, 1976), 287.

20. Jón Jóhannesson, "Aldur Grænlendinga sögu," in *Nordæla. Afmæliskvedja til Sigurdar Nordals 14. september 1956* (Reykjavik: Helgafell, 1956), 152.

21. Dag Strömbäck, *Sejd: Textstudier i nordisk religionshistoria* (Nordiska texter och undersökningar, 5) (Stockholm: Gebers, 1935), 59; Jón Jóhannesson, "Aldur Grænlendinga sögu," 152. Willem van Eeden, "Vínland-studiën I," *Tijdschrift voor Nederlandse Taal- en Letterkunde*, 41 (1922), 61 assumed that the passage derived from a lost and otherwise unknown saga about Gudrid, but his suggestion failed to win support.

22. Dag Strömbäck, *Sejd*, 59.

23. The thirteenth century author of the saga was apparently thinking of Bishop Brand of Hólar (d.1201), and bishop Thorlak of Skálholt (d.1133), both descendants of Gudrid. In AM 557 qv. (cf. note) no mention is made of the failing power of the *völva*. Here the allusion is tied to Gudrid's progeny, over which "there shall shine a bright light." However, if we juxtapose this bright [Christian] future to the semi-pagan setting of the prediction, the deliberate contrast is obvious, and suggests a wider perspective.

24. See the remark in the *Grænlendinga Saga* referring to the same episode: "At this time, Christianity was still in its infancy in Greenland," trans. Magnusson and Palsson, *The Vinland Sagas*, 62.

25. Interestingly enough, they are at a loss how to do it until Christian Gudrid lends them a hand.

26. It is an artistic device that, albeit in different form, is also found elsewhere in Old Norse literature, e.g. the story of Thorhall the Prophet in *Flateyjarbók*, ed. Gudbrandur Vigfússon and C.R. Unger (Christiania, 1860), 1, 220.

27. Sigurdur Nordal, *Völuspá* (Reykjavik, 1923) thought the poem to have been composed in the last decade of the tenth century, a date still advocated by many scholars. In my opinion, there is nothing in the poem that speaks against a composition around the year 1050, or even later.

28. It was no guarantee however, as is shown by the Eddic poem Helgakvida I, one of the younger heroic lays, where the word *völva* is used to insult the male opponent.

29. *Edda: Die lieder des codex regius nebst verwandten denkmälern*, ed. Gustav Neckel (Heidelberg: Carl Winter, 1914).

30. See Jan de Vries, *Altnordische Literaturgeschichte*, vol. 2 (Grundriss der germanischen Philologie, 16) (Berlin: Walter de Gruyter, 1967), 103; Einar Ólafur Sveinsson, *Íslenzkar bókmenntir í fornöld* (Reykjavik: Almenna Bókfélagid, 1962), 286.

31. Lee M. Hollander, *The Poetic Edda* (Austin: University of Texas Press, 1962), 5.

32. It could refer to necromancy, as is instanced by the phrase "hinn frægasti at útisetum," which occurs in the Old Norse translation of the *Vitae patrum*, rendering Latin "sepulcrorum violator," see *Heilagra Manna søgur: Fortællinger og legender om Hellige Mænd og Kvinder*, ed. C.R. Unger (Christiania, 1847), 411.

33. *Norges gamle Love*, ed. Gustav Storm and Ebbe Hertzberg (Christiania, 1846–1895), 1, 19.

34. *Norges gamle Love*, 2, 497.

35. *Diplomatarium Islandicum* (Copenhagen: Hid Íslenzka Bókmenntafélag, 1857–76), 1, 243.

36. Ursula Dronke, "Völuspá and Sibylline Traditions," in *Latin Culture and Medieval Germanic Europe*, ed. Richard North and Tette Hofstra (Germania Latina, 1) (Groningen: Egbert Forsten, 1992), 17.

37. An account of the first settlers and their descendants. Compilation may have started around 1150, or even earlier, but only revised and greatly altered versions from the thirteenth century have been preserved, see Jónas Kristjánsson, *Eddas and Sagas* (Reykjavik: Hið íslenska bókmenntafélag, 1988), 124–127.

38. *Landnámabók 1–3 (Hauksbók. Sturlubók. Melabók)*, ed. Finnur Jónsson (Cøpenhagen: Det Konglige Nordiske Oldskrift-Selskab, 1900), 46, 171ff, trans. Hermann Pálsson and Paul Edwards, *The Book of Settlements* (The University of Manitoba Icelandic Studies, 1) (Winnipeg: University of Manitoba, 1972), here used with some alterations.

39. Sawyer, "Women," 281.

40. According to *The War of the Irish with the Foreigners*, ed. James H. Todd, *Cogadh Geadhel re Gallaibh* (1867), 41 and 207, one woman warrior *Ingen Ruaidh*, "the Red-haired Maid," commanded a Norse fleet that raided Munster in the tenth century, cf. Duald Mac Firbis, *On the Fomorians and the Norsemen* (Christiania: Norske historiske kildeskriftfond, 1905), 24. Difficult to assess is the significance of the tenth century grave at Åsnes, Norway, in which the skeleton of a young woman was surrounded by sword, shield, spears, axe, whetstone, bridle, with the skeleton of a horse at her feet, see Ursula Dronke, *The Poetic Edda 1: Heroic Poems* (London: Oxford University Press, 1969), 58.

41. H. Wesche, *Der althochdeutsche Wortschatz im Gebiete des Zaubers und der Weissagung* (Untersuchungen zur Geschichte der deutschen Sprache, 1) (Halle a.d. Saale: Max Niemeyer, 1940), 102ff.

42. Helmut de Boor, "Zum althochdeutschen Wortschatz auf dem Gebiet der Weissagung," *Beiträge zur Geschichte der deutschen Sprache und Literatur*, 67 (1944), 108: "niedersitzen, um auf etwas zu lauschen." In his view OHG "hliodarsaza" did not necessarily refer to necromancy, though he admitted that the oldest occurrence of the derivate agent noun "hleotharsazzo" glosses Latin "negromanticus." His main argument was that the gloss is conspicuously missing in those other cases where the Latin text clearly refers to necromancy. Instead we meet the words "dohotrunu vel helliruna" glossing Latin "necromantia;" see Wesche, *Wortschatz*, 48ff. For our investigation the distinction is less relevant.

43. Wesche, *Wortschatz*, 49: "Wir haben in unseren Belegen beide Bedeutungen. Einmal das Abstraktum *helliruna*—'necromantia,' dann aber auch das Konkretum *-runa* 'Zauberin'."

44. Jente, *Die mythologischen Ausdrücke*, 330.

45. *Jordanis Romana et Getica*, 24, *Monumenta Germaniae Historica Auctores Antiquissimi (MGH AA)*, vol. 5/1, 89.

46. *Capitulatio de partibus Saxoniae*, in *Texte zur germanischen Bekehrungsgeschichte*, ed. W. Lange (Tübingen: Max Niemeyer, 1962), 155: "Divinos et sortilegos ecclesiis et sacerdotibus dare constituimus," trans. Henry R. Loyn and John Percival, *The Reign of Charlemagne* (Documents of Medieval History, 2) (London: Edward Arnold, 1975), 53. See also Hans Vordemfelde, *Die germanische Religion in den deutschen Volksrechten* (Religionsgeschichtliche Versuche und Vorarbeiten, 18/1) (Giessen: Alfred Töpelmann, 1923), 125.

47. Tacitus, *Historiae*, 4.65.4, ed. J. Borst (München: Heimeran Verlag, 1969), 474: "ipsa edita in turre, delectus e propinquis consulta responsaque ut internuntius numinis portabat."

48. This platform on which the Germanic seeress was seated reminds us of the tower in which Saint Barbara was said to have resided.

49. Elard Hugo Meyer, *Völuspá: Eine Untersuchung* (Berlin: Meyer & Müller, 1889), 10; Vilhelm Kiil, "Hliðskjálf og seiðhjallr," *Arkiv för nordisk filologi*, 75 (1960), 84–112.

50. Tacitus, *Historiae*, 4.65, ed. Borst, 474.

51. T. Lewis and C. Short, *A Latin Dictionary* (London: Oxford University Press, 1955), sub voce.

52. C. Julius Caesar, *De Bello Gallico* 3.14, ed. G. Dorminger (Munich: Heimeran Verlag, 1973), 126.

53. Strömbäck, *Sejd*, 116.

54. Kiil, "Hliðskjálf," 87.

55. *The War of the Irish with the Foreigners*, ed. Todd, 13; Peter Sawyer, *Kings and Vikings: Scandinavia and Europe* AD *700–1100* (London [etc.]: Methuen, 1982), 22.

56. Dronke, "Völuspá," 20.

57. Magnus Magnusson, *Viking Expansion Westwards* (London: Bodley Head, 1973), 63; Sawyer, *Kings and Vikings*, 22.

58. P.G. Foote and D.M. Wilson, *The Viking Achievement* (London: Sidgwick & Jackson, 1970), 408–411. Ibn Fadlan's account has been translated into various European languages, for instance: Harris Birkeland, *Nordens historie i middelalderen etter arabiske kilder* (Skrifter utgitt av Det Norske Videnskaps-Akademi i Oslo, 2: Historisk-Filosofisk Klasse) (Oslo: Dybwad, 1954), 22. I have considered the possibility of some connection between Ibn Fadlan's description and a scene depicted on a Gotlandic picture stone from Ihre, but as the differences are considerable, I refrained from pursuing the idea further. An illustration of the Ihre Stone can be found in Erik Nylén & Jan Peder Lamm, *Stones, Ships and Symbols* (Stockholm: Gidlund, 1988), 97.

59. Sven B.F. Jansson, *Runinskrifter i Sverige* (Stockholm: Gebers, 1977), 155 (fig. 81); Foote and Wilson, *The Viking Achievement*, plate 26b. Here fig. 1.

60. G.W. Weber, "Das Odinsbild des Altunasteins," *Beiträge zur Geschichte der deutschen Sprache und Literatur*, 94 (Tübingen: Niemeyer, 1972), 232–334.

61. *Die Goldbrakteaten der Völkerwanderungszeit*, ed. Karl Hauck, 1,3 (Ikonographischer Katalog, Tafeln) (Munich: Wilhelm Fink, 1985), 23 (nr. 20 Beresina). Here fig. 2.

62. See Karl Hauck, "Zur Ikonologie der Goldbrakteaten, IV," in *Festschrift Siegfried Gutenbrunner zum 65. Geburtstag* (Heidelberg: Carl Winter, 1972), 47–70, and, by the same author, "Brakteatenikonologie," in *Reallexikon der Germanischen Altertumskunde* (Zweite, völlig neu bearbeitete und stark erweiterte Auflage Berlin: Walter de Gruyter, 1978), vol. 3, 389.

63. Saxo Grammaticus, *Gesta Danorum*, 1.7.14, ed. Alfred Holder (Strassbourg: Trübner, 1886), 31, lines 5–31. See also *Balder's Dreams*.

64. The episode seems inspired by Vergil's description of Aeneas' journey to the underworld, and as such it is of limited value, but it does have some original traits, among which is the decapitated cock.

65. Johnny Roosval, *Die Steinmeister Gottlands* (Stockholm: Fritze's Hofbokhandel, 1918), 83–89, plates 8 and 14; Bengt G. Söderberg, *Mäster Sighmunder i Dädesjö* (Malmö: Allhems Förlag, 1957), 45; Bengt Thordeman, "Rustningarna i Kalevala," *Fornvännen* (1940), 182, fig. 4: altar front from Broddetorp (Sweden) and Rune Norberg, *Nordisk Medeltid* (*Bildkonsten i Norden* 1, H. Arbman and E. Cinthio, *Vår äldsta konst* 1) (Stockholm: 1974), 142 [in Skara Domkyrka].

66. In Homeric Epic a rod was the attribute of the witch-like Circe, who used to turn men into pigs. The episode has vague overtones of erotic fertility magic.

67. Tacitus, *Historiae*, 4.65, ed. Borst, 474.

68. Often, as in Delphi, they are situated at what is claimed to be the navel of the world.

69. Tacitus, *Germania*, 9.2 and 40.2, ed. Fehrle, 24 and 52.

70. Christoph B. Rüger, "Beobachtungen zu den epigraphischen Belegen der Muttergottheiten in den lateinischen Provinzen des Imperium Romanum," in *Matronen und verwandte Gottheiten* (Beihefte der Bonner Jahrbücher Band, 44) (Cologne: Rheinland-Verlag, 1987), 25.

71. M. Schönfeld, "De Kelties-Germaanse Matronenverering," in *Handelingen van het zevende Nederlandse filologen-kongres* (Groningen: Wolters, 1913), 75.

72. In the following I will use the terms *Matres* and *Matronae* interchangeably.

73. It brings to mind the fruit-baskets with which Saint Anne, mother of the Virgin Mary, is iconographically associated, and the bowl with which Saint Bridget of Kildare is often depicted.

74. Schönfeld, "De Kelties-Germaanse Matronenverering," 75. It is tempting to consider whether names like *Audrinehae* and *Aufaniae* cannot be derived from *Aldrinehae* and *Alfaniae*, the first parts of which could be cognate with respectively ON *aldr*, "life, lifetime" and ON *alf(r)* "elementary mythological being (connected with Frey in Old Norse tradition)."

75. Isabella Horn, "Diskussionsbemerkungen zu Ikonographie und Namen der Matronen," in *Matronen und verwandte Gottheiten*, 155.

76. Harald von Petrikovits, "Matronen und verwandte Gottheiten: Zusammenfassende Bemerkungen," in *Matronen und verwandte Gottheiten*, 249: ". . . , daß die mütterliche Fruchtbarkeit zu allen Zeiten und überall als eine der engsten Verbindungen zu dem 'ganz Anderen' angesehen wurde." One could compare the Pythagorean logic of the transmigration of souls: if the soul migrates when we die, then it must come from somewhere when we are born. It only needs to substitute "the other world" for "somewhere."

77. Rüger, "Beobachtungen," 21.

78. Horn, "Diskussionsbemerkungen," 155, see also Julianus E. Bogaers, "Nehalennia en de epigrafische gegevens," in *Deae Nehalenniae* (Gids bij de tentoonstelling: Nehalennia de Zeeuwse godin: Zeeland in de Romeinse tijd, Romeinse monumenten uit de Oosterschelde) (Middelburg: Koninklijk Zeeuwsch Genootschap der Wetenschappen, 1971), 39. The occurrence and the distribution of these *Offenbarungsinschriften* have been studied by Bernardus H. Stolte, "Die religiösen Verhältnisse in Niedergermanien," in *Aufstieg und Niedergang der Römischen Welt*, 18/1, ed. Hildegard Temporini and W. Haase (Berlin [etc.]: Walter de Gruyter, 1986), 592–671, esp. 662–668.

79. Heinz Günther Horn, "Bilddenkmäler des Matronenkultes im Ubiergebiet," in *Matronen und verwandte Gottheiten*, 53.

80. Jens Peter Schjødt, "The 'fire ordeal' in the Grímnismál—initiation or annihilation?" *Mediaeval Scandinavia*, 12 (1988), 39ff.

81. A Celtic origin was advocated by Siegfried J. De Laet, "Nehalennia, déesse germanique ou celtique?" *Helinivm*, 11 (1971), 154–162. De Laet's main argument, the occurrence of a fairy named *Nehaliéna* in a French novel by Eugène Le Roy published 1899, was mildly doubted by Maurits Gysseling, "Over de naam van de godin Nehalennia," *Naamkunde*, 4 (1972), 228, who pointed out that the intervocal *-h-* ought to have disappeared long ago if the name had lingered on in oral tradition. Since then it has been established by C.A. Kalmeyer that Le Roy must have got his information from a French catalogue printed in Paris 1811, see Stolte, "Religiöse Verhältnisse," 620f.

82. Julianus E. Bogaers, "Nehalenninae," *Berichten van de rijksdienst voor het oudheidkundig bodemonderzoek*, 12–13 (1962–1963), 581–583. The stone (CIL XIII 8798) is also depicted in Elisabeth Cramer-Peeters, "Frija—Isis—Nehalennia," *Amsterdamer Beiträge zur älteren Germanistik*, 3 (1972), 17f.

83. Ada Hondius-Crone, *The Temple of Nehalennia at Domburg* (Meulenhoff: Amsterdam, 1955), 104.

84. Harald von Petrikovits, "Matronen und verwandte Gottheiten," 245.

85. Edgar C. Polomé, "Muttergottheiten im alten Westeuropa," in *Matronen und verwandte Gottheiten*, 211. Maybe she was a goddess of the sea, who took lives, and who gave riches; it should be noted that of the dedicants several were merchants of fish. In Old Norse mythology the goddess of the sea was called *Rán* "the one who

robs [lives]," because of the ships and sailors she drew down in her net.

86. Gysseling, "Over de naam," 229, prefers to explain the name as "rectrix," derived from the Indo-European root *nei- "to guide." This meaning was welcomed by Stolte, "Die religiösen Verhältnisse," 619.

87. Bogaers, "Nehalennia en de epigrafische gegevens," 39.

88. Jan de Vries, *Altgermanische Religionsgeschichte* (Grundriss der germanischen Philologie 12/2 (Zweite, völlig neu bearbeitete Auflage Berlin: Walter de Gruyter, 1957), vol. 2, 319ff.

89. *Denkmäler deutscher Poesie und Prosa aus dem VIII–XII Jahrhundert* (ed. Karl Müllenhoff and Wilhelm Scherer) 3d ed. E. Steinmeyer, 1: *Texte* (Berlin: Weidmann, 1892), 16.

90. Lotte Motz, "Sister in the Cave: the stature and function of the female figures of the Eddas," *Arkiv för Nordisk Filologi*, 95 (1980), 168–182, esp. 169–172; Jenny Jochens, "Old Norse Sources on Women," in *Medieval Women and the Sources of Medieval History*, ed. Joel T. Rosenthal (Athens, GA [etc.]: University of Georgia Press, 1990), 162. Hans Kuhn, "Die Religion der nordischen Völker in der Wikingerzeit," in *Normanni e la loro espansione in Europa nell'alto medioevo* (Settimane di studio del Centro italiano di studi sull'alto medioeva, 16) (Spoleto: 1969), 119: "Die Göttinnen standen im allgemeinen deutlich hinter den Göttern zurück. Hiermit steht die Wikingerzeit im Gegensatz zu früheren Perioden der germanischen Kultur mit der grossen Rolle der Muttergottheiten (Matronen) und der Nerthus."

91. Both are reflexes of Germ. *nerþuz, an u-stem. The exact etymological correspondence has been explained in various ways. Axel Kock, "Die Göttin Nerthus und der Gott Njörþr," *Zeitschrift für deutsche Philologie*, 28 (1896), 289–304 stressed the fact that in Primitive Germanic u-feminines and u-masculines had identical case-endings. Already at an early stage the feminines were on the retreat: few are found in Gothic, and none in Old Norse. In Kock's view this disappearance of feminine u-stems caused people to allot a new grammatical gender to *nerþuz: it became a masculine noun, that in due course was interpreted as representing a male god. This solution is hardly convincing. The Gmc. feminine u-nouns *handuz and *kinnuz (Gothic handus and kinnus), the gender of which is irrelevant, still appear as feminines in Old Norse, and simply followed other declensions. A better explanation was given by Hans Kuhn, "Die Wanen," in *Kleine Schriften* (Berlin [etc.]: Walter de Gruyter, 1978), 4, 271, who argued that the frequent plural use of *Njörðr* by the skalds echoed an original coexistence of a god and a goddess, venerated together, and simultaneously. These namesakes were denoted by a neuter dualis, which later, when the dual forms went out of use, and the female Nerthus had been forgotten, was reinterpreted as masculine plural: "Es wird dann anfangs ein (neutraler) Dual gewesen sein, der dann später, als die Sprache die Dualformen aufgab, *die weibliche Nerthus vergessen war* [my italics], und der Name vielleicht auf andere Angehörige ausgedehnt wurde, die Form des maskulinen Plurals erhielt." Indeed, in spite of all theories, the basic fact remains that in Roman times we have a goddess *Nerthus*, whereas its Old Norse cognate *Njörðr* denotes a male god. Of course the change was not a deliberate one; it probably represents the outcome of a long process.

92. Snorri Sturluson, *Heimskringla*, 4 and 7, ed. Finnur Jónsson (Copenhagen: Gad, 1911), 5–7, trans. Lee M. Hollander, *History of the Kings of Norway* (Austin: University of Texas Press, 1964), 7–11.

93. Saxo Grammaticus, *Gesta Danorum*, 1.7.2, ed. Holder, 25f.

94. Paulus diaconus, *Historia Langobardorum* 1.8, in *Monumenta Germaniae Historica Scriptores Rerum germanicarum in usum scholarum (MGH SRG)*, 48, 58.

95. Paulus diaconus, *Historia* 1.3, ed. *MGH SRG*, 54: "mulier quantum inter suos et ingenio acris et consiliis provida; de cuius in rebus dubiis prudentia non minimum confidebant."

96. J.O. Plassmann, "Agis: Eine Untersuchung an Wörtern, Sachen und Mythen," *Beiträge zur Geschichte der deutschen Sprache und Literatur*, 82

(Sonderband Elisabeth Karg-Gasterstädt zum 75. Geburtstag am 9. Februar 1961 gewidmet) (1961), 107.

97. Plassmann, "Agis," 110.

98. *Jordanis Romana et Getica*, 24, ed. *MGH AA* 5/1, 89: "magas mulieres quas patrio sermone Haliurunnas is ipse cognominat."

99. Preben Meulengracht Sørensen, "Thor's Fishing Expedition," in *Words and Objects: Towards a Dialogue Between Archeology and History of Religion*, ed. Gro Steinsland (Oslo: Norwegian University Press, 1986), 257–278. If the scene depicts Odin on *hlidskjálf*, the man on horseback just underneath may have to be interpreted as a dead warrior arriving in Valhalla carrying a drinking horn in his right hand, cf. Nylén & Lamm, *Stones, Ships and Symbols*, 68.

100. As Mircea Eliade, *Shamanism* (Princeton: Princeton University Press, 1974), 381, puts it: "Indeed, we may ask if Odin's two crows, Huginn ('Thought') and Muninn ('Memory') do not represent, in highly mythicized form, two helping spirits in the shape of birds."

101. See n. 91.

102. Jochens, "Old Norse Sources," 163.

103. Tacitus, *Germania*, 7.1, ed. Fehrle, 22: "Reges ex nobilitate, duces ex virtute sumunt. nec regibus infinita aut libera potestas."

104. Rudolf Much and Herbert Jankuhn, *Die Germania des Tacitus* (3d ed. Heidelberg: Carl Winter, 1967), 231. The little we learn about their rules resembles the laws of the Old Norse Jomsvikings.

105. Lucien Musset, *Les invasions: les vagues germaniques* (Paris: Presses universitaires de France, 1965), 50.

106. Dietrich Claude, "Beiträge zur Geschichte der frühmittelalterlichen Königsschätze," *Early Medieval Studies*, 7 (Antikvariskt arkiv 54. Kungl. Vitterhets Historie och Antikvitets Akademien) (Stockholm: Almqvist & Wiksell, 1973), 8ff.

107. See for instance the lists of genealogies of Anglo-Saxon kings in the ninth century Cotton MS. Vespasian B 6, fol. 108ff., ed. Henry Sweet, *The Oldest English Texts* (London: Early English Text Society, 1885), 170f.

108. *Jordanis Romana et Getica*, 13, ed. *MGH AA* 5/1, 76: "Gothi proceres suos . . . non puros homines, sed semideos, id est Ansis, vocaverunt." (The Goths called their ancestors . . . not ordinary men but half-gods, i.e. *ansis*.) The philological implications of the ending *-is* need not concern us here, see Winfred P. Lehmann, *A Gothic Etymological Dictionary* (Leiden: Brill, 1985), 38.

109. It became the king's duty to conduct religious ceremonies in order to obtain good harvests and peace, as expressed in the recurrent Old Norse phrase "at blóta til árs ok fridar."

110. Matthias Zender, "Die Verehrung von drei heiligen Frauen im christlichen Mitteleuropa und ihre Vorbereitungen in alten Vorstellungen," in *Matronen und verwandte Gottheiten*, 213–228, esp. 227. Overtones of a fertility cult are present in the Life of Bridget of Kildare. She turned a stone into bread in time of famine, the cows she milked produced enormous amounts of milk, and barns filled miraculously with grain through her prayer. Her veneration had a stronghold in Flandres, with relics kept in Bruges. See Bynum, *Holy Feast and Holy Fast*, 90, and Otto Wimmer, *Handbuch der Namen und Heiligen* (Innsbruck [etc.]: Tyrolia, 1966), 161.

111. Jan Huisman, "Moedergodinnen en heiligen," *Jeugd en samenleving*, 10 (1980), 41. Huisman mentions a number of additional similarities, which would imply some degree of continuity. However, the nature of his sources makes it advisable to regard the parallel, if accepted, as merely typological.

112. Maurits Gysseling, "Inleiding tot de toponymie, vooral van Oost-Vlaanderen," *Naamkunde*, 10 (1978), 3.

113. Bynum, *Holy Feast and Holy Fast*, 89 and 412.

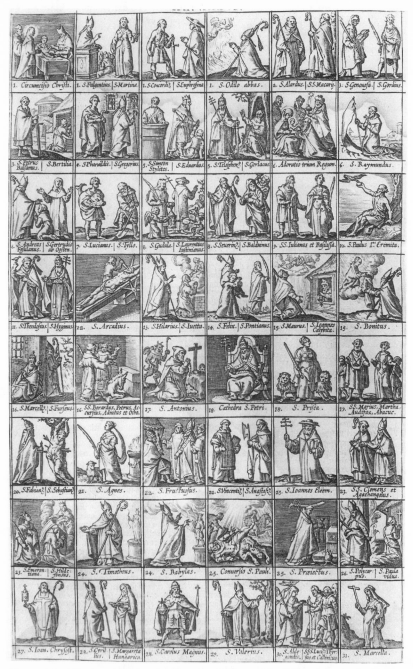

Figure 4.1. *All saints of the month January in Rosweyde, Generale Legende (Antwerp, 1649)* (U.B. Groningen)

4. "Consciousness Fecund through God"

From Male Fighter to Spiritual Bride-Mother in Late Antique Female Sanctity

Giselle de Nie

After Mary, who was "in the Christian tradition, . . . the preeminent Good Mother," Augustine's mother Monica is perhaps the most prominent late antique mother to be recognized as a saint: but not in any substantial way until the twelfth century.[1] In the preceding period, were motherhood and sanctity mutually exclusive?

Late fourth-century western men and women who had renounced the world and physical progeny to embrace the ascetic life could encounter this heady promise in their edificatory reading:

> Christ's birth took its beginning from the shadow: not only in Mary did his birth take its beginning from the shadow, however, but also in you, if you be worthy, will God's Speaking be born (*sed et in te, si dignus fueris, nascitur sermo Dei*).[2]

What is urged here is the rejection of physical conception and motherhood to achieve the imitation of the infinitely greater spiritual conception and motherhood of Christ as it had been realized in Mary.

In the sixth century, a childless Frankish queen turned nun, Radegund, is praised with the epithet "consciousness fecund through God."[3] Looking back from her actualization of it, I will give a few glimpses of the theme of spiritual motherhood as it occurs in the late antique female saints' *Lives* that are reported to have inspired her, and then describe what she did with these models. What we see is that, in this period—contrary to what the Church Fathers' diatribes against sexuality and the married life would lead one to believe—sanctity could, in the deepest and fullest sense, be conceived of as motherhood, albeit of an invisible kind.[4]

But, first, something more needs to be said about the ideal itself. The above passage, occurring in Origen's *Homily on the Song of Songs* as it was translated into Latin by the Church Father Jerome (c.347–420), is the allegorical interpretation of the latter's verse 2:3:

> As an apple tree among the trees of the wood, so is my beloved among young men. With great delight I sat in his shadow (*In umbra eius concupivi, et sedi*), and his fruit was sweet in my throat.

Origen (c.183–c.254) associates this shadow with the "overshadowing" by the Deity that made Mary conceive Christ in Luke's report: "'The Holy Spirit,' [the angel] said, 'will come upon you and the power of the Most High will overshadow you (*virtus Altissimi obumbravit tibi*) . . . .'" (Lk. 1:35). As the masculine gender of the adjective "worthy" shows, however, Origen—perhaps the first to designate Mary as Theotokos or "she who gives birth to God"[5]—is talking to men as well as to women.

A central level of meaning here is also the tasting in the throat of the actual spoken word about the Kingdom, in which Christ, as the Word, would be regarded as present.[6] For Origen, this has further consequences; elsewhere he says:

> For he is the Bridegroom and the Husband of the pure and virginal soul, the Word of God, who is Christ the Lord . . . . Therefore, as much as the soul clings to her bridegroom, and listens to his word, it fills [her], and without doubt she receives from him the seed of the Word: and as that [prophet] has said, "Out of the awe for you, Lord, I have conceived in my womb;" likewise he also said, "From your Word, Lord, I conceived in my womb and gave birth, and produced the spirit of your salvation over the earth" [cf. Isa. 26:18]. If, therefore, the soul thus conceives from Christ, it produces children . . . . Truly happy, therefore, is the *fecundity of the soul* [italics added] (*Est itaque vere beata soboles*), when her union with the Word of God will have taken place, and when they will have exchanged embraces. From this, a noble progeny will be born . . . .[7]

Here not Christ himself is born of the virgin, but, through the seed of his word—he himself also being the Word—spiritual "children" are born.[8] The overlapping and sliding into each other of the various interpretative levels in Origen's passages is typical for the allegorical manner of understanding Bible texts which he did so much to develop.[9]

The Greek-speaking Church Father Origen was one of the first Christians to interpret the sensuous biblical love song as an allegory of the chaste soul and God.[10] This fact should be seen in connection with his view that, through spiritual exercise, the human person was capable of gradually discarding the sexual nature it had acquired through the Fall, thereby returning to man's paradisiacal state and anticipating the life of the angels; a view which, after 393, was to be rejected by the Church.[11] Accordingly, at the beginning of his career, and also in order to be able to teach women as well as men without incurring suspicion, he literally made himself a eunuch for the Kingdom by having himself castrated.[12] In the first passage cited above, he presents an ideal of a spiritualized bridal communion that is simultaneously a conception and a giving birth: as the lover is also the fruit or child, so the bride is also his mother.[13]

This was the ideal that the most prominent Church Fathers held up for imitation. But, as I will show, it also captured the hearts of a number of prominent late antique saintly women. What was the essential appeal of such a view for women in this period? To what extent were their lives shaped by it, and to what extent did they give it the form of their own lives, as models for holy life to be transmitted to later generations?

In what follows I will show how the image of the Virgin Mother[14]—although extensively discussed, now also by feminist theologians,[15] but not yet investigated as a role model for late antique female sanctity outside the prescriptive literature[16]—could become, in Peter Brown's phrase, "an ideogram for one's own soul" in various types of female holiness: that of the virgin, the mother, the widow, and the whore.[17] This occurred alongside the earlier model, also for both sexes, of the male fighter against the Enemy, the latter being the image of the temptations, especially the sexual ones, of the world.[18] For, as Brown has shown, the stirrings of human sexuality had become a symbol of the fallenness of the human condition and its abolishment as the remedy for the latter: "The doctrine of sexuality as a privileged symptom of personal transformation was the most consequential rendering ever achieved of the ancient Jewish and Christian yearning for the single heart."[19] For the eastern monastic tradition, this state was the precondition for union with the One.[20]

Some feminist critique sees in this overcoming of the material by the spiritual the overcoming of the female by the male principle.[21] In my opinion, this is dangerously close to agreeing with the late antique tendency to limit femaleness to affect and sensuality,[22] as well as reading the weight of one's own mental categories into the textual evidence. The Roman state was an urban patriarchy, and male dominance was taken for granted.[23] After its first century, in which the Christian movement tended to follow

Jesus' call to spiritual rather than traditional role patterns, the Church began to take over the male-dominated structure of the surrounding society.[24] If we wish to find evidence of "male dominance" in the image of Mary, it would be in her self-characterization as "maidservant," not in the spiritualization of her motherhood. Even though in the apostolic letters the male had seemed to be identified with the spirit and the female with the body (Ephes. 5:28), this change from a charismatic to a hierarchical structure, or the assertion of male over female leadership, need therefore not be directly connected with, or the equivalent of, the assertion of the spiritual over the material. The latter thought is reductionism: an underestimation of the category of spirituality as a separate though all-encompassing dimension of human experience for women as well as for men. Not because males were out to appropriate female roles,[25] but, I would say, because actual physical gender is profoundly irrelevant in a reality in which all is possible for everyone (Gal. 3:28, Mt. 19:26) do we see male and female roles assumed—metaphorically—by persons of the opposite sex in this sphere.[26]

As Brown continues to point out, moreover, by overcoming what was thought of as "the flesh" or the body, the individual transcended human society, which was dependent on physical procreation for the continuation of its existence. A consequence of Origen's words could be that through a spiritualized bridal union with the divine, the soul participated in an idealized society in heaven instead.[27] One could go further and say that in acting out the Christian imaginary on their bodies, late antique ascetics were delineating the contours of a new, better society in place of what was then perceived as the abuse of power in the later Roman empire.

In one of the fullest portraits we have of a late antique woman saint, that of the former Thuringian princess and later Frankish queen turned nun, Radegundis or Radegund (c.520–87), we see the antique tradition of female holiness summed up. Her friend, the Italian poet, later Bishop of Poitiers, Venantius Fortunatus (c.530–c.604) wrote one of the two prose *Lives* that have come down to us. It is in his poems to and about her, however, that his—and, presumably, her—models of female sanctity are explicitly named. These models will serve as the starting point of this brief survey of the types of holiness, and their stance toward motherhood, described in women of the late antique period.[28] A later, complementary biography of Radegund by a younger fellow nun, Baudonivia, combines elements she had found in Fortunatus's and Bishop Gregory of Tours's (539–594) writings about Radegund with what must have been personal experience, and shows us Radegund regarded as a spiritual queen, reigning a spiritual kingdom in Gaul. This tradition was still alive during the First World War, when she was prayed to in France as "la mère de la patrie."[29]

We find the late antique woman's models for sanctity in condensed form in one of Fortunatus's poems. He describes the royal nun in terms of the virtues of women saints whom he evidently expects to be known to Radegund and her nuns:

> Overcoming Eustochium in the sparingness of her food, and Paula in her fasting, / She has learned from Fabiola how to cure her moral wounds; / She renews Melania through assiduity, Blesilla through piety, / Equalling Marcella through her prayers; / She renews Martha through her service and Mary through her tears, / Eugenia through her vigils, Thecla through her patience.[30]

Elsewhere, he states that, although Sara, Rebecca, Rachel, Esther, Judith, Anna and Naomi—all married women or mothers—are in heaven (but not pointed to as examples to follow), the leader of the choir of virgins there is "the Holy Virgin Mary, the Mother of God."[31] Missing in Fortunatus's list of models—virgins, martyrs, and widows, and no mothers, except Mary, described in that role—is the martyred mother Perpetua and her companion Felicitas, whose cult was well established by this time.[32] I will suggest a reason for this below. The Mary who is mentioned may be Mary of Bethany, but could also be Mary Magdalene, or a conflation of both: the type of the sanctified repentant whore that would play a not inconspicuous role in the later Middle Ages.[33]

We will look briefly at a representative of each type. The transformed image of the almost invisible wife of Joseph into the glorified Virgin Mother of Christ will be described as it appears in a second-century apocryphal gospel which has been called "the central text for the construction of the medieval Mary."[34] I will show how this image is increasingly implicated in descriptions of ascetic women from the third century onward: those of the mother and martyr Perpetua, the virgin and martyr Eugenia, the widow and mother Paula, and a penitent whore whose tradition is better attested in this period than that of Mary Magdalene: Thais. In the sixth century, the energetic royal nun Radegund—whose *Life* was the first of a member of reigning royalty—managed to combine the then existing role models for women into a new and powerful image: that of a queen and "mother" through grace, or through God.

Mary's Role in the New Testament

Only two of the four Gospels mention the nativity of Christ. Matthew first gives the ancestry of Joseph, as the husband of Mary, going back through David to Abraham, and thereupon relates that "before they came together she was found to be with child of the Holy Spirit" (Mt. 1:18), and that "he knew her not until she had borne her first-born son; and he called his name Jesus" (Mt. 1:25). Later, during his ministry, Jesus is presented as paying little attention to his earthly family:

> While he was still speaking to the people, behold, his mother and his brothers stood outside, asking to speak to him. Someone told him, "Your mother and your brothers are standing outside, asking to speak to you."
>
> But he replied to the man who told him, "Who is my mother, and who are my brothers?" And stretching out his hand toward his disciples, he said, "Here are my mother and my brothers! For whoever does the will of my Father in heaven is my brother, and sister, and mother." (Mt. 12:46–50)

Matthew does not mention Jesus' mother as being present at the Crucifixion: only Mary, the mother of James and Joseph,[35] and Mary of Magdala (Mt. 27:56). Mark says something very similar (Mk. 15:40). There is no glorification in either of Mary's motherhood, virginal or otherwise.

Luke is the source for the two similarly structured and detailed stories about the divinely arranged, almost simultaneous, conceptions and births of John the Baptist and Jesus (Lk. 1:5–2:39). The central text in what became the image of Mary as the handmaid of the Lord and the Virgin Mother of Christ follows:

> In the sixth month the angel Gabriel was sent from God to a city of Galilee named Nazareth, to a virgin betrothed to a man whose name was Joseph, of the house of David; and the virgin's name was Mary.
>
> And he came to her and said: "Hail, O one full of grace, the Lord is with you! Blessed are you among women!"
>
> But she was troubled at the saying, and considered in her mind what sort of greeting this might be. And the angel said to her: "Do not be afraid, Mary, for you have found favor with God. Behold you will conceive in your womb and bear a son, and you shall call his

name Jesus. He will be great, and will be called the son of the Most High; and the Lord God will give to him the throne of his father David, and he will reign over the house of Jacob forever; and of his kingdom there will be no end."

But Mary said to the angel: "How can this be, since I do not know a man?"

And the angel replied to her: "The Holy Spirit will come upon you, and the power of the Most High will overshadow you (*Spiritus Sanctus superveniet in te et virtus Altissimi obumbravit tibi*); therefore the child to be born will be called holy, the Son of God. And behold, your kinswoman Elizabeth in her old age has also conceived a son; and this is the sixth month with her who was called barren. For with God no word will be impossible (*Quia non erit inpossibile apud Deum omne verbum*)."

And Mary said: "Behold I am the handmaid of the Lord. Let it be to me according to your word (*Ecce ancilla Domini. Fiat mihi secundum verbum tuum*)."

And the angel departed from her. (Lk. 1:26–38)

As we shall see below, in late Antiquity, this passage was understood as a creation-conception through the hearing, and thus receiving, of the divine word, just as God had created the world through his word.[36]

About the birth in Bethlehem, we are told: "And she gave birth to her first-born son and wrapped him in swaddling cloths, and laid him in a manger because there was no place for them in the inn" (Lk. 2:7). Then follow: the story of the angel appearing to the shepherds, Jesus's circumcision, and the presenting at the Temple, meeting Simeon and the prophetess and widow Anna (Lk. 2:8–39).

Central in the story of the virginal conception and birth is the idea that the God-man Christ, beginning a new age, cannot have been conceived through the ordinary human procreative process: a late antique notion that is also found outside the Christian tradition.[37] Herewith, the storyteller makes two important points. First, human procreation is demoted from being a possibly sacred act of the transmission and creation of life to being something not worthy of the God-man: potentially or actually obscene.

This thought should be seen in the context of the coalescence of two anti-body traditions in first-century Palestine: that of Platonic philosophy and that of the indigenous biblical rules about ritual purity.[38] Moreover, speaking of early Christianity, Mary Douglas has said: "The idea that virginity had a special positive value was bound to fall on good soil in a small persecuted minority group. . . . these social conditions lend themselves to beliefs which symbolise the body as an imperfect container which will only be perfect if it can be made impermeable."[39] We will see, however, that this mentality lasts well beyond the persecutions; mentalities change much more slowly than social conditions.[40]

Second, God's Fatherhood is asserted at the expense of human fatherhood, which was evidently not good enough. With this assertion, not only woman, but also the human male is diminished in stature over against what is thought of as the divine Patriarch.[41] In short: again, the spiritual is the real, the body at most an instrument. This attitude was to gain strength in late Antiquity and remain dominant until the high Middle Ages.

The same idea underlies Luke's report of the incident of the adult Jesus' not wishing to see his family:

> Then his mother and his brothers came to him, but they could not reach him for the crowd. And he was told, "Your mother and your brothers are standing outside, desiring to see you." But he replied, saying to them, "My mother and my brothers are those who hear the word of God and do it (*verbum Dei audiunt et faciunt*)." (Lk. 8:19–21)

Jesus chooses for the spiritual family rather than the carnal one. At the Crucifixion only "the women who had come with him from Galilee" are mentioned (Lk. 23:49); at the tomb, these turn out to be Mary of Magdala, Joanna and "Mary the mother of James" (evidently not his mother, Mary) with their companions (Lk. 24:10).

The Gospel of John does not mention Christ's birth as such:

> In the beginning was the Word (*Verbum*), and the Word was with God, and the Word was God. He was in the beginning with God; all things were made through him, and without him nothing was made that was made. In him was life, and the life was the light of men. The light shines in the darkness, and the darkness has not overcome it. . . .
>
> The true light that enlightens every man was coming into the world. He was in the world, and the world was made through him, yet the world knew him not. He came to his own home, and his own people received him not. But to all who received him, who believed in his name, he gave power to become children of God: who were born, not out of blood nor out of the will of the flesh nor out of the will of man, but out of God (*ex Deo nati sunt*).

And the Word became flesh and dwelt among us, full of grace
and truth; we have beheld his glory, glory as of the only Son from
the Father (*a patre*). . . . And from his fullness have we all received,
grace upon grace. For the law was given through Moses; grace and
truth came through Jesus Christ. No one has ever seen God; the only
Son, who is in the bosom of the Father, he has told [us] about him
(*enarravit*). (Jn 1:1–5, 9–14, 16–18)

What could this passage have meant to the ordinary Christian believer?
Christ is identified as the Word, God, and the creative principle of and in
the world; he is also life, which is the light or spirit of man; and he is full of
grace, truth, and glory.

Christ's being referred to as the Word must point to God's having effected the Creation through speaking (Gen. 1:3–31). In Luke's version of the
parable of the Sower, Christ had said that "the seed is the word of God (*semen est verbum Dei*)" and that the seeds in the good soil are like those of
good heart who, having heard it, would "bring forth fruit (*fructum
adferunt*)" (Lk. 8:11, 15). Mark's version says that "(w)hoever sows, sows
the word (*verbum*)," and that "those [seeds] that were sown upon the good
soil are the ones who hear the word and accept it and bear fruit (*qui audiunt
verbum et suscipiunt et fructificant*), thirty-fold, and sixty-fold, and a hundredfold" (Mk. 4:14, 20). The late second-century Church Father Irenaeus
was to say that Mary "through the speaking of the angel received the glad
tidings that she would bear God by obeying his Word (*per angelicum
sermonem evangelizata est, ut portaret Deum, obediens ejus verbo*)."[42] Here
the obedient reception of the word heard is itself the conception, the event
of generation. Irenaeus' emphasis on obedience is another way of formulat-
ing the *ancilla* idea. The degrees of fruitfulness were later applied by ecclesiastical writers to the orders of the married, the widows and the virgins respectively.[43]

The word of God, then, is a seed that germinates in the receiving heart,
and brings forth fruit there. The same attitude toward the word is evident
in the apostolic letters. Most explicit on this point is the Epistle to the
Thessalonians, that sees God's word as immanent in the apostles' preaching: "And we also thank God constantly for this, that when you received
from us the word of the heard God, you accepted it not as the word of men,
but as what it really is, the word of God that works in you who have believed (*cum accepissetis a nobis verbum auditus Dei, accepistis non ut verbum
hominum, sed sicut est vere verbum Dei qui operatur in vobis qui
credidistis*)" (1 Th. 2:13). This is the word that, also through men, creates

children of God. What we have here again, then, is the substitution of spiritual generation and bonding for carnal procreation and family relations. The carnal and spiritual relations that could have been regarded as a harmonious combination were somehow put in terms of bitter separation and alienation. Genesis having pointed the way (Gen. 3:16), biological motherhood was regarded as a most painful emotional as well as physical fact; Jerome was later to contrast the untroubled life of consecrated virgins with the nastiness of life as a wife and mother.[44] This is not to say that the notion of the spiritualization of human reproduction as the "higher" form went uncontested. In the fourth century, the ascetic Jovinian firmly asserted the equal value of all forms of Christian life, married and celibate. Although he was silenced by Ambrose and Jerome, this need not mean that popular practice followed the guidelines of the Church's official spokesmen.[45]

Nevertheless, John does pay more attention to Mary. He records her presence at the Crucifixion, and reports that Jesus charged him, as the most beloved disciple, to take care of her from then on as his own mother (Jn 19:25–7). In his account, however, it is Mary of Magdala alone who first meets the risen Jesus (Jn 20:1–18). Like Matthew, he shows us that Jesus was otherwise not particularly concerned with his mother:

> On the third day there was a marriage at Cana in Galilee, and the mother of Jesus was there; Jesus was also invited to the marriage, with his disciples. And when there was not enough wine, the mother of Jesus said to him: "They have no wine."
>
> And Jesus said to her: "What is it to me and to you, woman (*Quid mihi et tibi est mulier*)? My hour has not yet come."
>
> His mother said to his servants: "Do whatever he will say to you." (Jn 2:1–5)[46]

After the jars had been filled with water that thereupon turned into wine, John says: "This [was] the first of the signs that Jesus did," and concludes with the statement that: "After this he went down to Capernaum, with his mother and his brothers and his disciples; and there they stayed for a few days" (Jn 2:11–12). Here Mary, although rebuffed, seems to expect her son's first miracle, that was probably intended by the storyteller as a symbol for the Eucharist.[47] Again, she is mentioned as having other sons, and therefore is the wife of Joseph, and not a perpetual virgin. Noteworthy too, however, is that she is said to accompany Jesus and his disciples for at least a short while. In all this, there is no hint of any glorification of Mary's motherhood of Jesus, nor of her perpetual virginity.

After an almost complete silence about Mary in the official ecclesiastical writers since the New Testament, Origen is the first to mention a book of James that may have been what we know as the *Protevangelium of James*.[48] This gnostically influenced apocryphal gospel[49] is a creation of circles that would later be declared to be outside mainstream Christianity; Jerome was to characterize such literature as "the delirious nonsense of the apocrypha."[50] From the end of the fourth century, however, ecclesiastical writings, contain many allusions to statements made in the Protevangelium. It must have been an influential strand in the traditions that merged to become the cult of Mary.

Sometime in the second century, then, a story that may have been an unofficial oral tradition and/or based upon someone's prophetic vision of "how it must have been" was given literary form in writing. Whose needs are addressed? The subtitle of this apocryphal Gospel is programmatic: *The birth of Mary the Holy Mother of God, and very glorious Mother of Jesus Christ.* Is this a late antique forerunner of today's feminist historiography: "cherchez la femme"? Could it have been, in connection with the fact of the diminishing role of flesh-and-blood women in the increasingly male-dominated church,[51] an anonymous prophetess' vision of the compensatory establishment of a woman leader in the spiritual sphere?

In the Protevangelium, the human person of Mary herself, as well as the physical birth of Jesus, have become completely spiritualized:

> [W]hen she was six months old, her mother set her on the ground to try whether she could stand, and she walked seven steps and came into her bosom; and she snatched her up, saying: "As the Lord my God lives, you shall not walk on this earth until I bring you into the temple of the Lord." And she made a sanctuary in her bed-chamber, and allowed nothing common or unclean to pass through her. (James 6)

When, in her third year, Mary was brought to be raised in the Temple, "she danced with her feet, and all the house of Israel loved her." The story continues: "And Mary was in the temple of the Lord as if she were a dove that dwelt there, and she received food from the hand of an angel." In her twelfth year, the widower Joseph, an old man, with children—this to account for the mention of Jesus' having brothers—was chosen by oracle to receive and keep her. The Annunciation is related in essentially the same form as in Luke's Gospel. Joseph's reaction is told in more detail; both he and Mary are made to undergo an oracle at the temple but are found to be without sin (James 7–16).

When, on the way to Bethlehem, the time for her delivery came, Joseph

took her down from off the ass and said to her: "Where shall I take you, and cover your [intimate nakedness]?[52] For the place is a desert."

And he found a cave there, and led her into it; and leaving his two sons beside her, he went out to seek a midwife in the district of Bethlehem. [When he returned with a midwife,] they stood in the place of the cave, and behold a luminous cloud overshadowed the cave. And the midwife said: "My soul has been magnified this day, because my eyes have seen strange things—because salvation has been brought to Israel." And immediately the cloud disappeared out of the cave, and a great light shone in the cave, so that the eyes could not bear it. And in a little that light gradually decreased, until the infant appeared, and went and took the breast from his mother Mary. And the midwife cried out, and said: "This is a great day to me, because I have seen this strange sight."

And the midwife went forth out of the cave, and Salome met her. And she said to her: "Salome, Salome, I have a strange sight to relate to you: a virgin has brought forth—a thing which her nature admits not of."

Then said Salome: "As the Lord my God liveth, unless I thrust in my finger, and search the parts, I will not believe that a virgin has brought forth." (James 17–19)

When Salome had looked and found Mary to be indeed a virgin, her hand began to burn as if with fire; it was healed as soon as she had carried the infant. The stories of the Magi and of Herod's slaying of the innocent children follow. Upon hearing of the danger, Mary swaddled the infant and put him in an oxstall (James 20–22). There the work takes leave of her and the child. It is a vindication, in story form, of Mary's glorious qualities: her ever sinless state and her miraculous virginity before, during and after the birth of Jesus; as Bishop Ambrose of Milan (c.340–97) was later to defend it, depending upon this tradition.[53]

The imaged story of Mary, the Virgin Mother of God, must stand— as so many of the miracle stories springing up in this time—for an overwhelming interior experience that can be communicated only in an indirect manner through a narrative about visible events, an extended metaphor.[54] It seems to me no accident that Origen mentions what is probably the Protevangelium. I suggest that the latter presents a feminine counter-image to that of the Crucifixion.

A letter of the late first-century Bishop and martyr Ignatius of Antioch seems to show that this view may have been around from the beginning. After a number of exhortations to the community of the faithful, he writes:

> And the virginity of Mary and her giving birth concealed the Ruler of this world, as did the death of the Lord; three mysteries clamored [around the world], which were performed in the silence of God. . . . A star shone in the sky, conquering all other stars by its splendor, and its light was indescribable. . . . For this reason all magic was dissolved, and the whole chain of evil abolished; ignorance was destroyed, and the old kingdom brought to ruin, upon the manifestation of God in the manner of men leading to the newness of eternal life.[55]

The abolition of the old order, then, was accomplished already in the virgin birth, and not only after the Passion.

Is it too much to say that this view is likely to have contributed to the celibates' and ascetics' later looking to Mary as a model for their way of life? A life that, instead of, or alongside, achieving eternal life in (living) death through the imitation of the suffering in the Passion, achieved it in (continuous) giving birth in imitation of the Mother of God: the same process as that which Origen had seen in the Song of Songs. The image of the fight through suffering, as we shall see in the next section, is explicitly said to have informed the experience of women martyrs. The image of continuous spiritual generation was perhaps found to be at least as appealing after the persecutions had ceased early in the fourth century.

The generative dynamic of the spiritual bride-and-mother image is, of course, analogous to that of the ancient near Eastern Mother Goddess who was still being worshipped in late Antiquity, for instance in the form of Artemis, Isis, and Cybele. In a number of cases, archeological evidence seems to indicate that the cult of Mary replaced that of the Great Mother.[56] Further, the generative dynamic is similar to that of the contemporary neo-Platonic notion of the overflowing Godhead—or "self-transcending fecundity"—and also resembles the then current Christian image of the spring of eternal life in Paradise, sometimes conflated with Christ.[57] Further, it must be connected with the occurrence of maternal God-images in second-century gnostic writings.[58] Origen's teacher, Clement of Alexandria (150–c.215), had characterized God in masculine and feminine terms simultaneously:

> The Word is everything to the child, both father and mother, teacher and nurse. . . . The nutriment is the milk of the Father, by Whom

alone the littlest ones are fed. . . . and the Word alone supplies us children with the milk of love, and only those who suck at his breast are
truly happy. . . . Thus, for Christ, nourishment was to do the will of
the Father; but for us, the littles ones, nourishment is Christ himself:
we drink the heavenly Word. For this reason seeking is called suck-
ing; to those infants who seek the Word, the Father's breasts of be-
nevolence supply milk (*quod infantibus, qui Verbum quaerunt,
paterna benignitatis ubera lac suppeditent*).[59]

The image of Christ as a nursing mother occurs in Irenaeus, who had written of the latter feeding the faithful (with his doctrine) "as if from the breast
of his flesh,[60] and Augustine, too, later referred to Christ as "mother" and
as "nursing."[61] In the sources, we find these God-images as such much less
verbalized than that of the divine Father. The maternal image is, however,
transposed onto the Church. Ambrose, for instance, says that her motherly
attributes derive from Christ:

Who is this virgin, who is moistened by the springs of the Trinity,
whose waters flow from the rock, whose breasts never dry up, who
pours out honey? The Rock, according to the Apostle however, is
Christ [1 Cor. 10:4]. Therefore, from Christ [comes her] breasts not
drying up, from God [comes] her brightness, from the Spirit her river
(*Ergo a Christo non deficiunt ubera, claritas a deo, flumen ab spiritu*).
For this is the Trinity that moistens her church: the Father, Christ and
the Spirit.[62]

The underlying image of continuously creative, overflowing grace also becomes visible in the dynamic pattern of God's action as in the miracle of the
overflowing lamp in Radegund's convent which was regarded as an epiphany
of the power of the particle of the Holy Cross near it.[63] I suggest that, in
the image of the bride-mother, we see an analogous God-image becoming
an "ideogram for one's own soul." After all, according to Genesis, the original human being to whose condition one tried to return, had been created
in God's image (Gen. 1:27).

The apocryphal gospels also describe the horrors of biological parenthood, again a theme that would be taken over by the fourth-century
Church Fathers.[64] By the fourth century, the ideal of the spiritual motherhood of virgins somehow began to become extremely powerful. It is spelled
out in prescriptive literature by Church Fathers such as Jerome and Augustine,[65] and, as I will show, it emerges now and then as a scarcely expressed

substratum, taken for granted, in the biographies below. An early sixth-century author of a poetical treatise in praise of virginity, Bishop Avitus of Vienne (450–518), more explicitly held Mary up to his sister as a model: for the spiritual motherhood she, as a consecrated virgin, and according to Origen's interpretation, could also achieve.[66] As we saw, later in the sixth century, Fortunatus describes Mary, implicitly in a similar role, as leading the choir of virgins in heaven.

Ascetic women in their then developing independence from family obligations resulting from their new role of virgin consecrated to Christ,[67] but equally all male celibates and ascetics, needed a glorious archetype or model to look up to. This is the basic reason that serious churchmen continued to exercise their ingenuity in arguing Mary's virginity before, during and after birth. She was the model for the life of the Church's élite as well as the Mother of the Church as Christ's mystic body.[68] In a sermon to the people, Augustine, for instance, citing Christ's words at the wedding of Cana—"whosoever does the will of my Father Who is in Heaven is my brother, sister and mother" (Jn 2:5)—tells his hearers: ". . . you too are the members of Christ and you are the body of Christ. . . . Let the members of Christ give birth in mind, as Mary, a virgin, gave birth to him in her womb; and thus you will be mothers of Christ."[69] At the same time, however, the image of Mary as Virgin Mother of a flesh-and-blood God-child made any real imitation impossible. Hence mortal women could never aspire to leadership in the patriarchally organized church in this world. Brown has stressed that the late antique church's model of human relationships to the divine was one of complete dependence upon and subjection to a father-figure.[70] Even Mary, since the Gospels, had been described as regarding herself as in obedience to a male: "the handmaid of the Lord." In Antiquity, moreover, the male seed was regarded as the sole creative element in the procreative process; women were thought to contribute only the blood that nourished it. Similarly, the male was thought to contribute the spirit, the female the flesh.[71] Motherhood, however idealized, was therefore still regarded as no more than a passive receptivity and nurturing. Nevertheless, the notions of spiritual marriage and motherhood are images of spiritual experiences, communicated through the metaphors of more earth-bound events. They must have provided an ecclesiastically sanctioned imaginary giving direction and shape to the natural yearnings of many ascetic women.

At the same time, however, Mary was viewed—for instance by the influential Jerome—as the rehabilitation of the woman through whom sin had come into the world and thus the bringer of death: Eve.[72] The glorification of Mary's spiritual motherhood may thus be seen as a reversal of this persistent tendency. It is a vindication of women's dignity as the forth-bringer of spiritual life, through her generative capacity. As we shall see, this gave them opportunities for power and leadership in the religious context alongside men.

PERPETUA: THE MOTHER WHO BECAME A MAN

From the late second century on—in the same period that the Protevangelium is first mentioned—imagery of the spiritual bride and mother begins to appear in the biographies of female saints. In the *Passion* of Perpetua and her companion Felicitas, martyred in Carthage in 203, it is not yet very prominent. The imagery may be latent, however, in the fact that both are actual human mothers with young infants. There is only one instance of explicit bridal imagery, and it is the first to occur in the Christian saints' lives:[73] of Perpetua the anonymous author says that, when she entered the arena, she did so "as the wife of Christ, as the beloved of God (*ut matrona Christi, ut Dei delicata*)."[74] This qualification could also imply a simultaneous reference to an imitation of the suffering of Christ, the model of all martyrs. In the earlier part of the *Passion*, however, in what claims to be an autobiographical prison diary,[75] Perpetua herself does not mention any nuptial imagery.

The story line of Perpetua and Felicitas' *Passion* is as follows. The recently converted Lady Vibia Perpetua, married and nursing an infant son, was imprisoned with her eight months pregnant maidservant Felicitas, the latter's husband Revocatus, and two male catechumens, Saturninus and Secundulus, for refusing, on account of her Christian belief, to offer sacrifice to the Emperor and the gods. Perpetua's husband is not mentioned. Her father, with whom she had had an especially close relationship, tried, at the beginning and at other crucial moments, to persuade her to give priority to her earthly family bonds. His repeated failure to do so is the measure of Perpetua's strength and of the debacle of earthly paternal authority:[76] an important point, showing that earthly and divine patriarchy are here regarded as definitely not continuous. In the first of her four visions in prison, she presents what seems to be an anticipatory, dream version of her martyrdom, describing her way out of earthly society to a transformed father figure:

> I saw a bronze ladder, of wondrous height, reaching as far as heaven, and narrow. . . . And on the sides of the ladder every kind of iron implement was fixed: there swords, lances, hooks, knives, javelins, so that if anyone went up carelessly or not looking upwards, he would be torn and his flesh caught on the irons. And beneath the ladder

7. *S. Perpetua et Felicitas.*

Figure 4.2. The holy Mothers Perpetua and Felicitas (Idem)

lurked a serpent of wondrous size, who laid ambushes for those mounting, terrifying [people] to prevent them from ascending. But Saturus climbed up first (he was the one who at a later stage gave himself up spontaneously on account of us . . .). And he reached the top of the ladder, and turned and said to me: "Perpetua, I am sustaining you; but take care that the dragon does not bite you."

And I said: "He will not harm me, in the name of Jesus Christ." And under that ladder, almost, it seemed, afraid of me, the serpent showly thrust out its head. And, as if he were the first rung I stepped on, I trod on its head, and went up.

And I saw an immense space of garden, and in the middle of it a very tall grey-haired man sitting in shepherd's clothing, milking sheep. And, standing around him, many thousands of people dressed in white garments. And he raised his head, looked at me, and said: "You are welcome, child." And he called me, and gave me, as it were, a mouthful of the curds that he was milking; and I accepted it in both my hands together, and ate it. And all those standing around said: "Amen."[77]

The image—from Genesis (Gen. 3:15)—of treading upon the Devil/serpent's head returns in her last vision, when, as a male athlete, she defeats her Devil-opponent. The grey hair of the old man recurs in the various references to her human father: in the very next episode, in her father's self-description when he comes to the prison in another attempt at persuasion. It is then that he prostrates himself at her feet and addresses her as "lady (*domina*)."[78]

Later on, as she mounted the tribunal for the judicial hearing of her case in the Forum, her father appeared with her infant son and appealed to her maternal feelings. That she very much had these is evident earlier in her diary. There she describes her entry into the dark prison: "Oh harsh day: intense heat, because of the crowds, beatings by soldiers. Above all, I was tormented there with anxiety about my child." Later she received her child, already weakened with hunger, for breast-feeding, and spoke to her mother about him. She continues: "Then I managed to have the child allowed to stay with me in prison. And at once I grew well again, relieved of the strain and the anguish for him. And suddenly the prison became a palace to me, where I would rather be than anywhere."[79]

Before the hearing, evidently, her son had been taken away again. She tells us:

And my father appeared there with my son, and pulled me off the step, saying: "Perform the sacrifice! Have pity on your child!" So too the governor, Hilarianus, who had been given judiciary power . . . : "Spare your father's grey hair, spare your little boy's infancy! Perform the ritual for the Emperor's welfare." And I answered: "I will not." Hilarianus asked: "Are you a Christian?" And I replied: "I am a Christian." And when my father persisted in trying to make me change my mind, Hilarianus ordered him to be shoved away, and he was struck with a rod. And I grieved for my father's downfall as if I'd been struck myself: that's how I mourned for his pitiful old age. Then the governor sentenced us all and condemned us to the beasts of the arena. And joyful we went back to the prison.

Then, as the baby had been used to breast-feeding and staying in the prison with me, I at once sent the deacon Pomponius to my father, imploring him to have it back. But my father did not want to give it. And somehow, God willed that it no longer needed the breast, and that my breasts did not become inflamed, so that I would not be tormented with worry for the child, or with soreness.[80]

In the next episode, Perpetua sees another vision, this time of her younger brother Dinocrates who had died unbaptized at the age of seven, dirty and suffering from a wound on his face as well as of thirst in a dark place near a pool of water that he could not reach. After praying for him to be released from this condition for a number of days, she had a new vision in which Dinocrates looked clean, healed and refreshed:

> . . . and the pool I had previously seen had its rim lowered: it was down to the boy's navel. And he was drinking from the pool incessantly. Above the rim was a golden bowl full of water. Dinocrates came near it and began to drink from that, and the bowl never ran dry. And when he had drunk his fill, he began to play happily with the water, as children do. And I awoke. Then I realized that he had been delivered from his punishment.[81]

Here, Perpetua's prayers have mediated between God and her dead brother: just as her visions have exhibited her mediatory position. In the early Church, female leadership had often been exercised through visions.[82] At the same time, I suggest, the visions Perpetua relates may have another level. They may exhibit in image-form her transformation of her relation with her living infant son: his weaning from her breast-feeding. If so, her motherhood is thereby spiritualized. In the image of Dinocrates, she is now feeding him through her prayers. Her words about the little boy happily playing with the water reveal her own happiness at the motherly care she has been able to give by spiritual means.

There was, however, no way for her to endure the final collision with earthly society through an acting out of the role of motherhood. It seemed to call for the—male—role of an athlete.[83] In her fourth and last vision, "the day before our fight," Perpetua was led to the amphitheatre and surprised that no beasts were sent out against her:

> Out against me came an Egyptian, foul of aspect, with his seconds: he was to fight me. And some handsome young men came up beside

me: my own seconds and supporters. And I was stripped naked, and became a man. And my supporters began to rub me with oil, as they do for a wrestling match; and on the other side I saw the Egyptian rolling himself in the dust.

And a man of amazing size came out; he towered even over the vault of the amphitheatre. He was wearing the purple, loosely, with two stripes crossing his chest, and patterned sandals made of gold and silver, carrying a baton like an athletic trainer and a green bough laden with golden apples. He asked for silence, and said: "This Egyptian, if he defeats her, will kill her with his sword; she, if she defeats him, will receive this bough." And he drew back.

And we joined combat, and fists began to fly. He tried to grab my feet, but I struck him in the face with my heels. And I was raised up into the air, and began to strike him as if I were not touching ground. But when I saw there was a lull, I locked my hands, clenching my fingers together, and so caught hold of his head; and he fell on his face, and I trod upon his head. And the populace began to shout, and my supporters to sing psalms. And I went to the trainer and received the bough. He kissed me and said: "Daughter, peace be with you!" And triumphantly I began to walk towards the Gate of the Living. And I awoke. And I knew I should have to fight not against wild beasts but against the Fiend; but I knew the victory would be mine.[84]

Here, the towering trainer, calling her "daughter," seems to be another form of her heavenly Father. Are these the apples from the Tree of Eternal Life, because of which she may proceed to the peace of that eternal life through the Gate of the Living? Or is there, also, a pointer to the apple tree in the Song of Songs? In any case, the senseless fight against wild beasts is transformed into a fight with the Devil in the appearance of a dark Egyptian. In order to be able to defeat him in this guise, Perpetua finds herself transformed into the appearance of a man. The trainer/Father, however, continues to speak of and address her as a woman. Again we see the typical late antique thinking of reality as consisting of various levels simultaneously, just as in dreams: here this perception is presented as an actual dream.

The story of the eight months pregnant Felicitas, and the subsequent martyrdom of both, told by the anonymous author of the *Passion*, seems to wish to show traces of current attitudes of sexist abuse. Because even Romans then drew the line at pregnant women, Felicitas was afraid she would not be permitted to suffer with the rest, recognizably as a Christian martyr, but later, after her delivery, unrecognized, with common criminals. Everyone therefore prayed for her to be delivered as soon as possible:

> Immediately after their prayer, the birth pains came upon her. And while, because of the natural difficulty of labor in the eighth month, she was in great pain, one of the prison guards said to her: "You who suffer so much now, what will you do when you are thrown to the beasts, whom you didn't think of when you refused to sacrifice?"
>
> And she answered: "What I suffer now, I suffer by myself; but then, another will be inside me who will suffer for me, because I shall be suffering for him." And thus she gave birth to a girl, who was raised by one of the sisters as her daughter.[85]

The imitation of Christ through suffering and death as well as the presence of Christ (as the Bridegroom of the soul?) within are clearly experienced. Here, motherhood again stood in the way of participating in the spiritual companionship in martyrdom.

When the women are, finally, in the arena—Perpetua as the *matrona Christi*, and Felicitas "glad that she had safely given birth so that she could fight the beasts, from blood to blood, from the midwife to the gladiator, ready to wash after childbirth with a second baptism"[86]—the anonymous author again gives us the shivers. The men had been exposed to a leopard, a bear and a boar:

> [f]or the young women, however, the Devil had prepared an unusual animal: a most fierce cow. This was chosen so that their sex might be matched with that of the beast. So they were stripped naked, placed in nets and thus brought out into the arena. The crowd was horrified when they saw that one was a delicate young girl and the other was a woman fresh from childbirth with the milk still dripping from her breasts. And so they were brought back again and dressed in unbelted tunics.
>
> First Perpetua was hit in the loins and fell. Then, where she sat, she pulled down her tunic that was ripped along the side so that it covered her thighs, thinking more of her modesty than of her pain. Next she asked for a pin to fasten her untidy hair: for it was not right that a martyr should die with her hair in disorder, lest she might seem to be mourning in her hour of triumph.
>
> She got up, and, when she saw that Felicitas had fallen, she went to her, gave her her hand and lifted her up. And the two stood side

by side. And the cruelty of the populace now being appeased, they were called back through the Gate of the Living.[87]

It is difficult not to get the impression that even this presumably sympathetic and religiously motivated author experienced some measure of pleasurable horror—or expected his audience to do so—in such an almost strip-tease style of sadistic description. Similarly, contemporary apocryphal stories ostensibly propagating asceticism are at the same time decidedly erotic.[88] There is evidence, moreover, of a contemporary revulsion against the messiness of the human body[89] that was then often projected primarily onto the feminine one.[90] Traces of the Old Testament notion, for instance, that a woman, during her menstruation and after birth, might not be "pure" enough to receive communion began to circulate in the Church at least from the fourth century.[91] I adduce all this more specific evidence to give the modern reader some taste of the late antique patterns of feeling behind the more formal and distanced protestations of revulsion against what Peter Brown has so aptly characterized: the body as a symbol of society.[92]

At the Gate of the Living, Perpetua was held by a catechumen. "As though awaking from sleep—up to that point she had been in the spirit and in ecstasy:" she had begun to sing psalms and imagine herself treading upon the dragon and the Egyptian when she first entered the arena[93]—she began to look around and ask when they were going to be thrown to the beasts, believing only that this had already happened when she saw the marks on her dress and body.[94] Then she exhorted all to stand fast in the faith. When the mauled martyrs were to be finished off with the sword on a platform in the arena, Saturus—as in the vision—was the first to mount the stairway and thus to die. After him, Perpetua cried out as she was struck between the bones, and then guided the hand of the young, beginner, gladiator to her throat: "Perhaps so great a woman, who was feared by an evil spirit, could only be killed if she herself wished it."[95]

I find a fundamental ambivalence in the anonymous author's description of the mother martyrs: admiration for their courageous spirituality and a hint of an idea of their being spiritual brides of Christ, but also a deep horror of their soft, vulnerable, maternal bodies. This dread of the formless is found also in other sources.[96] In this period, the ideal human being was the firm, impermeable, closed, dominating male.[97] That is why Perpetua had to become a man to be able to overcome her opponent. The redactor's description of her paying attention to her hair in the midst of being gored in the loins—an image with definite sexual connotations—may tell us more about him than about her. In her *Porneia*, Rousselle has inferred from the male-oriented prescriptive medical treatises of this period that the manner in which women's bodies were then "dominated" in marriage may have been one important reason for an increasing number of ladies to prefer virginity to marriage.[98]

Perpetua and Felicitas, however, were forced to choose. There was no middle way between the two extremes of, on the one hand, denying their inmost conviction by sacrificing to the Emperor as a proof of loyalty to the Roman state, and, on the other, denying their bonds of loyalty to their children and their family by choosing to die for their conviction. The persecuting state left no way for her to continue being a mother except by formally betraying her deepest experience of the Way, the Truth, and the Life exemplified by Christ. Without there being any hint of an ascetic life style for religious reasons—and this may be the reason that Fortunatus did not adduce them as a model for the nuns—in these circumstances, motherhood could not be integrated with the spiritual life. This was not their own choice; it was that of the representatives of the Roman state. The decision, by so many men and women in this period, for a spiritual realm of Love must have been at least in part a decision against the contemporary earthly authorities' exercise of power over men and women in a cruel, dehumanizing way. Seeing this, it is less difficult to understand how rejection of life in "the world," i.e. human society, in order to realize its opposite became a deep urge for many Christians, nor how, as a result, antithesis and inversion came to be dominant rhetorical figures in the depiction of Christian aims and practices.[99] What we also see in the *Passion of Perpetua and Felicitas* is a choice—in this case, a forced one—for the spiritualization of human bonding patterns that was to become a dominant theme in the medieval Church.

EUGENIA—VIRGIN: FROM MAN TO SPIRITUAL BRIDE AND MOTHER OF FUTURE CITIZENS OF HEAVEN

Eugenia, the extremely well-educated daughter of the Roman prefect of Egypt in the late second century, started becoming a Christian when she came across "the doctrine of the most blessed apostle Paul."[100] Outside the city, she heard Christians sing day and night, but women were forbidden to join their community. Because of this, she decided to cut her hair and disguise herself as a man. Together with her two equally educated eunuchs, whom she henceforth regarded as "brothers," she managed to get inside the "monastery" or monastic community in the bishop's house. Then, it was "the power of the songs," and the hearing of a story in which their Bishop Helenus walked unharmed into a fire to prove the truth of his religion against a magician, that made her decide to join this community permanently. Since she expected that her pagan parents would try to stop her, she did not inform them, but simply disappeared from sight. Understandably, they were shattered. Her father even had a statue made in her likeness which "began to be so venerated [by the family] that they showed no less honor to it than to their gods."

Before the three "young men" were presented to Bishop Helenus with their request for entry, the latter had a dream. In it, as he himself is made to tell the story, he was ordered to make a sacrifice before the statue of a female goddess, but, instead, said to the statue:

> "Understand that you are a creature of God, and come down [from your pedestal]—don't allow yourself to be worshiped!" Upon hearing this she came down and placed herself in my train, saying: "I will not leave you until you will have given me back to my Creator and Maker." Therefore, while he was turning these things over in his mind, Eutropius, with whom Eugenia had spoken, came into his presence [to request him to receive the three]. . . .[101]

The dream is obviously meant as an allegorical revelation of what follows. In a typically dreamlike compression, however, the goddess statue may simultaneously point to Eugenia's effigy being adored by her family (which is related in the next section), as well as her later converting them. After the three had been presented, the bishop took Eugenia's hand and prayed. Then he began to ask about their origins. Eugenia said: "We are Roman citizens: one of these, my two brothers, is called Protus, the other Hyacinthus, and my name is Eugenius." The bishop thereupon replied:

> "Rightly are you called Eugenius, for you act in a manly way, and your heart is strengthened on account of your faith in Christ (*viriliter enim agis, et confortetur cor tuum pro fide Christi*). So you are rightly called Eugenius. Therefore, know this too, that through the Holy Spirit we foresaw you, Eugenia, in the body before this, and how you would come here and what these men of yours are has not been allowed to escape me. But the Lord has deigned to reveal to me that you have prepared a most pleasing dwelling for him in your body, by preserving the treasure of your virginity and rejecting the false blandishments of the present age. Know, however, that you will suffer much on account of your chastity; but the One to whom you have wholly given yourself over shall not desert you."[102]

What we see here is the dominant image behind the idea of virginity, for men as well as for women: that of the body as a temple of the Holy Spirit (1 Cor. 3:16). Since Paul's words about the mutual exclusiveness of living according to the desires of "the flesh"—often, less abstractly, interpreted as the body[103]—and "the spirit" (Rom. 8:7–8), there had been individuals and small groups of Christians awaiting what was believed to be the imminent end of the world, like the apostle himself, in chastity.[104] Eugenia formulated this view when she later said at her trial: "My Lord Jesus Christ, whom I serve, taught chastity, and promised those preserving the integrity, i.e. inviolate condition, of the body (*integritas corporis*) eternal life."[105] As we saw, the image of the "closed" body has been interpreted as a symbol of the individual over against the group, on the one hand, and of the (minority) group as a coherent unit over against the rest of society on the other.[106]

Having spoken to the two others, the bishop with no one else present, i.e. in secret, "ordered Eugenia to remain thus in her masculine dress,"[107] and did not leave them until they had been baptized and hastened to join the monastery. We must conclude that there was, then and there, no alternative for a woman desiring to enter the Christian religious life.

After her manner of entry, Eugenia's conduct in the monastery is described. We will later recognize many of her virtues in the sixth-century descriptions of Radegund:

> The blessed Eugenia remained in the aforementioned monastery of men through her manly dress and [like] mind (*virili habitu et animo*); and she made such progress in divine erudition that before her second year was over she had memorized all the Scriptures of the Lord. So great was her peace of mind that all unanimously said that she was one of the angels.
>
> For who [could] detect her being a woman when the power of Christ and her immaculate virginity protected her so that she was wonderful even to men? For her speech was humble in love, clear in modesty, lacking in faults, and, avoiding verbosity, she overcame all in humility. No one was found to precede her in prayer. However, she was made [to be] all to everyone: she consoled the sad, delighted with the joyful, appeased the wrathful with one speech; the proud she edified so much with her example, that they were delighted to believe themselves turned from wolves into sheep. And so much grace from God followed, that when she had visited anyone who was in pain, all pain disappeared at once, and all health arrived.[108]

When, in her third year, the abbot died and all wished to elect her as abbot, she "fear[ed] that she, as a woman, would be placed over men against the rule."[109] This is the view of women in the Pauline letters; it was current in the contemporary Church as well as in contemporary society. The strategy that Eugenia found to avoid leadership may, for more purely spiritual reasons, have been Radegund's model: quoting Christ's words that the first would be the last, and whoever wished to be the leader of the faithful, should be their servant (Mk. 9:35), she was able to decline the new position. The following description of her activities—in implementation of her position—also very much resembles those found in Radegund's *Life*:

> . . . she herself, before all, took it upon herself to do the work that the lowest person used to do; in all [opportunities] she carried water, chopped wood, and cleaned. Finally, in that place she chose for herself as a living quarter there where the doorkeeper of the monastery lived, lest she should show herself to be superior to him. She fixed the brothers' meals with care, and kept the sequence of singing to God with strength: she persisted in the hours of tierce, none, vespers, nocturns and matins so that it seemed as though she would perish for God if any hour or part thereof would pass without divine praises. In this way she finally became so much more beloved by God, that she drove demons from possessed bodies and opened the eyes of the blind.[110]

Then follows a dramatic and detailed description of how an Alexandrian lady of standing, Melanthia— meaning the black and explicitly associated with her being inhabited by the Devil—became so incensed that the handsome young monk [Eugenia] did not accept her amorous advances that she accused him to the prefect. After the young monk, in chains and an iron collar, had obtained that her proof of innocence would not be used to punish Melanthia, she spoke forth to the prefect, who happened to be her father:

> "Now is the time to speak. . . . I had wished indeed to uncover the crime in the future Judgment, and only to show my chastity to the One through whose love I have been preserved. However, so that false audacity will not overcome the servants of Christ, I will reveal the truth with few words, not for pride in human speech, but for the glory of the name of Christ. For so great is the power of his name, that even women placed in reverent fear of him will obtain a manly dignity (*virilis dignitas*). And for him there is—in the faith—no superiority

in one sex or the other, when the blessed apostle Paul, the teacher of all Christians, said that with God there is no distinction between men and women, since we are all one in Christ [Gal. 3:28]. Therefore, accepting his rule with a burning soul, through the confidence that I had in Christ, I did not wish to be a woman (*nolui esse femina*), but—preserving my immaculate virginity with the whole intention of my soul—I lived, as a man, constantly in Christ (*virum gessi constanter in Christo*). For I did not take on an intemperate simulation of decency, as if I were a man pretending to be a woman; but, being a woman, I lived as a man by acting in a manly way by embracing with strength the virginity which is in Christ (*sed femina viriliter agendo, virum gessi, virginitatem quae in Christo est fortiter amplectendo*)."

And having said this, she tore down the tunic she was wearing, and appeared as a woman.[111]

What we see here is that fortitude is thought of as something that can only be "manly," even when exhibited by a woman.[112] There does not seem to be a way of being strong which is essentially feminine. Therefore Eugenia, like Perpetua, felt that she did not wish to be a woman, because this would mean that she could only lose the fight. This image of maleness, however, may also have a gnostic background. The recently discovered *Gospel of Thomas*, for instance, concludes with the following passage:

Simon Peter said to them [the disciples]: "Let Mary be excluded from among us, for she is a woman, and not worthy of Life. Jesus said: Behold I will take Mary, and make her a male, so that she may become a living spirit, resembling you males. For I tell you truly, that every female who makes herself male will enter the Kingdom of Heaven."[113]

The underlying (gnostic) idea is that maleness is spirituality, and femaleness carnality. When Eugenia says that "embracing with strength the virginity which is in Christ" is "living as a man" she is in fact not very far from this position.

After this, she said to the prefect that he was "her father according to the flesh," and told him what she had done since she left the family: with her companions, she had "rejected the world with its delights as though it were dung" and entered "the school of Christ," where the latter was such a good teacher that "through his mercy, he made me the victor over all desires for pollution (*victricem libidinum omnis pollutionis*)."[114] The mutual association of world, sex and "dirt"—that which is non-functional[115] and offensive—is clear. Christians rejected the present world because they expected to find their fundamentally opposite values realized in the next, and wished to live so as, ultimately, to deserve to enter it.

After a dramatic reunion, Eugenia's whole family was baptized. As prefect, her father gave the Christians the privilege of living in the city again, and "the whole city of Alexandria was as it were one church." As a "proof of [Eugenia's] chastity, fire was seen to come out of the sky which so enveloped Melanthia's house that no trace was left of anything that belonged to her."[116] "The Devil's advice" later caused Eugenia's father to be relieved of his office, however; he became bishop of the city instead until he achieved his desired martyrdom through being killed by assassins sent by the new prefect. Eugenia then founded a convent of virgins near the atrium of the church where he was killed and then buried—thereby creating the alternative that, presumably, had not been open to her. Her mother Claudia had an endowed hostel for pilgrims built in the vicinity. After this, the remaining family returned to Rome.

There, Eugenia collected many "mothers (*matronae*)" and even more virgins, and made them believe in Christ as well as "remain in the Lord's virginity." A virgin of royal—imperial?—blood, Basilla, sought such instruction from Eugenia through intermediaries; Eugenia sent her "brothers" Protus and Hyacinthus "in the guise of servants (*famuli*)" to her to "make her a maidservant in Christ (*in Christo . . . ancilla*)." This qualification—one that is prominent in all later descriptions of Radegund, who had been a queen—is purposely an inversion of her position in the world and, no doubt, points to the evangelical inversion of positions practiced by Eugenia herself in the male monastery. At the same time, Eugenia's words seem to be reminiscent of Mary's self-qualification in her answer to the angel: "Behold, I am the handmaid of the Lord (*ancilla Domini*)" (Lk. 1:38), which would mean that the image of the Virgin Mary is an ideal to which they now aspire. After she had persisted day and night in holy conversation and prayers, Basilla was baptized and able to see Eugenia many evenings. Probably in the family house, two groups of religious women were formed: "O how many virgins did the Saviour find through Eugenia! how many brides (*sponsae*) did Christ obtain even through Basilla! how many preserved their widowhood with resolute will through Claudia!"[117] In a community of women instead of men, the more feminine image of the bride of Christ comes to the fore.

When rumors of an impending persecution of Christians reached her, Eugenia "spread out her hands and said: 'Lord Jesus, Son of the Most High, who came for our salvation through the virginity of your Mother, lead all those whom you entrusted to me through the treasure of virginity to the Kingdom of your glory.'"[118] This is the first passage in this *Life* in which the virginity of Mary and that of the brides of Christ are explicitly connected. Eugenia thereupon spoke to her community of virgins, saying that it was time for the grape harvest in which wine for the royal meals was made by treading the grapes underfoot; they should be prepared to be the shoots, the grapes, and to give their blood as the wine for the heavenly feast. She continued:

> For virginity is the sign of the first virtue of being close to God, resembling the angels (*similis angelis*), the generator of life (*parens vitae*), the friend of sanctity, the way of safety, the mistress of joy, the leader of virtue, the furtherance and crown of faith, the aid and support of charity.[119]

The crucial point here is that she makes virginity, barrenness of the body, not only "angelic" but also a "generator of life." Both qualities will also be seen in Radegund. Of one's own eternal life only, or also of that of others? If the latter, virginity would be equivalent to motherhood as it had been in Mary.

In the story that follows, the theme of motherhood is central. When Basilla rejected a suitor, the latter complained to the emperor himself that "Eugenia's new gods which she brought with her from Egypt" are "injuring the state." They "overthrow the laws of nature" by rejecting marriage. How can the Roman state and the Roman army continue to be renewed if there is no wedlock to produce children? When Basilla refused an imperial order to accept him as her husband, saying "that she had the King of kings, who is Christ, the Son of God, as her husband," she was struck down with a sword.[120]

Next, after Protus' and Hyacinthus' prayers had made a statue of Jupiter, to which they had been ordered to sacrifice, fall at their feet—a variation on Bishop Helenus' dream—Eugenia is asked by the prefect of the city to say something about what he regarded as their "magic arts (*magici artes*)." Her words are programmatic and reveal a central Christian inversion:

> I promise you that our art is vehemently greater; for our Teacher has a Father without any mother, and a mother without a father. In short, his Father generated him in such a manner that he never in any way knew a woman; and his mother generated him in such a manner that

she did not know a man in any way. This man [our teacher] himself has a virgin as a wife, who creates children for him every day, [who] even bears him innumerable children [since] she joins her flesh with his flesh every day (*hic ipse habet uxorem virginem, quae illi quotidie filios creat, etiam innumerabiles ei filios parit, quotidie suam carnem eius carnibus coniungit*). His kisses around her are joined without pause, they wholly persist in their reciprocal love, and remain in such integrity that all virginity, and all charity, and all integrity may be discerned in their marriage (*coniugium*).[121]

This looks very much like Origen's image of the bride-mother, but with a difference. The superbly educated Eugenia may or may not have come into contact with Origen and his group before she left Alexandria; but she seems to have been well-acquainted with epithalamic imagery. Or the author of her *Life* had read a commentary on the Song of Songs along the same lines: three of these are known to have been written in the west before 350, but have been lost.[122] What Origen had said about "God's Speaking" being born in every worthy soul has here been extended, it seems, to spiritual children in human bodies.

As we saw, Ambrose regards the Church as the spiritual mother of all Christians; in the following passage, he extends this spiritual motherhood to all individuals:

The burden of the womb is not known, nor the pain of birth, and yet the offspring of the pious consciousness, that has all as its children, is more numerous; fruitful in its descendants, it is sterile in losses of children (*suboles piae mentis, quae omnes pro liberis habet; fecunda successoribus, sterilis orbatibus*); unacquainted with funerals, it knows [only] heirs. . . . A virgin, not filled by a man, but by the Spirit, gives birth to us. A virgin gives birth to us, not with the pain of her body, but with the rejoicings of angels. A virgin suckles us, not with bodily milk, but with that of the Apostle [1 Cor. 3:2]. . . . Our [virgin-mother] does not have a husband, but she has a bridegroom through the fact that either the Church among the peoples, or the soul among individual persons, becomes—through the [W]ord of God, without any rupture of her virginity—as it were the bride of the eternal Bridegroom, empty of injury, pregnant of [divine] Reason (*Nostra virum non habet, sed habet sponsum, eo quod sive ecclesia in populis sive anima in singulis dei verbo sine ullo flexu pudoris quasi sponso innubit aeterno effeta iniuriae, feta rationis*).[123]

The virgin's bringing forth children to Christ can then be through His presence—also as God's Reason or Speaking—in her as a bride, which generates spiritual children through the example of her life and through her words of exhortation and teaching. We will see Fortunatus using some of the same terms—*mens, fecunda*—to describe Radegund. Through the image of Mary as the Virgin Mother, which begins to take hold in the third and fourth centuries,[124] the ideal motherhood is now regarded as a spiritual motherhood.

In Bishop Avitus of Vienne's early sixth-century poem praising virginity, Eugenia too is celebrated. After mentioning her martyrdom, he continues: "Before that, however, the woman went forth in strong deeds, /

26. *S. Polycar:* | *S. Paula*
    pus. | *vidua.*

Figure 4.3. Holy Mother Paula (Idem)

When she was made abbot of a large group of saints, / And fulfilling [the functions of] a father, concealed beneath her disguise a mother (*patrem conplens celaret tegmine matrem*)."[125] With all its restrictions, spiritual motherhood was thus an ideal that gave new opportunities for freedom and leadership to second-class citizens of the male-dominated Roman state. After three attempts to kill Eugenia—by throwing her, weighted with a stone, in the Tiber (she floated) and in the furnaces of the baths (they were immediately extinguished), and by starving her in a dark prison (where Christ himself fed her)—she was finally cut down by a gladiator in her prison cell.[126] At her funeral, a brilliant light appeared and angels came by singing hymns: glimpses of the other, "real" reality into which she had journeyed.

PAULA—WIDOW: "SHE DID NOT [WANT TO] KNOW OF HER [HUMAN] MOTHERHOOD SO AS TO PROVE HERSELF THE MAIDSERVANT OF CHRIST"

In a long letter, including not only Paula's life story but also her itinerary around the biblical Holy Places, as well as elucidations of various doctrinal points, Jerome celebrates the Roman lady who made his own extended work in Bethlehem possible.[127] Noble through her ancestry, he says, she is even more so through her holiness. Fortunatus says almost the same of Radegund, but for the rest the parallels with Paula are primarily in the general sphere of self-punishment. As we shall see, their views of the possibilities of spiritual life were sadly different.

Jerome continues about Paula: once powerful through her riches, she is now more famous for her poverty of Christ. Married to an illustrious husband, she bore him five children, of which—at the time of writing—three daughters had already died, one prematurely: "which . . . had thrown her devoted soul as a mother (*pium matris animum*) into consternation."[128] At the death of her husband, "she mourned him so much that she herself almost died; then she converted herself to the service of the Lord in such a manner that it seemed as though she had wished his [her husband's] death."[129] She began by giving away so much to the poor that her children were almost disinherited. Then, when she had met bishops from the East who had come to Rome for church business,

> [s]he was fired by their virtues [and] began at once to think of leaving her fatherland. Forgetting her palace, her children, her household, her possessions, everything that pertained to the world, she desired passionately to go, alone (if one could say that) and unaccompanied to the desert of Anthony and Paul.[130]

After the winter was over, all her family and her children escorted her to the harbor:

> Already the sails billowed, and, guided by the oars, the ship was drawn towards the deep. On the shore, [her youngest child and only son] the small Toxotius stretched out his entreating hands [towards her]. Rufina, already of marriageable age, beseeched her to wait for her marriage by weeping silently. Nevertheless, [Paula] turned her dry eyes to heaven, overcoming her devotion to her children by faith in God (*pietatem in filios pietate in Deum superans*). She did not [want to] know of her [human] motherhood, so as to prove herself the maidservant of Christ (*Nesciebat matrem, ut Christi probaret ancillam*). Her insides were tortured, and she was as it were stretched out of her body when she fought with her grief: in this she was more admirable to all in that she overcame a great love. In the hands of enemies and the hard necessity of captivity nothing is more cruel than for parents to be separated from their children. She endured this, which is against nature, full of faith, her rejoicing soul even desired [it]. And disdaining the love of her children through her greater love for God, she acquiesced only in [the presence of her daughter] Eustochium, who was her companion in her plan and her voyage.
>
> Meanwhile the ship cleaved through the waves, and while all who sailed with her looked ardently toward the shore, she kept her eyes averted, so that she would not see those whom she could not see without suffering. I confess: no other [mother] thus loved her children, to whom she gave all before she sailed, disinheriting herself on the earth so that she would find her inheritance in heaven.[131]

All this sacrifice can only be explained by her wishing to follow Christ's words, then intended for those who would dedicate their lives to his itinerant preaching:[132] "If anyone comes to me and does not hate his own father and mother and wife and children and brothers and sisters and even his own life, he cannot be my disciple" (Lk. 14:26). Radegund, as we shall see, continued warm contacts with her adopted family. But, for Paula, there was something else as well. After a long pilgrimage to all the Holy Places, she settled in Bethlehem. Jerome turns to a description of her virtue. He stresses her humility, generosity and modesty, but also her asceticism: no baths, sleeping on small goats' hair shirts on the ground, almost continuous prayer and weeping. When he advised her to save her eyes so as to be able to read the Gospels, she said:

This face, which, against the command of God, I often painted with purple, cerussa and antimony, must be made ugly. My body, which has given itself over to many delights, must be chastised. My prolonged laughing must be compensated by perpetual weeping. The soft linens and costly silks must be exchanged for the roughness of goats' hair. I, who pleased a man and the world, now desire to please Christ.[133]

In short, this is penitence for a life lived according to the world, an attempt at purification so as to deserve heaven after all in the end. Some of Radegund's self-punishment can also be interpreted in this manner. Paula took all this so seriously that she contracted a physical disability through excessive fasting and work. Jerome insists on her patience in enduring all this.

When she heard by letter that one of her children was seriously ill, she would quote Jesus' words in the Gospel: "he who loves son or daughter more than me, is not worthy of me" (Mt. 10:37).[134] And this brings us to a crucial passage in this portrait of a mother trying not to be one. Further on, the author permits himself to say something about her weakness: "I write history and not a panegyric, and her faults are others' virtues (*illius vitia, aliorum esse virtutes*)."[135] Others' virtues indeed! Practiced in this manner, Christian asceticism—blindly following the letter and not the spirit of Jesus' saying, shattered by the feeling of guilt and pollution about the physical aspect of life, and self-destructively imitating Christ's suffering as a manner of purification (read: punishment) so as to deserve eternal life— was an inversion of human living at its most miraculous and best: motherhood and motherly love. Origen, whose father had been martyred when he was very young, appears to have realized this. His ascetic teaching had stressed the desire to become one with all of the Creation; it was an encouragement of a slow personal transformation into a wider, deeper, more real and more creative life: that of the generative quality of spiritual joy of all in all.[136]

Jerome had already hinted that Paula's grim masochism may have been a violent reaction to the loss of her husband and children: she was determined to forget about her grief by forgetting about motherhood *tout court*, by finding a new direction in her life. The following view of Jerome—expressed in a letter, full of martial imagery, to a young man—must be held at least partially responsible for the lady's choice: "The battering ram of affection [for one's family] which shakes faith must be beaten back by the wall of the Gospel."[137] It was Paula's individualism in desiring this—leading to the neglect of sacred bonds—that accounts for her own suffering as well.

She could have stayed home to be the mother her children needed, and worked on her spiritual development there. But, in addition to her unendurable grief, she may have resented her new, more limited possibilities as an ordinary widow, and have opted for a better one as a monastic leader in one of the spiritual centers of Christianity, Bethlehem.[138] In the following, Jerome shows that—understandably—she never quite managed to subdue her natural inclinations:

> The one who had such steadfastness in the contempt of food, was tender in sorrow, and shattered by the deaths of her friends, especially those of her children (for the deaths of her husband and daughters remained a trial for her); and when she would sign her lips and her stomach, trying to mitigate the grief of a mother with the impression of the Cross, her feelings were stronger, and her consciousness so full of faith was put into confusion by her motherly heart (*credulam mentem parentis viscera consternabant*); and overcoming [all] through her spirit, she was [also] conquered by the fragility of her body, [a situation] which—when, as often, an illness seized her and possessed her for a long time—brought us anxiety and her a critical situation. She rejoiced in this, [however,] constantly calling to mind [the apostolic saying]: "Miserable human being that I am, who will deliver me from the body of this death?" (Rom. 7:24)[139]

One can only feel a deep compassion for this tormented and constricted lady, tormented by her natural grief, and constricted by her misguided view of the Christian message, which made her try to excise and destroy this grief by suffering to the limit, instead of widening and transforming it into a warm, liberating, and generative spiritual motherhood of all. Brown has shown that this very conception of the new human relations possible in Christianity was gaining ground in the East in her time.[140] One feels that she must have lacked the self-esteem and have been too busy punishing herself to notice. At the Rome she had left behind too, however, there was clerical opposition to Jerome's extreme views; he was forced to leave the city. It is likely that the majority of the Roman clergy held a view that marriage was completely compatible with sanctity.[141]

Jerome then describes her monasteries, one for men and another for women, and their organization. Then, he turns to praising Paula's erudition. She knew the Bible by heart, sang the Psalms in Hebrew and spoke that language without any accent. Paula died in 404 and, as was then customary among the great, with a multitude of notables around her, including the bishops of Jerusalem and other cities, as well as many monks and nuns. Her passing away is presented—and this is the first time we hear of him in her biography—as a call by the heavenly Bridegroom:

> As soon as she heard the Bridegroom calling: "Rise, come, my love, my fair one, my turtle-dove, for behold, the winter is past, the rain is over," she joyfully replied: "The flowers appear on the earth, the time of cutting [them] has come," and: "I believe I see the good things of the Lord on the earth of the living." (Cant. 2:10–11, 12; Ps. 26:13)[142]

Only here do we finally get a glimpse of a positive image that directed her conduct, and—no doubt, connected—an affirmation of the visible Creation. The ideal of the spiritual bride-mother that Jerome almost passes over in his biography of the widow Paula, is stressed in his prescriptive letter to her virgin daughter Eustochium. And here he translates Origen's words into plain language: "You too can be the mother of the Lord (*Potes et tu esse mater Domini*)."[143] Why did he not hold this transforming image out to the grieving mother Paula? I think because physical virginity was something of a fetish for him.[144] For him, as he explicitly says, motherhood was good only in that it produced virgins.[145]

During her funeral, the multitude of the poor mourned in her the loss of the one whose funds had supported them, their "mother and nurturer (*mater et nutricia*);" Jerome never describes her in fact mothering any of these, however. He and the rest of the religious wept for her as "the reigning one (*regnans*)" or governor of the monastery; as we shall see, Baudonivia's portrait of Radegund may be somewhat indebted to this notion. He adds that she is now crowned after a long martyrdom, "for it is not only the spilling of blood that counts in the confession [of Christ], but also the immaculate service of the daily martyrdom of a devoted mind."[146] As we shall see, martyrdom in the general sense was still an ideal in Fortunatus's *Life of Radegund*. Martyrdom as service, however, or service as martyrdom, is a negative and egocentric ideal. Radegund never confused the two. Mothers, as such, give and serve because they find joy in making others happy.

Jerome's inscription near the doors of the chapel in the cave in Bethlehem—mentioned in the Protevangelium—where Paula was buried read:

> This is the home of Paula, now living in the heavenly kingdoms. Leaving behind her brother, her family, and her Roman fatherland, as well as her riches and her children, she is buried in the cave in Bethlehem.

Here [was] your manger, Christ, and here the Magi, carrying mystic gifts, gave them to the man and God.[147]

And so Christ was thought of not only as the Lord, the King and the Bridegroom, but also as the Child. Jerome says that, when reading the Bible, Paula "followed especially the spiritual understanding (*intelligentia spiritalis*) [*sic*], and through this roof protected the building of her soul."[148] Seeing her preoccupation at the moment of death with the Song of Songs, it is not unlikely that she had read Jerome's translation of Origen's homily from which our title quotation comes. Perhaps she felt then that her soul had finally been made worthy—also through her biblical erudition and teaching—to give birth, like Mary, to God's Speaking or Word.

A Tearful Mary: The Virgin's Antitype Forgiven because of Her Great Love for Christ

As we saw in Fortunatus's poem describing Radegund's models of sanctity, the conflation of Mary of Bethany, Lazarus's sister, Mary of Magdala, witness of the Resurrection, and the (tearful sinner) woman who anointed Jesus, into one woman named Mary Magdalene was evidently in the air in his time.[149] Nevertheless, her cult does not arise until after the late antique period.[150] We will see below that Radegund may have felt that her involuntary, temporary married life with the polygamous and violent King Clothar called for some kind of purification such as Mary's tears.

In the course of the centuries, the figure of Mary Magdalene, as it came down to the Middle Ages, was somehow transformed into that of a hermitess, "the perfect embodiment of Christian repentance."[151] Already in the sixth century, however, as we shall see, Radegund secluded herself completely during Lent, a mode of penitence that would also afford an opportunity to meditate upon Christ's Passion. I believe that her practice of seclusion may be connected with the legend of another repentant whore, Thais, who appears in the fourth-century monastic *Lives of the Fathers*.[152] According to modern research, her story is almost identical with that of Pelagia and is a pious invention. Because representations of Thais in medieval art take on the characteristics of Mary Magdalene,[153] it seems justified to look at her story as a possible model for Radegund's ideas and practices. She was a beautiful whore "in a certain Egyptian city," who was persuaded by Abbot Paphnutius to leave her profitable business in order to save her soul. He placed her in a convent of virgins, in a small cell with only a tiny window to receive food through, and fastened the door with a lead seal. When she asked him how she should pray, he replied:

You are not worthy to pronounce the name of God, nor to bring the name of his divinity onto your lips, nor to extend your hands toward heaven, for your lips are full of your iniquity, and your hands are polluted with filthiness. But only sit and look towards the East, and repeat this one speech frequently: "One who formed (*plasmasti*) me, have mercy upon me!"[154]

When, after three years, Abbot Paphnutius went to consult with the famous hermit Anthony and his greatest disciple, Abbot Paul as to whether Thais's sins would now have been forgiven, they decided to spend the night in prayer. During this vigil, Abbot Paul saw a vision:

> he suddenly saw, in heaven, a bed, adorned with costly garments, that was guarded by three virgins with shining faces. When Paul then said: "This can only be the [heavenly] gift for my [monastic] father Anthony," a voice said to him: "It is not your father Anthony's but the whore Thais's."
>
> When Abbot Paul had told him this openly, Abbot Paphnutius, apprehending the will of God, left, returned to the convent in which she had been shut up and loosened the door which he had fixed in place. She who had up to then been shut up in this manner asked him why he was opening the door.
>
> He said to her: "Come out, for God has forgiven you your sins."
>
> She replied: "I call God to witness that, from the time that I went into this place, I have placed all my sins as a heavy burden before my eyes, and my sins did not disappear from my eyes, but I wept while I was constantly seeing them."
>
> Abbot Paphnutius then said: "God has forgiven you not on account of your penitence, but because you always had the thought of these things in your soul."
>
> And when he had led her out of there, Thais lived for only fifteen [more] days, and thus she passed away in peace.[155]

Praying with the image of her sins constantly before her mind's eye is, of course, the real penitence; being shut up in a cell is, in itself, not enough. In Radegund's convent, one of the nuns would also decide to have herself built into the wall. She gave as her reason a vision she had just had of her becoming the bride of Christ in Paradise.[156] An influence upon her of the story of Thais's being rewarded for her seclusion with a heavenly marriage bed cannot be ruled out.

Abbot Paul's words, however, put the ideal of the spiritual marriage into its proper perspective: although it was later to become institutionalized in connection with women,[157] it then still belonged, in principle, just as much to men. For the soul, *anima*, of both men and women was regarded as feminine, and as such, as the potential bride of Christ.[158] If this is so, one would expect spiritual motherhood to become available to men as well. And in fact Fortunatus, probably pointing back to Jesus's self-reference as a hen with her chicks (Mt. 23:37), describes certain bishops as motherly birds shielding him and others under their wings.[159] The image of generation that he uses for men is a masculine one, however: that through words as seeds.[160] However, we have seen and will see again in the description of Radegund as a teacher, that this latter image applies equally to women. In the spiritual sphere, as Eugenia had said, there is no difference between men and women, and all is possible.

QUEEN RADEGUND AS INHERITOR OF LATE ANTIQUE IMAGES OF SANCTITY: MOTHER THROUGH GRACE

In the limited space here available, it is not possible to give a comprehensive treatment of the relatively copious material about Radegund, who, after being forced to become her captor's queen, finally found her vocation as a queenly nun.[161] In her period, Roman imperial power had long since retreated to the East, and what had been a state based upon cities was, in the west, slowly turning into a more primitive, agrarian society. Her new fatherland, Gaul, was ruled by quarrelsome and warlike Frankish kings. In such a society, a woman was at the mercy of the armed male, unless she could mobilize her family or her grown children.[162] Another possibility, however, was patronage of the Church, which, as in Radegund's case, meant protection by church authorities in case of need.[163] Clothar's queen was able to leave her lawful husband and found a convent in Poitiers only because she was supported by powerful churchmen. Her life shows clearly how the choice for the ascetic life could—in this exceptional case—liberate a woman from subjection to a harsh husband.

We have four sources about her: the writings of Bishop Gregory of Tours, Fortunatus's poems, his prose *Life*, and a complementary prose *Life* by Baudonivia, one of her pupils.[164] Radegund is the first Christian female saint who is consistently described in the role of spiritual mother. Looking only briefly at many other aspects in which she is presented as following male as well as female saintly models, to what extent does she emerge as a holy mother in each source?

In 567, when she had just accepted the Rule of Caesarius for her community, a gathering of bishops wrote Radegund a solemn letter confirming their continuing protection of her convent. It is included in the *Histories* written by Bishop Gregory of Tours (539–94). The wording makes clear that these churchmen thought of Radegund as a spiritual mother:

> For, although the time is getting worse through the decrepitude of the age, . . . that faith which was growing cold . . . at last becomes warm again through the ardor of your glowing heart. . . . With the brilliance of St. Martin lighting up before you, you cause the hearts of those listening to you to be so suffused by a heavenly glow, that the souls of the virgins called forth from everywhere, ablaze with the spark of divine fire, come in great haste, longing to be refreshed in Christ's love at the spring of your heart; having left their families, they prefer to be with you, whom grace, not nature, makes their mother (*quam matrem facit gratia, non natura*).[165]

It is important to notice that Radegund is addressed as the head of the community, whereas out of humility—perhaps in imitation of Eugenia—she has decided to let her spiritual daughter Agnes hold the office of abbess.

In another matter, however, she did act as a leader, and, so to say, already as "mère de la patrie;" and this, although it pleased everyone else, earned her the lasting enmity of the Bishop of the city, Maroveus. As Gregory tells us, "Queen Radegund, in merit as well as faith to be compared to [Empress] Helena" sent messengers to the East to ask the reigning Emperor and Empress for a particle of the true Cross, which Helena, the mother of Constantine, had found early in the fourth century.[166] Miffed by what seemed to be the bypassing of his superior authority in the city, Maroveus absented himself when it arrived, and its festive arrival was officiated over by the Bishop of Tours in his stead. The same was to happen twenty years later at Radegund's funeral. He may have felt that the lady did not know her place as a nun: one who had, presumably, left the world.

The wandering Italian professional poet Fortunatus, who arrived in Poitiers around this time, wrote several hymns for the arrival of the Cross. The opening line of one of them shows what was really happening: "The banners of the King go forth (*Vexilla regis prodeunt*)"[167] for, with his contact-relic, Christ the King himself had come to reside in the Convent! Thereby, it became, potentially, the center of spiritual power of Gaul. Gregory's comparison of Radegund with Empress Helena seems to show that he realized this.[168] It was Baudonivia, however, who later formulated conclusions from this fact which we do not find elsewhere.

Fortunatus's Poems

Fortunatus's poems exhibit a spiritual friendship with the royal nun. His loving veneration of her is evident in many, sometimes playful, poems: although he sometimes calls her "powerful queen (*regina potens*)," the essence of his attitude toward her is expressed in the many variations on the epithet "beloved mother (*mater amata*)."[169] In a poem written to lament her absence during her Lent retreat, however, Fortunatus addresses her in a suggestive manner as: "Consciousness fecund through God (*Mens fecunda Deo*), Radegund, life of the sisters."[170] Here, with what is perhaps part assonance, part play, on her name,[171] Fortunatus seems to be saying that Radegund is the spiritual mother of the nuns. Elsewhere he says: "Her faith conceiving by the love of Christ (*Concipiente fide Christi . . . amore*), Radegund / venerates what the Rule of Caesarius prescribes."[172]

Later in the same poem, a panegyric on virginity, probably written for the consecration of Radegund's spiritual daughter Agnes as Abbess in 567,[173] he paints the obscenity of physical coitus and the pain and possible grief of physical motherhood,[174] and develops the theme of the virgin who is the bride of Christ, repeating the phrase *concipiente fide*, but now as referring to Mary:

> Behold him who wished to be born from the womb of a virgin, / And how the highest Lord as flesh came from the flesh: / The venerable Spirit arrived at the untouched womb, / Wishing to inhabit a virginal dwelling / . . . Conceiving through faith (*Concipiente fide*), [the womb] did not deceive itself with any [human] seed, / and the man made by this was not any man. / Happy virginity, which is worthy of giving birth to God, / Which merited to bring forth (*progenerare*) its Lord! / The chaste body of the virgin is the temple of the Creator, / And he lives there as in his own marriage-bed. / . . . [God] now loves in the interior of his bride / That which he, the Sacred one, earlier loved in his mother (*Hoc ergo in sponsae nunc viscera diligit ipse / Quod prius in matrem legit honore sacer*).[175]

In all this, the spiritual birth of Christ in Radegund and the other virgins too—as Origen had put forward—is strongly suggested without actually being said. Besides Jerome's translation of Origen's treatise, Fortunatus and the nuns certainly knew the former's letter to Paula's daughter Eustochium, in which, as we saw, he had said: "You too can be a mother of God (*Potes et tu esse mater Domini)*."[176] Or they could have read the—now lost—commentary on the Song of Songs by Bishop Hilary of Poitiers (c. 315–c. 367).[177] Augustine had taught that Mary conceived first through the belief or faith of her heart, and that "they [all holy virgins] are mothers of Christ with Mary if they do the will of their Father *(ipsae cum Maria matres Christi sunt, si Patris eius faciunt voluntatem)*.[178] In Avitus's already-mentioned poem, however, both the words *fecunda* and the equivalent of *concipiens fide*, as well as the gist of Origen's statement may be found:

> She indeed was fecund, who merited to carry her Maker as a chaste burden and to bring forth her perpetual Lord; but the glory of such a deed will not have been lacking to you, if, conceiving Christ through a believing heart, you will bring forth pious seeds of works to heaven.
>
> [*Illa quidem fecunda fuit, quae pondere casto / Factorem portare suum dominumque perennem / Edere promeruit; sed nec tibi gloria tanti / Defuerit facti, si Christum credula corde / Concipiens operum parias pia germina caelo*].[179]

Fortunatus's use of the same phrase—conceiving through faith—also in the context of Christ's love, for Radegund makes clear that this generation is not restricted to virgins in the physical sense: it is also applicable to one who is and always has been a virgin in spirit. In his prose *Life*, he would later mention people saying that Radegund's husband had married a nun instead of a queen.[180] Here, then, is the notion of virginity as spiritual marriage to and motherhood of Christ, and celebrated as the essence of holy living.

Elsewhere, Fortunatus returns to the theme of Radegund's fecund consciousness being the life of the sisters and addresses her as the spiritual mother of Agnes:

> Excellent and beautiful mother, rejoice in the accomplishment of your blessed wish, / Be happy: today is the birthday of your dear daughter. / Your womb did not make this child for you, but grace did; / Not the flesh, but Christ gave her in love. / The Author brought her to you to be with you forever, / The Father gives perpetual offspring without end *(Perpetuam prolem dat sine fine pater)*. / Happy posterity that will never cease, / And which will remain undying with its mother![181]

The spiritual family, begotten—through faith—by God, is the better one. As we have seen, Eugenia had said something similar. Although she had been married for a number of years, Radegund—no doubt at least in part because, as her *Life* says, she used to spend the night hours praying in the cold chapel instead of in bed with the King[182]—had no (recorded) children. At the end of the poem for his sister Fuscina, Avitus had told her:

> . . . you will receive your reward, / Worthy through your acts, and be made into a mother of mothers (*materque effecta parentum*), / You will associate with the throng of virgins as a joyful victor (*victrix*).[183]

Although the image of the victor is reminiscent of the male athlete, Fuscina's leadership through virginal motherhood is central: she is a mother of mothers! What we see here in Fortunatus's poems is, in essence, the image of Radegund, too, as a mother of mothers.

A last poem, written at Easter, upon her return from her retreat, images the dynamic of a more diffuse kind of inner generativity that her presence brought about in the poet and probably in others:

> Even though the seeds are only just beginning to rise in the furrows, / Today, upon seeing you again, I reap them. / Already I gather the harvest, I make the bundles: / What the month of August usually does, now April does. / And even though the first vine shoots come out only as buds, / Already my autumn comes together with the grape. / The apple and the high pear trees only spread their pleasing fragrances, / But with the new flower they already bring me fruit. / Although the bare field is not adorned with any ears of grain, / Now that you have returned, all are full and shine.[184]

Fortunatus is probably too subtle to be thinking of a fertility goddess.[185] Is it going too far to see in his words, also, a—perhaps playful, because Fortunatus is almost always playful—reminiscence of royalty's onetime priestly function as guarantors of fertility?[186]

Fortunatus's Prose Biography

It has been suggested that Fortunatus's prose *Life* of Radegund was probably written shortly after her death in 587.[187] His prologue shows that the model of the male athlete has not yet completely disappeared:

> The generosity of our Redeemer is so unbounded that he celebrates powerful victories in the female sex, and renders those who, as women, are vulnerable of body, glorious through the fortitude of a

lofty spirit. Those who are born with soft bodies, Christ makes strong in faith; so that those who seem weak, being crowned through their merits, thereby gather praise for their Creator, who has stored the hidden treasures of heaven in earthen vessels: for in their bosoms, Christ the King dwells with all his riches.[188]

But the athlete is also, or especially, bride, and, implicitly, even queen. Mentioning Radegund's royal origin in Thüringen, Fortunatus adds—as we saw, possibly following Jerome about Paula: "Nevertheless, however elevated her origin may have been, she became even more so through her deeds."[189] Her capture on the battlefield as a child and her education in the royal country villa until she should be ready for marriage to King Clothar is then described. Martyrdom was already on her mind (but as persecution, and not confused with her charitable services), and, as Eugenia, "already then did the young maiden show signs of the merits of old age."[190] She gave the small children of the estate whatever food was left of her own meal and cleaned the floor of the chapel with her robe—an indirect pointer to Mary Magdalene? All of these deeds prefigure her later activities first as queen and later as nun.

She was forced into marriage: "Although she married an earthly king, she was not therefore separated from the heavenly one . . . she felt more one with Christ than joined to her husband in wedlock." As queen, she imitated St. Martin and always gave to the poor, "believing the body of Christ to be hidden under the garment of a needy person."[191] Perhaps imitating Paula, she made a hospital for poor women and a refectory for needy men, caring for them herself: "Thus the devout lady, by birth and by marriage a queen and the mistress of the palace, waited on the poor as a maidservant (ancilla)."[192] The image of the Virgin Mother Mary as maidservant seems to be the subtext here. At meals, she would secretly eat only vegetables (as the three youths in Babylon [Dan. 1:3–16]), and leave early to sing psalms in the chapel. At night, as we saw, she would find a pretext to escape the bedroom and prostrate herself in prayer on the cold ground in the chapel. During Lent, she fasted and wore a hair shirt—possibly like Paula—under her royal robes. Further, and significantly, she not only furnished all the nearby chapels with her handmade candles, but showed great veneration for all visiting churchmen, washing their feet and listening avidly to their words about the heavenly life. When a criminal was about to be executed, she would do everything to obtain his pardon; once, prisoners' chains broke spontaneously when she was singing in church. Jo Ann McNamara regards all such acts as constituting a "ritual of queenship," and says that in this way women could use "sanctity as an alternative avenue to power."[193]

When her brother, who had come with her to Gaul, was found killed, however, she decided to leave her husband (whom she suspected of complicity) for the religious life. Notwithstanding the violent resistance of a number of magnates, who said that the deed would be against the laws of the Church (as indeed it was),[194] Radegund managed to pressure a bishop into consecrating her a deaconess. After this, she traveled via a number of hermits and monasteries, to whom she gave many gifts, to pray and serve for a while at the church of Saint Martin in Tours. Then she settled for a while on a country estate at Saix, there continuing her eating habits and her feeding and elaborate and loving personal care of the poor and the sick, showing her "sweetness (*dulcedo*)" in washing and kissing even lepers—the latter again in imitation of Martin.[195] Clearly, Martin was at least as important a model for her as the women saints. Here, Fortunatus says that "she was busy as a new Martha." Did her service have some connotation of penitence, as it did for Paula? If so, what Fortunatus says about her sweetness lets us see that she experienced it not as martyrdom but as joy. This appears too in the following: after having washed and cared for the poor and served them a meal, feeding some personally with a spoon, "she would remove herself from the [dining room] to wash her hands [before her own meal], she was already wholly gratified (*gratificabatur*) by the well-served community-meal."[196] And, as with Eugenia, her life-style led to some miraculous cures being effected through her.

In the new convent in Poitiers, the Rule forbade the direct contacts with the poor and the sick. She continued with her frugal meals, fasting, keeping vigils, singing, wearing a goats' hair shirt and sleeping on ashes. Moreover, and here we recognize something of Eugenia, "nothing of the monastic duties pleased her unless she was the first to carry them out;" "(s)he did not delay even in cleansing the toilets but, busy with carrying the filthy-smelling excrement, she believed herself to be less if she did not ennoble herself through the meanness of service."[197] A description of her enthusiasm in carrying out kitchen duties follows. Then Fortunatus tells us, with horror, how the lady—planning "to be made a martyr by herself"—secretly tortured herself with tight iron chains, the branding of the sign of the Cross, and the burning of holes in her flesh (the stigmata?) with glowing coals. "The lady thus suffered so much bitterness on account of the sweetness of Christ," Fortunatus concludes; but he adds at once: "[h]ence it happened that what she had hidden, her miracles made manifest."[198] A number of miraculous cures, a resurrection and other miracles follow. The *Life* ends with a tribune's dream announcing her death. Fortunatus concludes with a pointer to the future:

But let briefness about the miracles of the blessed one suffice, lest an abundance become tiresome; and let [this report] not be thought to be too short since the amplitude of her miracles may be known through a few [of them]—[showing] with what piety, soberness, love (*dilectio*), sweetness (*dulcedo*), humility, integrity, faith and fervor (*fervor*) she lived, so that after the passing of her glorious journey, wondrous things will follow (*mirabilia prosequantur*).[199]

The word "mother" does not occur in the *Life*, but Radegund's acts from the first—washing, nursing, feeding, clothing and liberating the needy, the sick and the unfortunate, and all this with humility and, especially, with sweetness—are those of a mother.

The Prose Life by Baudonivia

The nun Baudonivia, writing in the early seventh century,[200] says in her prologue that she will only add the deeds and miracles (*miracula*) which Bishop Fortunatus omitted in his fear of prolixity. After a brief paraphrase of the earlier *Life's* picture of Radegund's life at court, she tells us that in this period the queen managed to have a pagan shrine burned down, again probably imitating Martin.[201] At Saix, moreover, she had a vision of Christ: ". . . she saw a man-shaped ship, with people sitting on every limb and she was sitting on his knee. He said to her: 'Now, you are sitting on my knee, but in time you will find a place in my bosom.'"[202] The image was probably a visualization of the traditional notion of the faithful as "the body of Christ" (Rom. 12:5). While she was there, King Clothar made an attempt to get her back. Radegund, terrified, multiplied her self-torment, vigils and prayers in an attempt to obtain her request to God to avert this: "For she scorned to rule her fatherland and she rejected the sweetness of marriage; excluding worldly love, she chose exile lest she wander from Christ."[203] Via a revelation to a venerable hermit, however, she learned that God would prevent it from happening.

Her former husband thereupon gave her permission to build a convent for herself in the city of Poitiers, where she gathered a congregation of virgins. "She felt [then] that Christ had come to dwell within her."[204] Then, however, Clothar tried once more to repossess his queen. This time the powerful Bishop Germanus of Paris interceded and permanently changed the King's mind.

The saint's "ceaseless prayers and vigils," her devotion to reading, her feeding of the poor, her abstinence, "her patience, charity, fervor of spirit, prudence, beneficence, holy zeal, and incessant meditating on the law of God by day and night" (Ps. 1:2) are praised.[205] Perhaps in imitation of Eugenia, she let nothing be done by others which she herself had not done first. But according to Baudonivia, too, she did all this not in a grim, self-tormenting manner (as Paula had done), for

> [s]he so loved her flock, which, in her deep desire for God, she had gathered in the Lord's name, that she no longer remembered that she had a family and a royal husband. So she would often say when she preached to us: "Daughters, I chose you. You are my light and my life. You are my rest and all my happiness, my new plantation. Work with me in this world that we may rejoice together in the world to come. . . ."
>
> . . . from pious concern and maternal love (*pia sollicitudine maternoque affectu*), she never ceased to preach on what the readings offered for the salvation of the soul. . . . Who could ever imitate the ardent charity (*caritatis . . . ardor*) with which she loved (*dilexit*) all mankind?[206]

She is mother and teacher here, begetting daughters by her words, but essentially through the limitless outpouring of her loving heart. This dynamic spiritual pattern seems to be reflected in the following miracle story as a metaphor. When her wine barrel never became empty, Baudonivia, pointing to the Lord's feeding five thousand with five loaves and two fishes (Jn 6:1–14), says that, likewise, "his maidservant (*sua ancilla*) [Radegund] refreshed the needy wherever she saw them from this little cask for the whole year."[207] This, I suggest, is a metaphor of the current God-experience as ceaseless flow or self-transcending generativity that we have already encountered in Gregory of Tours's description of the overflowing lamp as epiphany of the power of the Holy Cross.[208]

Then, Baudonivia introduces an element that does not occur in earlier *Lives* of saintly women—the royal nun as peacemaker[209] and spiritual queen:

> She was always solicitous for peace and worked diligently for the welfare of the fatherland (*patria*). Whenever the different kingdoms made war on one another, she prayed for the lives of all the kings, for she loved them all. And she taught us also to pray incessantly for their stability. Whenever she heard of bitterness arising among them, trembling, she sent such letters to one and then to the other pleading that they should not make war among themselves nor

take up arms lest the fatherland perish. And, likewise, she sent to their noble followers to give the high kings salutary counsel so that their power might work to the welfare of the people and the fatherland.

She imposed assiduous vigils on her flock, tearfully teaching them to pray incessantly for the kings. And who can tell what agonies she inflicted on herself? So, through her intercession, there was peace among the kings. Mitigation of war brought welfare to the fatherland.

Despite having secured the triumph of the kings' peace from the King of Heaven, she devoted herself all the more eagerly to God and gave herself up to the service of all men, not caring what slavish task that might involve. For she was eager to fill the needs of everyone. She washed the feet of all with her own hands, cleansing them with her veil and kissing them. If it had been permitted, like Mary, she would have wiped them clean with her own loosened hair.

In return for this multitude of great good deeds which Divine Grace empowered her to perform, the Lord, the bountiful giver of virtue, rendered her famous for her miracles throughout all Francia. There, where she had been seen to reign, he prepared a kingdom for her more celestial than terrestrial (*magis caeleste quam terrenum . . . regnum*).[210]

Here, the reference to a tearful Mary's service seems to indicate that Radegund did see her service, at least in part, as a kind of penitence, perhaps for her sexual life in marriage. As for her spiritual queenship, Baudonivia elsewhere also refers to Radegund as "a good governess (*gubernatrix bona*)" and it is possible that the memory of Jerome's qualification of Paula as *regnans* helped the lady nun to image her beloved saint in this manner.[211] Certainly, Radegund's feeling no qualms about bending the Church's rules to do what she felt needed to be done exhibited the attitude of one accustomed to rule. After two miracles and a visionary dream, Baudonivia tells us that Radegund collected relics of saints. And then she proceeds to fill Fortunatus's greatest lacuna: the story of Radegund's procuring of a particle of the Cross so that Christ might "visibly live here (*visibiliter hic habitare*)." She is again compared to Helena, now qualified as "holy (*beata*)." First, however, she had asked her stepson King Sigebert for permission to do this "for the welfare of the whole fatherland and the stability of his kingdom. Most graciously, he consented to the petition of the holy queen (*sancta regina*)." After it had been installed in the monastery by the Bishop of Tours, it worked many miracles. Some of her own miracles follow.[212]

Then another vision, this time with bridal imagery, and which appears to fulfill the promise made in the first one at Saix, is related:

> Before the year of her transition, she saw the place prepared for her in a vision. A very rich youth came to her. He was most beautiful and had, as the young do, a tender touch and a charming way with words as he spoke to her. But she jealously protected herself and repelled his blandishments.
>
> So he said to her: "Why then have you sought me, with burning desire, with so many tears? Why do you plead, groaning, and call out with copious prayer, afflicting such agony upon yourself for my sake who am always by your side? Oh, my precious gem, you must know that you are the first jewel in the crown on my head."
>
> Who can doubt that this visitor was He who had her whole devotion while she lived in the flesh and that He was showing her what she was to enjoy in her glory?[213]

Remembering "her love (*amor*), nurturing (*nutrimenti*), charity (*caritas*) [and] preaching (*praedicatio*)," Baudonivia says, causes grief. The first three qualities appear to be specifically motherly ones: they are culled, however—as much more of the material in Baudonivia's biography[214]—from the *Life* of the extremely energetic early sixth-century Bishop Caesarius of Arles.[215] But there is more. The term "sweetness (*dulcedo*)" is used to describe the male saint too, and the latter is there said to have loved his people not only with fatherly, but also with motherly love: "*ille tamen eos non solum paterno, sed etiam materno, diligebat affectu.*" In late Antiquity, at least from the time of the Apostle Paul (1 Thess. 1:7), tender care was not considered to be a monopoly of women.[216]

The sentence "Thus her holy little body came to the end of its life, that long drawn-out martyrdom for the love of God"[217] shows that the idea of martyrdom—much less than in Fortunatus's *Life*, however—was not yet forgotten. The saintly queen was buried in the church of the holy Mary, the burial church for the convent. Why the dedication to Mary? It must be because, as we have seen in Fortunatus's poem *On Virginity*, Mary is the leader of the choir of virgins in heaven.[218] The description of Radegund's death and funeral includes an audition of angels' voices; Baudonivia closes with a few posthumous miracles.

GENERAL CONCLUSION: "CONSCIOUSNESS FECUND THROUGH GOD"

The portraits of women saints that were investigated show a shift of emphasis from the model of the male fighter to that of the spiritual bride-mother: the new image of Mary as Virgin Mother developed in second-century apocryphal literature, became the "ideogram for their souls." The former role model had inspired energy and endurance when women martyrs were attacked by wild animals in the arena. Outside the arena too, there was no model of feminine fortitude except that of becoming a man, in consciousness and/or in appearance. This attitude is still noticeable in the sixth century.

Mary's emerging from obscurity into the limelight as the Virgin Mother of God is most intimately connected with the ascendance of an otherworldly attitude, involving an alienation toward the body's natural functions. I have argued that it is the (also very conspicuous) emphasis upon the Virgin Mother as the maidservant of the Lord, and not that upon her virginity, which reflects patriarchal thinking. Male dominance was an accepted tradition in late antique society, and eventually came to prevail in the Church as well. The emphasis on the spiritual as the only "real" reality, and the resulting disparagement of biological motherhood, is not connected with this. The latter almost certainly has to do with disillusion with the prevailing human society and the reaching out to a new, better one in the spiritual sphere.

I have also argued that the new role model of spiritual motherhood through ascetism (if not virginity) and faith, available to men as well as to women, is a crucial contrapposto to that of the suffering Christ on the Cross: instead of eternal life through suffering, the same through generation. In the *Lives* of Eugenia and Radegund, the acting out of the role of spiritual mother becomes leadership and joy in giving. Paula believed that she should first seek purification for her married sexuality through penitential service. She tried to suppress her human motherhood without transforming it into a more inclusive spiritual one (as far as we can judge from Jerome's description), and seems to have suffered more than anything else. The tearful Thais, in no way connected with motherhood, purified herself of the stain of her sexual experience through penitential seclusion in the hope that she too, in the end, might become the joyful bride of Christ.

The late antique obsession of some influential circles with the body and sexual relations as obstacles to union with the divine must be responsible for the fact that the virtues of human marriage and biological motherhood are not conspicuously celebrated as models for a saintly life. The essence of saintliness, by definition, then tended to be seen as a living outside of ordinary life and ordinary human relations, as the pagan philosopher had done. The ideal was contemplation in the spirit, not action in this world. Another reason may be that the relative absence of adequate obstetrical knowledge and care made biological motherhood painful, dangerous and not seldom fatal. It is quite clear that women could then experience monastic life and spiritual motherhood as liberating.

It is time we stopped using biological functions to construct anachronistic gender-images or roles for women in other periods, and began recognizing the positive content of the experience of powerful personalities, male and female, in the late antique period: that "there is neither male nor female in Christ" and that "all is possible to those who believe." Eugenia and Abbot Paul, too, knew this. Biological motherhood was the metaphor used for an experience that has nothing to do with human gender: a "consciousness fecund through God." It was the contemporary image of God—self-transcending fecundity—as an ideogram for one's soul. Through Fortunatus's celebration of his revered friend Radegund, it was an ideal that was transmitted to the Middle Ages.

Which model-image the nuns experienced as central in their "mother" and leader of virgins (mothers) on earth may be glimpsed in Baudonivia's rendering of Bishop Gregory's reaction upon first seeing the dead Radegund:

> When he came to the place where the holy body lay—as he himself was later wont to tell, with an oath and weeping—he had seen, in the appearance of a human being, the face of an angel, shining as a rose and a lily; and he was so awe-struck and reduced to trembling, that the devout man, wholly in God, stood there as though he were in the presence of the holy Mother of the Lord (*beata genetrix Domini*).[219]

NOTES

1. Clarissa W. Atkinson, "'Your Servant, My Mother': The Figure of Saint Monica in the Ideology of Christian Motherhood," in her *Immaculate and Powerful: The Female in Sacred Image and Social Reality* (Boston: Beacon Press, 1985), 139–72, here 139 and 144.

2. Eusebius Hieronymus, *Origenis in Canticum Canticorum Homilia*, 2.6, in Migne, *Patrologia Latina*, vol. 23, 1190f: "Nativitas Christi ab umbra sumpsit exordium: non solum in Maria ab umbra eius nativitas coepit, sed et in te si dignus fueris nascitur sermo Dei." The date of the translation may be 383, ten years before Jerome, when the mood in the church changed, was to turn from an enthusiastic admirer of the great Alexandrian into his bitter detractor (conjecture of Ferdinand Cavallera, *Saint Jérôme, sa vie et son oeuvre* (Paris-Louvain: Champion, 1922), vol. 1/2, 26, referred to in *Origène, commentaire sur le Cantique des Cantiques*, 1, ed. and trans. Luc Brésard et al. (Paris: Cerf, 1991), 11, n. 3). Cf. Elizabeth A. Clark, "The Uses of the Song of Songs: Origen and the Latin Fathers," in her *Ascetic Piety and Women's Faith: Essays on Late Ancient Christianity* (Studies in Women and Religion, 20) (Lewiston: Mellen, 1986), 386–427. Ambrose of Milan uses the same passage as nuptial imagery for female virgins as brides of Christ, but does not connect it with his discussion of the spiritual motherhood of all, see Ambrosius Mediolanensis, *De Virginibus Libri Tres*, 1.46, ed. Egnatius Cazzaniga (Corpus Scriptorum Latinorum Paravianum) (Torino: Paravia, without date), 23f., trans. H. de Romestin in *The Select Library of Nicene and Post-Nicene Fathers of the Christian Church* (2d ser., 10)

(1890–1900, rpt Grand Rapids: Eerdmans, 1979), 361–87. Cf. Hervé Savon, "Un modèle de sainteté à la fin du ive siècle: la virginité dans l'oeuvre de saint Ambroise," in *Sainteté et martyre dans les religions du Livre,* ed. P. Marx (Problèmes d'Histoire du Christianisme) (Brussels: Editions de l'Université de Bruxelles, 1989), 25.

3. Venantius Fortunatus, *Carmina,* 8.9.1 in *Monumenta Germaniae Historica. Auctores Antiquissimi (MGH AA),* vol. 4/1, 195. The Latin text from another manuscript, plus a translation, is found in M. Charles Nisard, ed. and trans., *Venance Fortunat: Poésies melées* (Collection des Auteurs Latins avec la Traduction en Francais) (Paris: Librairie de Firmin-Didot, 1887).

4. John Bugge, *Virginitas: An Essay in the History of a Medieval Ideal* (International Archives of the History of Ideas, Series Minor, 17) (The Hague: Nijhoff, 1975), 59–64, here 64, states that this ideal "seems to have passed out of the picture after the less than whole-hearted treatment of it by Ambrose." I will show that this is not the case.

5. Hilda Graef, *Mary: A History of Doctrine and Devotion* (Westminster: Christian Classics, 1985), 46, states (without further source reference) that this phrase "occurs in two Greek fragments on Luke (numbers 41 and 80 in the Berlin edition), though his authorship is not absolutely certain." The edition referred to (not available to me) is, *Origenes Werke,* ed. Max Rauer (Griechische Christliche Schriftsteller, 9) (2d ed. Berlin: Akademie-Verlag, 1959). In Origène, *Homélies sur Luc,* ed. and trans. Francois Fournier et al. (Sources Chrétiennes, 87) (Paris: Cerf, 1962) the content of the passages with these numbers (493 and 537) does not accord with her statement.

6. 1 Thess. 2:13. I have used Jerome's so-called Vulgate translation of the Bible throughout and made my own translations. On the biblical view of the presence of God's word in that of man, see Bertold Klappert, "Word," *New International Dictionary of New Testament Theology,* vol. 3 (Grand Rapids: Zondervan, 1971), 1112f.

7. Origenes, *In Numeros Homilia,* 20.2, in Migne, *Patrologia Graeca,* vol. 12, 728: "Est ergo sponsus et vir animae mundae et pudicae, Verbum Dei, qui est Christus Dominus. . . . Donec igitur anima adhaeret sponso suo, et audit verbum eius, et ipsum complectitur, sine dubio ab ipso semen suscipit verbi: et sicut ille dixit, De timore tuo, Domine, in utero concepi, ita et haec dicit, De verbo tuo, Domine, in ventre concepi, et parturivi, et spiritum salutis tuae feci super terras. Si ergo sic de Christo concepit anima, fecit filios . . . . Est itaque vere beata soboles, ubi concubitus factus fuerit animae cum Verbo Dei, et ubi complexus ad invicem dederint. Inde nascetur generosa progenies. . . ."; French translation: *Origène, Homilies sur les Nombres,* ed. and trans. André Méhat (Sources Chrétiennes, 29) (Paris: Cerf, 1951), 395f. I have not been able to identify the first reference. The Vulgate translation of Isaiah 26:17–18 (the reference suggested by the editor) has the following: "Sicut quae concipit cum adpropinquaverit ad partum dolens clamat in doloribus suis, sic facti sumus a facie tua Domine. Concepimus et quasi parturivimus et peperimus spiritum."

8. Some hold the origin of this epithalamic imagery for union with the divine to be gnostic. Rejecting the contamination of spirit with matter as in physical conception and birth, gnosticizing Christians would nevertheless have used the latter as a central metaphor of spiritual life. See on gnostic epithalamic imagery of begetting new life: Bugge, *Virginitas,* 63.

9. Robin L. Fox, *Pagans and Christians in the Mediterranean World from the Second Century AD to the Conversion of Constantine* (Harmondsworth: Penguin, 1988), 524.

10. Peter Brown, *The Body and Society: Men, Women and Sexual Renunciation in Early Christianity* (New York: Columbia University Press, 1988), 172f.

11. Bugge, *Virginitas,* 32; Brown, *The Body and Society,* 162–177, 379.

12. Mt. 19:12; cf. Brown, *The Body and Society,* 168.

13. Cf. Julia Kristeva, "Stabat Mater," in *The Kristeva Reader,* ed. Toril Moi (Oxford: Blackwell, 1986), 169.

14. Graef, *Mary,* 50f., 55; Thomas J. Heffernan, *Sacred Biography: Saints and*

Their Biographers in the Middle Ages (Oxford: Oxford University Press, 1988), 190.

15. Graef, *Mary*, 356–361 and 154–157 gives a general bibliography. Marina Warner, *Alone of All Her Sex: The Myth and the Cult of the Virgin Mary* (London: Weidenfeld and Nicolson, 1976) offers a more feminist approach, and a bibliography. On Mary as a contemporary symbol see Ivone Gebara and Maria C. Lucchetti Bingemer, *Maria, Mutter Gottes und Mutter der Armen* (Bibliothek Theologie der Befreiung) (Düsseldorf: Patmos, 1988).

16. Clarissa W. Atkinson, *The Oldest Vocation: Christian Motherhood in the Middle Ages* (Ithaca: Cornell University Press, 1991), mentions Jerome's statement that, like Mary, virgins could conceive Christ, and says that "the ideology of spiritual motherhood [was] firmly established in monastic communities and spheres of influence by the late fourth century" (111); and that the notion of spiritual motherhood provided the only position of leadership for women in late Antiquity (99f.); but does not specifically mention or show this idea as recurring in *Lives* of holy women until eighth-century England (95).

17. Peter Brown, "The saint as exemplar in Late Antiquity," in *Saints and Virtues*, ed. J. Stratton Hawley (Berkeley: University of California Press, 1987), 13.

18. Cf. Bugge, *Virginitas*, 19f., 47f. Alison Goddard Elliott, in her *Roads to Paradise: Reading the Lives of the Early Saints* (Hanover: University Press of New England, 1987), 16–76, distinguishes between the "epic" style of the martyr's passion and the "romance" style of the ascetic saint's life.

19. Peter Brown, "Late Antiquity," in *A History of Private Life*, vol. 1: *From Pagan Rome to Byzantium*, ed. Paul Veyne, trans. Arthur Goldhammer (Cambridge, Mass.: Belknap, 1987), 300.

20. Bugge, *Virginitas*, 16, 37.

21. As in Gail P. Corrington, "The Milk of Salvation: Redemption by the Mother in Late Antiquity and Early Christianity," *Harvard Theological Review*, 82 (1989), 413.

22. Klaus Thraede, "Zwischen Eva und Maria: das Bild der Frau bei Ambrosius und Augustin auf dem Hintergrund der Zeit," in *Frauen in Spätantike und Frühmittelalter: Lebensbedingungen—Lebensnormen—Lebensformen*, ed. Werner Affeldt (Sigmaringen: Thorbecke, 1990), 133.

23. Atkinson, *The Oldest Vocation*, 9–12. On Roman motherhood: Suzanne Dixon, *The Roman Mother* (London: Croom Helm, 1988). See also: Sarah B. Pomeroy, *Goddesses, Whores, Wives and Slaves: Women in Classical Antiquity* (New York: Schocken, 1975); Teresa Carp, "Two Matrons of the Late Republic," in *Reflections of Women in Antiquity*, ed. Helene P. Foley (New York: Gordon and Breach, 1981), 343–54; Judith P. Hallett, *Fathers and Daughters in Roman Society: Women and the Elite Family* (Princeton: Princeton University Press, 1984). Further: Graham Gould, "Women in the Writings of the Fathers: Language, Belief and Reality," in *Women in the Church*, ed. W.J. Sheils and Diana Wood (Studies in Church History, 27) (Oxford: Blackwell, 1990), 1–13; on all aspects: Gillian Clark, *Women in Late Antiquity: Pagan and Christian Life-styles* (Oxford: Clarendon Press, 1993). Cf. Atkinson, *Immaculate and Powerful*.

24. Elizabeth S. Fiorenza, "Word, Spirit and Power: Women in Early Christian Communities," in *Women of Spirit: Female Leadership in the Jewish and Christian Traditions*, ed. Rosemary Ruether and Eleanor McLaughlin (New York: Simon and Schuster, 1979), 30–44. Likewise: Atkinson, *The Oldest Vocation*, 14, 18, 66.

25. Corrington, "Milk of Salvation," 412f.

26. Fiorenza, "Word, spirit, and Power," 44–51, shows that gnosticizing Christians "employed the categories of 'male' and 'female', not to designate real women and men, but to name cosmic-religious principles or archetypes" (50). Elaine Pagels, *The Gnostic Gospels* (New York: Random House, 1979), 48–69, shows that the Gnostic Trinity was regarded as having both male and female characteristics.

27. Brown, "Late Antiquity," 171.

28. On woman in the Bible, see: H. Vörlander et al., "Woman, Mother, Virgin Widow" in *New International Dictionary of New testament Theology*, vol. 3, 1055–1078. In late Antiquity: Elena Giannarelli, *La tipologia femminile nella biografia e nell'autobiografia cristiana del IVo secolo* (Studi Storici, 127) (Roma: Istituto Storico Italiano per il Medio Evo, 1980); Joyce Salisbury, *Church Fathers, Independent Virgins* (London: Verso, 1991), who gives the views and stories of women who did not choose to follow the Fathers' directions for female living, and a useful bibliography of the subject, including English translations of the relevant sources; and Clark, *Women in Late Antiquity*, with a large, up-to-date bibliography. In late Antiquity and early Middle Ages: Marie-Louise Portmann, *Die Darstellung der Frau in der Geschichtschreibung des Früheren Mittelalters* (Basel: Helbing and Lichtenhahn, 1958), 7–59.

29. Brian Brennan, "St Radegund and the Early Development of Her Cult at Poitiers," *Journal of Religious History*, 13 (1985), 340.

30. Fortunatus, *Carmina*, 8.1.41–46, ed. *MGH AA* 4/1, 189. The virgin Eustochium was the daughter and companion of the widow Paula, about whom more will be said below. The widows Fabiola and Marcella were ascetic correspondents of Jerome. Their lives are described in Eusebius Hieronymus, *Epistola* 77 and 127; together with *Epistola* 22 to Eustochium these are edited and translated in: *Select Letters of St Jerome*, ed. and trans. F.A. Wright (Loeb Classical Library, 262) (London: Heinemann, 1975), 308–337, 438–466, and 52–158 resp. The life of the widow Melania, a spiritual friend of Rufinus, is described in Palladius, *De vitis patrum sive Historia Lausiaca*, 8.117, in Migne, *Patrologia Latina*, vol. 73, 1198f. The young widow Blesilla was also Paula's daughter and died (of excessive fasting?) at twenty years of age (Hieronymus, *Epistola*, 39, in *Saint Jérôme, Lettres*, ed. and trans. Jérome Labourt (Collection des Universités de France) (Paris: Les Belles lettres, 1951), vol. 2, 71–85). See on Jerome and these women: Brown, *The Body and Society*, 366–386. Martha is she who served Christ (Lk. 10:38–42); the tearful Mary, and the virgin and martyr Eugenia will be investigated below, and the virgin Thecla was a literary creation in an apocryphal Gospel: she fled from her fiancé, survived martyrdom and thereafter lived as a hermitess (*Vita Theclae*, ed. G. Dagron, *Vie et Miracles de Sainte Thècle* (Subsidia Hagiographica, 62) (Brussels: Société des Bollandistes, 1978). See on her, Brown, *The Body and Society*, 156–159.

31. Fortunatus, *Carmina*, 8.3.99f and 25f resp., ed. *MGH AA* 4/1, 183, 182 resp.: "Dei genetrix pia virgo Maria."

32. Heffernan, *Sacred Biography*, 193.

33. Warner, *Alone of All Her Sex*, 224–235. The standard work about Mary Magdalene is: Victor Saxer, *Le culte de Marie Madeleine des origines à la fin du Moyen Âge* (Cahiers d'Archéologie et d'Histoire, 3) (Auxerre-Paris: Clavreuil, 1959). See also Carolyn M. and Joseph A. Grassi, *Mary Magdalene and the Women in Jesus' Life* (Kansas City: Sheed and Ward, 1986) and Susan Haskins, *Mary Magdalen: Myth and Metaphor* (New York: HarperCollins, 1993).

34. Atkinson, *The Oldest Vocation*, 106.

35. Cf. Warner, *Alone of All Her Sex*, 344f.

36. Graef, *Mary*, 57, 59.

37. Ibid., 4.

38. Ibid., 18.

39. Mary Douglas, *Purity and Danger: An Analysis of the Concepts of Pollution and Taboo* (1966, rpt London: Ark, 1984), 158.

40. As, for instance, Jacques Le Goff, "Culture ecclésiastique et culture folklorique au Moyen Age: saint Marcel et le dragon," in his *Pour un Autre Moyen Age: Temps, travail et culture en Occident: 18 essais* (Paris: Gallimard, 1977), 243.

41. Sallie McFague, *Metaphorical Theology: Models of God in Religious Language* (London: SCM Press, 1983), 145–164, discusses the radical feminist view that this image is the "root-metaphor" of Christianity.

42. Irenaeus, *Adversus Haereses*, 5.19.1. Editions: Book 2, ed. A.R. and L.

Doutreleau; Book 3, ed. F. Sagnard; Books 4 and 5, ed. Adelin Rousseau et al. (Sources Chrétiennes, 294, 34, 100, 153 resp.) (Paris: Cerf, 1982, 1952, 1965, 1969 resp.).

43. Bugge, *Virginitas*, 67.

44. Eusebius Hieronymus, *De Perpetua Virginitate Beatae Mariae adversus Helvidium*, 20, in Migne, *Patrologia Latina*, vol. 23, 214.

45. Brown, *The Body and Society*, 359ff., 377. Cf. David G. Hunter, "'On the Sin of Adam and Eve': a Little-known Defense of Marriage and Child-bearing," *Harvard Theological Review*, 82 (1989), 283–299.

46. Graef, *Mary*, 19–24, discusses various renderings of the Greek which do not accord with this one in the Vulgate.

47. Graef, *Mary*, 20; cf. Howard C. Kee, *Miracle in the Early Christian World: A Study in Sociohistorical Method* (New Haven: Yale University Press, 1983), 230f.

48. Berthold Altaner, *Patrologie: Leben, Schriften und Lehre der Kirchenväter* (5th ed. Freiburg: Herder, 1958), 56f. *Protoevangelium Jacobi (Graece)*, in *Evangelia Apocrypha*, ed. Konstans von Tischendorf (Hildesheim: Olms, 1966), 1–50, trans. Alexander Roberts and James Donaldson, *Apocryphal Gospels, Acts and Revelations* (Ante-Nicene Christian Library, 16) (Edinburgh: Clark, 1870), 1–15.

49. Graef, *Mary*, 35ff.

50. Hieronymus, *De Perpetua Virginitate*, 8, ed. *PL* 23, 201.

51. Atkinson, *The Oldest Vocation*, 66.

52. My own rendering of the Greek *aischêsynê*, instead of Musurillo's "disgrace."

53. Charles W. Neumann, *The Virgin Mary in the Works of Saint Ambrose* (Paradosis, 17) (Fribourg: Presse Universitaire, 1962) 254f.

54. The term is that of Sallie McFague, *Speaking in Parables: A Study in Metaphor and Theology* (Philadelphia: Fortress, 1975), 120.

55. Ignatius, *Epistola ad Ephesios*, 19, in Migne, *Patrologia Graeca*, vol. 5, 659 (Latin translation of Greek text).

56. Joseph A. Grassi, *Mary, Mother and Disciple: From the Scriptures to the Council of Ephesus* (Wilmington: Glazier, 1988), 67ff., 131. On male and female images of the divine see Rosemary R. Ruether, *Sexism and God-Talk: Toward a Feminist Theology* (Boston: Beacon Press, 1983), 47–71.

57. "Self-Transcending Fecundity": Arthur O. Lovejoy, *The Great Chain of Being: A Study in the History of an Idea* (1936, rpt New York: Harper Torch, 1960), 49. The spring of eternal life: Jn 4:14; Christ as the Spring: Eucherius, *Formularum Spiritualis Intelligentiae ad Uranium Liber Unus*, 4, in Migne, *Patrologia Latina*, vol. 50, 747.

58. As presented by Elaine Pagels in "What Became of God the Mother? Conflicting Images of God in Early Christianity," *Signs*, 2 (1976), 293–303.

59. Clemens Alexandrinus, *Paidagogos*, 1.6.42.3, 43.3–4, 46.1; Greek text and French translation: *Clement d'Alexandrie, Le Pedagogue*, ed. and trans. Henri-Irénée Marrou and Marguerite Harl (Sources Chrétiennes, 70) (Paris: Cerf, 1960), 186–189, 192–195. Somewhat reduced English translation and reference in Pagels, "What became of God the Mother?" 302 (n. 43).

60. Irenaeus, *Adversus Haereses*, 4.38.1, in *Irénée de Lyon, Contre les hérésies, Livre IV*, ed. and trans. Adelin Rousseau (Sources Chrétiennes, 100) (Paris: Cerf, 1965), 946: "quasi a mammilla carnis eius."

61. Irenaeus cited in Corrington, "Milk of Salvation," 412, and Augustine, *In Johannis Evangelium Tractatus*, 15.7 and 21.1, cited in Caroline Walker Bynum, "Jesus as Mother and Abbot as Mother: Some Themes in Twelfth-Century Cistercian Writing," in her *Jesus as Mother: Studies in the Spirituality of the High Middle Ages* (Berkeley: University of California Press, 1982), 126, n. 54.

62. Ambrosius, *De Virginibus*, 1.5.22, ed. Cazzaniga, 11f.

63. Gregorius Turonensis, *In Gloria Martyrum*, 5, in *Monumenta Germaniae Historica. Scriptores Rerum Merovingicarum (MGH SRM)*, vol. 1/2, 484–561, trans. Raymond van Dam, *Glory of the Martyrs* (Liverpool: Liverpool University Press,

1988). An investigation into this incident in Giselle de Nie, "A broken lamp or the effluence of holy power? Common sense and belief-reality in Gregory of Tours' own experience," *Mediaevistik*, 3 (1990), 269–279.

64. Atkinson, *The Oldest Vocation*, 16f, referring (n. 24) to *Acts of Thomas*, 1.12, in *New Testament Apocrypha*, vol. 1, ed. Wilhelm Schneemelcher (Philadelphia: Westminster Press, 1983), 449.

65. Graef, *Mary*, 94ff.

66. Alcimus Ecdicius Avitus, *Poematum*, 6.201–224, in *Monumenta Germaniae Historica. Auctores Antiquissimi (MGH AA)*, vol. 6/2, 281.

67. Suzanne Wemple, *Women in Frankish Society* (Philadelphia: University of Pennsylvania Press, 1981), 149f.

68. Grassi, *Mary, Mother and Disciple*, 119; Graef, *Mary*, 97; Atkinson, *The Oldest Vocation*, 110.

69. My own translation of: Augustine, *Sermo* (Denis), 15.8, ed. Germanus Morin, *Sancti Augustini Sermones post Maurinos Reperti* (Roma: Tipografia Polyglotta Vaticana, 1930), 163f.: ". . . et vos membra Christi estis, et vos corpus Christi estis. . . . Ergo in mente pariant membra Christi, sicut Maria in ventre virgo peperit Christum; et sic eritis matres Christi." Translated in Graef, *Mary*, 97 (n. 3).

70. Peter Brown, *The Cult of the Saints: Its Rise and Function in Latin Christianity* (Chicago: University of Chicago Press, 1981), 113, 118.

71. Graef, *Mary*, 14; Atkinson, *The Oldest Vocation*, 113.

72. Hieronymus, *Epistola*, 22.21., in *Saint Jerôme*, ed. Labourt, vol. 1, 132.

73. Heffernan, *Sacred Biography*, 190.

74. [Anonymous], *Passio Sanctarum Perpetuae et Felicitatis—The Martyrdom of Saints Perpetua and Felicitas*, 18.2 (BHL 6633–6636), ed. and trans. Herbert Musurillo, *The Acts of the Christian Martyrs* (Oxford Early Christian Texts) (Oxford: Clarendon Press, 1972), 106–131, here 126. A more recent edition and translation, with bibliography, which was not available to me is that of James W. Halporn, intr., *Passio Sanctarum Perpetuae et Felicitatis* (Bryn Mawr, 1984). I have chosen to make my own translation.

75. On this see Peter Dronke, *Women Writers of the Middle Ages: A Critical Study of Texts from Perpetua (d. 203) to Marguerite Porete (d. 1310)* (Cambridge: Cambridge University Press, 1984), 1–17; and Heffernan, *Sacred Biography*, 199f.

76. Heffernan, *Sacred Biography*, 194ff.

77. *Passio Perpetuae*, 4.3–9, ed. Murillo, 110ff.

78. Ibid., 5.5., ed. Murillo, 112.

79. Ibid., 3.6 and 3.9, ed. Murillo, 108, 110.

80. Ibid., 6.2–8, ed. Murillo, 112–114.

81. Ibid., 8.2–4, ed. Murillo, 116.

82. Heffernan, *Sacred Biography*, 216.

83. Corrington, "Milk of Salvation," 396, says that her "maleness" and that achieved by virginity—according to gnosticizing apocryphal gospels—tended to be seen as a prerequisite for salvation. A contrary view is that of Rosemary Rader, *Breaking Boundaries: Male/Female Friendship in Early Christian Communities* (Theological Inquiries) (New York: Paulist Press, 1983), 47, who sees the incident as "reflect[ing] conditions conducive to the establishment of egalitarian attitudes and practices."

84. *Passio Perpetuae*, 10.6–14, ed. Murillo, 118.

85. Ibid., 15.5–7, ed. Murillo, 122ff.

86. Ibid., 18.2–3, ed.Murillo, 126.

87. Ibid., 20.1–7, ed. Murillo, 128.

88. Kee, Mira*c*le, 276.

89. J.M. Mathieu, "Horreur du cadavre et philosophie dans le monde romain: Le cas de la patristique grecque du IVe siècle," in *La Mort, les Morts et l'Au-Delà dans le Monde Romain: Actes du Colloque de Caen 20–22 Novembre 1985*, ed. F. Huiard (Caen, 1987), 311–320. This persists into the sixth century: Giselle de Nie, "Le corps,

la fluidité et l'identité personelle dans la vision du monde de Grégoire de Tours," in *Aevum Inter Utrumque: Mélanges offerts à Gabriel Sanders*, ed. Marc van Uytfanghe and Roland Demeulenaere (Instrumenta Patristica, 23) (Steenbrugge: Abbatia S. Petri, 1991), 75–88.

90. Atkinson, *The Oldest Vocation*, 71.

91. Ibid., 79, 89. Wemple, *Women*, 22, exaggerates the influence of this idea in the sixth-century church, however; see Giselle de Nie, "Is een vrouw een mens? Voorschrift, vooroordeel en praktijk in zesde-eeuws Gallië," *Het raadsel vrouwengeschiedenis*, ed. Francisca de Haan et al. (Jaarboek voor Vrouwengeschiedenis, 10) (Nijmegen: SUN, 1989), 51–74.

92. Brown, *The Body and Society*, passim.

93. *Passio Perpetuae*, 18.7, ed. Murillo, 126.

94. Ibid., 20.8–9, ed. Murillo, 128.

95. Ibid., 21.8–10, ed. Murillo, 130.

96. Mathieu, "Horreur," passim, and de Nie, "Le corps," passim.

97. As Aline Rousselle, *Porneia: De la maitrise du corps à la privation sensorielle. IIe–IVe siècles de l'ère chrétienne* (Paris: Presses Universitaires de France, 1983), 13–36. English translation: *Porneia: on Desire and the Body in Antiquity* (Oxford: Blackwell, 1988). On Jerome's view of male-like roles for women see, for instance, Jan Willem Drijvers, "Virginity and Ascetism in Late Roman Western Elites," in *Sexual Asymmetry: Studies in Ancient Society*, ed. Josine Blok and Peter Mason (Amsterdam: Gieben, 1987), 241–273, here 266f.

98. Rousselle, *Porneia*, 37–63, 244. See also Rosemary Ruether, "Mothers of the Church: Ascetic Women in the Late Patristic Age," in *Women of Spirit*, ed. Ruether and McLaughlin, 72f.

99. Henry Maguire, *Art and Eloquence in Byzantium* (Princeton: Princeton University Press, 1981), 83ff.

100. [Anonymous], *Vita Sanctae Eugeniae Virginis ac Martyris*, (BHL 2666), in *De Vitis Patrum*, 1, in Migne, *Patrologia Latina (PL)*, vol. 73, 606–24, quotation 607 (also in *Rufini Opera*, in vol. 21, 1105–1122). Hippolyte Delehaye, *Étude sur le Légendier Romain* (Subsidia Hagiographica, 23) (Brussels: Société des Bollandistes, 1936), 176, 182f., 186, regarded Eugenia and her story as completely fabulous, conflating two known periods of persecution (late second and mid-third centuries), and dates the text as before the early sixth century (since Avitus of Vienne first shows knowledge of it).

101. *Vita Eugeniae*, 7, ed. *PL* 73, 610.

102. Ibid.

103. Brown, *The Body and Society*, 48.

104. Ibid., 33f, 53–57.

105. *Vita Eugeniae*, 14, ed. *PL* 73, 613.

106. See n. 39.

107. *Vita Eugeniae*, 7, cd. *PL* 73, 610.

108. Ibid., 9, ed. *PL* 73, 611.

109. Ibid., 10, ed. *PL* 73, 611.

110. Ibid., 10, ed. *PL* 73, 611f.

111. Ibid., 15, ed. *PL* 73, 614.

112. Cf. Caroline Walker Bynum, "'. . . And Woman His Humanity': Female Imagery in the Religious Writing of the later Middle Ages," in her *Fragmentation and Redemption: Essays on Gender and the Human Body in Medieval Religion* (New York: Zone Books, 1992), 151–180.

113. *The Gospel According to Thomas*, logion 113–4, ed. A. Guillaumount et al. (London: Collins, 1959), trans. Pagels, "What Became of God the Mother," 294 I have added the quotation marks.

114. *Vita Eugeniae*, 15, ed. *PL* 73, 614f.

115. Douglas, *Purity and Danger*, 2f.

116. *Vita Eugeniae*, 16, ed. *PL* 73, 615.

117. Ibid., 19–21, quotation 21, ed. *PL* 73, 616f.

118. Ibid., 22, ed. *PL* 73, 617.

119. Ibid., 23, ed. *PL* 73, 617.

120. Ibid., 26, ed. *PL* 73, 619.

121. Ibid., 27, ed. *PL* 73, 619.

122. Bugge, *Virginitas*, 62.

123. Ambrosius, *De Virginibus*, 1.30, ed. Cazzaniga, 15f. *Ratio* as divine Reason: *Dictionnaire Latin-Francais des Auteurs Chrétiens*, ed. Albert Blaise (Turnhout: Brepols, 1954), 696, *ratio* 10 and 11. See on Ambrose's position: Thraede, "Zwischen Eva und Maria."

124. Graef, *Mary*, 42.

125. Avitus, *Poematum*, 6.505ff. ed. *MGH AA* 6/2, 289.

126. *Vita Eugeniae*, 28f., ed. *PL* 73, 620. The date is uncertain according to Migne's rendering of Rosweyde's n. 16 on p. 624.

127. Hieronymus, *Epistola* 108, in *Saint Jérôme*, ed. Lacourt, vol. 5, 159–201. Cf. Brown, *The Body and Society*, 367f. On Paula and her family, see Jo Ann McNamara, "Cornelia's daughters: Paula and Eustochium," *Women's Studies*, 11 (1984), 9–27.

128. Hieronymus, *Epistola* 108.4, ed. Lacourt, vol. 5, 162.

129. Ibid., 108.5, ed. Lacourt, 163.

130. Ibid., 108.6, ed. Lacourt, 163.

131. Ibid., ed. Lacourt, 164.

132. Atkinson, *The Oldest Vocation*, 15f.

133. Hieronymus, *Epistola* 108.15, ed. Lacourt, 177.

134. Ibid., 108.19, ed. Lacourt, 184.

135. Ibid., 108.21, ed. Lacourt, 189.

136. Brown, *The Body and Society*, 172.

137. Hieronymus, *Epistola* 14.3, ed. Lacourt, vol. 1, 37.

138. The panegyricist Jerome, at least, says that she has exchanged the lesser glory of being known to all Rome for that of being known everywhere: in the Roman as well as "barbaric" countries (*Epistola.* 108.3, ed. Lacourt, vol. 5, 161).

139. Hieronymus, *Epistola* 108.21, ed. Lacourt, vol. 5, 188.

140. Peter Brown, "The Notion of Virginity in the Early Church," in *Christian Spirituality: Origins to the Twelfth Century*, ed. Bernard McGinn et al. (World Spirituality, 16) (New York: Crossroad, 1978), 436–439.

141. Cf. Hunter, "'On the Sin of Adam and Eve.'"

142. Hieronymus, *Epistola* 108.28, ed. Lacourt, 198.

143. Hieronymus, *Epistola* 22.38, ed. Lacourt, vol. 1, 155; trans. Wright, *Select Letters of St Jerome*, 52–157.

144. Averil Cameron, "Virginity as Metaphor: Women and the Rhetoric of Early Christianity," in *History as Text. The Writing of Ancient History*, ed. Averil Cameron (London: Duckworth, 1989), 181–205, sees the theme of virginity as a central rhetorical element in the Fathers' expression of paradoxical Christian truth. Patricia Cox Miller, "The Blazing Body: Ascetic Desire in Jerome's Letter to Eustochium," *Journal of Early Christian Studies*, 1 (1993), 21–45, says that Jerome attempted "to erase the literal body by reimagining it as an assembly of textual metaphors" (44), "a 'textual' body that is the object of Jerome's desire" (24).

145. Hieronymus, *Epistola* 22.20, ed. Lacourt, vol. 1, 130.

146. Ibid., 108.29–31, ed. Lacourt, vol. 5, 200.

147. Ibid., 108.33, ed. Lacourt, 201.

148. Ibid., 108.26, ed. Lacourt, 195.

149. Pope Gregory the Great (590–604) made this interpretation official: "Hanc vero quam Lucas peccatricem mulierem, Joannes Mariam nominat, illam esse Mariam credimus, de qua Marcus septem daemonia ejecta fuisse testatur," see Hom*ilia,*

33.1 in Migne, *Patrologia Latina*, vol. 76, 1238, quoted in Saxer, *Le Culte de Marie Madeleine*, 3. Pagels, *Gnostic Gospels*, 64, mentions the fact that one of these—*The Gospel of Philip*—describes Mary Magdalene as Jesus' most loved and intimate companion, and that a similar tradition is found in the others. All this literature had evidently been suppressed after the second century by what became the official church. Is Fortunatus's mentioning her as a model for sanctity a vague reminiscence of this tradition? Cf. Grassi, *Mary Magdalene*.

150. Saxer, *Le Culte de Marie Madeleine*, 9.

151. Warner, *Alone of All Her Sex*, 229.

152. [Anonymus], *Vita Sanctae Thaisis Meretricis*, (BHL 8012), in *De Vitis Patrum*, 1, in Migne, *Patrologia Latina*, vol. 73, 661–664. The translation is my own. An English translation and a comparison with similar stories in Benedicta Ward, *Harlots of the Desert: A Study of Repentance in Early Monastic Sources* (London: Mowbray, 1987), 76–84.

153. Agostino Amore, "Taisia," in *Bibliotheca Sanctorum*, vol. 12 (Roma: Città Nuova, 1969), 97ff.

154. *Vita Thaisis Meretricis* 2, ed. PL 73, 662.

155. Ibid.

156. Gregorius Turonensis, *Historiarum Libri X*, 6.29, ed. and trans. Rudolf Buchner (Ausgewählte Quellen zur deutschen Geschichte des Mittelalters, Freiherr vom Stein-Gedächtnisausgabe, 3) (Darmstadt: Wissenschaftliche Buchgesellschaft, 1967), 48–51. English translation by Lewis Thorpe, *The History of the Franks* (Harmondsworth: Penguin, 1974). In this vision, "the source of living water springing up into eternal life (fons aquae vivae salientis in vitam aeternam, see Jn 4:14) is prominent."

157. Brown, *The Body and Society*, 259–262, 356; Bugge, *Virginitas*, 66f.

158. In the late sixth century, Gregory of Tours still uses the notion to refer to male saints: Gregorius Turonensis, *Vita Patrum*, 2, prol., in *Monumenta Germaniae Historica. Scriptores Rerum Merovingicarum*, vol. 1/2, 669. English translation by Edward James, *Life of the Fathers* (Liverpool: Liverpool University Press, 1985).

159. Fortunatus, *Carmina*, 3.17.9f; 3.21.9, ed. *MGH AA* 4/1, 70, 71.

160. "Corde parens, pastu nutrix, bonus ore magister, / Dilexit, coluit, rexit, honesta dedit. / Ille pio studio sulcata novalia sevit: / Quod pater effudit, hoc mihi semen ale" (*Carmina* 3.19.7–10, ed. *MGH AA*, 4/1, 71).

161. Brennan, "Radegund," gives useful bibliographical information, and summarizes the state of research on Fortunatus in his "The career of Venantius Fortunatus," *Traditio*, 41 (1985), 49–78. Some more recent discussions are: *La riche personalité de Sainte Radegonde: Conférence et homilies* (Poitiers: Comité du XIVe Centenaire, 1988); Jean Leclercq, "La Sainte Radegonde de Venance Fortunat et celle de Baudonivie," *Fructus Centesimus: Mélanges offerts à Gerard J.M. Bartelink*, ed. Antonius A.R. Bastiaensen et al. (Instrumenta Patristica, 19) (Steenbrugge: Abbatia S. Petri, 1989), 207–216; Sabine Gäbe, "Radegundis: Sancta, Regina, Ancilla. Zum Heiligkeitsideal der Radegundisviten von Fortunat und Baudonivia," *Francia*, 16 (1989), 1–30; Cristina Papa, "Radegonda e Batilde: Modelli di santita regia femminile nel regno Merovingio," *Benedictina*, 36 (1989), 13–33; Robert Folz, *Les saintes reines du Moyen Age en Occident (VIe–XIIIe siècles)* (Subsidia Hagiographica, 76) (Brussels: Société des Bollandistes, 1992), 13–24; Judith George, *Venantius Fortunatus: A Latin Poet in Merovingian Gaul* (Oxford: Clarendon Press, 1992), 161–177. On the position of women in Frankish Gaul, see also Hans-Werner Goetz, "Frauenbild und weibliche Lebensgestaltung im Fränkischen Reich," in *Weibliche Lebensgestaltung im frühen Mittelalter* (Cologne: Böhlau, 1991), 7–44.

162. Wemple, *Women*, 27–74.

163. Ibid., 61.

164. Gregorius Turonensis, In *Gloria Confessorum*, in *Monumenta Germaniae Historica. Scriptores Rerum Merovingicarum (MGH SRM)*, vol. 1/2, 744–820. En-

glish translation by Raymond van Dam, *The Glory of the Confessors* (Liverpool: Liverpool University Press, 1988). Fortunatus: *Vita Sanctae Radegundis*, (BHL 7048), in *Monumenta Germaniae Historica. Auctores Antiquissimi (MGH AA)*, vol. 4/2, 38–49. Baudonivia: *Vita Sanctae Radegundis*, (BHL 7049), in *MGH SRM* 3, 377–95. Both *Lives* are translated in Jo Ann McNamara and John E. Halborg, *Sainted Women of the Dark Ages* (Durham: Duke University Press, 1992), 60–105.

165. Gregorius Turonensis, *Historiarum Libri X*, 9.38, ed. Buchner, 298ff.

166. Gregorius Turonensis, *Gloria Martyrum*, 5, ed *MGH SRM* 1/2, 489; and *Historiarum Libri X*, 9.40, ed. Buchner, 302.

167. Fortunatus, *Carmina*, 2.6.1, ed. *MGH AA* 4/1, 34.

168. According to Jan Willem Drijvers, "Helena Augusta: Exemplary Christian Empress," in *Studia Patristica*, 24, ed. Elizabeth A. Livingstone (Leuven: Peeters Press, 1993), 89: ". . . in the West Helena was especially celebrated for her discovery of the True Cross and not so much because she was the first Christian Empress." Cf. his *Helena Augusta: The Mother of Constantine the Great and the Legend of Her Finding the True Cross* (Leiden: Brill, 1992).

169. Fortunatus, *Carmina*. 8.8.1; Ibid. App. 22.2, ed. *MGH AA* 4/1, 194 and 286 resp. Other instances: "mater opima," "mater honore mihi," "cara mater" (*Carmina*. 11.3.1, 6.1, 7.1 resp., ed. *MGH AA* 4/1, 259, 260, 261 resp.), and esp.: "Cara, benigna, decens, dulcis, pia semper habenda, / Cuius in affectu stat mihi patris honor, / Per quam, quae genuit, recolunt mea viscera matrem, / Et mores aviae te renovante colo" (*Carmina*. App. 12.7–10, ed. *MGH AA* 4/1, 283).

170. Fortunatus, *Carmina*, 8.9.1, ed. *MGH AA* 4/1, 195.

171. In old Germanic languages *raede* or *rede* is wisdom, mind, consciousness (as in Ethelred "the Redeless," Aelred: the noble mind); *gund* appears often (as in Gundobad, Guntchramn) and may mean favor, cherish, as in the modern German *Gunst*.

172. Fortunatus, *Carmina*, 8.3.47f., ed. *MGH AA* 4/1, 182.

173. Wilhelm Meyer, *Der Gelegenheitsdichter Venantius Fortunatus* (Abhandlungen der Königlichen Gesellschaft der Wissenschaften zu Göttingen. Philologisch-Historische Klasse, NF. 4) (Berlin: Weidmann, 1901), 98f.

174. Fortunatus, *Carmina*, 8.3.325–84, ed. *MGH AA* 4/1, 189ff.

175. Ibid., 8.3.85–88, 91–96, 105f., ed. *MGH AA* 4/1, 183, 183, 184.

176. Hieronymus, *Epistola* 22.38, ed. Lacourt, vol. 1, 155.

177. Bugge, *Virginitas*, 62.

178. Augustine, *De Sancta Virginitate*, 5, ed. Migne, *Patrologia Latina*, vol. 40, 399.

179. Avitus, *Poematum*, 6.214–223, ed. *MGH AA* 6/2, 281.

180. Fortunatus, *Vita Radegundis*, 15, ed. *MGH AA* 4/2, 40.

181. Fortunatus, *Carmina*, 11.3.1–8, ed. *MGH AA* 4/1, 259.

182. Fortunatus, *Vita Radegundis*, 15, ed. *MGH AA* 4/2, 40.

183. Avitus, *Poematum*, 6.664ff., ed. *MGH AA* 6/2, 294.

184. Fortunatus, *Carmina*, 8.10.5–14, ed. *MGH AA* 4/1, 195f.

185. Cf. on the occasional late antique association of Mary with a fertility goddess: Atkinson, *The Oldest Vocation*, 107. Cf. Matthias Zender, "Die Verehrung von drei heiligen Frauen im christlichen Mitteleuropa und ihre Vorbereitungen in alten Vorstellungen," in *Matronen und verwandte Gottheiten: Ergebnisse eines Kolloquiums* (Beihefte der Bonner Jahrbücher, 44) (Cologne, 1987), 213–228.

186. As, for instance, Karl J. Leyser, *Rule and conflict in an Early Medieval Society: Ottonian Saxony* (London: Arnold, 1979), 80, quoting a letter of Alcuin to the Northumbrian King Aethelred (*Monumenta Germaniae Historica. Epistolae Karolini Aevi*, 2, 51, nr. 23). Frantisek Graus, *Volk, Herrscher und Heiliger im Reich der Merowinger: Studien zur Hagiographie der Merowingerzeit* (Prague: Czechoslovakian Akademy, 1965), 326–329, however, finds no evidence of kingly charisma before the Carolingian period and sees the idea as a borrowing from Irish sources.

187. Brennan, "Radegund," 343.

188. Fortunatus, *Vita Radegundis*, 1, ed. *MGH AA* 4/2, 38. Cf. Hieronymus, *Epistola* 108.19, ed. Labourt, vol. 5, 183.

189. Ibid., 3, ed. *MGH AA* 4/2, 38.

190. Ibid., 5, ed. *MGH AA* 4/2, 38. On the late antique topos of the mature youth (*puer senex*): Ernst R. Curtius, *European Literature and the Latin Middle Ages*, trans. Willard R. Trask (Bollingen Series, 36) (New York: Pantheon, 1953), 98–101.

191. Fortunatus, *Vita Radegundis*, 9 and 11, ed. *MGH AA* 4/2, 39. Cf. Sulpicius Severus, *Vita Sancti Martini*, 3.1–6, ed. J. Fontaine (Sources Chrétiennes, 133) (Paris: Cerf, 1967), 256–259.

192. Fortunatus, *Vita Radegundis*, 12, ed. *MGH AA* 4/2, 39.

193. Jo Ann McNamara, "The Need to Give: Suffering and Female Sanctity in the Middle Ages," in *Images of Sainthood in Medieval Europe*, ed. Renate Blumenfeld-Kosinski and Timea Szell (Ithaca: Cornell University Press, 1991), 199f.

194. Wemple, *Women*, 140.

195. Fortunatus, *Vita Radegundis*, 35–46, ed. *MGH AA* 4/2, 42f; Sulpicius Severus, *Vita Martini*, 18.3, ed. Fontaine, 292.

196. Fortunatus, *Vita Radegundis*, 42, ed. *MGH AA* 4/2, 43.

197. Ibid., 55 and 56, ed. *MGH AA* 4/2, 44.

198. Fortunatus, *Vita Radegundis*, 62f, ed. *MGH AA* 4/2, 45.

199. Ibid., 91, ed. *MGH AA* 4/2, 49.

200. Brennan, "Radegund," 343.

201. Baudonivia, *Vita Radegundis*, 2, ed. *MGH SRM* 2, 380; cf Sulpicius Severus, *Vita Martini*, 14.1f, ed. Fontaine, 282.

202. Baudonivia, *Vita Radegundis*, 3, ed. *MGH SRM* 2, 380.

203. Ibid., 4, ed. *MGH SRM* 2, 381. On such practices, see Clare Stancliffe, *St Martin and His Hagiographer: History and Miracle in Sulpicius Severus* (Oxford: Clarendon Press, 1983), 241ff.

204. Ibid., 5, ed. *MGH SRM* 2, 382.

205. Ibid., 8, ed. *MGH SRM* 2, 383.

206. Ibid., 8 and 9, ed. *MGH SRM* 2, 384f.

207. Ibid., 10, ed. *MGH SRM* 2, 384.

208. Gregorius Turonensis, *Gloria Martyrum*, 5, ed. *MGH SRM* 1/2, 490.

209. Suzanne F. Wemple, "Female Spirituality and Mysticism in Frankish Monasticism: Radegund, Balthild and Aldegund," in *Medieval Religious Women 2: Peace Weavers*, ed. Lillian T. Shank and John A. Nichols (Cistercian Studies Series, 72) (Kalamazoo: Cistercian Publications, 1987), 44f.

210. Baudonivia, *Vita Radegundis*, 10, ed. *MGH SRM* 2, 384f.

211. Ibid., 16, ed. *MGH SRM* 2, 389; Hieronymus, *Epistola* 108.30, ed. Lavourt, vol. 5, 199.

212. Baudonivia, *Vita Radegundis*, 16ff., ed. *MGH SRM* 2, 388–391.

213. Ibid., 20, ed. *MGH SRM* 2, 391.

214. William E. Klingshirn, "Caesarius's Monastery for Women in Arles and the Composition and Function of the 'Vita Caesarii,'" *Revue Benedictine*, 100 (1990), 474–480.

215. *Vita Sancti Caesarii*, 2.37, ed. *MGH SRM* 3, 497: "de amore, de nutrimentis, de caritate, de praedicatione." The following quotations are from 2.35 and 1.53.

216. de Nie, "Is een vrouw een mens?" 71ff. Cf. Corrington, "Milk of Salvation," 406.

217. Baudonivia, *Vita Radegundis*, 21, ed. *MGH SRM* 2, 392.

218. Fortunatus, *Carmina*, 8.3.25f., ed. *MGH AA* 4/1, 195. Bishop Caesarius and the nuns of the convent he founded were also buried in a church dedicated to Mary.

219. Baudonivia, *Vita Radegundis*, 23, ed. *MGH SRM* 2, 392f; cf. Gregorius Turonensis, *In Gloria Confessorum*, 104, ed. *MGH SRM* 1/2, 814ff.

PART III
HOLY MOTHERS
IN THE MIDDLE AGES

9. **S. Waldetrudis.**

Figure 5.1. Waldetrudis not with her own children but with two relatives (Idem)

FAMILY TIES
MOTHERS AND VIRGINS
IN THE NINTH CENTURY
Ineke van't Spijker

As we saw in the previous study, Venantius Fortunatus's *Vita Radegundis* can be regarded as a summary and culmination of the ideals of female sanctity in Late Antiquity. Radegund, the bride of Christ, was also a spiritual mother, fertile, nursing and nurturing. In Western Europe in the subsequent centuries the society of Late Antiquity made way for early medieval society and the changes involved in this transition had an impact on the ideals of sanctity. Although female religious were still, or perhaps even more often than before, called *Sponsa Christi*, the title acquired a completely different meaning.

One of these changes in society was the increasing role the aristocracy came to play in the Church and in monasteries—an aristocracy in which the Gallo-Roman and the Germanic populations were mingling. Family relationships and ties of loyalty between various (aristocratic) families were very important. Marriage, choice of godparents and various other patronage relationships were used to reinforce the family. Ecclesiastical offices played an important role: a bishopric was sometimes used by a prince as an instrument to establish links with a certain family. Noble families were involved in building monasteries, which were then more or less regarded as family establishments. Of course the Merovingians and later the Carolingians were very important, but there were other prominent families as well. The founder—whether male or female—of a religious house was often venerated as a saint and that sainthood endowed the family with a certain prestige. In the case of the recently Christianized Germanic aristocracy this prestige helped to legitimize their power in the changing society.[1]

These developments made an impact on religious life in general. Seclusion from the world was still an essential concept of monasticism, but the position of monasteries in the world had changed: they were no longer manifestations of protest against urban society, but spearheads of Christianization, centers of culture representing the "politische Religiosität," which was to become so characteristic of the Middle Ages and to reach its peak under the Carolingians.[2] Like marriages, the founding of monasteries and donations to monasteries could be instrumental in the politics of inheritance.

Female sainthood in this period must be seen within the context of these developments. If a widow preferred to enter a convent rather than re-marrying, part of the motivation may have been to keep the family property intact, even though the hagiographers do not state this directly. In the Merovingian and early Carolingian eras women often played an important role within family structures, not only as nefarious queens, but also as founders of convents and as abbesses.[3] If, as sometimes happened, they had originally entered the convent against the wishes of their parents, this did not necessarily lead to a rift within the family. The family maintained its ties with that convent, often after a reconciliation, and sometimes had children brought up there who became successors to the abbesses. Sometimes women founded a convent or entered one with the approval of their husbands, or they were converted to the religious life after their husbands' deaths. Possibly there are more mothers to be found among saintly women in this period than in other periods. We shall see that this did not lead to greater importance being attached to physical or spiritual motherhood as a component of sanctity. However, sometimes these women along with their children, sisters or other relations, did belong to a family of saints. Although the saintly women, according to their hagiographers, complied with the evangelical command to relinquish all earthly ties, broader family structures did in fact play an important part in their lives, even after they had become full-time religious.

In the Carolingian era the role of women as founders of convents or abbesses declined.[4] But the memory of such women was preserved in *vitae*. In this study the ninth-century *vitae* of two (families of) seventh-century saints will be examined: that of Waldetrude and that of Rictrude. Another ninth-century *vita*, that of the virgin martyr Maxellendis, will also be discussed. Naturally these *vitae*, which were written long after the deaths of the saints themselves, reveal at least as much about Carolingian ideals of sanctity as about actual events in the seventh century, and it is those ideals of sanctity which concern us here. In this study, it is not my aim to present an exhaustive analysis of Carolingian female sanctity,[5] but merely to highlight some of its important aspects.

"COMPANION AND CO-HEIRESS": *SPONSA* BY PARTICIPATION

The first family of saints to be discussed here lived in the seventh century: Waldetrude and her sister Aldegund, the daughters of Waldebert and Bertilla, respected members of the nobility in the reign of king Dagobert. Waldetrude's husband Madelgar, also called Vincent, and their daughters, Aldetrude and Madelberta, were, like Waldetrude and Aldegund, venerated as saints.

In the ninth-century *Vita Waldedrudis* we are told that when the saint had become nubile, she had been married, in accordance with the wishes of her parents.[6] The marriage is given an aura of piety: the parents decided to give their daughter in marriage "according to divine ordinance and the example of the patriarchs." But "this carnal tie could not alter God's secret plan, through which she had already been betrothed by the ring of faith (*subarraverat*) and through which she had been predestined to be the companion and co-heiress (*socia ac coheres*) of her previously mentioned sister Aldegund"—who had dedicated herself to God at a very early age. Waldetrude turned away from worldly cares and started to cherish eternal longings. She carried out works of charity and attempted to banish vice "not only from her corporal deeds, but also from the deliberations of her heart."[7] In the *Life of Waldetrude* herself it is she who urges her husband Vincent on to a conversion. (In the eleventh-century *vita* of her husband, which in fact consists mainly of quotations, including many from the *Vita Waldedrudis*, this part of Waldetrude's role is brushed aside.[8]) In the following description of her ever-increasing aversion to the physical aspects of marriage, we find the sole allusion to her motherhood:

> Since carnal affections tend to obscure the intentions and acuity of the mind, she came to abhor physical union, *not because of the task, permitted by God, of producing offspring,* (italics added), but because she knew the words of the apostle, that an unmarried woman, a virgin, is occupied with divine affairs, so that she is holy in body and spirit, whereas a married woman is occupied with worldly affairs, how to please her husband. (I Cor. 7:34)[9]

She prayed to God to release her from the constraints of her marriage. When Vincent himself conceived the plan of entering a monastery, he received her approval, and her desire to serve God only was fulfilled. In accordance with Church views a married couple could take such a step only by mutual consent. The marriage ties were dissolved, but *caritas* remained. In the rest of the story there is no further mention of Vincent.

God, "who knows how to cultivate every fruitful palm and to make it bear more fruit," spurred her on to even greater saintliness through a vision in which the holy Gaugeric appeared to her and predicted her future status as an anchoress. When she told her maids about this, they started spreading malicious rumours, accusing her of bragging—a trap set up by the devil in order to frustrate her plan right from the beginning. This gossip made Waldetrude very sorrowful, as she was as yet inexperienced (*utpote adhuc rudis*). An angel appeared to her in the form of a man, and asked her why she was so dejected. He comforted her and told her to be strong (*robusta*), for these trials were a normal part of a saint's struggle. "A disciple is not above his teacher" (Mt. 10:24). Then her "useless sorrow" made way for spiritual joy.[10]

Another saint, Gislenus, became her adviser: he often came to visit her, under divine orders, in order to strengthen her "with the food of God's word." When he saw that her desire for the religious life and the habit which went with it (*sanctae conversationis habitum*) was increasing steadily, he helped her by indicating a site where she could have a cell built, close to his own hermitage, "far from the busy world, but all the more suited to the religious life: a wild and uncultivated spot (*spinarum et veprium densitate nemorosus atque incultus*)"—the usual description of a hermit's dwelling-place.[11] Waldetrude bought the site from the nobleman who owned it and he built a cell there for her which she in fact thought was too luxurious. It was destroyed by a (divinely sent) whirlwind and then rebuilt more in accordance with her wishes. She was given the veil by Bishop Autbert. The devil, jealous of her piety, opposed her; having lost the "public battle"—her maids' smear campaign—he started to prepare for a secret battle. His weapons consisted of recollections of her past wealth and nobility, her love of worldly possessions, the arduousness of her lifestyle. Realizing she was involved in a battle, Waldetrude took up arms: she gave herself over to fervent prayer. Then the devil appeared to her at night, in the shape of a man who leapt on her and put his hand on her breast; but when she made the sign of the cross, he fled. Undaunted, strengthened by the angels' help, she heaped mockery and humiliation on her enemy, saying: "Look at you, banished from heaven because of your pride, justly condemned to death in hell, and now driven away by a woman."[12] The devil blushed with shame, vanished in a puff of smoke, and bothered her no more.

Now that the thorns of temptation had been uprooted, Waldetrude began to bear fruit: many noble ladies came to her. Sometimes her sister came to visit, and together they spoke sweet words, *dulcia verba*. Moved by human love, Aldegund felt sorry for her sister, because her housing was so austere. In this respect Waldetrude surpassed Aldegund, the indisputable bride of Christ, for when Aldegund invited her to accompany her to her own more comfortable convent, Waldetrude persisted in her poverty, "the security of which she guarded like a rich man guarding his perishable possessions."[13]

Eventually sisterhood proved powerful: it was revealed to Waldetrude in a vision that she would dwell in the same mansion in God's kingdom and enjoy the same beatitude, "for some come to salvation in one way, others in another."[14] In what is probably a later addition,[15] a story is told to illustrate this assertion: two sisters, of whom one was married but preserved her chastity (*et castitatem suam servavit*), while the other remained a virgin (*in virginitate permansit*), nevertheless both received the same reward (*aequale praemium*). Waldetrude died old, and was welcomed by the angels as a holy virgin (*virgo haec sancta*). She "lives with Christ, shares in the joy of the holy apostles and the triumph of the martyrs, she is the companion of the confessors and *the equal of virgins* (italics added), she rejoices forever in the Curia of the angels, in the presence of our Lord Jesus Christ," concludes the writer.[16]

This outline of the *vita* may serve to demonstrate a certain ambiguity in the sanctity of married women. Marriage is justified as a divine institution, which is later defined more precisely: God has given mankind the task of producing offspring. This is completely in accordance with the views of the Carolingian clergy, who in general had a positive attitude towards marriage, provided of course it was subject to Christian rules.[17] Although married people, or lay people in general, could not hope to reap the hundredfold reward which was reserved for virgins, there was no need for them to despair of gaining salvation in the next world.[18] In their "mirrors for the laity" Jonas of Orleans and Alcuin, for example, expressed a positive view of marriage as an institution desired by God. They based this view on the works of authors such as the Church Father Augustine, who in his *De Bono Conjugali* had presented marriage as an institution with a threefold purpose. Begetting offspring is one purpose. The physical union which this involves is in itself not evil, but the lust, which inevitably accompanies it, is. But just as it is not wrong for a lame person to get from one place to another, even though lameness itself is a bad thing, begetting children is not wrong in itself. Secondly, marriage is a symbol of the relationship between Christ and the Church. The third element is the unity of spouses, the *naturalis societas*. Apart from Augustine's works, the pastoral writings of Gregory the Great provide a source; in his *Regula Pastoralis* he created an appropriate place for each of the various states, showing great psychological insight.[19]

However, within the sphere of sanctity, virginity continued to be regarded as the highest possible achievement. So the author of the *Vita Waldedrudis* makes use of the idea of Predestination—a preoccupation of Carolingian theologians since the controversy which had arisen around the views of Gottschalk [20]—in order to cancel out the disadvantage which married people normally had: however respectable the institution of marriage may have been, the emphasis is still given to the idea that Waldetrude was destined to be the companion and co-heiress of her virgin sister. Although she is not directly named *Sponsa Christi*, she was "betrothed by the ring of faith" (see above).

Her marriage ties were annulled, but love (*caritas*) remained: *solutis vinculis conjugalibus, manente autem caritate.*[21] In this way the marriage is placed—almost in retrospect—in a monastic or at least a religious context. It was this same *caritas* which God had caused to burn in her heart and which Waldetrude had then also kindled in her husband. Even though they were no longer united by marriage ties, they were still united by *caritas*, which permanently enveloped the futures of both of them.

The ideal of virginity was just as valid for men as for women. In the *Life of Vincent* himself, we are told that he initially resisted marriage plans, but eventually yielded to the objections of his father, who complained to his only son that all his work would be in vain if he had no heir.[22] Vincent was forced to wait until the marriage could be annulled with Waldetrude's consent. When his own son expressed the wish to devote his life to God, Vincent made no objections.

There was also a lasting tie between Waldetrude and her sister Aldegund, whose *socia* and *coheres* she was supposed to be. They visited each other and spoke of the "sweet food of the heavenly homeland which they could not yet fully taste, but of which they could have a wistful foretaste."[23] In the ninth-century *Vita Aldegondis* the two sisters also visit each other and talk about love and the holy way of life (*conversatio*) of the group who followed Aldegund's teaching and example.[24] In the eleventh-century version of the *Vita Aldegondis* this sisterly tie is given more depth: the sisters are compared to the New Testament sisters Mary and Martha, although it cannot be said that one of them is Mary and the other Martha, as both fulfil both roles: they both sit at the Lord's feet, like Mary, but they are also occupied with exterior things, like Martha, although against their wishes (*invita*).[25] So the spiritual equality of these two sisters presented in the *Vita Waldedrudis* continued to be valid in later centuries.

In the *vitae* of Aldegund, Waldetrude's role in her sister's spiritual career is even more significant than in the *Vita Waldedrudis* itself. Waldetrude, already in a convent, asked her mother to send her younger sister Aldegund to visit her. In the second version this took place after Aldegund had had a talk with her mother, who had tried to persuade her to marry, using the family's wealthy property as an argument. But Aldegund had answered that she wanted a husband who was Lord of both heaven and earth.[26]

The mother gave Aldegund permission to visit Waldetrude, in order to comfort her. Waldetrude wanted Aldegund to take the veil too, undoubtedly "at the instigation of the Holy Spirit, who wanted to ensure that those who were of one spirit should have the same dwelling place":[27] a confirmation of the oneness of spirit between the sisters expressed in the *Vita Waldedrudis*. In the eleventh-century version these elements—the dialogue with the mother and Waldetrude's role in the story—are developed even further. Waldetrude wanted to protect her sister from the bondage of carnal love, but also wanted her as a companion in her religious life. When Aldegund returns from her visit at her mother's command, there is no longer just a friendly discussion between mother and daughter, but vigorous opposition on the mother's part.[28] Waldetrude had adjured her sister to prepare herself for her immortal *Sponsus*, but her mother made it so difficult for her that Aldegund had to run away. It was only after a difficult journey, including the miraculous crossing of an unfordable river, that Aldegund was able to found her convent.[29] Eventually, when the mother was mourning for her daughter as though she were dead, a reconciliation followed—and the mother's conversion.[30] These additions, with all sorts of extra trials which the future saint has to overcome—such as impassable rivers and intractable suitors—are a familiar phenomenon in eleventh-century revisions of earlier *Lives*.[31]

Aldegund is known mainly for her visions.[32] According to the first two versions, when she was still at home Aldegund had visions in which an angel appeared to her, announcing that she was to have no other[33] and must seek no other bridegroom[34] than Christ. This promise was repeated in later visions, in which Christ himself also appeared to her. The visions were a sign of Aldegund's status as an elected saint, and served to encourage her and confirm her in her spiritual career. The theme of the saint as bride of Christ recurs continually, as it does in the descriptions (most of which are taken from the *Vita Aldegondis*) of Aldegund's nieces Aldetrude and Madelberta—Waldetrude's daughters—who were brought up by Aldegund in her convent.[35] Quotations are taken from the Song of Songs about the bridegroom who brings the bride, the holy one, "into the wine-cellar" (Song of Songs 2:4),[36] and stars who ask Aldegund to come to the wedding feast of the Bridegroom.[37]

Reminiscences of Mary, in Aldegund's answer to the angel, also fit into this context of the *virgo* as bride. When the angel announces to her that she is to be Christ's bride, Aldegund answers in the words of Mary, Christ's first and foremost Mother and Bride: "[L]et it be to me according to your word" (Lk. 1:38).[38] After an attack by the devil another angel appears to her, saying in the words of the Annunciation: "Blessed are you among women

(Lk. 1:28), for your name is written in the Book of Life."[39] In the second version these correspondences have become mere hints. However, they definitely imply triumph—and not an annunciation of spiritual motherhood. "The Holy Spirit will come upon you, and the power of the Most High will overshadow you" (Lk. 1:35), again a reminiscence of the Virgin Mary, is what Aldegund is told in a vision in which she is standing in a street, surrounded by a host of people, and sees a fiery globe coming from heaven;[40] and in a final eulogy, after the saint's death, it is said that she "was not less than martyrs. Overshadowed by the Holy Spirit, she vanquished the power of the devil, overcame the weakness of the female sex, rose manfully above worldly delights."[41]

As an abbess she had a vision in which she was told that the Lord had betrothed her forever, so that she might gain the incorruptible crown. At once she was clad in wedding garments. When she asked the name of the angel who had appeared to her, the answer was: "Glorious is my name (*gloriosum est nomen meum*),"[42] in the second version, with a reference to the parents of Samson, to whom the angel had made his name known in this way (Judges 13:18).[43] In this second version it was revealed to Waldetrude that Aldegund deserved to have Christ as a bridegroom, and according to the same *vita*, a monk had a vision in which he saw that Christ had sent messengers to fetch his bride Aldegund, since she had prepared a worthy habitation for him in her body and an undefiled bridal bed in her soul.[44]

Unlike some other *vitae*, the *Vita Aldegondis* does not seem to present the *Sponsa*-idea primarily as a religious alternative, a defense strategy against a parental marriage plan. (It only develops into this sort of strategy in the eleventh-century version, when the influence of the mother's threat is expanded).[45] But the bridal imagery used here does not have the same connotations as similar imagery in the patristic era or the mystical bridal imagery which is so characteristic of the later Middle Ages. Neither the intimacy of the later mystical interpretation nor the subtle stratification of the patristic era[46] seems to prevail here. It is not the intimate shade of the orchard from the Song of Songs, but the massive shadow of an imposing *Virtus Altissimi* which falls over Aldegund.[47] The correlation made in the second version between a "worthy habitation in the body" and an "undefiled bridal bed of the soul" should perhaps remind us of the emphasis on cultic purity which is so characteristic of the Carolingian era.[48] It is this cultic purity and the importance attached to liturgy—another characteristic feature of the period—which provide us with a key to understanding the bridal imagery in these ninth-century *vitae*. A hieratic Christ appears to Aldegund, as if in an imposing liturgy: a Bridegroom, sometimes radiant in rich attire and splendid jewels, sometimes in full shining glory which seems to illuminate the whole world. He even shows her the riches and glory of the heavenly Jerusalem.[49] We see a stately bridal procession which is at the same time a triumphal procession, with wedding garments, a crown, a glorious name; the whole picture is more reminiscent of the glorious manifestations of the Lamb of the Apocalypse than of the bridegroom from the Song of Songs, whose "left hand is under my head."

An important element in the *Vita Waldedrudis* is her defeat of the devil. The gossip, which had distressed Waldetrude so much, was the devil's work. After she had been comforted and urged on by heavenly powers (*esto robusta*), she realized that these trials were to be expected. In this respect the *vita* shows an evolution: at first she was still inexperienced (*rudis*), but later, when her opponent renewed his attacks in a secret battle, she sought inner strength, in prayer. This second attack, which used the weapons of past wealth, the position of her family, the defense of her family and the difficulties of the road which lay ahead of her, is formulated in the same words as attacks by the devil described in the *Vita Antonii*.[50] So the monastic reader, who would probably have been familiar with Anthony's story, would of course have been even more convinced of Waldetrude's prestige. The figure of a man laying his hand on her breast is the equivalent of similar female appearances to Anthony and other male saints. In these battles with the ancient enemy there is no trace of female weakness. On the other hand, it was even more humiliating for the devil to be defeated by a woman, as is implied in the words Waldetrude uses to mock him when he has to retreat. Nevertheless, the devil, who "deliberately joins battle, is forced against his will to offer an opportunity of victory" to the saint. In this way the devil's attack is incorporated into a divine plan of redemption; it was through these trials that Waldetrude "bore more fruit, like cultivated ground."[51]

In Aldegund's *Life*, the same humiliating words which Waldetrude flung at the devil—who then vanished in a puff of smoke—are again used to combat the devil's attacks. The devil had no chance of making any headway with Aldegund, who like her sister before her, ridiculed him. He approached her with the words "through your obedience you have received the secrets of Paradise, which I lost through my disobedience."[52] The constantly recurring contrasts in the *vitae* between the proud devil or the first humans on the one hand and the saint on the other, make the saint's ultimate victory more dramatic; it is like a reverse image of the Fall—of both Satan and man—and has the same connotations of triumph as the *Sponsa-Dei* imagery with its apocalyptic colors.

Although Waldetrude's marriage was annulled, love remained; and the ties of sisterhood also form part of the setting for Waldetrude's sainthood. In contrast, the natural tie of motherhood apparently constituted so great an impediment to her sanctity that it is not even mentioned; it is almost impossible to deduce from the passage about her marriage that Waldetrude was a mother. It only becomes clear in the *vitae* of the other members of the family: in the *vitae* of Aldetrude and Madelberta their mother is mentioned, and in the eleventh-century *Vita Vincentii* the names of her children are given. Abhorrence of sexuality, as an obstacle to concentration on a saint's divine goals, is discussed explicitly, and seems to serve here as an approximation of virginity; perhaps an outright mention of motherhood would have made it too difficult to maintain the suggestion of virginity. In relation to the fact that she remained in the world while her husband was already in a monastery, the most obvious reason is not stated, i.e., that she had to look after her children. Evidently it is only through suppression of her motherhood that Waldetrude is able to share in the status of *Sponsa-Christi*, which for her sister is incontestable. In this case literal, biological motherhood does not open the way to spiritualization of motherhood but impedes it. When a comparison is made between married women or widows and virgins in the lives of saints, there is often a reference to Matthew, as we shall see in other examples: the harvest for virgins is a hundredfold, for married people thirtyfold. In Waldetrude's case this text or any allusion to it is missing altogether. There are two instances of fruit-bearing imagery in the story: when God, who knows how to care for every fruit-bearing palm, urged her to become even more saintly, and after her defeat of the devil (see above). But this imagery—like the text from Matthew in fact—is taken from the (impersonal) world of nature and vegetation, and is the consequence of her "almost-virginity," not of her motherhood. It was after the defeat of sexual temptation, when the devil had manifested himself for the second time and "the thorns of temptation had been uprooted," that "she bore more fruit, like cultivated ground," that her fame grew and noble ladies started to come to her.[53] However, when she was delivered from temptation, she became a *magistra virtutum*, not a mother.[54]

Within the framework of other family relationships, where no literal tie of motherhood existed, spiritualized motherhood was possible: in the *vitae* of both Aldegund and her nieces Aldetrude and Madelberta, Waldetrude's daughters, we are told that these girls were brought up by their aunt. She was their nurse, *nutrix*, and Waldetrude gave her little daughter Aldetrude to her sister to bring up and educate,[55] or to feed with spiritual milk.[56] It is not taken for granted that holiness is passed on directly within the "saintly family"; it is not the biological mother who transmits holiness, it seems, but the aunt. This is also true on a literary level: the *Lives* of Aldetrude and Madelberta consist mainly of quotations from the *vita* of Aldegund.

Aldegund is also called mother of her community, in a spiritual sense: her convent sisters, who knew about her visions, rejoiced and thanked Christ for having placed them under the yoke of such a spiritual mother.[57] However, this spiritual motherhood is not worked out in any depth. Aldegund's role as a mother is continually overshadowed by her other roles: leader, *magistra*. She "has won a crowd of girls from her bridegroom, as a battle prize."[58]

In the *Lives* of Waldetrude's daughters spiritual motherhood does not receive much attention either. There is very little mention of motherhood in relation to their sisters in the convent; the saint is presented rather as a *magistra* at the head of a stately line of virgins, the leader of a procession of wise virgins awaiting the arrival of the Bridegroom. Like a leading lady, Madelberta, through her death, takes the souls of the holy virgins which have been won with her to glory,[59] to the court of the angels, *curia angelorum*, where her mother, the equal of virgins, *aequa virginibus*, awaits her with joy.

MOURNING BECOMES RICTRUDE

If Waldetrude's motherhood was completely suppressed in her *vita*, in Hucbald of Saint-Amand's *Vita Rictrudis* (written around 907) motherhood constitutes an important element, so that this *vita* is quite revealing about the consequences of motherhood for sanctity. Rictrude was the mother of a whole family of saints. Her husband, a grandson of the holy Gertrude of Hamay—herself a noble lady who founded a convent after marriage and motherhood—was venerated as a saint after his death, and her daughters went with her to the convent. One of them became an abbess, while her son became an abbot.[60]

Hucbald, one of the last representatives of the Carolingian renaissance, wrote his *Vita Rictrudis* at the request of the clerics and nuns of the monastery of Marchienne, the house where Rictrude had been abbess.[61] He says in his prologue that he had hesitated at first to accept the task because he lacked data. But when he realized that various stories in circulation matched up and after inhabitants of the monastery had assured him that these data had formerly been written down but had been lost during the Norman raids, he acquiesced.[62] His story combines great vitality with a theological appraisal of the various aspects of Rictrude's life.

Again, the events take place in the Merovingian era, in the social environment of noblemen and bishops, partly at the royal court. According to Hucbald's description, Rictrude's marriage complies with the rules given by Jonas of Orleans in his *De Institutione Laicali*. Adalbald married Rictrude "not through lack of self-control (*incontinentia*) but in order to have beloved offspring."[63] So in this case the marriage was honorable and the marriage bed undefiled (*honorabile connubium, torus immaculatus*, Hebr. 13:4). Evidently in this case this means not a virginal, but a chaste marriage, in which the Church rules of abstinence are kept. Unanimity prevailed between the spouses; they served God in unity of flesh and heart. So the marriage was entirely respectable. Parenthood and childraising are given full approval, on the basis of the commandment in Genesis to the first married couple to multiply: *Crescite et multiplicamini*.[64] Both they themselves and their servants brought these children up in the fear of the Lord. The children had distinguished godparents: the holy Abbot Richarius, the holy Bishop Amand and Queen Nanthild. In this part of the story, the contours of a spiritual family are already becoming apparent. Amand and Richarius will reappear on the family stage several times.

One day Adalbald set off on a journey, on political business. Rictrude accompanied him for some distance, but returned home at his orders, saddened by sinister premonitions. Adalbald was ambushed and killed. Rictrude was overcome with grief, which was multiplied by the mourning of her children and domestics. When the time for mourning had passed, she finally turned to friends who shared her love for Christ (*philochristis sibi familiaribus*), including Amand. Amand comforted her, not by disparaging her marriage in retrospect, but by using texts from the Apostle Paul to point out to her the possibility of a positive future: after the death of her husband, a married woman can remarry, but it is better to remain unmarried (I Cor. 7:39–40). Texts about renunciation, ("If any man would come after me, let him deny himself and take up his cross and follow me" (Mt. 16:24), and "So whoever of you does not renounce all that he has cannot be my disciple" (Lk. 14:33) lose their usual inexorability here: instead, they constitute a sweet gospel (*dulcem et amplectendam Christicolis evangelicam vocem*).[65] As we shall see, in this case renunciation did not entail giving up the ties of motherhood.

Rictrude, widowed by Adalbald (*Adalbaldi relicta*) but loving God and loved by God (*Dei dilectrix et a Deo dilecta*), was threatened in her intentions by the king himself, who wanted to marry her to one of his optimates.[66] When he was unable to persuade her by other means, he tried threats. However, she managed to achieve her goal by a clever ruse: after asking Amand's advice, she pretended to have given up her plan not to remarry and invited the king and noblemen to a banquet. When all had eaten and drunk their fill, she carried out her plan. She asked the king's permission to do what she liked in her own home, and the king, thinking she was going to propose a toast to them all, granted her permission. However, she covered her head with a veil which had already been blessed by Amand. The king left her house in a rage, but she had faith in God; she divided all her possessions, and she who had formerly—in her married state—borne thirtyfold fruit, now, as a widow, bore sixtyfold fruit. She had become Mary instead of Martha. When she changed the "disposition of her mind" (*habitus mentis*), she also changed her outward clothing (*habitus corporis*). She renounced the fine garments she had worn during her marriage. Then, after all, she had been anxious about worldly affairs, how to please her husband (I Cor. 7:34). Now she put aside the cares of the world, so that as a widow (*vidua*) she was divided (*divisa*) from her husband, but not divided in her mind (*non divisa animo*); on the contrary, her spirit was now focused only on the affairs of the Lord.[67] In this story there is an echo of the ideal of simplicity (*simplicitas*) which was so predominant in the early Christian era.[68] And "in order to overcome the delights which her body had tasted and the insinuations of the devil"—this is practically the only allusion to the physical side of her marriage—she practiced asceticism, "so that in spite of her fragile body, she might have the strength to overcome physical desires."[69] After a reconciliation with the king, she withdrew into the convent of Marchienne, in order to gain victory in a spiritual battle.

She offered not only herself as a living sacrifice, but also her daughters, "the first fruits of the earth, that is of her womb," so that they, "unblemished in body and soul, could preserve their virginity forever and follow the Lamb, son of the Virgin Mother, wherever he might go. They would be able to sing the new song, which others could hear, but which could be sung only by virgins," a reference to the hundred and forty-four thousand chosen who accompany the Lamb of the Apocalypse (Rev. 14:4).[70]

Rictrude withdrew into Marchienne. She betrothed all three of her daughters to one man, Christ, so that the song which she herself could not sing could be played on the cithers of her daughters. Just as Waldetrude shared in the inheritance of her sister, the *Sponsa Christi*, Rictrude shared in the virgins' song through her daughters. In the course of her spiritual struggle, she in turn taught her daughters by her example how to live. The apocalyptically musical context of her daughters' virginity and their betrothal to Christ suggests a wedding procession, reminding us of the story about Waldetrude's sister and daughters. Hucbald continues with an appeal to his readers to follow the example of Rictrude's daughters, in which reminiscences of Lot's wife and of the wise and foolish virgins intensify the suggestion of an insistent procession: "Make haste, run, come quickly and remember Lot's wife, don't look back. Flee from stinking lechery, trample on carnal passions." He himself says that he is quoting Augustine's words: "Gird up your loins and light your lamps and wait for the Lord to come to the wedding. You will bring to the wedding of the Lamb a new melody which you will play on your cithers as no one else can."[71]

Within the convent community it was possible for Rictrude to give vent to her maternal feelings. This is illustrated by the story about the death of her youngest daughter, Adalsendis,[72] who died at Christmas, the celebration of Christ's coming—Christ, the "remedy for death." Rictrude was trapped between two emotions: joy at the feast of Christmas and grief at the death of her daughter, for whom the human condition itself forced her to mourn. However, with manly strength of mind she overcame her womanly emotions and celebrated Christmas, the birth of the Lord. But this did not mean that she had to suppress her grief permanently: she found an opportunity to mourn when the day of remembrance for the Massacre of the Innocents of Bethlehem and the sorrow of their mothers arrived. After Mass, in which God and the holy martyrs were venerated, she summoned the sisters and said: "[T]he occasion now permits us to follow the example of the *dominae* whose weeping and lamentations are heard today and to weep for my innocent little girl, for she too has been torn away from us prematurely."[73] She found a secluded place where she could give vent to her grief. The *naturae conditio* which compels mourning is placed in a wider, monastic context and is even integrated into the history of redemption, rather than detracting from it. Within this context, Rictrude is able not only to reconcile her personal grief with her monastic commitment, but to make it part of it and to ritualize it. Even more clearly than in the case of the sisterly affection between Waldetrude and Aldegund, in Rictrude's case biological ties function as a substratum rather than as an obstacle.

The fact that control of the emotions is regarded as masculine is in itself not proof of a misogynous attitude. One may find it regrettable that weakness was described as feminine, but we must not forget that both aspects were ascribed to both men and women. Rictrude's self-control is not presented as a triumph over her sex. Apparently characteristics categorized as masculine and feminine are complementary, and as such can be present in both men and women. The same observation can also be applied to the earlier description of the way Rictrude carried out her plan to enter the convent, against the wishes of the king, "not hesitantly but firmly, not coolly but warmly, not sluggishly but wisely, not womanlike but manlike."[74] The parallelism of these pairs of concepts does not imply an identification of the woman Rictrude with hesitation, sluggishness and coolness.

In the story about a visit by Richarius, the godfather of Rictrude's son Maurontus, (maternal) feelings are also given free rein.[75] Richarius came on a visit, both for the sake of holiness and friendship (*tam pro sanctitate quam pro familiaritate*): spiritual intimacy shines through in their venerable conversations (*sacra colloquia*). A touching scene provides the background for emotional reactions and for a miracle, both of which are presented with cinematographic precision. Richarius was about to leave, and had already mounted his horse; Rictrude, the *Dei famula*, walked along with him a little way, out of love, carrying Maurontus, her natural and Richarius's spiritual son, in her arms. Richarius picked the child up, in order to kiss him or to bless him. But the horse bolted: "[A] double fear seized both of them, one and the same fear was felt by the priest and the mother." The priest feared both for himself and for the boy, the mother for the priest and for her son. Faced by death, almost lifeless herself, she turned her face away, so as not to see both of them wretchedly destroyed; her whole household joined in the panic and grief. The servant of God held on to the little boy and prayed; the child landed on the ground unhurt and the horse came to a standstill. The mother took the child into her arms again, laughing; great sadness was turned into great joy.[76] This event must be attributed to the merits of both, concludes Hucbald, whereas Alcuin, in his *Vita Richarii*, attributes the miracle solely to Richarius. Richarius decided that the moral of the story was that he should no longer ride a horse, but a donkey.[77] The story illustrates, in Hucbald's version even more than in Alcuin's version, the affinity within a spiritual *familia*, and is reminiscent of the visits the sisters Waldetrude and Aldegund paid each other.

When her son, at Amand's suggestion, opted against married life, Rictrude had reservations. She was afraid his decision would only lead to a later outburst of lasciviousness, "as so often happens with young people." She asked Amand to help her as he had done before, and he "soothed her with soft medicines and restored her former cheerfulness."[78]

This was not the last family drama. After the death of Adalbald's grandmother Gertrude, the abbess of the convent of Hamay where Rictrude's daughter Eusebia was being brought up, Rictrude wanted to bring the twelve-year-old Eusebia to Marchienne.[79] A conflict arose between parental rights to obedience and claims to wisdom on the one hand and, on the other, the spiritual liberty of the daughter, who wanted to live a stricter life than her mother thought fitting for a twelve-year-old. Eusebia did not want to go to Marchienne. After a royal command had been issued, she finally came, with the relics of her great-grandmother, like a medieval version of Rebeca in

A Hundred Years of Solitude. Rictrude gave Eusebia instructions, but was unable to turn her daughter's mind from her love of the place she regarded as her bridal home. The girl returned to Hamay secretly at night, leaving her shoes beside her bed so that no one would notice her absence. When her mother found out, she tried to admonish her, knowing that she could hold on to her body, but not her mind. When nothing seemed to help, even the words of other friends, she consulted with her son and decided to try physical punishment. When the bishops, abbots, and noblemen who were summoned saw that it was impossible to dissuade Eusebia, the only thing they could think of was to advise the mother to acquiesce to her daughter's wishes. Eusebia returned to the place she loved, again with her great-grandmother's relics. There, while still in her adolescence, she was "called away to the chamber of the heavenly bridegroom."[80]

Hucbald anticipates possible questions from persons who "raise their mouths up to heaven" (Vulgate Ps. 72:9) and "do not hesitate to malign those who are already reigning with God in heaven, as to what sort of saintliness this can be, in which a mother prevents her daughter from serving God, a brother whips his sister and a daughter refuses to obey her mother."[81] But in Hucbald's justification of Rictrude's mistake, her motherhood does not enter the discussion. Rictrude was concerned because of her daughter's tender years, knowing that there is a time for everything. She preferred to keep Eusebia with her, in order to lead her to perfection by admonitions and her own good example. Eusebia, betrothed to the heavenly King, did not spurn or despise her mother, but was unwilling to show love for anyone else, even her mother, because she did not want to be separated from her love of God. There is a hiatus here in the biological tie as substratum of spiritual kinship, or rather, it seems to work only in one direction. When Maurontus punished her he was also acting from love for his younger sister. It is a matter of human and therefore fallible judgment, says Hucbald: Rictrude and Maurontus were not yet aware of the divine grace present in Eusebia. Their deeds "sprang from the root of love, as Truth itself witnesses: if your eye is single, your whole body will be full of light" (Mt. 6:22).[82]

Although the limitations attached to Rictrude's sanctity are not denied—she herself cannot sing the bridal hymn, she can gain only a sixtyfold reward, she makes mistakes through *humano judicio*—the portrait presented is that of a woman who continues to practice motherhood. The *vita* does not create the impression that she is a saint *in spite of* her motherhood, let alone that her motherhood has to be suppressed; on the contrary, her exemplary behavior as a mother—even if her judgment sometimes fails—is of overriding importance. Motherhood takes its place as a natural relationship alongside of spiritual *familiaritas* or is integrated into it. Family structures remain intact and are even expanded in a certain sense. Rictrude is surrounded by a spiritual *familia*, which includes men like Richarius and Amand, who give her counsel and support.

At the same time it must be said that Rictrude scarcely acts as a *spiritual* mother, neither for her convent sisters, nor for her children. The role of spiritual counsellor or father is reserved for *familiares* like Amand and Richarius.

Considering the emphasis on virginity, the fact that motherhood usually does not play an important role in the *vitae* is perhaps less surprising than the space given to Rictrude's motherhood. However, this was not unique. In the German empire, for instance, noblewomen and queens were venerated as saints, and the dynastic element was predominant. There was plenty of scope for conjugal love—provided it complied with Church ideals of marital chastity and continence—and also for motherhood.[83] However, whether we should regard the *Vita Rictrudis* as part of a trend towards a more positive view of marriage and motherhood, and towards the spiritualization of virginity, as Corbet does,[84] is open to question. Corbet himself observes that this trend reached its peak around 1000 and then stagnated, to be continued only in *vitae* such as that of Ida of Boulogne.[85] Perhaps there were merely co-existent alternative views rather than a simple linear development towards more appreciation of motherhood as a component of sanctity.

"I Am Already Betrothed to Another Man"

Only a virgin could be truly and completely a *Sponsa Christi*, as we saw in the stories about Waldetrude and Rictrude. It was this unconditional bridal role which was the goal, at any cost, of Maxellendis, a seventh-century girl who was no less resolute than Rictrude's daughter Eusebia. In her *vita*—again from the ninth century—this bridal ideal is set in an extremely harsh light. Family interests and even age-old traditions are forced to make way for the aspirations of the future saint.

As soon as Maxellendis reached the age of reason, the author tells us, she made a total commitment to Christ, dedicating herself to be his bride forever.[86] She devoted herself to churchgoing, prayer and almsgiving, did not behave like a *domina* among her servants, did not wear fine clothes and jewelry. Love vanquished all her earthly desires and all carnal temptations; just as fire is quenched by water, in her all these things were quenched by her love of Christ. She was well-spoken, humble and modest, and avoided the company of men, especially young men.

Her behavior represented an ideal which was of course valid not only for future saints, but also for young girls in general. This is shown by the approbation which, according to the author, she gained by these qualities, which together with her constancy, attracted many suitors. One of these, a certain Harduin, was so insistent that her father could not refuse him and according to Germanic custom, he promised him his daughter. Maxellendis was much grieved by this, and decided she would rather die than accept marriage to an earthly man and its physical consequences. Just as in the *Lives* of Aldegund, the most important point seems to be the desire to keep her body undefiled, *incontaminatum*, for Christ. Her father pressed the suitor's case—he was handsome, pleasant and rich—and her mother urged her to do what so many women do: both strive to serve God, to whom she had dedicated herself, and also have a legitimate marriage according to the custom of all the women of the land. Maxellendis asked for one night's respite, after which she would reveal the secret of her heart. Her parents agreed to this, thinking they would achieve their goal by kindness. However, Maxellendis did not need to think about her decision; she merely needed time for prayer, in order to find the right way to make it known, and to "find a way to escape from the snares of her foes." She drew strength from the text, "[H]e who loves mother or father more than me is not worthy of me" (Mt. 10:37).[87] After her nocturnal deliberations, at dawn she hastened to meet her parents. Her determination did not prevent her from observing form. The *vita* subtly describes how she waited for them to say something first, before giving her answer. Her father asked what she had decided. Again, she explained that from her childhood she had dedicated herself to God. The combination her mother had suggested—serving God and also being married—was out of the question for her. "That I shall certainly not do," she said. "I have nothing against marriage, and I would not have the temerity to condemn it, for it is good for those who want both things." In answer to her father's objections, she claimed the right to make her own decision: "I am entitled to choose the bridegroom I want." The betrothal took place nevertheless; the father was afraid of the possible consequences of breaking his promise to Harduin. Maxellendis thought this was unlawful, because she was already betrothed to Another (*subarrata sum ab alio viro*)[88]—and she was backed by the views of the Church, which required the consent of both partners. Besides, a dedication to Christ was regarded as an indissoluble tie. Maxellendis's constancy had not been so highly praised without good reason: she declared that her betrothed would never gain her consent, even if he were to pierce her with his sword—an allusion to what was eventually going to happen. But first she devoted herself even more fervently to prayer, fasting and works of charity, so that her choice might be quite clear. She prayed that her body be kept intact by the Lord, just as her soul was kept free from every impurity by the Holy Ghost.

One day Maxellendis's parents went to a banquet. Maxellendis stayed at home: she avoided such occasions because of the lewd songs and coarse bantering she might hear, for "while she was trying to devote herself even more fervently to prayer, she did not want indecent words to intrude into her memory and burden her mind." Apparently Harduin knew she was at home alone, as he came with his retinue to fetch her. In vain she tried to hide, helped by her nurse, who told the intruders that Maxellendis had gone with her parents to the banquet. They took no notice of this, but stormed into the house and searched it, in vain it seemed at first. When they were about to leave, one of them thought of looking in a corner under a pile of clothes—and there they found Maxellendis. She wrestled herself free manfully (*viriliter*), telling her persecutors that she would rejoice in the heavenly bridal chamber with her companions. "I am not afraid, for my bridegroom Christ has said: do not fear those who kill the body but cannot kill the soul." In a rage, Harduin killed her. As soon as he saw her blood flowing to the ground, he was struck blind. The others were appalled at what they had done, and scattered. They were too frightened to speak to each other, and justly pierced by God's judgment, they went home in confusion.[89]

The confusion and dispersion of the villains contrasts with the unanimity of the priests, faithful and relatives who gathered at Maxellendis's funeral. If Maxellendis had broken with family traditions during her life, through her death she succeeded in consolidating communal ties. Miracles took place, proving that Maxellendis's martyrdom had not been in vain. Under divine orders Vindician, the Bishop of Cambrai, had her bones translated. The conciliatory power of the saint even extended to the chief villain: one of the miracles which took place during the translation was the healing and conversion of Harduin. His cruelty was changed into devotion: according to the later version he thanked the virgin *intimo affectu*.[90]

The *Vita* illustrates the conflict between traditional Germanic views on marriage and the Church view, which apart from its sexual morality—which in a twentieth-century perspective seems oppressive for both sexes—definitely signalled an improvement for women, because it required their consent. The violence that men sometimes used to get what they wanted was certainly one of the factors that caused some young women to choose the convent.

This story also shows that it is not marriage and motherhood in themselves which are reprehensible—as Maxellendis herself says in so many words—but the defilement of the body that inevitably accompanies them. For Maxellendis, bodily integrity was all-important and although it is presented as an exterior quality, corresponding to her inner purity, eventually it seems to grow into an absolute *sine qua non*. In the eleventh-century version the passage in which Maxellendis hides from Harduin contains some interesting comments on this subject.[91] First the author points out that she was suddenly struck by terror, as young girls often are because of their weakness (*imbecillitas*), but that she did not hide because she shrank from the suffering she would have to endure; she had long expected that and was ready for it. What she feared was losing her chastity (*pudicitia*) to Harduin's incestuous violence (incestuous because Maxellendis had already dedicated herself to God). But why, the author asks himself? For if the spirit does not consent, and the flesh does not experience pleasure, the *claustra* of virginity can never be broken by violence.[92] This precursor of an ethical standpoint which was to gain in strength throughout the twelfth century—i.e., that sin can be committed only by consent[93]—seems hardly to fit into this *vita*: it is probably an indication that the eleventh-century writer did not consider it necessary for everyone to go as far as Maxellendis.

Conclusion

In the Carolingian era, virginity continued to be the most important road to saintliness, as we see again in the *Vita Maxellendis*. Moreover, this was just as true for men as for women, at that time and long after. Both nuns *and* monks, for whose edification the *vitae* were originally written,[94] were encouraged to emulate the holy virgins portrayed to them: as we saw, Hucbald, after describing Rictrude's daughters' entrance into religious life, appeals to his readers to follow them and to hurry to the heavenly wedding: *properate, currite, festinate*. He quotes Augustine's exhortations to the virgins: follow Christ, the Lamb, himself a virgin.[95] In his prologue, the author of the *Vita Maxellendis* urges his brothers to follow the example of the holy saints of the past, and like the crowd which prepared the way for Christ with palm branches, to prepare a way for the Lord in their hearts, just as this virgin had prepared herself, so that when devil came, he found no access, and was forced to retreat in humiliation, defeated by a member of the weaker sex.[96] Equal standards regarding the ideal of virginity were in fact not limited to saints: Jonas of Orleans points out to his male readers that if a man wishes to marry a virgin, he should remain a virgin himself.[97] Sometimes male saints too had to fight for their virginity; sometimes without success, as in the case of Vincent, Waldetrude's husband. If they fulfilled the requirement of virginity, or—as in Vincent's case—their marriage was annulled after mutual consent, they could become bishops or abbots, practice typically monastic virtues or excel in spiritual leadership.[98]

What distinguishes the female saint in the *vitae* examined in this study is mainly the idea that the saintly woman is a *Sponsa Christi*, sometimes through her sister or daughters. The connotations this image had in the patristic era—i.e., fruit bearing and motherhood—have almost disappeared. The imagery of the bride of Christ and of Christ himself as bridegroom is extremely hieratic. It supports the familiar characterization of the Carolingian era as a "*civilisation de liturgie.*"[99]

However, this austerity, which is most evident in relationships with the divine, is at the same time embedded in an earthly *familiaritas*. Family structures, whether based on biological ties or not, are often an important component of religious life. The bridal procession sets off; although the solemnity of the destination is never forgotten, there is plenty of time on the way for *dulcia colloquia*. Just as an earthly wedding did not touch only one man and one woman but also their families, betrothal to Christ was not an exclusive affair. In spite of the many texts quoted about renunciation of all earthly ties, these ties very often seem to play an important role. It is as though ordinary family relationships were incorporated into the marriage to Christ, rather than being annulled. Here we see none of the uncompromising renunciation of Columbanus, who, when his mother tried to stop him by lying down on the ground in front of the threshold, jumped over her, as the Church Father Jerome had recommended.[100] Family ties may be transformed through spiritualization, but they remain present as a substratum, underlying both monastic maternal mourning and also sweet conversations, *dulcia verba*, whether these are between two sisters or between a biological mother and a spiritual father. Marriage and motherhood of saints in this period have to be seen within this wider—and sometimes paradoxical—context. Waldetrude's *Life* is ambiguous to a certain extent, the *Vita Maxellendis* is a strong plea for the ideal of virginity but nevertheless contains an explicit defense of marriage, and in the *Vita Rictrudis* there is complete recognition of motherhood taking its place in the midst of spiritual ties. Within the spiritual kinship structures, the distinction between unmarried virgins and mothers remains: the first are the *Sponsae Christi*, but the second can share in that status on the basis of family ties.

NOTES

1. See Friedrich Prinz, "Aspekte frühmittelalterlicher Hagiographie," in *Agiografia nell'Occidente Cristiano, secoli XIII–XV* (Atti dei Convegni Lincei, 48) (Rome, 1980), 21f with a warning as to regarding this all too simply as mere political propaganda. It should rather be seen as the sort of "politische Religiosität" which was

typically medieval but which is so strange to twentieth-century readers.

2. Ibid. For developments in monastic life and their impact on hagiography: Katharina Weber, "Kulturgeschichtliche Probleme der Merowingerzeit im Spiegel frühmittelalterlicher Heiligenleben," *Studien und Mitteilungen zur Geschichte des Benediktinerordens und seiner Zweige,* NF 17 (1930), 347–403; Franticek Graus, *Volk, Herrscher und Heiliger im Reich der Merowinger: Studien zur Hagiographie der Merowingerzeit* (Prague: Czechoslovakian Akademy, 1965).

3. See Suzanne Fonay Wemple, *Women in Frankish Society: Marriage and the Cloister 500–900* (Philadelphia: University of Pennsylvania Press, 1981).

4. For the decline in the power of abbesses see Wemple, *Women in Frankish Society,* 165–174. See also Jane Tibbets Schulenburg, "Strict Active Enclosure and its Effects on the Female Monastic Experience (c. 500–1100)," in *Medieval Religious Women 1: Distant Echoes,* ed. John A. Nichols and Lillian Thomas Shank (Cistercian Studies Series, 71) (Kalamazoo: Cistercian Publications, 1984), 51–86. For a corresponding decline in the number of female saints after about 750, see Jane Tibbets Schulenburg, "Sexism and the Celestial Gynaeceum—from 500 to 1200," *Journal of Medieval History,* 4 (1978), 117–133.

5. For the *vitae* discussed here see L. van der Essen, *Étude critique et littéraire sur les vitae des saints mérovingiens de l'ancienne Belgique* (Louvain-Paris, 1907); Yvonne Scherf, "Zij was mooi en goed en zij hield van Christus: Onderzoek naar de mogelijkheden van heiligenlevens als bron voor de geschiedenis van vrouwen van de zesde tot de twaalfde eeuw," in *Vrouw, familie en macht: Bronnen over vrouwen in de Middeleeuwen,* ed. M. Mostert et al. (Hilversum: Verloren, 1990), 259–278. For an exhaustive study of Carolingian hagiography about women, see Katrien Heene, *Vrouw, huwelijk, moederschap: norm en beeld in de belerende literatuur van het Karolingische Frankenrijk* (thesis Faculty of Letters and Philosophy Ghent: Universiteit Gent, 1992–1993); the English version: *Women and Women's Business: the Attitude towards Marriage, Motherhood and Women in Carolingian Edifying Writings* will be published in 1995. For a general discussion of ideals of sanctity in the ninth and tenth century see also Joseph-Claude Poulin, *L'Idéal de sainteté dans l'Aquitaine carolingienne d'après les sources hagiographiques (750–950)* (Québec, 1975); L. Zoepf, *Das Heiligenleben im 10. Jahrhundert* (Beiträge zur Untersuchung des Mittelalters und der Renaissance, 1) (Leipzig-Berlin, 1908).

6. *Vita Waldedrudis* (BHL 8776), edited in *Analectes pour servir à l'histoire ecclésiastique de la Belgique,* 4 (1867), 218–231; trans. in *Sainted Women of the Dark Ages,* ed. and trans. Jo Ann McNamara et al. (Durham [etc.]: Duke University Press, 1992), 254–263. On this cycle as a whole see Henri Platelle, "Elle était belle et bonne; elle aimait le Christ: Que savons-nous au juste de Sainte Waudru?" *Mélanges de science religieuse,* 64 (1987), 147–169; Van der Essen, *Étude critique,* 219–244.

7. *Vita Waldedrudis,* ed. *Analectes* 4, 220.

8. *Vita Vincentii* (BHL 8672–73), edited in *Analecta Bollandiana (AB),* 12 (1893), 422–440. On this *Vita* see J. Nazet, "La transformation d'abbayes en chapitres à la fin de l'époque carolingienne: le cas de Saint-Vincent de Soignies," *Revue du Nord,* 49 (1967), 257–280. For the ties between Waldetrude and Vincent in their biographies see G. Bavay, "Sainte Waudru: de l'hagiographie montoise à l'hagiographie sonégienne: Trace cultuelle et genèse hagiographique," in *Mélanges offerts à Christiane Piérard: Études d'histoire montoise et hainuyère,* in *Annales du cercle archéologique de Mons,* 74 (1990), 41–70.

9. *Vita Waldedrudis,* ed. *Analectes* 4, 221.

10. Ibid., 222, 223 resp.

11. Ibid., 224.

12. Ibid., 226.

13. Ibid., 227.

14. Ibid., 228.

15. Ibid., 228, n. 1.

16. Ibid., 231.

17. These rules were mainly about periods of sexual abstinence, in connection with the demands of cultic purity, see Heene, *Vrouw, huwelijk, moederschap*; Jean-Louis Flandrin, *Un temps pour embrasser: Aux origines de la morale sexuelle occidentale (VIe–XIe siècle)* (Paris: Éditions du Seuil, 1983).

18. Cf. Alcuinus, *De Virtutibus et Vitiis Liber*, 36, in Migne, *Patrologia Latina*, vol. 101, 638: "Nec te laici habitus vel conversationis saecularis terreat qualitas, quasi in eo habitu vitae coelestis januas intrare non valeas. Igitur sicut omnibus aequaliter regni Dei praedicata est beatitudo, ita omni sexui, aetati, et personae aequaliter secundum meritorum dignitatem regni Dei patet introitus."

19. Jonas of Orleans, *De Institutione Laicali*, especially book 2, in Migne, *Patrologia Latina*, vol. 106, 167–234; on Jonas' work, see P.A. Maccioni, "'It is Allowed, neither to Husband nor Wife . . . ' The Ideas of Jonas of Orleans on Marriage," in *Vrouw, familie en macht*, ed. Mostert et al., 99–125. For Carolingian views on marriage see also Pierre Toubert, "La théorie du mariage chez les moralistes carolingiens," in *Il matrimonio nella società altomedievale* (Settimane di studio del Centro Italiano di Studi sull'Alto Medioevo, 24) (Spoleto, 1977), 233–285. See also Janet L. Nelson, "Les femmes et l'évangélisation au IXe siècle," *Revue du Nord*, 68 (1986), 471–485.

20. See (among others) Henri Platelle, "Le thème de la conversion à travers les oeuvres hagiographiques d'Hucbald de Saint-Amand," *Revue du Nord*, 68 (1986), 511–531, here 520. On the ninth-century debate about predestination see Jean Devisse, *Hincmar archevêque de Reims (845–882)* (Geneva: Droz, 1975), vol. 1, 115–279.

21. *Vita Waldedrudis*, ed. *Analectes* 4, 221.

22. *Vita Vincentii*, 6, ed. *AB* 12, 428: "Casso enim labore exercemur ad operandum, si possessor deerit et ad fruendum." See Comm. praev., 423f: taken from Gregory of Tours on Leobard, *Vitae Patrum*, 20, in *Monumenta Germaniae Historica. Sriptores Rerum Merovingicarum*, vol. 1, 741.

23. *Vita Waldedrudis*, ed. *Analectes* 4, 227.

24. *Aldegondis Vita Prima* (BHL 244), in *Acta Sanctorum (AASS) Belgii*, vol. 4, ed. Josephus Ghesquierus (Brussels, 1786), 315–326. For the possibility that this *Vita* was written by a female author, see Rosamund McKitterick, "Frauen und Schriftlichkeit im frühen Mittelalter," in *Weibliche Lebensgestaltung im frühen Mittelalter*, ed. Hans-Werner Goetz (Cologne [etc.]: Böhlau, 1991), 100. *Aldegondis Vita Secunda* (BHL 245), *Acta Sanctorum (AASS)*, 30 Jan., (3d ed. Brussels, 1863), vol. 3, 651–655. A *Vita Quarta* attributed to Hucbald of Saint-Amand (BHL 247), ibid., 655–662 actually dates from the eleventh century. See L. van der Essen, "Hucbald de Saint-Amand (c. 840–930) et sa place dans le mouvement hagiographique médiéval," *Revue d'Histoire Ecclésiastique*, 19 (1923), 333–355, 522–552, for a correction of the attribution to Hucbald of Saint-Amand (527–531): the *Vita* quotes Rainerus, the author of the *Vita Gisleni*, which was written around 1052. This is a correction of Van der Essen's own attribution of this *Vita* in *Étude critique et littéraire*, 225. On the *Vita Prima* of Aldegund as a document from the beginning of the eighth century, see Anne-Marie Helvetius, "Sainte Aldegonde et les origines du monastère de Maubeuge," *Revue du Nord*, 74 (1992), 221–237, also for a discussion of this dating. For a translation of this *Vita* (including fragments from the ninth-century version) see *Sainted Women of the Dark Ages*, ed. McNamara et al., 237–254.

25. *Aldegondis Vita Quarta*, 8, ed. *AASS* 3, 657.

26. *Aldegondis Vita Secunda*, 3, ed. *AASS* 3, 651.

27. Ibid., 4, 651.

28. *Aldegondis Vita Quarta*, 7–9, ed *AASS* 3, 657f.

29. Ibid., 10–11, 658.

30. Ibid., 12, 658.

31. Cf. additions of the same sort in the *Vita Tertia Gertrudis* (BHL 3494), and in the *Vita* of Gertrude's sister Begga (BHL 1083–1085). For various sorts of nar-

rative, with varying proportions of legendary elements, see also the contribution in this volume by Renée Nip, "Godelieve of Gistel and Ida of Boulogne."

32. See Edouard De Moreau, *Histoire de l'Église en Belgique*, vol. 1 (Brussels, 1945), 138, for the view that Aldegund had her visions written down and that later this book of visions and an older biography were incorporated into the surviving *Vita*. Suzanne Fonay Wemple, "Female Spirituality and Mysticism in Frankish Monasteries: Radegund, Balthild and Aldegund," in *Medieval Religious Women 2: Peaceweavers*, ed. John A. Nichols and Lilian Thomas Shank (Cistercian Studies Series, 72) (Kalamazoo: Cistercian Publications, 1987), 39–53, uses these visions to characterize a certain kind of female spirituality, in which the emphasis is given to "caritas" as the chief virtue instead of the masculine emphasis on "humilitas." For further discussion of this interpretation of Aldegund's piety as mysticism, see below.

33. *Aldegondis Vita Prima*, 5, ed. *AASS Belgii* 4, 317.

34. *Aldegondis Vita Secunda*, 5, ed. *AASS* 3, 652.

35. *Vita Aldetrudis* (BHL 253), *Acta Sanctorum (AASS) Belgii*, vol. 5, 160–164; *Vita Madelbertae* (BHL 5129), ibid., 490–496 (fragmentary edition).

36. *Vita Madelbertae*, 5, ed. *AASS Belgii*, vol. 5, 493. For the influence of the Song of Songs in the Middle Ages, see the recent publication by E. Ann Matter, *The Voice of My Beloved: The Song of Songs in Western Medieval Christianity* (Philadelphia: University of Pennsylvania Press, 1990); Ann W. Astell, *The Song of Songs in the Middle Ages* (Ithaca, N.Y. [etc]: Cornell University Press, 1990).

37. *Vita Aldetrudis*, 12, ed. *AASS Belgii* 5, 162.

38. *Aldegondis Vita Prima*, 6, ed. *AASS Belgii* 4, 317.

39. Ibid., 8, 318.

40. *Aldegondis Vita Secunda*, 12, ed. *AASS* 3, 653.

41. Ibid., 26, 655.

42. *Aldegondis Vita Prima*, 13, ed. *AASS Belgii* 4, 320.

43. *Aldegondis Vita Secunda*, 6, ed. *AASS* 3, 652.

44. Ibid., 11, 653.

45. In Carolingian *Vitae* of contemporary saints the wishes of the saint do not come into conflict with those of the parents, whereas in several revisions of the biographies of Merovingian saints they do. See Heene, *Vrouw, huwelijk, moederschap*, 202.

46. See Giselle de Nie's contribution "Consciousness Fecund through God." in this volume. One of the "strata" of female sanctity in the patristic era is inner fertility. In the *Vitae* of that period, identification of a saint with Mary by means of Gospel texts often culminates in a birth of Christ in the saint.

47. For the bridal concept in the patristic era, cf. the study by De Nie in this volume.

48. *Aldegondis Vita Secunda*, 11, ed. *AASS* 3, 653. On this preoccupation with ritual purity, see Wemple, *Women in Frankish Society*, 143–148. For a possible alternative meaning of bodily integrity, see the study by De Nie in this volume.

49. Ibid., 9, 652: "Nunc ipsa videt sponsum suum diversis fultum apparatibus, nunc in splendore quasi totum illuminantem orbem, aliquando etiam ostendentem illi divitias et gloriam coelestis Jerusalem."

50. *Vita Waldedrudis*, ed. *Analectes* 4, 225–226: "Et primo quidem immisit ei memoriam possessionum, generis nobilitatem, familiae defensationem, amorem rerum praesentium, fluxam seculi gloriam, escae variam delectationem, et reliqua vitae remissioris blandimenta; dehinc virtutis arduum finem, et maximum perveniendi laborem, nec non corporis fragilitatem et aetatis spatia prolixa. His igitur et hujuscemodi temptationibus maximam cogitationum caliginem suscitabat, temptans, si quomodo posset, hanc a sancto proposito avocare."

Vita Antonii, 4, in the Latin translation in Migne, *Patrologia Latina*, vol. 73, 129: "Et primo . . . immittebat ei memoriam possessionum, sororis defensionem, generis nobilitatem, amorem rerum, fluxam saeculi gloriam, escae variam delectationem, et reliqua vitae remissioris blandimenta; postremo virtutis arduum finem, et maximum perveniendi laborem, necnon et corporis fragilitatem suggerebat, et aetatis spatia prolixa: prorsus maximam ei cogitationum caliginem suscitabat, volens eum a recto proposito revocare."

51. *Vita Waldedrudis*, ed. *Analectes* 4, 227.

52. Cf. *Vita Madelbertae*, 9, ed. *AASS Belgii* 5, 494: through obedience, Madelberta desires to return to Paradise, from which the first humans had fallen through pride.

53. *Vita Waldedrudis*, ed. *Analectes* 4, 227.

54. Ibid.: "Liberata namque a temptatione, jure facta est magistra virtutum."

55. *Vita Aldetrudis*, 8, ed. *AASS Belgii* 5, 161.

56. *Vita Madelbertae*, 4, ed. *AASS Belgii* 5, 492.

57. *Aldegondis Vita Prima*, 12, ed. *AASS Belgii* 4, 320.

58. *Aldegondis Vita Secunda*, 8, ed. *AASS* 3, 652.

59. *Vita Madelbertae*, 12, ed. *AASS Belgii* 5, 495.

60. Hucbald, *Vita Rictrudis* (BHL 7242), *Acta Sanctorum*, 12 Maii (3d ed. (Paris-Rome, 1866), vol. 16, 81–88. Translation in *Sainted Women*, ed. McNamara et al., 195–219. For the *Vitae* of Rictrude and her family see Van der Essen, *Étude critique et littéraire*, 260–270. See also next note.

61. On the *Vita Rictrudis* and on Hucbald himself and his other *Vitae*, see also Platelle, "Le thème de la conversion." On the later hagiographical production at Marchienne see Henri Platelle, "La religion populaire entre la Scarpe et la Lys d'après les miracles de Sainte Rictrude de Marchienne (XIIe siècle)," in *Alain de Lille, Gautier de Châtillon, Jakemart de Giélée et leur temps: Actes du colloque de Lille 1978*, ed. Henri Roussel and François Suard (Lille, 1978), 365–402.

62. Hucbald, *Vita Rictrudis*, Prologue, ed. *AASS* 16, 81.

63. Hucbald, *Vita Rictrudis*, 9, ed. *AASS* 16, 82f.

64. Ibid., 10, 83.

65. Ibid., 12, 83.

66. Ibid., 13, 83.

67. Ibid., 15, 84.

68. See De Nie's contribution to this volume "Consciousness Fecund through God."

69. Hucbald, *Vita Rictrudis*, 16, *AASS* 16, 84.

70. Ibid., 17, 84f.

71. Ibid., 18, 85.

72. Ibid., 20–21, 85.

73. Ibid., 21, 85.

74. Ibid., 14, 84.

75. Ibid., 22, 85. This story, here in a different version, was taken from Alcuin's *Vita Richarii*, 9, (BHL 7223), in Migne *Patrologia Latina*, vol. 101, 681–694, here 687f.

76. Hucbald, *Vita Rictrudis*, 22, ed. *AASS* 16, 85.

77. Alcuin, *Vita Richarii*, 9, ed. *PL* 101, 688.

78. Hucbald, *Vita Rictrudis*, 23, ed. *AASS* 16, 86.

79. Ibid., 25–27, 86f.

80. Ibid., 27, 87.

81. Ibid., 28, 87.

82. Ibid., 30, 87.

83. Patrick Corbet, *Les saints ottoniens: Sainteté dynastique, sainteté royale et sainteté féminine autour de l'an Mil* (Beihefte der Francia, 15) (Sigmaringen: Thorbecke, 1986).

84. Corbet, *Les saints ottoniens*, 205f.

85. But see Renée Nip's contribution on "Godelieve of Gistel and Ida of Boulogne" and her critique on Corbet in this volume.

86. *Vita Maxellendis* (BHL 5794), *Acta Sanctorum (AASS) Belgii*, vol. 3, 580–

589. An eleventh-century adaptation, *Vita Maxellendis Secunda* (BHL 5795), in *Catalogus codicum hagiographicorum Biliothecae Regiae Bruxellensis*, vol. 2 (Brussels, 1886–1889), 19–27. On the *Vita* see Van der Essen, *Étude critique et littéraire*, 277–281.

87. *Vita Maxellendis*, 6, ed. AASS Belgii 3, 582.

88. Ibid., 7, 583.

89. Ibid., 12, 584f.

90. *Vita Maxellendis Secunda*, 26, ed. *Catalogus Codicum* 2, 27.

91. Ibid., 18, 24.

92. This line of reasoning recalls Augustine's arguments against suicide, *Sancti Aurelii Augustini De Civitate Dei*, 1.16–20, ed. Bernardus Dombart et al. (Corpus Christianorum Scriptorum Latinorum, 47) (Turnhout: Brepols, 1955), 17–23.

93. See Robert Blomme, *La doctrine du péché dans les écoles théologiques de la première moitié du XIIe siècle* (Louvain [etc.]: Publications de l'Université de Louvain, 1958).

94. See Katrien Heene, "Merovingian and Carolingian hagiography: Continuity or change in public and aims?" *Analecta Bollandiana*, 107 (1989), 415–428.

95. Hucbald, *Vita Rictrudis*, 18, ed. AASS 16, 85.

96. *Vita Maxellendis*, ed. AASS Belgii 3, 581.

97. Jonas of Orleans, *De institutione laicali*, 2.2, in Migne, *Patrologia Latina*, vol. 106, 170ff.

98. For ideals of male saintliness in this period see Poulin, *L'idéal de sainteté*.

99. Etienne Delaruelle, "La Gaule chrétienne à l'époque franque," *Revue d'Histoire de l'Église en France*, 38 (1952), 64–72, quoted by André Vauchez, *La spiritualité du Moyen Age occidental VIIIe–XIIe siècles* (Paris: Presses universitaires de France, 1975), 14. For the liturgical character of the Carolingian period see also Arnold Angenendt, *Das Frühmittelalter: Die abendländische Christenheit von 400 bis 900* (Stuttgart [etc.]: Kohlhammer, 1990), esp. 327–348.

100. Jonas of Bobbio, *Vita Columbani Discipulorumque eius* (BHL 1898), *Monumenta Germaniae Historica. Scriptores Rerum Merovingicarum*, vol. 4, 61–152, quotation on 69, taken from Jerome's Letter to Heliodorus, in Migne, *Patrologia Latina*, vol. 22, 348. For Jerome's severity, see also De Nie's study in this volume.

6. GODELIEVE OF GISTEL AND IDA OF BOULOGNE

Renée Nip

This contribution is about two women from the eleventh century, who spent most of their lives in the Flemish coastal area. Godelieve of Gistel was born near Boulogne; when she married, she moved north to Gistel. Ida of Boulogne, daughter of the Duke of Lorraine, married Eustace II who was Count of Boulogne. Both women were to become saints: Godelieve (c. 1052–1070) as a result of her short and tragic life, and Ida (c. 1040–1113) more as a result of her long and successful one. To this day, Godelieve of Gistel is worshipped in Belgium, with the Abbey of Saint Godelieve in Gistel as its center. Ida of Boulogne was never venerated to such an extent; her worship remained centred around the priory of Waast, where she found her last resting place. As the mother of the two most famous leaders of the first crusade and the first Christian rulers of Jerusalem (Godfrey of Bouillon and Baldwin of Boulogne) she was, however, well-known throughout the Middle Ages. In his study of medieval marriage, the French historian Duby presents the marriages of the two women as opposites, that is to say as examples of a good and a bad eleventh-century marriage.[1] It is well worthwhile elaborating on this comparison of two women who led such different lives, and looking for answers to the kinds of questions which are presented in this collection of studies.

GODELIEVE OF GISTEL

On July 30, 1084, about fourteen years after she died, the remains of Godelieve of Gistel were taken from her grave and ceremoniously interred in the church at Gistel, in the coastal area of Flanders.[2] This ceremony was performed by Radbod, Bishop of Noyon and Tournai, the diocese to which Gistel belonged. With this elevation and translation, he granted her ecclesiastical recognition of her sainthood. Until the Pope took over the right of canonization in the thirteenth century, this was common procedure with a canonization. The presence of Gertrude of Saxony, Countess of Flanders, and many noblemen and prelates added lustre to the occasion.

Shortly before these events took place, Drogo, a monk from Saint Winocsbergen, had chronicled her life.[3] In the prologue he explains that he was urged to do so by many worshippers, who hoped that this would help to secure Godelieve's canonization. An experienced hagiographer—author of sainted King Oswald's *Vita*, a book of the miracles of Saint Winnoc and an account of the translation of Saint Lewinna[4]—he illuminated the path that led to her canonization. To the bishop, Drogo's *Life* served as evidence for her election. Most important for her canonization were the miracles she had performed, and in particular the miracles she performed posthumously. As with all hagiographies, this account of a saint's life also served to instruct the faithful.

Drogo had not known Godelieve personally; he used eyewitness accounts from people who had survived her.[5] He could not wish for better sources. The story still rings with the voices of neighbors and others who did know her personally, even though the monk had adapted it to the hagiographic tradition. We can hear their admiration for this remarkable woman and their indignation at the suffering endured by her.

Our knowledge of Godelieve is entirely based on hagiographical texts. In the thirteenth century, the original *Life* was adapted.[6] We also have a comprehensive account of Godelieve's life from the fourteenth century.[7] It is generally believed that she actually did exist, because her father's name, Heinfridus, can be found in the records of the counts of Boulogne.[8] The portrayal of Godelieve in this contribution, unless specified otherwise, is based exclusively on the earliest version of the *Vita*. Her life story almost reads like a fairy tale.

Cinderella

Once upon a time, there was a girl named Godelieve. Her name means "God's favorite" in Dutch. She was of noble birth, and she lived near Boulogne. She was sweet and obedient and always cheerful; she was a source of joy to her parents. She was also very beautiful, with silky raven hair and a lily-white skin. Small wonder that many a young man asked her parents for her hand in marriage. In the end they chose Bertolf, a knight from Gistel, to become her husband, because he was the most powerful and richest of them all.

However, this Bertolf had a wicked and jealous mother, who had a great influence on him. When she heard about her son's wedding plans, she became furious. "Why do you insist on marrying this black crow from the

Figure 6.1. Devotional statue of Godelieve in the Godelieve Abbey Church (Godelieve Abbey, Ghistel)

farthest corners of the country? Don't we have enough pretty girls right here? Why did you only ask your father for advice, and why didn't you let me choose your bride?" She made his life so miserable that he came very much to regret his decision.

When the wedding day came, Godelieve and her retinue came to Gistel and three days of festivities followed, which was customary in those days. But the bridegroom was not there. He was seen with his friends in all sorts of unlikely places, but not at the wedding, where his mother in his place put on a great display of cordiality. When the feast came to an end, Bertolf took his young bride to their new home, but he himself stayed at his father's house. He simply abandoned her, and what is more, he ordered his servants not to look after her. She was given less and less to eat and to drink, only a morsel of bread and some water. Godelieve endured all this with cheer and sought comfort in God. What she had, she shared with those who had even less. She did not complain, and she reproached those who pitied her or spoke ill of her husband.

But one day she had clearly endured enough, and she ran away, back to her parents. Her father felt sorry for her and went to the count of Flanders in order to ask him to call Bertolf to order. But the count said that there was nothing he could do, because this was a matter for the bishop. Godelieve's father then went to the bishop. He ordained that Godelieve should return to Gistel. He reprimanded Bertolf and ordered him to treat his wife as a good husband should.

The result was that Bertolf hated his wife more than ever. He said to his friends: "My mother does not speak to me any more and that is all because of *her*. I wish I had never started it. How will I get rid of this woman?" Blinded by hatred, he devised a fiendish plan. His servants, Lantbert and Hacca, were to kill her. Then he would be rid of her once and for all. But it had to be done in secret, of course. One day he went to Godelieve and said to her in his sweetest voice: "Come and sit with me awhile, my love. Do not be afraid. I know I have been unkind to you. It matters not for what reason. I want everything to be different from now on, and I want us to find pleasure in our marriage. I know a woman who can solve our problems. If you wish, Lantbert and Hacca can take you to her, and if you do exactly as she says, then everything will be fine." Godelieve hesitated, but after a while she said: "If there is no witchcraft in it, I will meet her." They agreed that the servants would take her to this woman. Bertolf jumped on his horse and headed for Bruges.

That night, when everybody was fast asleep, Lantbert and Hacca came to Godelieve's bed and woke her up. "Come quickly," they said, "This woman is waiting for you outside and we've got to do it now, before dawn, otherwise it will not work." They did not even give her time to put something on over her nightgown. Once outside, they strangled her with a rope and just to be sure, they tossed her dead body into the well. Then they dragged her out of the well, put her back to bed and arranged the covers so that it looked as if she were asleep. She was not found until well into the afternoon and she did not appear to be wounded (apart from a couple of red streaks across her neck) so that some people thought she had died of natural causes. But others knew better. There were signs which indicated that God had made her a saint. At the exact spot where she had been murdered, the earth had changed to a priceless white marble, and the water in the well cured everyone who drank from it.

This story does not end as we would expect a fairy tale to end. The girl is not saved, and the villains are not brought to justice. And yet, any Christian can see that the story has a happy ending. Godelieve is rewarded, because she is saved from this valley of tears and she is given a place in the Kingdom of God.

In a world in which most people were illiterate (which was certainly the case in the high Middle Ages) stories were passed on from one generation to the next by oral tradition; this was the only way in which knowledge was transferred. Oral tradition ensured that standards and values were handed down and that role models were explained. Folk tales, fairy tales and legends, myths and sagas, it is difficult to distinguish between the various kinds of tales. They often represent conflicts between ideals and day-to-day practice, and in this way they offer an escape from harsh reality. Justice always prevails in these stories: he that mischief hatches mischief catches. What they have in common is that they all offer an account of reality which may serve as an example, or which may offer hope and comfort through recognition. They reflect a body of ideas which has taken shape under the many influences of a society in which the majority of the population has had no education whatsoever.[9] In the Middle Ages, religion and the church were interwoven with daily life in a way that is unknown to us now.

In our western society, religion is one of the many aspects of our lives which is more important to some than to others. You can be a good person and never run into trouble with any kind of authority, without being religious. In the Middle Ages this was unthinkable; in those days, religion provided all the answers to Christians. You only needed to know what God expected from man and what His divine intentions were. It was the task of the clergy, the men of letters, to find the right answers. In doing so, they tried to organize society in accordance with God's wishes wherever possible. To this end, theorists formulated ideas which were founded on the Bible. Monks and priests propagated these ideas in their sermons, and as a matter of course they used the means which were familiar to them as well as to their audiences. It comes as no great surprise that the lives of saints, which have the same function as the folk tales mentioned above, sometimes closely resemble such stories. This is particularly true for a life story such as that of Godelieve, which finds its origins in a popular legend. Such a resemblance will be less obvious as the texts become more highly cultivated, and the saint evolves into a stereotype. Naturally, these stories may change in form and content, depending on the time and circumstances in which they are used. In some cases the themes are no longer understood, or lose their function and are replaced by others.

Godelieve's life story can be interpreted as a Christian version of the fairy tale of Cinderella. According to scholars such as Baring and Cashford, this tale as we know it is based on ancient myths, with common themes such as transformation, banishment of the soul to darkness and the process which ends in her return to divine light.[10] In Christian terms, this means that the human soul is expelled from paradise after the Fall of Eve, and that she has to undergo the ordeals to which she is submitted without protest in order to return through death to the heavenly light.

Godelieve is also associated with the goddess Nehalennia, who was worshipped in the Schelde-region in pre-Christian times as the guardian of farmers, sailors and hunters. The elements in Godelieve's biography which are mentioned in evidence of this, however, are first encountered in a fourteenth-century *Life*.[11] One might argue that Drogo deliberately omitted these "heathen" elements, and that his account is nothing more than an expurgated and Christianized version of stories that already existed. It seems more likely to me that these pre-Christian elements, which survived in popular culture, became associated over the years with the image of this extremely popular saint.

Furthermore, there is a certain similarity between the life of Godelieve and the life of the holy virgin Pharaildis, or Veerle in the vernacular. According to the eleventh-century *Life* of this saint (the earliest that we know of) Pharaildis was also treated very badly by her husband, who was not very happy with the fact that she tried to keep her virginity by avoiding him and spending the night praying in church.[12] In spite of his brutal attempts to have his way, with God's help she succeeded in her resolve to remain a virgin. The number of people who worshipped her increased rapidly, and in 754, a few years after she died, her remains were, it seems, taken to Saint Bavo's Abbey in Ghent.[13] The Church of Saint Veerle, a tenth-century fortified church in Ghent, is also dedicated to her.[14] Just as Pharaildis is the latinized form of "Vrouw Hilde" (Lady Hilde), one of the Valkyrie (the nightly companions of Wodan), it is possible to identify aspects of German mythology in her cult.[15]

Marriage and Sexuality

What can we learn from the *Vita Godeliph* by the monk Drogo? The text has raised many questions, which in turn are based on one basic question: how was it possible for this woman to become a saint? She was no martyr in the traditional sense, because she did not die a violent death for her faith. She was no queen or noblewoman who had protected or benefitted her Church in some special way. She had not founded monasteries, nor was she an abbess who was a source of inspiration to the faithful because of her exemplary conduct. She was not even a widow who had devoted her life and her children's lives to God, nor was she renowned because she had managed to keep her virginity. She was an ordinary married woman who had a particularly hard life.

Most scholars have looked at her unlucky marriage, and wondered why Bertolf detested his young spouse to the extent that he did and why he only managed to end his marriage by means of a cowardly murder. Some considered the question of her virginity to be essential: had the marriage been consummated or not? Many hypotheses were raised, most of which will not be discussed here.[16] Most authors of these hypotheses based their views on the various versions of her life story, without realizing that these were the products of entirely different ages. The most recent and comprehensive hypothesis was proposed by Duby.[17] His ideas are based on the two earliest versions of the *Vita Godeliph,* on the unjustified assumption that these were written at approximately the same time.

All these hypotheses in themselves are an interesting source for those who wish to study developments in modern scholarship. The medical scientist Elaut, for instance, suggested in 1965 that there was only one possible explanation for Bertolf's hatred.[18] His behavior could only be explained from the fact that the couple were unable to consummate their marriage on their wedding night. For the causes we had to turn to Godelieve, who undoubtedly suffered from vaginismus, as a result of which she was physically incapable of sexual intercourse. Elaut does not consider the possibility that Bertolf was impotent and was therefore unable to fulfil his duties. He does, however, put the blame on rough Bertolf, who undoubtedly scared off his sensitive bride with his crude behavior.

Huyghebaert and Duby also consider crude and boorish behavior of husbands in matters of sex as the prime cause of the failure of marriages during the high Middle Ages.[19] Marriages were arranged in order to continue a family's lineage and, if possible, to add to their power and wealth. The happy couples themselves—least of all the women—had virtually no say in these matters. The bride and groom were sometimes very young; the age difference could also be considerable. These factors were of course not particularly constructive in trying to make a marriage succeed, especially when the couple failed to have children.

In a society in which the wife was submissive to her husband and in effect belonged to him, respect for her as a woman or consideration for her feelings was not to be expected. Whether women were indeed more sensitive than men, as a result of which they might have had to be introduced to the secrets of life with the utmost caution, is far from certain. Men and women were part of one and the same culture and many examples can be found of women who committed excesses to the same extent as men. Furthermore, was it not true that the subordinate position of women was often regarded as justified, because of the licentiousness of their nature? Apparently, women were not particularly timid in matters of sex; ignorance about what they could expect in relations with men is hard to imagine in a world in which privacy was totally unknown.

A rich source of knowledge about life and attitudes towards it in Northern Europe of that age is provided by the autobiography of Abbot Guibert of Nogent (c. 1064—c. 1125).[20] This clergyman held strict views, which fit the so-called Gregorian Reform movement. The existence of sexual desire in women as well as in men is an accomplished fact to him, although he does not think we should be pleased about it. In his eyes, lust was one of the main causes of misery in the world. Guibert praises God because He had helped his mother to keep her chastity in the beginning of her marriage, which was not consummated until years after the wedding. She was harassed by admirers who thought they saw their chance: "[B]ut Thou, O Lord, the builder of inward chastity, didst inspire her with purity stronger than her nature or her youth. Thy grace it was that saved her from burning, though set in the midst of flames."[21] In the end, this marriage also took its course and Guibert's mother performed her duties as was expected of her. The abbot even wondered if a woman who was particularly renowned for her lasciviousness would have behaved more decently if her husband had not been away from home so often in order to fight: "Would she have kept herself in check if he had paid her the marriage debt as often as she desired?"[22]

A passage in the *Vita Godeliph* also indicates that it was considered normal for women to enjoy sex and that Godelieve herself had no objections whatsoever.[23] When people pitied her for her misery and said that the world had nothing good to offer her, and that she had never known the physical pleasures of marriage, she said that she did not care for this earthly, transitory existence. Drogo explains that people pitied her out of ignorance: those who love the world value everything according to worldly standards. Godelieve added that however unhappy she might be now, she would at one time be rewarded. This firm belief gave her the strength to endure her suffering. She was, however, very much prepared to live her married life to the full, and her hagiographer Drogo expected no different.

When Bertolf visits his wife for the last time and tries to gain her confidence with his sweetly voiced deceptions, the physical side of their marriage crops up once more. He says that he is sorry he treated her so roughly, that his presence and sweet words were not enough to comfort her and that he denied her the physical pleasures of their marriage. He does not know what could have got into him; it has to have been an evil spirit, but now he wishes to end all the misery and hatred, to honour her as his wife and to become as one with her in body and soul.[24] It is not clear whether or not Godelieve was denied physical pleasure because her husband did not fulfil his duties, or because his performance was so poor. There is no mention of physical incapabilities on either part. Bertolf appears to blame himself for their problems: he has behaved badly. However, he leaves it to Godelieve to solve them; he asks her to meet a woman who may be able to help her. Does this indicate that he believes the cause of his behavior lies with her?

It must be said that in the Middle Ages, there was nothing unusual about calling on the help of a woman who specialized in solving marital difficulties. For instance, the marriage of the parents of Guibert of Nogent was saved by "a certain old Woman" who managed to remove the "bewitchment by which the bond of natural and lawful intercourse was broken."[25] From the thirteenth century onwards, the Church appointed "wise women" in investigations which were required in case of a request to dissolve a marriage on the grounds of sexual inadequacy.[26] Furthermore, witchcraft was often seen as the cause of sexual inadequacy without obvious physical causes.[27] According to Drogo, Bertolf considers the devil to be the cause of his marital misery. In Drogo's version, Godelieve hesitates a moment before she agrees to call in the help of a woman, who claims that she can relieve their suffering. After all, she might be involved in the practice of some kind of blasphemous witchcraft.[28] This would have indicated that Bertolf was impotent, and that he had made use of the fact that Godelieve (and others) believed that a wise woman could break the spell that caused it. The fact that it was Godelieve rather than Bertolf who had to turn to such a woman indicates that she was the one who was bewitched and that as such, she was the sole cause of his impotence, possibly since the day they were married.

Mothers- and Daughters-in-Law

Drogo has no doubts about the origins of the sudden hatred Bertolf feels for his bride; it was caused by his mother's reaction. Bertolf complains about it to his friends. "With this marriage," he says, "I have vexed my mother. I am lost if I do not find another way out."[29] Wicked mothers-in-law are of all ages, like wicked stepmothers. Drogo agrees with one worldly scholar (he refers to the Roman comic dramatist Terence) who said that all mothers-in-law hate their daughters-in-law.

There is a good explanation for this. A woman always walked in the shadow of a man. She could only exercise power indirectly, by means of the influence she had on her husband and sons. From them she derived status, respect and certain rights, and they provided protection. The loss of her husband and sons made her extremely vulnerable. It is therefore not surprising that a new woman in the life of a son could be considered a threat.[30] In addition, all kinds of changes, such as the restriction of hereditary rights to the first-born son, and increasingly negative views on women as a result of, among other things, a greater emphasis within the church on clerical celibacy, made the already vulnerable position of women from about 1050 until the thirteenth century even weaker.[31]

The story of Guibert of Nogent's parents, for instance, is remarkably similar to that of Bertolf and Godelieve. The first years of the marriage of Guibert's parents were made a hell by his father's stepmother. "It was said that their marriage drew upon them the envy of a stepmother, who had some nieces of great beauty and nobility and who was plotting to slip one of them in my father's bed. Meeting with no success in her designs, she is said to have used magical arts to prevent entirely the consummation of their marriage."[32] Guibert's father had incurred his stepmother's wrath by not marrying one of her candidates. She still tried to have her way by trying to make married life impossible for them.

Of course, women tried to reduce the threat by having as much influence as possible on the choice of their sons' brides. The more they could manipulate the young bride, the safer they would be. A woman from their own clan, with whom they would have more in common, was therefore to be preferred. This was one of the issues in Bertolf's case; his mother blamed him for choosing a girl from somewhere far off and not asking her advice, as he had his father and others. In short, she had had no influence whatsoever on the choice of girl that was to take her place and as a result, her son brought home a woman who was a total stranger to her. She just had to wait and see whether Godelieve would be at all well-disposed towards her. To be on the safe side, she tried to get rid of her by turning Bertolf against the girl. In this she did succeed where the stepmother of Guibert of Nogent's father failed. The question remains, however, as to why Bertolf selected such a radical and drastic solution.

Marriage Laws

Apparently it was not possible for Bertolf to have the marriage dissolved; something which was not otherwise uncommon in those days, and usually on the grounds of a family relationship between the bride and groom, or because the marriage had not yet been consummated. But why did he not repudiate his wife, as some of his contemporaries did? The French historian Duby suggests that nobility of that age set great store by the episcopal recognition of a marriage. According to the Church, marriage was indissoluble; a man was only allowed to marry again if his wife had died or had entered a convent. In some hopeless cases, the latter option was the only way to prevent murder.[33] To my mind, in order to understand Bertolf's motive, we should look to the very nature of marital union in those days. Marriage was an agreement between two families, not between bride and groom; it was usually concluded by the bridegroom and his father on the one hand, and the bride's parents on the other. As regards the position of the women, this was first and foremost a man's affair. True enough, Godelieve's mother was involved, but it is doubtful whether she was truly indispensable to the arrangement. The presence of the groom's mother, in any case, was not required. Bertolf's mother at least had had no share in the matter. Apparently, the notion that the bride to be should give her consent had not yet taken root and this also appears in a passage from the *Vita Arnulfi*. Arnulf, Bishop of Soissons, originally came from Flanders and he and Godelieve were contemporaries. His *Vita* dates from the beginning of the twelfth century. In this passage, a married couple, at their wits' end, consult the bishop about their daughter, who does not want to marry the man her parents have chosen for her. The girl has set her heart on another man. The bishop explains that according to canon law, it is forbidden to marry the girl off against her will. He comforts the couple with the prediction that when she marries the man of her choice—rather a violent character—she will soon be a widow, in which case she is bound to fulfil her parents' wish after all.[34]

The ecclesiastical rule that the bride and groom should both agree to the marriage is often seen as one of the attempts by the Church to strengthen its influence on society.[35] However, it can equally well be explained as part of the task which the Church had set itself of protecting the weak, as the rule involved a considerable improvement in the position of women, at least in theory. Apart from the fact that they had a say in the matter, it was now the bridal couple themselves who were responsible for the marriage, and not their families. The indissolubility of the marriage was also to the woman's advantage. Women could no longer be repudiated on the grounds of sterility or the fact that their fertile period had come to an end. As long as marriage, apart from the convent, was virtually the only possibility for a woman to secure a roof over her head, this was of the utmost importance. It was only to be expected that the nobility would object to this when one considers their views on marriage.

The marriage contract was a mutual agreement, comparable to the relationship between a lord and his vassals, its main objective being to continue the bridegroom's line. The purpose of the union was therefore to produce offspring. The two parties may not have been socially equal, but both derived their rights and duties from the agreement. The bride's father appears to have been the weakest party, because he was dependent on his daughter's wishes; on the other hand, he was usually of higher social standing than the bridegroom.[36] A breach of such an agreement usually resulted in war or other acts of violence. Apart from death, such a contract in theory could only be dissolved by mutual consent of the parties, for instance if no children were born, or if either of the parties did not fulfil their obligations.

In this respect, a marriage could not easily be dissolved in a feudal society. The marriage was confirmed by the vows taken by the various parties; its actual consummation was of secondary importance.[37] If we are to believe the *Vita Pharaildis*, Pharaildis had been married for thirty years without having had sexual intercourse.[38] According to the *Life*, the reason for this was that God supported her in her desire to keep her virginity by, if needs be, curbing her husband's lust or making it impossible for him to accomplish the deed. It was not a question of her denying him what he was entitled to. It is true that she avoided him by spending night after night praying in church, but ultimately she kept her virginity because of his impotence. The hagiographer considers this to be an act of God. There is no question of ill will on either part, and dissolving the marriage would undoubtedly have had serious financial consequences. In principle, impotence was reasonable grounds for divorce, but only in case of absolute incapability.[39]

Since the marriage was aimed at reproduction, according to standards of feudal society as well as religious standards, it was of course important for the couple to be able to consummate their marriage. The validity of the marriage, however, was not determined by its consummation, but by their mutual agreement. The marriage could only be dissolved if either of the couple could be proved to be actually physically incapable of having sexual intercourse. In this light it is understandable that the marriage of Guibert of Nogent's parents was not dissolved, in spite of his father's lasting impotence, because during this period, he did succeed in fathering a child, albeit through another woman.[40] If Godelieve's marriage had not been consummated (as was assumed earlier) because of her husband's impotence, and if his impotence was caused by her, it is clear why this could not result in divorce.

If a man wanted to have his marriage dissolved without a valid reason, he had to find a way to declare his wife in default. For instance, in the year 1000 the count of Anjou either justly or unjustly accused his wife Elizabeth of adultery, and had her sent to the stake.[41] Guibert of Nogent describes a failed attempt by John, Count of Soissons, to discredit his wife Adeline.[42] John of Soissons, a consummate villain according to Guibert, instructed another miscreant to get into Adeline's bed as soon as the lights were out and to pretend that he was the count. The count could then get rid of his wife by accusing her of adultery. However, Adeline immediately saw through the exchange, and she managed to get rid of the impostor. This did not keep the count from accusing her of adultery, and he demanded that she should be submitted to a trial by ordeal, in this case red-hot iron. The famous Bishop Ivo of Chartres managed to prevent this by requiring the count to produce witnesses first.[43]

Another option was for a husband and his family to make his wife's life so miserable that she would run away. Guibert of Nogent gives an account of such a scheme: for three years, his father had managed to keep his impotence a secret, but when it finally came out, his relatives urged him to divorce his wife in order to become a monk. According to Guibert, they did this in their own interest rather than in his, because they hoped to acquire his possessions. "When their suggestion produced no effect, they began to hound the girl herself, far away as she was from her kinsfolk and harassed by the violence of strangers, into voluntary flight out of sheer exhaustion under their insults, and without waiting for divorce."[44] We have already seen that in this case, Guibert's father's impotence was probably not valid grounds for divorce. The most acceptable alternative for the family was to try to blame the failure of the marriage on the other party and to get her to break the contract. Guibert's mother, however, remained firm. According to the *Life*, Bertolf of Gistel was more successful.

Drogo tells us how Godelieve, no longer able to endure the suffering caused by her husband and his entire family, fled to her father, barefoot and with only one person to accompany her. He pitied her of course, and he took her in until he had decided upon the best solution, for his honor as well as his daughter's well-being. He decided to consult Count Baldwin of Flanders, whom Bertolf certainly could not refuse to obey. However, the count referred Godelieve's father to the bishop. The bishop had to order Bertolf to take back his wife and the count could only intervene further if Bertolf were to ignore the bishop's orders. According to Drogo, Bertolf was in the end forced by both these men to return to his wife. He also had to swear under oath that he would no longer treat her badly.[45] In this way, a bloody feud between the families—or worse—was prevented, but for Godelieve it amounted to nothing more than a death sentence.

For the sake of completeness, we should investigate how it was possible for Bertolf's mother to play such a dominant role. There is not always a rational explanation for such matters. In this case as well, we can make a comparison with Guibert of Nogent's parents. According to Guibert, his mother had barely reached marriageable age when she married his father, "a mere youth." This means that she cannot have been much older than twelve, and that the groom was probably very young as well.[46] The marriage was said not to have been consummated until seven years after the wedding. Drogo does not mention Godelieve's or Bertolf's age, but according to a fourteenth-century *Life* of Godelieve, she was fifteen when she was married off. She died three years afterwards.[47] She may well have been even younger, and perhaps the bride as well as the groom had been unable—because they were so young—to oppose their wicked mothers. It is not surprising that in the end even Bertolf's father and his family turned against Godelieve. To them, the marriage served no purpose whatsoever. If it was to continue there would never be any children, whatever the cause. After the bishop and the count had ordered the couple's reunion, so Drogo tells us, Bertolf lost many of his supporters. They accused him of not submitting to the rules of the Almighty and to the authority of the bishop and the count. They said that he persisted in his stubbornness, that he refused to live according to accepted rules of conduct and that he did not keep his marriage vows.[48]

A Saint

It will be clear that a marriage such as Godelieve's was not uncommon. Then why, might we ask, did she become a saint? We need to distinguish between what made her a saint in the eyes of the people around her and what made her a saint in the eyes of her hagiographer, since it is our ultimate objective to determine why the Church decided to canonize her. The people around her were moved in the first place by the circumstances of her death. Many people were outraged because a young woman who meant well was continually maltreated for no good reason by a family into which she had married. One day she does what anyone in his or her right mind would have done much earlier: she runs away. She returns at the order of the bishop and the count, only to be brutally murdered. She dies because she obeys those who act on God's authority; this makes her a martyr. Where ecclesiastical authority and aristocratic authority fail, who would be more suited to act as an intermediary between God and the faithful than someone who has fallen victim to it? That the worship of Godelieve originated from the people and was only later recognized by the Church is beyond question. But this is not about a class struggle between peasants and nobility; it is an indictment of the failure of ecclesiastical and worldly authorities.[49]

What makes her a saint in the eyes of Drogo? At the beginning of the *Vita*, the monk argues that God calls various kinds of people to Him. Some are called to Him after they have endured many hardships, others are rewarded and become martyrs, yet others are rewarded according to their deserts, simply because they spread virtue and love of God and man in the name of the Church. In order to withstand all devilish schemes and temptations, one has to stand firm, be humble and be patient. One is wreathed with roses as a token of such martyrdom, the other with lilies as a token of purity and love. But they are all equally rewarded with eternal life, while here on earth their remains are honored with miraculous signs.[50] Godelieve is considered a martyr by Drogo. Naturally, he describes her as a good mistress and housewife. She runs the house, sees to it that the servants have everything they need and gives to the poor what they lack. She spends her days spinning and weaving and during her lonely nights, she prays to God in tears and begs Him to soften her husband's heart. As a wife she is obedient, humble, submissive, and docile. She does not question Bertolf's behavior, nor does she allow others to criticize him. Her motives are not in the first place aimed at pleasing her husband, but at pleasing God. She wants to keep her promises to Him, to live up to His expectations, so that He will reward her. She hopes that He will bedew Bertolf's heart with His mercy, so that he will no longer hate her and will start to honor her as his wife. She is confident that she will be truly rewarded: "Once I shall rise above all the women in Flanders and before the eyes of the world I will appear with a wealth which will be far greater than any I have ever seen."[51] This foreknowledge already proved her saintliness.

Virginity does not play a part in this life history. This is a sharp contrast to the *Vita Pharaildis*, in which virginity is the central theme. The role of the female virtue of obedience is remarkable in this respect. According to the author, Pharaildis does not submit to her husband's wish to let their marriage take its natural course. Instead, she devises all kinds of schemes to avoid him. She interprets his impotence as a sign that this is indeed the right choice. She sees it as proof of God's will that she should keep her virginity. From this *Life*, we can learn that obedience to God is more important than obedience to the husband. The *Vita Godeliph* contains a similar message. When Bertolf asks his wife to save their marriage by consulting a woman, Drogo says that she hesitates. She agrees, but only on condition that there will be nothing sinful about it. To this the monk adds: "Fortunate are you, woman, if you entrust yourself to God. You do not wish to break with God. He cares for you! You fear that you may be parted from him by witchcraft. That is why you wish to strengthen the bonds of marriage, in order not to lose the Lord, who joins man and woman in matrimony."[52]

What Drogo admires most in her is her strength to persevere in spite of all her misfortunes. He says he has met monks—strong men, capable of facing any kind of adversity—who were prepared more than ever to take up the fight against evil once they heard her sweet-voiced words of encouragement—words spoken by a woman. Her charity, detachment and her role as intermediary—she spoke up for the weak, for whom she begged God for mercy—all this made her an exemplary Christian. The monk compares her suffering to that of Jesus. Betrayed by a Judas kiss, she let herself be brought like a lamb to the slaughter. Even if she was still unclean in some way, God saw to it that she was purged of all sin during her immersion in the well. The miracles which took place at the well and her grave provided absolute proof of her saintliness. According to Drogo, Godelieve not only cured those who were ill, but she also came to the aid of those who were punished by God because they had thwarted religious authorities. I do not think, however, that the conclusion that Godelieve was therefore worshipped "as the champion of resistance against clerical oppression" is justified.[53] On the contrary, the wondrous stories about transgressors of religious rules are meant to teach the readers and listeners that religious authorities cannot be ignored with impunity. Fortunately, thanks to saints like Godelieve, there is hope of salvation for sinners. Godelieve acts as an intermediary between God and those who are weak, after the example of Mary, a *mater misericordiae,* mother of compassion. In this representation, Mary embodies the last hope of salvation for earthly sinners. No son, not even Christ, can withstand such a passionate plea from any mother.[54]

That leaves us with the question as to why the Church decided to formalize this popular cult after so many years, by commissioning the writing of a *vita*, followed by the elevation and translation of Godelieve's remains. This should be interpreted as a joint attempt by the Flemish count and the bishop of Noyon and Tournai to consolidate their authority and to bring peace and order to the Flemish coastal region. In those days, Flanders was stricken with insurgence and violence. After the death of Count Baldwin VI (1070), a struggle for the succession broke out between, on the one hand, his widow Richilde of Hainault (and her young sons Arnulf and Baldwin) and his brother Robert the Frisian, on the other. Arnulf was killed in the Battle of Cassel (1071), as a result of which Robert the Frisian was able to conquer Flanders. Hainault remained in the hands of Richilde and Baldwin. But this was not enough to bring peace to the country. Many regarded Robert as a usurper, and his economic politics, with which he favored the cities, made him many enemies among the nobility. Continuous uprisings were the result, and in 1082 there was even a plot to depose him and to place the county under the authority of Baldwin of Hainault after all. During the struggle for the throne, most of Robert's support came from the Flemish coastal region. He therefore transferred the seat of his administration north, to Bruges. Most of his predecessors had taken up their abode in Lille and Arras.[55] It was not true, however, that Robert ruled West Flanders without difficulty. This is confirmed by the above-mentioned *Vita Arnulfi*.[56] By order of the Pope, Bishop Arnulf travelled the area between 1081 and 1087 on a peacekeeping mission; in his *Life*, the Flemish are depicted as barbarians.

The count and the bishop tried to consolidate their power in close cooperation. Episcopal authority was not too well-established in all parts of Flanders, which was part of the double diocese of Tournai-Noyon. Usually, the bishop maintained closer relationships with Noyon, as a result of which he met with a lot of opposition from Tournai, where people felt neglected. Bishop Radbod, however, had established a firmer foothold in Flanders than his predecessors, because he was related to a nobleman from the vicinity of Gistel named Cono, Lord of Eine, Oudenburg and Vladslo, one of the most powerful men in the county. The bishop was this knight's uncle, presumably because the bishop had a sister who married into Cono's family.[57] Cono's brother Everard was Viscount of Tournai. Cono of Eine was also related to Ingelbrecht, Abbot of Saint Winocsbergen, which explains why one of his monks was asked to write the *Vita Godeliph*.[58] According to Drogo, the worshippers who wanted to have her life story recorded, did not come from the ranks of riotous peasants, but from the ranks of knights or the nobility.

The count and the bishop formed a notorious team. The official canonization of Godelieve was certainly intended as a means of bringing peace to the region. The failure of the authorities, and the pointless death of a young woman which resulted from it, was now given some meaning. In a society which was governed by feuds, it also offered retribution to her family, and it unburdened her husband's family. It may even have helped to bring peace to the area for yet another reason: murder, that is to say killing someone in all secrecy and then trying to destroy the evidence, was just as unacceptable in the Middle Ages as it is now. It was even believed that the victim of such a cowardly act could never find peace (unlike those who had died of natural causes), but that they came out to haunt until the murder had been avenged. The clergy saw it as their duty to help. They promised to provide the much-needed repose by burying the victim in consecrated ground. Furthermore, magic powers were often ascribed to the victim's blood, and these were easily interpreted as miraculous signs.[59] By accepting an innocent victim of a brutal murder, to whom the people ascribed supernatural powers, into the Church as a saint and miracle worker, a form of superstition was rendered harmless; in this way, the canonization contributed to the pacification of a violent society.

Consequently, the most important message in this *Vita* is not about the views of the Church on marriage or on the role of women, nor is it about the view that in marital affairs, ecclesiastical authority precedes worldly authority.[60] The essence of the story is Godelieve's obedience to the God-given authority of the bishop and the count, with which she earns the highest possible reward. In this respect it is essential that her father decided after careful consideration not to take the matter in hand personally, but to go to a higher authority and in doing so, to recognize and to submit himself to the count's authority and, at his order, the bishop's authority. This contrasts sharply with Bertolf's behavior; he defies the laws of God, bishop and count, and resorts to crime.

It appears that the *Vita Godeliph* can only be satisfactorily interpreted in the light of its historical background: the situation in eleventh-century Flanders. This also goes—*mutatis mutandis*—for later life histories of this saint. It is only to be expected that these texts differ from each other, on the one hand because they are products of different ages and represent different ideas, on the other because they were composed long after the events had taken place, as a result of which they present a refined picture of the events; a picture which more closely resembles the hagiographic ideal. The more recent the text, the greater the distance to the historical reality. The thirteenth-century adaptation of Drogo's *Life* emphasizes Godelieve's virginity before, and her chastity during her marriage; her detachment develops into a rejection of the world. Most adaptations are elaborations on her piety and perseverance. This version also emphasizes the relation between ecclesiastical and worldly authority.

The fourteenth-century *Life* is centred on Godelieve's virginity. According to this version, she did not want to marry, a desire in which she was supported by her parents. The count of Boulogne, however, decided otherwise.[61] The marriage was not consummated, and she died a virgin and a martyr. Thereafter she watched over her husband, and finally, by means of miraculous signs, she caused him to repent. Bertolf had a daughter from a later marriage, who was born blind in punishment for his crimes. The girl turned to Saint Godelieve, and she was cured by sprinkling her eyes with water from the well in which the murderers had thrown Godelieve's body. In gratitude she founded a convent at Gistel, in the honor of Godelieve, her *mater misericordiae*. Bertolf finally died a monk at the monastery of Saint Winocsbergen.[62]

IDA OF BOULOGNE

It is possible that in 1057 Godelieve, as a little girl, feasted her eyes on the magnificent wedding of Eustace II, Count of Boulogne and Ida, daughter of the Duke of Lorraine, Godfrey with the beard. Eustace was a widower, and he had no children when he married Ida. He chose her because she was young, beautiful, well-behaved and of noble birth, according to her *Vita*.[63] He sent messengers to the duke to ask for her hand in marriage, so that as a result of this marriage, there would always exist an honorable bond between the families. After careful consideration, Ida's parents gave their consent. They placed the girl, still a virgin, in the hands of a number of related and honorable persons, who were to take her to the bridegroom. When they approached Boulogne, the entire city turned out in order to greet them.[64]

Most of what we know about Ida derives from the oldest *Life* that we know of, which was supposedly written between 1130 and 1135 by a monk from the priory of Waast near Desvres, southeast of Boulogne, where this saintly woman was buried when she died in 1113. After the prologue, the *Life* can be divided into three parts. The first part describes Ida's childhood, her marriage and her motherhood. The second part describes her life as a widow, until her death and burial. In the last part, the miracles and the other events that took place at her grave are described. There is only one manuscript of this *Life*; it dates from the fourteenth century.[65] In the fifteenth century, a summary was written by the hagiographer Johannes Gielemans.[66] For further knowledge of Ida of Boulogne, we can also turn to other literary sources and contemporary documents, in addition to these hagiographies.[67] She plays a role in the legends of the Swan Knight, which form part of a French narrative cycle on the first crusade.[68] But first, let us see what the monk of Waast has to tell us. His story does not read like a fairy tale, but it does fit the hagiographic tradition perfectly, interspersed as it is with customary commonplaces (*topoi*).

The Monk's Account

The hagiographer's account of her childhood and her married life is rather concise. Ida was an exemplary girl, who wished for heavenly love rather than worldly pleasures as she grew older.[69] One night, she saw in her dreams how the sun descended from the heavens and rested in her lap for a moment. She interpreted this as a sign from God, meaning that the sons she would have were to become famous.[70] This meant that God had destined her for motherhood. Once married, she faithfully fulfilled her marital obligations, but she did it in chastity, as if it did not involve having intercourse with a man. She had three sons. The eldest was Eustace, who was to succeed his father as Count of Boulogne. The second was Godfrey, who was to succeed her brother as Duke of Lorraine and, more importantly, who was to defeat the Turks to become the first Christian ruler of Jerusalem. The youngest was Baldwin, who was also to win his spurs in the Middle East; he would later succeed his brother as King of Jerusalem. Ida was a devoted mother, who insisted on breast-feeding her children herself, because she feared that her children might otherwise be exposed to bad influences.[71] She was an excellent housewife and performed her duties as a noblewoman should. She often went to church and generously gave alms to anyone who needed them. She cared for widows and orphans, the sick and the elderly, and especially the servants. She strengthened everyone in their faith. Ida did all this with the approval of her husband and only in the way he wanted it. She shone with humility, like Queen Esther, of whom it was said that in the presence of God, she regarded royal decorations to be of the same value as sanitary towels. In short, she was virtuous, obedient, pious and humble, caring and compassionate.[72] After the count died (1086/88[73]), although she was now deprived of her husband, she did not lay down her charitable work. On the contrary, she was more busy than ever, because she felt enriched by a higher, eternal love and uplifted by the knowledge that her sons were of noble character. She renovated churches, monasteries and convents and built new ones. She donated money, books and relics. She was advised by her eldest son and by her spiritual counsellors Gerard, Bishop of Thérouanne, and Hugh, Abbot of Cluny.[74]

Even during her lifetime, she effected a number of miraculous cures. Once when she was in England, she gave alms to a cripple. When he accepted the gift, he was cured on the spot. She refused to accept the praise she was given and emphatically denied that she had performed a miracle. And yet, the sick came to her from far and wide, and she cured them with her prayers and by laying on her hands.[75] Ida often stayed in the monastery of Capella in order to witness and to join in the services held by the monks. She had founded this monastery at the request of many, and she had dedicated it to the Virgin Mary. She had given funds and goods to the monastery from her own possessions, and she had given the monks some valuable relics, including eleven hairs from the Mother of God, which she had obtained from Bishop Osmond of Astorga.[76]

In this monastery, she once saw a deaf-and-dumb girl, hungry and shivering from the cold. Ida took her in her arms and covered her with her cloak. At once the girl, who had never heard—let alone spoken—a word in her life, cried out: "Mother, mother!" Out of joy over this miracle, the abbot took the girl in his care. Unfortunately, the girl soon fell from grace, lost her virginity and had an illegitimate child. Her old problems returned, and once again she was cured by Ida. The countess had to come to her rescue three times, after which the girl lived in absolute chastity until she died.

After a fruitful life, Ida died in 1113, exhausted from her deeds of charity. The monks of Waast stood by her in her final hours. At her initiative, the monastery was reformed by the monks of Cluny and brought under the authority of their abbey. In accordance with her wishes, she was buried near the priory of Waast.[77] It was to be expected that after her death in 1113, the number of miracles only increased, some of which are of course also mentioned by her hagiographer. One of these miracles happened to Mathilda, a daughter of Ida's eldest son Eustace, Count of Boulogne, and his wife, Mary of Scotland. She was cured at her grandmother's grave.[78] That concludes the monk of Waast's account.

Various other sources give accounts of Ida's activities and describe how she donated most of her possessions to the church.[79] She maintained contacts with important clergymen, such as Anselm, Bishop of Canterbury and the Spanish Bishop Osmond of Astorga.[80] Chroniclers praised her as the honorable mother of Godfrey of Bouillon and his brothers.[81]

A Holy Mother

The *Vita*, along with other sources, tells us how Ida led a perfect life as a noblewoman and how she came to be an example to many, but was this enough to make her a saint? Her biography does not mention who commissioned the writing of her *Life*, nor does the hagiographer indicate his sources. Undoubtedly, its purpose was to prove Ida's saintliness and to persuade the

Church officially to recognize her sainthood. With respect to the latter, it remains to be seen whether it succeeded. The hagiographer describes the opening of her grave by the monks of Waast, in the presence of many people who had gathered from miles around. However, this event was not attended by a bishop or another dignitary, so that it is not likely that the rites which form part of an official canonization were actually performed at that occasion.

According to the author of the *Vita*, the reason for opening the grave was the speed with which her fame spread; it had to be proved that this fame was justified. The immediate occasion was an attempt by German relatives of Ida's to have her body transferred to their country. Furthermore, other churches and monasteries which had been founded by Ida or which she had helped in some other way, disputed the monks of Waast their right to her last resting place.[82] According to the monks of Waast, Ida had specifically asked to be buried at their monastery, which they were eager to prove by opening her grave. Her body appeared to be completely intact, as were her clothes.[83] A pleasant smell arose from the grave, which is always a sign of saintliness. Who would dare to disrupt a resting place such as this? This event has not been dated, but it is possible that the writing of the *Life* was commissioned as a result of it. The passage confirms the impression that the hagiographer specifically intended to justify and promote the cult around Ida and the monastery of Waast, ample reason for turning to this place in order to find the hagiographer's identity. Perhaps he had known Ida personally and received his information from the monastery; the information may have been completed by her granddaughter Mathilda. Apart from the *Life*, there is no other evidence of the existence of a thriving cult around the grave of Ida of Boulogne.

It is also possible that this Mathilda commissioned the writing of the *vita* in order to increase her family's fame.[84] In any case, the *Vita Idae* handed down to us must have been written in her lifetime. Mathilda of Boulogne married Stephen of Blois in 1125, who ascended the English throne ten years later. The *Life* refers to her by her title of Countess of Boulogne, strictly in combination with a reference to the *late* Bishop John of Thérouanne, who died in 1130; the *Life*, therefore, must have been written during the period of 1130–1135.[85] According to the *Life*, Mathilda worshipped her grandmother, who was a source of great relief to her. In addition, Margaret of Scotland, her grandmother on her mother's side, was also worshipped as a saint in those days. The earliest *vita* that we have of this Scottish queen was probably written after her death in 1093, and an adaptation of it was written at the beginning of the twelfth century at the request of one of her daughters, Edith/Mathilda, Queen of England.[86] Edith/Mathilda also worshipped Edward the Confessor (who died in 1066 and was canonized in 1163), whose cult was fervently promoted during the twelfth century. As a brother of the grandfather on Margaret of Scotland's father's side, this English king was one of her ancestors.[87] It is believed that the sainted King Stephen of Hungary (canonized in 1083) was her grandfather on her mother's side.[88] Margaret was finally canonized in 1250, after an investigation which took five years to complete.[89] If Mathilda of Boulogne trod in her aunt Edith/Mathilda's footsteps and indeed took the initiative regarding Ida of Boulogne's canonization, it seems to be an attempt to upgrade the count's authority by emphasizing ties with a sainted, in this case English, dynasty. Klaniczay explains the large number of canonizations of monarchs during the twelfth century as a reaction to the Pope's claim of the supremacy of ecclesiastical power.[90]

In any case, the *Life* is pervaded with the ideas of a Cluniac monk. In his prologue, the monk justifies the *Life* as the biography of a mother and virtuous wife. He argues that in a world full of evil, we should be guided by men as well as women of whom it can be proved that they have attained sainthood. Mothers are judged by God according to their merits and those of their sons. Virginity may be the highest good, but chastity after having borne sons, which is indispensable for a successful marriage, is also highly valued. He quotes a famous saying by Paul that it is better to be married than to burn.[91] The author's preferences are clear. His attention, incidentally, is focused on Ida's merits, rather than on her sons' achievements. Being a good wife is not enough to become a saint. Women saints are therefore always classed as martyrs, virgins or widows. The monk of Waast counts Ida as a holy widow.

The vision which she had in her childhood of the sun descending on her lap justified her choice for marriage instead of a life of virginity. The image of the sun is remarkable. The sun was a pre-Christian representation of the highest God, and an important step on the way towards monotheism.[92] Sun worship was condemned in early Christianity as idolatry, but this does not deter the hagiographer from using the image. Her vision is an "Annunciatio," with which God informs Ida that He has destined her to bear sons who have special missions to accomplish. In the same way as Mary was to be the mother of the Savior of Man, Ida was to be the mother of the saviors of Christianity. Even though the monk does not directly link Ida to Mary in this respect, her special adoration for the Mother of God can be explained via this similarity.

Corbet unjustly founds his observation that marriage in these days was highly valued by the clergy on the *Vita Idae*.[93] The notion that women are able to support their husbands in piety is nowhere to be found in this *Life*. There is no indication of a joint effort, as if they were equals. On the contrary, the monk of Waast describes how Ida chose to be led by her husband in all her actions. He is not positive about marriage. He regards it as second-rate, but in this case, Ida married because God wanted her to. The early twelfth-century *Vita Arnulfi* mentioned earlier contains a number of passages which indicate that it is the task of the women to reform their husbands.[94] If they succeed, their lives become more pleasant, but they do not become saints. Like Drogo of Saint Winocsbergen, the author of this *Life* is not opposed to marriage; he accepts it as a natural element of society. Actually, this does not illustrate a development in the appreciation of marriage; rather, the various hagiographies indicate to what extent the hagiographers were sound in their faith.

The way in which Ida led her married life as a devoted wife by not refusing to have sexual intercourse, but instead by undergoing it as if it did not involve a man, made it possible for her to keep her purity. The loss of her virginity was no detriment to her saintliness, because it was necessary for the fulfilment of God's intentions. That was the only thing she strived for. Her three sons formed the crown on her marriage, and their glorious lives proved that she had been a perfect mother. Was it not true that she had fed them herself, in order to keep them from bad influences? In those days a wet nurse was believed to pass on her qualities through her milk, just as a mother passed on her qualities through her blood.[95] That is why it was important to choose a wet nurse with the utmost care, but it was even better, at least according to theologians, for a mother to breast-feed her own children. This was no common practice, least of all for a woman of such standing as Ida, whom her hagiographer put on a par even with Queen Esther. But Mary, Mother of God, also breast-fed her son.[96] A woman who nursed her own children also created the possibility to live a chaste married life, because sexual intercourse was believed to reduce the quality as well as the quantity of the milk, and was therefore to be avoided as long as a woman had a child to suckle.[97]

The author of the *Life* admires Ida because she had the strength not only to pursue her efforts to live a perfect life after the death of her husband, but to do so with more vigor than ever. And all this without the support of a husband, which was indispensable to a woman. Her husband's death was not the worst thing that could have happened to her, because now there was room for a higher love. True enough, she lived as the widow of a mortal man, but also as the wife of an immortal husband. She is not referred to as *sponsa Christi*, but the idea is definitely there. For her it meant leading a chaste, celibate life, devoted to doing good for others, and above all, for the church.[98] This part of the *Life* does not mention her sons, apart from the remark that Eustace, by now Count of Boulogne, advises and assists his mother in founding a monastery near the church of Saint Vulmer, within the city walls.[99] His brothers have also come of age and are no longer dependent on her care. Ida exchanges physical motherhood for spiritual motherhood.[100] Just as she fed her biological sons with milk and a pure lifestyle, she feeds the Church and her faith as she does her spiritual children, with her possessions. To care is a mother's most important task. She is responsible for the physical, material and spiritual well-being of all those who have been entrusted to her care. It is her duty to extend her care to as many people as possible. It was the extent to which Ida succeeded in doing such a thing which made her into a saint.

A striking image is that of Ida taking a girl under her cloak, deaf-and-dumb and chilled to the bone. This is reminiscent of late-medieval *Cloak Madonnas,* representations of the *Mater misericordiae,* who offered shelter to the faithful under her cloak.[101] In this case it was Ida, as a *mater misericordiae*, who succeeded up to three times in saving a fallen girl from damnation. It is no coincidence that these events took place in the monastery of Capella, which was founded by Ida and dedicated to the Mother and Virgin Mary. That Mary was extremely important to Ida can also be inferred from Ida's efforts to obtain some of Our Lady's hairs as a relic for the monastery. The perfect mother was her example.

Like all saints, Ida sought out suffering. She died weakened and ill after hours and days of fasting and waking. Bynum argues that self-inflicted suffering and food deprivation as penitential asceticism is characteristic of female spirituality during the late Middle Ages.[102] One of her arguments for this observation is that women experienced sin as coming from within themselves, while men regarded it as a reaction to the outside world.[103] To my mind, it is more characteristic of hermits, men as well as women, at least in this period in history. Men and women alike regarded evil as something within them, whether it had always been there or whether it had got into them; in both cases, it provided ample reason for self-punishment. Their initial motivations, however, concern their desire to follow in the footsteps of Christ, a desire which is also demonstrated by the comparison which Drogo of Saint Winocsbergen made between the violent death of Godelieve and the death of Christ. Godelieve's suffering before her death, although it was not self-inflicted, also involved starvation. Even though He was hungry after forty days of fasting, Christ resisted the devil's temptations because, according to the Apostles, he says that it is written that "Man cannot live on bread alone;

he lives on every word that God utters" (Mt. 4:1–4). In a society which is impossible to imagine without hunger, a voluntary refusal of food is bound to have been regarded as the highest form of detachment. The notion that fasting was used as a coercive method, with reference to the Irish pre-Christian tradition of fasting and to present-day hunger strikes, seems to me to be equally untenable for the eleventh and twelfth centuries.[104] The strong emphasis on humility in those days, which is also evident in the way that Ida denies having miraculous powers,[105] makes it impossible to approach God in such a way.

Daughter of a Swan Knight

Ida is depicted by her hagiographer in the first place as the mother of Christians and in particular of monks, but to the people she lived on as the mother of two heroes; the crusaders Godfrey of Bouillon and Baldwin. It was not her life story as it was told in the *Vita* that made her famous, but the legends that arose concerning the first crusade. Between 1170 and 1220, the story of the Swan Knight was included in the old-French *Cycle de la Croisade*.[106] This was presumably done at the request of Henry I of Brabant (who died in 1235) and his wife Mathilda of Boulogne (who died in 1211), granddaughter of the above-mentioned Mathilda of Boulogne, who is believed to have commissioned the *Vita Idae*.[107] The first part of this collection, *La Naissance du Chevalier au Cygne*, includes an account of how five of six princes who were robbed of their silver necklaces and consequently changed into swans regain their human shape as their necklaces are returned to them. The sixth prince is doomed to remain a swan forever, because his necklace was used for other purposes. He becomes the faithful companion of one of his brothers, who is called the Swan Knight from then on. In the second part, *Le Chevalier au Cygne*, the Swan Knight marries Beatrice, Duchess of Bouillon. They have a daughter, Ida, who is married off to Count Eustace of Boulogne and who gives him three sons, one of whom is Godfrey of Bouillon. This legend is followed by the account of Godfrey's childhood years, *Les Enfances de Godefroi*. The earliest other records that link the story of the Swan Knight to the houses of Bouillon and Boulogne date from about 1180.[108]

The existence of a direct relationship between the *Vita Idae* and the narrative cycle of the Swan Knight cannot be proved.[109] They only have two elements in common, the fact that Ida breast-fed her sons and the motif of the cloak, two examples of the fact that she was a caring mother. The story of her breast-feeding is expanded with an anecdote, in which Ida goes to church one day to attend Mass after she has fed her three sons; she leaves the boys in the care of a maid. In her absence, one of the boys starts to cry and cannot be silenced. The girl decides in the end to send for a wet nurse in order to satisfy the child's needs. No sooner said than done, but Ida discovers it upon her return; she becomes furious and does what she can to let the child vomit in order to get rid of this strange milk. It works, but the damage has been done. In later life the child always lags behind his brothers.[110] This proves once more that Ida was right in feeding her children herself. The child in question must have been her first-born son, Eustace. He succeeded his father as Count of Boulogne and married Mary, daughter of the sainted Margaret of Scotland. Like his brothers, he took part in the first crusade; at the end of his life he retired to a monastery, where he spent his last years as a monk. Although he was devoted to the Church and his faith, he did not become as famous as his brothers, the first Christian rulers of Jerusalem.

In this version, the cloak is used to protect her own children. One day, Ida does not respectfully rise to greet her husband, as she should. When he rebukes her for it, she apologizes and explains that her boys have crawled under her cloak and have fallen asleep. She does not want to disturb them, because however honorable Eustace himself may be, her cloak hides a count, a duke and a king.[111] William, Archbishop of Tyrus (who died in 1186), tells a similar story.[112] In his account of the first crusade, the three children crawl under their mother's cloak while they are playing; there is a wriggling of arms and legs as their father enters the room. When he asks what is going on, Ida answers that she hides three great princes under her cloak: a future duke, a future king and a future count. William of Tyrus emphasizes Ida's predictive powers and the glorious futures of the boys. He depicts Ida as a saintly mother, because she has the gift of seeing into the future, a gift which is reserved only for saints. Ida's prediction that her sons will all have great futures is mentioned in several places in the legend, but in this case it is emphasized that Ida pays more attention to her sons than to her husband, because she knows they will become greater men than he is in terms of fame and honor. Here we see a combination of Christian and chivalrous values.

It goes without saying that the heroes of the first crusade appealed to the imagination, and it is likely that many a story was told about them, especially after the relatively early death of Godfrey of Bouillon in 1100. According to Guibert of Nogent, Ida contributed to the legend by telling everyone who would listen how her son Godfrey used to say to her when he was a child that he would go to Jerusalem, not as a pilgrim but at the head of a strong army.[113] Ida also made her contribution when it was time for her sons to prepare for their crusade. She travelled to Bouillon in 1096 to help Godfrey, and in 1098 she donated goods to the Abbey of Saint Bertin near Saint-Omer, for her own spiritual welfare and that of her husband and for the safety of her sons, who were on their way to Jerusalem.[114] Ida owes her fame on the one hand to the fact that she was chosen to bear exceptional sons, and on the other to the efforts with which she made it possible for her sons to rise to such heights. In the story about the crusades, the emphasis is therefore on her physical motherhood, whereas the *Life* emphasizes her spiritual motherhood, which she took up in an exemplary fashion after she had become a widow.

CONCLUSION

The two hagiographies which we have discussed here differ widely from each other. The *Vita Godeliph* presents a story which was passed down from popular tradition, cast by the Church in the form of a *Vita*. In the *Vita Idae*, however, the voice of the Church predominates; the contents are influenced by the hagiographic tradition. In popular tradition, a different image of this saint developed. Both hagiographies in their own way depict the ideal woman. A woman is subjected to the will of a man—her father, husband, son, guardian or spiritual adviser—but her love of God is more important to her than anything else. She is humble and pious, obedient and patient, caring and compassionate. She is strong, and she perseveres even in times of adversity, because she trusts in God. She does not care for worldly pleasures and riches. Those who do not own do not desire. Those who do own share their possessions with others. Both women fulfil their obligations as best they can with respect to the less fortunate. Godelieve feeds the poor, and Ida performs the duties of a monarch. She offers protection to widows and orphans, to the elderly and the sick, and to the clergy in particular. Both women look after the material and spiritual well-being of those who have been entrusted to their care.

In both hagiographies, marriages were arranged without the brides' consent. Both women are nevertheless prepared to make the best of it and to fulfil their marital obligations. Their hagiographers expected no different, but they do hold different views. Drogo of Saint Winocsbergen does not consider it necessary to justify Godelieve's marriage. To him, it is an accomplished fact and, furthermore, he assumes without question that she should find pleasure in sexual intercourse which is part of the union. That Godelieve accepted that this was not the case is regarded by Drogo as a wise and pious form of detachment. Whether or not she died a virgin does not matter to him. Nor is it of importance whether or not she tried to be chaste in her marriage. It is only important that she accepted the fact that she was denied worldly pleasures and that she did not give in to the temptation to look for them somewhere else. The people and the Church see her as a saint because of her suffering, in which chastity and virginity hardly play a part.

The monk of Waast, however, praises Ida for her chastity in the way in which she treated the sexual act. He clearly indicates that virginity is to be preferred to marriage, but that Ida was destined by God to bring forth exceptional sons. After her husband died, she still had ample opportunity to devote herself to a higher love in all virtue, the monk observes with some satisfaction. She had done her part by bearing three sons and raising them as best she could. She then voluntarily turned away from a sinful world. In the eyes of her hagiographer, Ida lived her life as virtuously as she could, and in this way she was perfect. Virginity is not a prerequisite for sainthood, but chastity is.

It is not justifiable to conclude from the differences in views between the two hagiographers that ideas on chastity and marriage had changed since Drogo's days. The difference lies in the tenor of each of the hagiographies. Ida is described as a saintly wife, mother and widow, in short, a saintly woman. Godelieve was an innocent victim, a martyr, in which her being a woman was of secondary importance. Her position as a woman made her an easy victim, but that was the way of the world in those days. Both life histories show us the extent to which women were dependent on men. Godelieve's suffering was the result of the conduct, and the rules of conduct, of men. The behavior of her mother-in-law is also an example of the difficult position of women in the Middle Ages. Ida's life, on the other hand, was a success precisely because of the men in her life. According to the monk of Waast, she had her husband and sons to thank for her success, but more importantly, her spiritual leaders. He highlights her life after the death of her husband and the completion of her sons' upbringing. He considers the spiritual motherhood to which she dedicated herself to be more important than her biological motherhood. The people, however, judged her by the glorious deeds of her sons.

That the cult of Godelieve came to be far more popular than the worship of Ida can be explained via the fact that many people recognize something of their own powerlessness in her. As one of them, she is best suited to act as their representative in heaven. Ida is a monarch and a mother of heroes. She earns respect, but she is distant from everyday life. In other words, since both women are related to popular tradition, Ida is the fairy-tale queen, but Godelieve is our Cinderella.

1. Georges Duby, *Le chevalier, la femme et le prêtre: Le marriage dans la France féodale* (Paris: Hachette, 1981), 142–150; Georges Duby, *Mâle moyen age: De l'amour et autres essais* (Paris: Flammarion, 1988), 50–73.

2. Drogo of Sint-Winoksbergen, *Vita Godeliph* (BHL 3591t), ed. and intr. Nicolaas-Norbert Huyghebaert, trans. Stefaan Gyselen (Tielt-Bussum: Lannoo, 1982), 74f: "Instrumentum primae elevationis sanctae Godelevae Anno Domini M° LXXX° IV°."

3. Ibid., 34–71.

4. Ibid., 19.

5. Ibid., 36f.

6. *Vita S. Godelevae Virginis et Martyris* (BHL 3592), in *Acta Sanctorum (AASS)*, 6 Julii (3d ed. Paris-Rome, 1867), vol. 29, 404–413; Huyghebaert, *Drogo, Vita Godeliph*, 17.

7. *Vita Altera S. Godelevae* (BHL 3593), also in *Acta Sanctorum (AASS)*, 6 Julii (3d ed. Paris-Rome, 1867), vol. 29, 414–436.

8. Maurice Coens, "La vie ancienne de sainte Godelieve de Ghistelles par Drogon de Bergues," *Analecta Bollandiana*, 44 (1926), 119; Duby, *Mâle moyen age*, 60.

9. Roland Barthes, *Mythologies* (Paris: Editions du Seuil, 1957), 193-247; see also Marina Warner, *The Absent Mother or Women against Women in the 'Old Wives' Tale* (Hilversum: Verloren, 1991), 17-25.

10. Anne Baring and Jules Cashford, *The Myth of the Goddess: Evolution of an Image* (London: Viking Cop., 1991), 655–658.

11. Jan Huisman, "Moedergodinnen en heiligen: Het voortleven van de verering der Moedergodinnen tussen Rijn en Schelde," *Jeugd en samenleving*, 10 (1980), 38; Eddy Valgaerts en Luk Machiels, *De keltische erfenis: Riten en symbolen in het volksgeloof* (Ghent: Stichting Mens en Kultuur, 1992), 110ff.

12 *Vita Pharaildis* (BHL 6791), in *Acta Sanctorum (AASS)*, 4 Jan. (3d ed. Brussels, 1863), vol. 1, 170–173; L. van der Essen, *Étude critique et littéraire sur les Vitae des saints Mérovingiens de l'ancienne Belgique* (Louvain-Paris, 1907), 303–306.

13. *Vita Pharaildis*, ed. AASS 1, 172; Huisman, "Moedergodinnen en heiligen," 43f.

14. *Vita Pharaildis*, ed. AASS 1, 173; Hans van Werveke, "'Burgus': Versterking of nederzetting?" in *Verhandelingen van de Koninklijke Vlaamse Academie voor Wetenschappen*, Letteren en Schone Kunsten van België, Klasse der Letteren, 27 (1965) nr. 59, 58.

15. Huisman, "Moedergodinnen en heiligen," 42ff.

16. Also see, except the studies of Duby, Coens, "La vie ancienne," 125–137; Michiel English, *Godelieve van Gistel* (Bruges-Brussels, 1944); and the various articles in *Sacris Erudiri*, 20 (1971).

17. See n. 1.

18. Leon Elaut, "Een onderzoek naar de redenen waarom Bertolf van Gistel zijn bruid Godelieve verstoten heeft," *Periodiek: Maandblad van het Vlaams geneesheren verbond*, 20 (1965), 86–94.

19. Nicolaas-Norbert Huyghebaert, "Les femmes laïques dans la vie religieuse des XIe et XIIe siècles dans la province ecclésiastique de Reims," in *I laici nella <<Societas Christiana>> dei secoli XI e XII* (Atti della terza Settimana internazionale di studio Mendola, 21–27 agosto 1965) (Milan: Vita e Pensiero, 1968), 350–356; Duby, *Mâle moyen age*, 38–41.

20. *Self and Society in Medieval France: The Memoirs of Abbot Guibert of Nogent (1064?–c. 1125)*, trans. John F. Benton (New York [etc.]: Harper & Row, 1970); Duby, *Le chevalier, la femme et le prêtre*, 151–172.

21. *Self and Society*, 1.12, trans. Benton, 64f.

22. Ibid., 3.3, p. 149.

23. Drogo, *Vita Godeliph*, 8, ed. Huyghebaert, 52f.

24. Ibid., 10, p. 58f.

25. *Self and Society*, 1.12, trans. Benton, 67.

26. Jacqueline Murray, "On the Origins and Role of 'Wise Women' in Causes for Annulment on the Grounds of Male Impotence," *Journal of Medieval History*, 16 (1990), 235–249.

27. Ibid., 240.

28. Drogo, *Vita Godeliph*, 10, ed. Huyghebaert, 60f.

29. Ibid., 3, p. 42f.

30. See also Warner, *The Absent Mother*, 38–52.

31. Sharon Farmer, "Persuasive Voices: Clerical Images of Medieval Wives," *Speculum*, 61 (1986), 518–521.

32. *Self and Society*, 1.12, trans. Benton, 64.

33. See Duby, *Le chevalier, la femme et le prêtre*, 95–116.

34. *Vita S. Arnulfi Episcopi Suessionensis*. Auctore Hariulfo abbate Audenburgensis coaequali & a Lisiardo episcopo Suessionensi, item coaequali, ut videtur, recognita (BHL 704), in *Acta Sanctorum Ordinis S. Benedicti: Saec. I–VI (500–1100) (AASS OSB)*, vol. 2, ed. Jean Mabillon (Paris, 1701), 502–557, here *Vita* 1.29, p. 525.

35. David Herlihy, *Medieval Households* (Cambridge, Mass.: Harvard University Press, 1985), 80ff.

36. Duby, *Le chevalier, la femme et le prêtre*, 156.

37. Ibid., 153f.

38. *Vita Pharaildis*, 7f., ed. *AASS* 1, 172.

39. Murray, "On the origins," 235.

40. *Self and Society*, 1.18, trans. Benton, 94.

41. Duby, *Le chevalier, la femme et le prêtre*, 99.

42. *Self and Society*, 3.16, trans. Benton, 210f.

43. Ibid., 211, n. 7.

44. Ibid., 1.12, p. 63f.

45. Drogo, *Vita Godeliph*, 6, ed. Huyghebaert, 48–51.

46. *Self and Society*, 1.12, trans. Benton, 63. Duby, *Le chevalier, la femme et le prêtre*, 153.

47. *Vita altera S. Godelevae*, 20, ed. *AASS* 29, 419f; according to the Prologue, Godelieve was born in 1052 and she died in 1070 (81).

48. Drogo, *Vita Godeliph*, 7, ed. Huyghebaert, 50–53.

49. Duby, *Mâle Moyen Age*, 70; a similar case seems to be that of the Danish Margaretha of Roskilde, who was also murdered by her husband (1176) and soon afterwards worshipped as a saint. Unfortunately nothing is known about her life and the circumstances of her death, so that we cannot make a comparison: *De S. Margareta, Martyre* (BHL 5324),in *Acta Sanctorum*, 25 Oct. (3d ed. Paris-Rome, 1870), vol. 59, 713–720, here 716.

50. Drogo, *Vita Godeliph*, 1, ed. Huyghebaert, 38f.

51. Ibid., 8, p. 54f.

52. Ibid., 10, p. 60f.

53. Duby, *Mâle moyen age*, 70.

54. Baring en Cashford, *The Myth of the Goddess*, 582ff.

55. Henri Pirenne, *Histoire de Belgique*, vol. 1 (3d ed. Brussels: Henri Lamertin, 1909), 105–108; Thérèse De Hemptinne, "Vlaanderen en Henegouwen onder de erfgenamen van de Boudewijns, 1070-1244," in *Algemene Geschiedenis der Nederlanden*, vol. 2 (Haarlem: Van Dishoeck, 1982), 372–376.

56. See also David Nicholas, *Medieval Flanders* (London [etc.]: Longman, 1992), 60f.

57. Ernest Warlop, "Het sociale kader: De Vlaamse adel in de tweede helft van de elfde eeuw," *Sacris Erudiri*, 20 (1971), 182f.

58. Nicolaas-Norbert Huyghebaert, "Un moine hagiographe: Drogon de Bergues-Saint-Winoc," *Sacris Erudiri*, 20 (1971), 221f; Huyghebaert, *Drogo, Vita Godeliph*, 23–26 and 76f.

59. *Handwörterbuch des deutschen Aberglaubens*, vol. 6 (Berlin [etc.]: De Gruyter, 1987), 570ff.

60. Duby, *Mâle moyen age*, 62, 66.

61. *Vita Altera S. Godelevae*, 20, ed. *AASS* 29, 419

62. Ibid., 90–95, p. 435f.

63. *Vita B. Ide Vidue* (BHL 4141), in *Acta Sanctorum (AASS)*, 13 April (3d ed. Paris-Rome, 1866), vol. 11, 141–146; and Migne, *Patrologia Latina*, vol. 155, 437–466.

64. Ibid., 3, ed. *PL* 155, 439.

65. Baudouin de Gaiffier, "Sainte Ide de Boulogne et l'Espagne: A propos de reliques Mariales," *Analecta Bollandiana*, 86 (1968), 67 and 70, n. 1.

66. Ibid., 75.

67. Ibid., 67–82; Nicolaas-Norbert Huyghebaert, "La mère de Godefroid de Bouillon: La comtesse Ide de Boulogne," *Publications de la section historique de l'institut Grand-Ducal de Luxembourg*, 95 (1981), 43–63; Henri Platelle, "Ide, comtesse de Boulogne," in *Nouvelle Biographie Nationale*, vol. 2 (Brussels: Académie Royale des Sciences, [etc.], 1990), 233f.

68. Jan A. Nelson and Emanuel J. Mickel, *The Old French Crusade Cycle* (Tuscaloosa [etc.]: University of Alabama Press, 1977).

69. *Vita Ide*, 2, ed. *PL* 155, 438.

70. Ibid., 3, p. 439

71. Ibid., 4, p. 439f.

72. Ibid., 5, p. 440.

73. Robert H. Bautier, "Boulogne-sur-Mer," in *Lexikon des Mittelalters*, vol. 2 (Munich: Artemis-Verlag, 1983), 500.

74. *Vita Ide*, 6f., ed. *PL* 155, 442.

75. Ibid., 8, p. 442.

76. Ibid., 9, p. 443 and De Gaiffier, "Sainte Ide," 79ff.

77. Ibid., 7, p. 442 and 11, p. 445 resp.

78. Ibid., 17, p. 448.

79. John C. Andressohn, *The Ancestry and Life of Godfrey of Bouillon* (Social Science series, 5) (Bloomington: Indiana University Publications, 1947), 25f.

80. De Gaiffier, "Sainte Ide," 70f.

81. Huyghebaert, "La mère de Godefroid de Bouillon," 54ff.

82. Ibid., 13, p. 446 and 12. p. 445.

83. Ibid., 13, p. 446.

84. Duby, *Mâle moyen age*, 58.

85. De Gaiffier, "Sainte Ide," 69; Huyghebaert, "La mère de Godefroid de Bouillon," 45.

86. Derek Baker, "'A Nursery of Saints': St. Margaret of Scotland Reconsidered," in *Medieval women*, ed. Derek Baker (Oxford: Blackwell, 1978), 130f.

87. Ibid., 122–125.

88. Gábor Klaniczay, *The Uses of Supernatural Power: The Transformation of Popular Religion in Early-Modern Europe* (Cambridge, Mass: Polity Press, 1990), 89.

89. Baker, "A nursery of saints," 120f.

90. Klaniczay, *The Uses of Supernatural Power*, 91.

91. Ibid., 1, p. 437.

92. Baring and Cashford, *The Myth of the Goddess*, 273–298.

93. Patrick Corbet, *Les saints Ottoniens: Sainteté dynastique, sainteté royale et sainteté féminine autour de l'an Mil* (Beihefte der Francia, 15) (Sigmaringen: Thorbecke, 1986), 206.

94. Hariulf, *Vita Arnulfi*, 1.26 and 31f, ed. *AASS OSB* 2, 423f and 526f.

95. Clarissa W. Atkinson, *The Old Vocation: Christian Motherhood in the Middle Ages* (Ithaca, N.Y. [etc.]: Cornell University Press, 1991), 60, see also 157f.

96. Ibid., 142.

97. Ibid., 60f.

98. *Vita Ide*, 9, ed. *PL* 155, 443.

99. Ibid., 6, p. 441.

100. See also Duby, *Mâle moyen age*, 54–58.

101. Jan J.M. Timmers, *Christelijke symboliek en iconografie* (3d ed. Haarlem: De Haan, 1978), nr. 364.

102. Caroline Walker Bynum, "'. . . And Woman His Humanity': Female Imagery in the Religious Writing of the Later Middle Ages," in her *Fragmentation and Redemption: Essays on Gender and the Human Body in Medieval Religion* (New York: Zone Books, 1992), 154.

103. Ibid., 177.

104. See the contribution of Anneke B. Mulder-Bakker, "Ivetta of Huy: *Mater et Magistra*," to this volume; Ludo Milis, "Pureté et sexualité," in *Villes et campagnes au Moyen Age: Mélanges Georges Despy*, ed. Jean-Marie Duvosquel and Alain Dierkens (Liège: Editions Du Perron, 1991), 503f.

105. *Vita Ide*, 8, ed. *PL* 155, 442.

106. Thomas Cramer, "Lohengrin," in *Lexikon des Mittelalters*, vol. 5, 2080–2082; Geert H. M. Claassens, "Zwaanridder" in *Van Aiol tot de Zwaanridder*, ed. W.P. Gerritsen and A.G. van Melle (Nijmegen: SUN, 1993), 380–384.

107. Claassens, "Zwaanridder," 384.

108. Cramer, "Lohengrin," 2080: a letter of Guido van Bazoche (c. 1180) and Willem van Tyrus (1184).

109. Huyghebaert, "La mère de Godefroid de Bouillon," 57–63.

110. As the new edition of Emanuel J. Mickel jr., *The Old French Crusade Cycle III: Les Enfances Godefroi* (Tuscaloosa [etc.]: University of Alabama Press, 1993) was not yet available to me, see: *La chanson du chevalier au cygne et de Godefroid de Bouillon*, ed. C. Hippeau (Paris: Auguste Aubry, 1877), 26.

111. Ibid., 27.

112. Huyghebaert, "La mère de Godefroid de Bouillon," 62; William of Tyre, *Historia Rerum Transmarinarum*, 9.6, in Migne, *Patrologia Latina*, vol. 201, 438.

113. Huyghebaert, "La mère de Godefroid de Bouillon," 62f.

114. Andressohn, *The Ancestry and Life of Godfrey of Bouillon*, 26.

13. *S.Hilarius.* | *S.Iuetta.*

Figure 7.1. Ivetta together with Hilarius, the other saint of the thirteenth of January in Rosweyde, Generale Legende *(Antwerp, 1649) (U.B. Groningen)*

7. IVETTA OF HUY

MATER ET MAGISTRA

Anneke B. Mulder-Bakker *

THE MATERFAMILIAS

When Ivetta (1158–1228),[1] a rich patrician widow of Huy at the end of the twelfth century, had herself enclosed in a cell attached to a lepers' chapel outside the city, she was not prevented from keeping a close eye on her family. Her oldest son caused her no worry. He had been called to religion before her and had entered the respected Cistercian abbey of Orval. He was soon to become abbot there—a source of pious joy to his mother.

Her second son was more of a problem; he enjoyed his freedom and lived in luxury, doing his part to dissipate the considerable family fortune. In Ivetta's opinion he was leading a wanton life. This distressed her and she often talked about it with the rest of the family. She did everything in her power to change his attitudes. She spent whole nights in prayer, tore her hair and wept copiously. It was, says her biographer, as if she were going through labor again, this time in order to bear for God the son she had first borne for the world.

When her son came to visit her she showered him with admonishments. He did not dare challenge her openly, knowing that she was regarded as a saint, but neither was he prepared to give in to her wishes. So eventually he demanded his portion of the inheritance and left for the city of Liège, out of his mother's reach (or so he thought). Although the sources do not give the impression that he was really headed for the gutter,[2] Ivetta was very distressed. At her wits' end, she called on God for help.[3]

Then it happened that her son had a terrifying nightmare, in which he saw himself being handed over to the demons of hell, but in which he also heard that his punishment would be postponed for three years for his mother's sake. The next day, when he was wandering in confusion through the streets of Liège, he was accosted by a beautiful, radiant woman. He did not know her, but she spoke to him and said: "Your mother greets you, and asks you to come and see her." Even more confused and full of remorse over his unholy life, he hurried to Huy and went to the window of Ivetta's cell. How happy his mother was, when she saw that her second son had repented and had been set on the right track by a subtle hint from an unknown Lady— who must have been Mary. Together they planned his future: first he was to study theology and then he would enter a monastery, Trois-Fontaines, another well-known Cistercian abbey.

Now Ivetta had all her close relatives grouped around her as a spiritual family. Her mother had been the first to enter the religious life, when Ivetta was still a child. When she was working at a lepers' shelter, before she was enclosed in her cell, Ivetta had persuaded her father to devote himself to a religious life. After various wanderings, he had ended up in Villers, probably the best-known Cistercian abbey in Belgium. Now both of her sons had also entered monasteries; she could be contented and devote the rest of her life to her spiritual progeny. She ran her community as a *sapientissima materfamilias*.

This information is to be found in the *vita* which was written shortly after Ivetta's death by the monk Hugh of Floreffe.[4] He had been asked to write it by his abbot John, who had been Ivetta's confessor. In the first part he had already told how Ivetta, as a young girl of thirteen, had been married against her will and how she had been left a widow with three children at the age of eighteen. As soon as her children had been old enough to manage without her, around 1181, she had gone to work in the lepers' shelter. Just outside the city gates—Huy was in the twelfth century one of the most important commercial centres in Europe[5]—on the river Meuse, next to an old chapel, a paltry shelter had been built for lepers,[6] who were not allowed to enter the city because of the risk of infection. Ivetta had moved in with them and taken care of the sick. She, the daughter of an important town official and a member of the urban elite, now laid the table of the poor and shared the life of outcasts. She had done this in order to become an outcast herself, to become one of the "rejected." What she wanted most was to become a leper herself, and she did everything in her power to do so: she had washed herself with infected bath water and had smeared herself with blood.

However, what actually happened was the opposite of what she had been aiming at. Not only had she not become ill, but she had gained the admiration of her fellow-townspeople and received their support. She had expanded the leprosarium into a flourishing hospital with a fine church and a convent in which she and a group of followers had founded a religious community. This community is thought to have been one of the very first Beguinages in Europe.[7] Ten years later, when Ivetta was about thirty-three years old (!), she had herself enclosed as a recluse in a cell which had been built on to the new chapel by her father. There she devoted herself to prayer, meditation and asceticism. But at the same time she remained available to believers who came to ask her advice and kept in touch with her family and friends. She led the community from the keep of her cell; she was the *domina*.

When her confessor, the abbot of the Premonstratensian abbey of Floreffe, wanted to hear her general confession, he had to have a hole cut in the wall in order to reach her deathbed. At that meeting she told him much of what we in turn know from his confidant, Hugh. After thirty-six years of reclusion she died, at the age of sixty-nine, on a bitterly cold day in January 1228. At the hour she drew her last breath, the snowstorm also held its breath for a moment, and birds sang a summer song. Like humanity, nature understood that a saint had died and paid her a last tribute.

Ivetta belongs to the oldest generation of *mulieres sanctae* in the Low Countries.[8] Although lesser known than her younger contemporaries such as Mary of Oignies (1177–1213) and Lutgard of Tongres (1182–1246), she is a good object of study, not only because she was a saint *and* a mother, but especially because her *vita* was written by a biographer who had an eye for the social and emotional aspects of her life. In describing Ivetta's life, Hugh of Floreffe—less of a Church politician than James of Vitry, who rigorously transformed Mary of Oignies into a model saint[9]—seems to be struggling how to express this saint's uniqueness. As though wanting to make sure not to miss a point, he incorporated various anecdotes about her ordinary life, her concerns as a mother and her social activities. For our study his *vita* is a mine of information.

In this study I will first give a brief account of the religious women's movement in the Low Countries around 1200 and then examine Ivetta's *Vita* in relation to the central issues of this book: female virginity, marriage and sexuality; mothering and motherhood; the construction of sanctity.

HOLY WOMEN IN THE LOW COUNTRIES

Around the middle of the thirteenth century a German cleric wrote about the new piety among women:

> Diu kunst ist bi unsern tagen
> in Brabant und in Baierlanden
> undern wiben ufgestanden.
> Herre Got, waz kunst ist daz
> daz sich ein alt wip baz
> verstet dan witzige man?[10]

[This art of religious living has begun in our days among women. Lord God, what kind of art is this that it is better understood by an old woman than by a wise man?]

This quotation has been widely used, as it expresses exactly the amazement felt both by contemporaries and by the modern historian on encountering so much unprecedented religious creativity, particularly among women, in the Low Countries in the thirteenth century, the time Ivetta lived in. Hundreds, possibly even thousands of women abandoned themselves to the love for Christ and made their mark in all sorts of ways. Thomas of Cantimpré speaks of two thousand Beguines just in the one small town of Nivelles.[11] He must have been exaggerating, but it does demonstrate the overwhelming character of this women's movement. King Louis IX of France was so impressed that he especially asked the pious women of Liège, "who are with you in such abundance,"[12] to pray for him and his family. What were these women like and what inspired them?

Many publications have been written about these pious women, often named *mulieres sanctae* in the sources, but most of them are about Beguines. The term *mulieres sanctae* is tacitly taken to refer to full-time religious, whose lives were similar to those of nuns.[13] In my view, this is incorrect and too limited a definition. The contemporary sources present a much more pluriform picture, depicting quite a variety of pious women, living within society, married or unmarried, or Beguines and, most often Cistercian, nuns.[14] Recently Ursula Peters concluded that there is in fact no evidence to be found in the sources that the Beguines formed a separate category with their own particular brand of spirituality; and what interested her more, their own particular literature.[15]

Caesarius of Heisterbach, a very important witness as regards the ordinary religious practice, concluded about the *mulieres sanctae*:

Licet enim huiusmodi mulieres, quales in dyocesi Leodiensi plurimas esse novimus, in habitu seculari secularibus cohabitent, multis tamen claustralibus caritate superiores sunt: inter seculares spirituales, inter luxuriosos celibes, in medio turbarum vitam ducunt heremiticiam.[16]

[Although these women, of whom a great many are known in the diocese of Liège, live amongst ordinary people, in charity they are superior to many conventuals: amongst the worldly they live as religious, amongst the luxurious as celibates, in the midst of the crowds they live like hermits.]

He regards it as typical that these women lived a hermit's life in their own villages or towns, in personal abstinence, but in contact with their fellow citizens and sensitive to their needs. They fasted and prayed a great deal, kept vigils in the church and chastized themselves. Many experienced mystical visions. This sort of life seems to him more redeeming than that of many who lived in seclusion. He encountered all sorts of pious women, of all ranks and classes, young and old, married and unmarried, virgins and mothers.[17] In the chronicle of Villers one such *femina valde religiosa* is portrayed. She excelled in faith, charity, and good works. During a mass a celebrant saw that she was accompanied by two angels and that a halo appeared around her head.[18] In his turn, Thomas of Cantimpré knew a young woman of noble birth following the Cistercian rule at home after her parents' death. She did not wear linen clothing, fasted, ate no meat, maintained silence, read the offices.[19] In Ivetta's *Vita* we read that the pious recluse made a deep impression on the women of Huy. Some of them joined her community, others paid frequent visits and gave her financial support. Still other women spent whole nights in vigils in the parish church.[20] In Liège pious women went to live near Lambert li Bègue, a popular preacher who would later be accused of heresy, one reason probably being that his activities included translating *Lives* of the saints and books of the Bible into the vernacular for the common faithful. One person who was deeply impressed was Odilia, a woman who after her husband's death wanted to devote herself to a religious life. Unfortunately she had fallen into the hands of a parish priest who had taken her into his house and forced her into a prolonged sexual relationship. It was only after his death that she was able to have herself enclosed as a recluse and devote herself entirely to penitence and prayer.[21]

What all these women had in common was that they all felt a deep desire for personal penance. They were strict ascetics and lived lives of great self-sacrifice. Their inspiration sprang from an intimate relationship with Christ. They prayed to him for hours on end and met him in mystical visions in which they would sometimes cradle him in their arms like a mother[22] or talk with him as a small child,[23] and sometimes be with him at the Cross or in a mystical union in heaven.[24] They also felt an intense craving for the Eucharist and were rife in the gift of tears, weeping for days on end for their sins.

What is striking in all the *exempla* and in the *vitae* as well, is that little is said of traditional monastic virtues such as renouncing one's family and the world, taking vows of chastity, preserving virginity. Quite a few exemplary women were either married or at least not obsessed with the ideal of virginity; whole families were choosing for God together, and relatively few discourses were set up about virginity and celibacy. Mary of Oignies was herself married and, together with her husband, joined a group of ascetics outside Nivelles. Later both of them, with their entire family, went to live in or near the priory of Oignies, where Mary's brother-in-law was prior. She and her husband lived in chastity at that time. In the *Vita*, James of Vitry ignores this marriage and the family ties as much as possible, as they did not fit in with his conception of sainthood, but whether Mary would have agreed with him is open to question. It is evident that in the latter part of her life she punished her body severely—to the point of self-mutilation—but it is not clear whether this was something she had wished to do all her life or something she did at that stage under pressure from the Church and tradition.[25] Thomas of Cantimpré describes Margaret of Ypres as a young girl: pious as she was, she never played games, sat in church and prayed all day long. At the same time, however, she fell in love and became engaged. It was the Dominican Zegher who persuaded her to take a vow of virginity. Margaret found this very difficult and could hardly bear to renounce her loved one. When she had finally decided to do so, she could no longer tolerate the presence of any man at all, an attitude which does not express great inner security.[26] In a later chapter Elizabeth of Thuringia, living in neighboring Germany in the same period, will be discussed. She too was married and loved her husband deeply, with what was described as a "leidenschaftliche, ja wilde Liebe," yet at the same time she led an ascetic, saintly life.[27] Apparently the two things were not mutually exclusive.

This concept was familiar to contemporaries. In his *Dialogue* between an experienced monk and a young novice, Caesarius of Heisterbach has his novice ask: So virgins are better than married women who live in chastity? In his answer the monk explains that this might be true in principle, but that many married women and widows were more deserving than virgins, because virginity is not a virtue in itself; after all, there are virgins amongst the heathens as well.[28] What matters is the right attitude and the part love and charity play. Were not most of the patriarchs, prophets and apostles married? When the novice then asks why the saints talk so much about *virginitas*, the monk shifts his attention to *castitas*: what we might call "not being unfaithful." This is the important thing: virgins must preserve their virginity and practise *continentia virginalis*, married women the *pudicitia coniugalis*, and widows the *continentia vidualis*. It may be the case that in principle virgins will reap a hundredfold in heaven and married women only thirtyfold, but in practice married women may well reap a much higher reward because of their works of love, their *caritas*.[29] Love, that is apparently the crux of the matter, as we also saw in the passage quoted above. Mechtild of Magdeburg had a vision in which she saw Mary, the patriarchs and the prophets standing higher in rank than apostles and virgins. She was surprised at this, since these people were married and possessed worldly goods. John the Evangelist explains to her that they were not further removed from Christ, because the Word had become flesh.[30]

In the oldest vernacular poem of Liège, the *Poème Moral*, believers who have the strength to withstand temptation, are encouraged simply to continue their role in society. By doing so, they can be of great support to others.[31] The faint-hearted, the irresolute, are the ones who need the seclusion of a convent or cell. James of Vitry regards the lives of devout peasants and town-dwellers as scarcely less deserving than the lives of those who spend the whole day in church singing the offices or the whole night in vigils.[32]

Nevertheless, many women were compelled to go and live in communities or to take refuge in convents. According to James of Vitry they did this because otherwise their lives were not safe. They ran the risk of falling into the hands of lewd men.[33] This seems to have been a great problem: many men were unable to keep their hands off and priests in particular found celibacy difficult. It was in this period that the Church officially commanded celibacy, while at the same time assuming that priests were probably not capable of it. Brundage wrote in a recent study: "[S]ome decretals of the late twelfth and early thirteenth century tolerated clerical fornication so long as it was discreet, directing prelates to take action only against notorious offenders. The legal writers treated this policy of selective enforcement as a dispensation from the full rigor of the law and thus achieved a precarious harmony between principles and practice."[34] This "precarious harmony" may have existed from the point of view of the clergy, but if so it was at the expense of women, both married and unmarried, for whom it caused a terrible moral dilemma. A priest's concubine once asked her confessor, who was not aware of her situation, what happened to priests' mistresses. He answered, in jest: "They cannot be saved, unless they enter a burning oven." The woman took this literally and, after baking her bread, crawled into the hot oven. At the moment of her death, people saw a shining white dove fly out of the chimney, straight into heaven.[35]

Priests, even monks and abbots, who did in fact live in celibacy, were regarded almost as saints. When Abbot William of Villers had died and women were washing his body, a halo appeared around his genitals: "This showed that he had always remained a virgin, pure and unsullied in body and spirit."[36] Conrad of Liège, another abbot of Villers who had risen to be a cardinal and a legate in Germany, wanted men who could not keep their hands off, dealt with much more severely and issued strict decrees to achieve this.[37]

Is it possible that the great emphasis on the physical virginity of young girls and their protection in separate houses sprang from a desire to make women partly responsible for men's failure? Were chaste young girls obliged to make sure that men could not give in to their sinful inclinations?

There is a second characteristic which is typical of all the *mulieres religiosae*: their attentive concern for those around them. As spinsters and housewives, but even as recluses locked up in cells or as nuns in Cistercian convents, they remained in contact with the outside world. Margaret the Lame of Magdeburg, a recluse, interrupted her visions when people came to her window to ask for help. She herself summoned known sinners to come to her. The Middle Dutch *vita* says:

> Sometimes it seemed to her that she had such great wisdom that even if all the oppressed hearts of the world should come to her she could have comforted them, each according to his own needs. She spoke to people with such sincerity and sympathy that her soul was quickened with pure charity [again emphasis on *caritas*] and her heart was almost torn asunder by eagerness.[38]

Critics called her a chatter-box. Alcantara Mens speaks of the Beguines's "irrepressible apostolic energy, which conquers by word and example."[39] These women also encouraged others to preaching and pastoral care, and taught them how to preach intelligibly and inspiringly. James of Vitry learned this from Mary of Oignies, Thomas of Cantimpré from Lutgard of Tongres. A young Dominican who had to preach in Ypres, the city in which Margaret had lived, and who was very apprehensive about it, had a vision in which he saw Margaret standing in front of him in the pulpit with an open book, so that he could simply read out what he had to preach.[40] Presumably, the women would have loved to preach themselves; Mary of Oignies at least wanted to pilgrimage to Southern France to fight the Albigensian heresy.[41]

Recent scholarship has often pointed out that the Beguines—I think we should say *mulieres sanctae* in general—devoted themselves to works of charity.[42] Women like Mary of Oignies and Ivetta of Huy were among the first to comprehend the needs of the new urban society and to attempt to meet them. They saw that the flourishing of trade and industry in Flanders and Brabant had brought not only new riches but also new poverty. Entrepreneurs, greedy for gain, were starting to exploit simple laborers, others were being excluded from work and care. The *mulieres sanctae* saw the dangers of the new prosperity. Sometimes they reacted quite drastically by giving away their own possessions or by going out begging, sometimes they gave alms very generously and supported the victims of the new morality. They also started to take care of the sick and lepers in hospitals outside town.

These women found some of their inspiration in the *Lives* of saints. Long before James of Voragine compiled his *Legenda Aurea*, thus making the stories of the saints accessible to a wide public, lay people were being inspired by stories of saints in the distant past. Lambert li Bègue from Liège (d. 1177) relates that he personally had translated the *Lives* of Mary and Saint Agnes as well as the *Acts of the Apostles*.[43] It seems significant that here in this circle evidence of saint's *Lives* in the vernacular crops up. These legends as well as the above-mentioned *Poème Moral* belong to the oldest parts of vernacular literature. The *Poème* includes a *Life of Thaïs*, a converted *meretrix*—which literally means whore, but in moralistic literature also stood for married woman.[44] Probably Ivetta too was inspired by them, and especially by the Life of another *meretrix* who continually crops up in Caesarius's *Dialogue*: Mary Magdalen.[45] In the twelfth and early thirteenth centuries the popularity of Mary Magdalen increased enormously everywhere in the southern Low Countries.

This is the religious climate in which we must place Ivetta of Huy. In the following section we shall see that a number of elements mentioned above will come back.

A YOUNG GIRL'S OPTIONS

In the world in which Ivetta grew up, the family was still the cornerstone of society. We might also say the clan, or even better, the House, for "the family" meant not only the family members but also their property. People and property were inseparable. The first and most important task of the members of the House was to maintain this unity and to pass it on intact to the next generation; the family members were supposed to devote all their energy to this. Women had to bear legitimate children so that there would be a next generation and also had to assume responsibility for the household, sometimes including the business affairs. Men begot the children (and usually a few illegitimate ones as well), worked on the land or in trade or occupied themselves with public administration. Every member was supposed to devote his or her energy to the honor and reputation of the family. The larger community kept a close watch on this lest it should be tainted in any way.[46] This was also the case in the urban society of Huy. But there were other options.

The official Church had always had objections to these clan communities. Not only had monks and ascetics been against marriage from conviction and rejected every form of sexuality—a true Christian did not marry—but even if they did not object to marriage as such, they disapproved of clan solidarity, which after all subordinated the individual responsibility of each Christian for his own salvation to the prosperity of the family. Obviously the Church had to be opposed to this.[47] It was in the twelfth century that this personal responsibility, also in matters of marriage, was gaining more emphasis. Brundage speaks of "a dawning consciousness of the importance of individual choice, coupled with a new awareness of marriage as a personal relationship."[48] But there was something else as well.

Commercial centres like Huy had evolved thanks to the private enterprise of their citizens. Their personal initiatives had yielded rich rewards. Their independent action and personal responsibility had brought them recognition. A greater pluriformity was the result, both from an economic as from a cultural and a religious point of view. This was even true of women.

This was the maze of contradictory expectations through which Ivetta had to find her way. A devout young girl, she had been impressed upon to dedicate her virginity to Christ. But as a member of a wealthy and powerful family she was expected to marry young and to bear many sons. If she had been able to follow her own feelings, she would have done neither. She saw marriage as something to be dreaded. To have to live under the yoke of a marriage, to have to go to bed with a man, to bear children and to shoulder the heavy responsibilities of running a household—for this was the role she was expected to assume—all of this, according to her biographer, was abhorrent to her. However, under the pressure of her parents, who were supported by the kith and kin and who were themselves being put under pressure by the town (!), she had agreed.[49] So at the age of thirteen she had been married; five years later she was the mother of three children. All the same, she had continued to resist her conjugal duties and to abhor all intercourse with her husband. She loathed him so much that she would have liked him to die. She was heavily censured for this. Eventually she herself realized that these thoughts were sinful and that she would burn in hell for them; but God brought her to repentance and offered her a new direction. So she resigned herself to her fate and possessed her soul in patience.[50]

From that moment, says her biographer, her life changed; she felt that she had become a different person. Inspired by the Holy Spirit, she started off on the road to sanctitude. Fortunately for her, her husband died soon afterwards. Her father wished her to remarry, but this time she refused outright, and managed to get her way.[51]

Three conclusions can be drawn from this story. The first is that no religious motivation is given for Ivetta's resistance to marriage. We assume almost automatically that Ivetta, being a budding saint, was against marriage because she wanted to preserve her virginity for Christ. But the text does not say so. Assuming that a popular *topos* like this will not have been omitted accidentally, the conclusion can only be that this was not Ivetta's (chief) motive.[52] Ivetta's case confirms what we have already seen in the lives of other pious women of that period and in Caesarius of Heisterbach's writings: that the ideals of virginity and renunciation were not as dominant as we might assume on the basis of our knowledge of the Church fathers and monastic authors.[53] Evidently virginity was not a prerequisite for Ivetta's later sainthood, nor was her marriage an obstacle. For a woman who did not wish to become a nun, marriage even provided an "alternative route" to sanctitude, as we shall see. We can only conclude that her refusal to marry kept her within the boundaries of what the Church, with its predilection for *virginitas*, required from a saint. Even a conservative monk could not object to this woman, who had been forced into marriage against her will, becoming a saint.

This is confirmed by my second point: the views of Hugh of Floreffe, author of the *Vita*. We might expect that this monk, having renounced all sexuality himself, would have expressed, either implicitly or explicitly, some aversion to marriage and sexuality in his story. This is not the case. He simply relates the facts in a neutral way, without betraying any negative attitude to marriage or even any sympathy for Ivetta's horror. Only when she has resigned herself to her fate does he indicate that she can now rely on God's help and protection and that hell and damnation have been averted. Apparently he completely agrees with the family, and his implicit message for girls is that they should marry and place their family's interests above their own desires. They should submit themselves and it is only then that they can count on God's support in their suffering.

This view also becomes evident in the following section,[54] in Hugh's description of Ivetta's father's attempts to have her remarried, even though she already has two healthy sons; the third child had died in childhood. When Ivetta refuses point-blank and stands her ground, her father calls in the help of the bishop, in order to persuade her to change her mind. The bishop does in fact try. Apparently he also takes it for granted that Ivetta should remarry, even though the Church was officially opposed to second marriages![55] Ivetta only finds support at the moment she turns to Christ: the bishop then promises her that he will be her guide and protector. Hugh expresses no disapproval of the marriage negotiations.

Finally I come back to Ivetta's aversion to marriage. What is so striking is that she so clearly has her own opinion; perhaps even more striking is that she dares to express it openly. Apparently this was possible at that time:

women could in fact expect their views to be taken seriously (not that they would automatically get their way, of course). When Ivetta had to appear before the bishop because of her obstinacy and defend herself in the face of a room full of dignitaries, she was visibly intimidated. The bishop saw this and took her aside. He put her at ease and had a private conversation with her. He too took her feelings into account.

To sum up, virginity was a much less dominant element, even in the attitudes of Church officials, than we are inclined to assume. On the other hand, marriage had a much higher status, even in the Church. Ivetta, with her personal aversion to marriage, kept within the boundaries which the Church regarded as desirable for saintly women.

THE BURDENS OF MOTHERHOOD

Now we come to motherhood: first the facts. However much Ivetta may have hated marriage and marital intercourse, once the children had arrived, she loved them deeply. They were everything to her. As long as they were dependent on her, the children determined the extent to which she could fulfil her spiritual vocation.[56] When after the death of her husband she gained access to the family property and started distributing large amounts to the poor,[57] her father thought she was depriving her children of their inheritance and took them away from her. Ivetta backed down a little and agreed to invest the children's inheritance with brokers in the city. For rich patricians in a commercial town like Huy, investing money in this way was a perfectly normal thing to do, but the Church regarded it as usury. Ivetta herself and her biographer regarded it as a grievous sin, for which she would be severely punished later. It is even the most grievous sin with which she was reproached. But she did it in order to get her children back, and for Hugh this was a justification. As a mother she could not bear to be without them.[58]

As an alternative Ivetta now devoted herself to strict asceticism and abstinence and offered hospitality to the poor and needy. Her house became a refuge for pilgrims and sojourners; she shared her bread with the poor and needy. In this way she gave back to the poor what she may have taken away from them by profiteering. Like Elizabeth of Thuringia, she gave a personal interpretation to the ideal of poverty. Neither of them formally renounced their property as the monks did, nor did they live from the work of their own hands as the hermits did, but they systematically refused to eat or use anything which had been gained by extortion or profiteering.

Whereas her initial way of life had been unacceptable to her family, she now had to confront critics in the church who thought her life style was half-baked. So Ivetta, when her sons had reached school age—she herself was 23 and had been a widow for five years—decided to give not only her money but also herself to the poor. As far as we know, she did not renounce her property at this point either, nor did she break off contact with her children and relatives. Once she had moved into the leprosarium and secured her own salvation, she regarded it as her first task to bring her family to God. In Hugh's imagery, she now wished to bear for God those she had first borne for the world.[59] So her motherhood is not denied, but raised to a higher level. Actually, it was only through her marriage and motherhood that this possibility was open to her. As an unmarried girl she would not have had any legal competence, as she would have remained under the custody of her father and family; as a nun, if she had chosen to go that way, she would have been cut off from her family and the world. Motherhood, and to an even greater extent her widowhood, had opened up a road to social independence for her; we shall see that the life of a recluse was to give her even more freedom.

I believe it is not unthinkable that Ivetta, as a widow, had originally intended to carry on fulfilling her devotion to Christ in a similar way as she had done before, in her own house. When it turned out that this was not acceptable to her family, who saw the inheritance disappearing, nor to the Church, which disapproved of this "part-time" sainthood, she felt compelled to withdraw from the world altogether. Her motherhood, and the status it had in society, now enabled her to go in a new direction, for which she could appeal to Mary for a theological basis. Ivetta is now called *mater misericors*,[60] which reminds us of the *Mater misericordiae*, Mary, the mother of Christ. According to Bernard of Clairvaux and his adepts, the Incarnation of Christ and the salvation of mankind would not have been possible without the cooperation of Mary. Mary's motherhood was essential; it had made of her an intermediary of redemption, a role which she still fulfilled from heaven as *Mater misericordiae*. Mary was "mother of all who are saved in our saviour," as Julian of Norwich was to write.[61]

Ivetta had a special relationship with this Mary.[62] After she had had herself enclosed in 1181, she had had a vision—her first—in which she had to appear before the judgment-seat of the Son of Man. Beside him Mary, the Queen of Heaven, was sitting on her throne. Through the intercedence of Mary, who had defended Ivetta, and taken her sins upon herself, Ivetta's sins had been forgiven, and she had been entrusted to the special care of Mary: "Mother, behold your daughter," Christ had spoken, "I entrust her to you as your own daughter, as your own special servant for eternity: guard and protect her and guide her as your own child;" a paraphrase of the words He had spoken to Mary and John from the Cross (Jn 19:27). From that moment onwards Ivetta had had a special bond with Mary, so much so that the clergy had some doubt as to the orthodoxy of her faith. As mother and son are of one flesh, more of one flesh than a father and his son, explains Hugh, as this is also, or especially true, of Mary and her Son, and less true of Joseph and Jesus' brothers (!), and since through the Resurrection Mary's carnality was raised above the stars, the whole of human nature, but most of all maternal nature, was elevated and venerated. I do not know why exactly Hugh explains this to us. He had heard it from his abbot, who as Ivetta's confessor had heard it from Ivetta herself. She had added that since that first vision she had frequently been with Jesus and his Mother in mystical visions. Both probably picked these images up from Cistercian thought, where Ivetta could find inspiration for her own ideas about motherhood, both spiritual and physical. Just like Mary, Ivetta, through her motherhood, was able to intercede for her physical and spiritual children to gain forgiveness of their sins and eternal redemption. It legitimized her role in the religious community, but also outside, in town.

As a sister in the leper house Ivetta transposed family duties into the spiritual sphere. As head of the Beguines she performed the same duties she had performed as a housewife: she saw to the (spiritual) education of her followers and trained them in virtue and discipline. Several young boys and girls were especially entrusted to her care.[63] It is touching to learn of Ivetta's concern for a certain young girl whom she had "adopted" at an early age. This girl was extremely pious, but also extremely naive, and Ivetta had frequently warned her about wicked men. Nevertheless, the child allowed herself to be taken in by a young clergyman and seduced away from Huy. For six months this man tried, sometimes by violence and sometimes by sweet words, to force her into a sexual relationship, without success, according to Hugh. "All that time faith stood fast against evil: the faith which the venerable Ivetta placed in the Lord on behalf of her daughter, *filia*. Her grief and sorrow, the tears and prayers with which she constantly sacrificed herself to the Lord, saved the daughter she had lost."[64] Just as Ivetta's tears had saved her own son from evil, they now did the same for this spiritual daughter. In a story about a young Premonstratensian monk who had also been entrusted to her care as a young boy, Hugh explicitly calls Ivetta *sapientissima materfamilias.*[65]

Discipline, virtue, good example: these are terms which recur continually in the *Vita.* Even when she felt death approaching, she felt so responsible for her daughters that she frequently called them to her bedside to give them all sorts of advice and instructions. Even her own prayers and offices suffered as a result! *[S]ic se habente cum filiabus matre, magistra cum discipulis*, she behaved like a mother with daughters, a teacher with pupils.[66]

She also took care of the property. She drew in vast sums of money and saw to it that the poverty-stricken colony of tramps grew into a flourishing hospital. Whereas she had started off with scarcely thirty pieces of silver, at the end of her life there were new buildings, a new convent, a fine church where three priests served; "you can scarcely imagine how all this was possible," writes Hugh.[67] Officially the hospital was run by the town authorities and the spiritual leadership was assigned to the prior and the brothers, or to secular curates, but in actual fact it was run by Ivetta, and this was accepted. She had transposed her tasks as a housewife and mother into the spiritual sphere and had stretched them to the utmost.

According to Hugh, Ivetta possessed all the virtues expected of a housewife and mother in her time. As a girl she was attractive, modest and demure, submissive and humble. For example, at her interview with the bishop, she did not speak at once, but listened to him in silence, in the meantime beseeching God that this tribulation should pass her by. Only when she was asked a question did she refute, "cautiously and thoughtfully," everything the bishop had said and explain "modestly and truthfully" that she could not obey. Her family's honor and reputation meant more to her than her own well-being; a public scandal had to be avoided at all costs. In the leprosarium the same thing was true: again, public scandal had to be avoided at all costs.[68]

In her penitence and complete submission to Christ in the leper house she was a model of humility. She considered herself to be nothing. In describing her way of life, Hugh uses terms like *humilis*, *humilitas* at least a dozen times. For him *humilitas* is the highest virtue a human being can achieve.[69] But her strength, too, lay in her humility. Hugh now calls her *virilis* and speaks of *virilitas*, masculine behavior. He uses masculine imagery, such as battle and chivalry, to praise her. This demonstrates what Bynum has stated: "Male biographers . . . felt that saintly women must be elevated or authenticated by male qualities."[70] But at the same time he shows how Ivetta eventually sheds her docility and begins to take initiatives herself. She is no longer the receiver of advice, but the giver; even her own father comes to her for advice. She now couples masculine authority with feminine concern. That, I believe, is something new. Ivetta could behave this way, because as a widow she was liberated from wardships *and* from the suspicion of being a dangerous seducer, at last she was free to play a social role. Like widows in late Antiquity she was expected to be wise and intelligent, a tutor of youngsters and people around her.[71] In her cell her (gendered) role in the social framework was to change again and her virtues were to adapt themselves to yet another situation.

Be this as it may, in Ivetta's case her motherhood was not a matter of secondary importance on the road to sainthood. On the contrary, she was able to use it to further her own independence and then to spiritualize her maternal role and extend it to the whole community. It provided her with the tools to shape that community. Just as in the early Church the ideal pattern of the Roman *familia*, with the *paterfamilias* as head of the family, had served as a model for the Benedictine monastic family under the father abbot, Ivetta used the socio-historical institution of motherhood to shape her religious community. As this was one of the oldest Beguine communities, if not the oldest, this is a matter of no small significance.

THE GIFT OF PROPHECY

Once she was enclosed in her cell, Ivetta was able to acquire even more authority. She was then 33, the same age as Christ when he preached the Gospel.

Through her visions she had prophetic gifts, which enabled her to act with authority. She also had the gift of insight; she could read people's minds. We read in the *Vita* that she "ordered priests to appear before her," and that they did not dare not to give heed. She also kept an eye on the common faithful in town. Once during a mass she "saw" little demons dancing around the head of a sinner gloating, because they saw in him a future victim. She also "beheld" the body of Christ withdrawing in shame from a consecrated host when it was given to a sinner. In dreams and visions she frequently saw fellow-townsmen being condemned before the judgment seat of heaven or in danger of ending up in hell. In order to save anyone she possibly could, she summoned these people and had them confess their sins.[72]

Besides she got involved in political matters. For instance, she opposed the dean and the chapter of the Church of our Blessed Lady, the principal church in town. This was a complicated but extremely interesting issue. Round about 1200 the chapter was involved in a radical process of change. The regular life of the canons was abandoned, prebends were privatized and the dean was accepted as general leader and administrator. He organized the property along "capitalistic" lines and forced tenants to pay high rents.[73] To Ivetta he was the prototype of the avaricious "exploiter." She summoned him to her window to give account.[74]

I have an idea she may actually have had another bone to pick with him. Nothing is said about it in Hugh of Floreffe's *Vita*; he only mentions the dean's avarice and Ivetta's moral indignation at it. But if we examine other sources, such as charters, we catch a glimpse of the power struggle which lay behind: did Hugh think Ivetta had gone too far? Is that the reason for his silence? Or did this sort of thing simply not fit into his concept of a *vita*?[75] The dean in question was invested with archdeaconal power; he had the right to appoint and supervise the priests in Huy. So he was responsible for the unworthy priests in the lepers' chapel who caused Ivetta and her convent much trouble. When through Ivetta's efforts money had finally come pouring in for the leprosarium, she and her sister Beguines found it intolerable that this money should go and enrich those worthless priests and their dean. In 1226, therefore, when two new altars were to be founded, one dedicated to Nicholas and the other to Mary Magdalen, one of Ivetta's confidants was sent to Liège—this is mentioned in the *Vita*, but the reason is not explained—to persuade the bishop, who after all had promised to protect Ivetta, to take these altars under his protection and have them served by priests who enjoyed the confidence of the convent. Ivetta's argument was that the pious gifts had been meant for her and her institution, not to enlarge the income of the town clergy. The bishop, Hugh of Pierrepont, a man who was highly respected, accepted this argument and appointed his confidant John of Huy, Abbot of Floreffe, to this task.[76] In this way both the dean and the town council, which had originally founded the leprosarium and regarded itself as its administrators, were bypassed, as were the prior and the brothers who were supposed to be responsible for the spiritual and material well-being of the holy women. But this state of affairs was not to last very long. After Ivetta's death a serious conflict ensued, which was to lead to court cases in 1236 and 1249. Eventually the dispute was settled amicably by the town council, the prior, and the bishop. Although the lay priests were legally in the right, it was agreed that Ivetta had the moral right on her side. One altar was allocated to the priory of Wanze, which belonged to Floreffe, and the other to the regular priests who were affiliated to the convent. So really Ivetta's side had won out in the end.[77]

Ivetta's role surpassed by far what was usually permissible for a woman. I believe she was aware of this and assented to it. Although she continually speaks of herself as "the sinner Ivetta," she was conscious of her special position and exploited it skilfully. For instance: she told of a vision she had had in which John the Baptist, when she was longing to receive communion, invited her to say a mass with him. She was allowed to stand next to him, saw him breaking the bread—something which ordinary faithful never saw and which she said she had herself never seen—and passing it to her. She was permitted to "assist": *coadesse*. The word has connotations of cooperation, "co-celebration," and so of a priestly quality. Did she see her position as something between that of a priest and that of an ordinary believer?[78]

At the end of her life, on the feast of Mary Magdalen—to whom the convent, as we have seen, had recently dedicated an altar, so that Mary Magdalen was one of the patron saints of the community—Ivetta had a vision in which the woman apostle had taken her by the hand and led her before Christ. Mary Magdalen then withdrew and Ivetta was able to fall before Christ and wash his feet with her tears: exactly what Mary Magdalen herself had done to earn her veneration. It was as though Ivetta had taken on Mary Magdalen's role; surely no small pretension![79]

What does this teach us? For instance, what does it teach us about sainthood and motherhood?

THE CONSTRUCTION OF SANCTITY

Sainthood, it should be recapitulated once and again, is not an absolute category, especially not for historians. As historians analyse the surviving evidence from the past, it is a concept which changes continuously, depending on place and time. If we follow the tradition of Max Weber and others, it can be regarded as a sort of charismatic power which a society is prepared to confer upon someone.[80] A person considered a holy man is accredited with supernatural powers, which give him the capacity to exercise power and influence. Historians infer from the sources that this accreditation, consciously or not, takes place on the basis of a number of criteria, which may in their turn vary according to the various groups within that society. The official Church, with its long and learned tradition, has to a certain extent different criteria from those of a peasant society or an urban community. Sanctitude conferred upon someone results from the total sum of various interwoven forces and powers. This was, of course, also the case in the southern Netherlands around 1200.

When the life of one of these charismatic personalities was later described in a *vita*, other factors, in their turn, had an influence on the concept: the traditions and ideals of the group for whom the *Life* was being written, the models of holiness which the author had at hand or church politics which had to be taken into account. In Ivetta's case the saint and the author were contemporaries and came from the same background, so it can be expected that their traditions and ideals were fairly similar. However, we can assume that in writing his *Vita* Hugh was influenced by his ecclesiastical and monastic background and that consciously or not he used the *Lives* of other saints as models, and that Ivetta, like the other faithful in town, was influenced by the views and ideas which were generally accepted in a town like Huy.

Several complexes of ideas played a determining role in the construction of sanctity in Ivetta's life. I distinguish the following: first, the social demands made on a girl from a wealthy family; the duties of a housewife within a family or clan. Second, the religious views existing in society, whatever their origins may have been; the religious needs people felt, for instance the need for prophetesses or seeresses or for (the replacement of) a mother goddess. Third, a different category consists of the views the Church had on women; ideals of *virginitas* and the *vita contemplativa* in the seclusion of a convent. And finally, Ivetta's own personal views and ideals, which were partly based on what she had heard at church, partly on what she had learnt "at home" and partly new and original ideas of hers. We should not underestimate this last category. Hugh was struck by the *novitas operum Dei*[81] in Ivetta. She was an extremely original and creative personality, with great charismatic gifts, who had a powerful influence on people. This made it possible for her to develop new ideals of sainthood.

Theology and intellectual history often seem to be limited to studying the ideas of Church Fathers and monastic authors; for historians it is challenging, however, to try to find out to what extent these ideas penetrated into everyday life. And even more, to discover whether other ideas and views besides the official ecclesiastical ones made an impact, and if so, what they were.

It seems to me that Ivetta's choice to live the life of a recluse is of crucial importance in an assessment of her sainthood. By withdrawing into her cell she acquired a special position. When Hugh describes how she was shut up in her cell, he observes that a new phase of her life has begun, that a *mutatio* has taken place.[82] He then describes Ivetta's first vision, in which she had received a general pardon for all her sins and entered into an intimate mystical relationship with Mary and her Son. She had finished Martha's work and, having chosen the *via contemplativa*, was now ready to assume Mary (Magdalen's) role, says Hugh. He places her in the tradition of the secluded women mystics who have withdrawn from the world.[83] This is how the monk Hugh first interpreted Ivetta's transition and her life in the *reclusorium*; but it is open to question whether Ivetta herself and the people around her saw it this way, too.

Through her seclusion in the cell and her strict asceticism Ivetta acquired the fame, and with it the charismatic authority, of a saint. To the medievals long and severe fasting was a certain proof of God's grace. Ordinary people simply couldn't do it! People possessed by the devil sometimes pretended, but they always turned out to be lying; for instance, they were caught gorging themselves at night.[84] The advantage of being a recluse was that the community could keep a close eye on her. Everyone could see what went into and came out of the cell; it was as though a recluse were living in quarantine. So a recluse living in asceticism was already surrounded by an aura of sanctitude; she was as it were predisposed to become God's chosen messenger, an intermediary between God and man.[85]

The signs of this sanctitude were: the gift of insight, clairvoyance, the ability to predict the future, especially the hour of one's own death, and sometimes also mystical visions. At least, that was the way the common faithful saw it. For them, a pious recluse was quite different from just any pious woman or Beguine. If a dividing line is to be drawn within the group of *mulieres sanctae*, as it has been in recent studies,[86] I believe that that line must lie between recluses and all the rest. Hugh seems to share this view and uses fitting terms and imagery to express it. Whereas at the beginning of his *Vita* he usually refers to Ivetta simply as *juvencula* or at most *ancilla Christi* when she is working in the leprosarium, she is later frequently called *beata* and when in her cell she is *sancta*. But there is something else.

In medieval society recluses often fulfilled the role which had previously belonged to fortune-tellers and seeresses.[87] In the Christian society of the late Middle Ages, the need for them was still felt, but there was no place for them within the Church, except for prophetesses who were directly inspired by God. It was quite natural that this role should be assigned to recluses. They were mediators between *God* and mankind. Ivetta was no exception.

But they were more as well. It seems to me that they introduced certain magical elements into the practice of faith. We know that in the pre-Christian society of Ireland people used to extract favours and compromises from their almighty ruler by strict fasting (a sort of hunger strike!). Milis proposes that this practice, when taken over into Christianity, led to penitential practices which had similar features.[88] Ascetics, and especially recluses, extracted from God forgiveness of sins and gifts of grace for ordinary believers. In this way they were mediators between *mankind* and God at the same time.

From a social point of view it is important to observe that recluses like Ivetta saw not only the material needs of their fellow citizens and tried to assuage them by giving alms and by working in poorhouses, but also their spiritual needs, their ignorance, their spiritual impoverishment. They saw that their fellow citizens yearned for wisdom and knowledge, for insight into religious truths. And they regarded it as their task to meet these needs as best they could.[89] In areas in which the clergy failed miserably, these women took on some of their tasks and educated, motivated and assisted the believers in their search for new forms of personal belief. They were the wise women. The ordinary people of medieval society were very grateful for this and willing to reward the recluses generously. Whether or not it pleased the Church, society bestowed money and gifts on the holy mediators and also believed in their mission. They assigned them a prominent role. The Church was displeased with some aspects of this development, though not all.

As far as discipline and morals were concerned, both the Church and society accepted the extreme pretensions of recluses like Ivetta and of pious women in general. This is borne out by what we know about some of Ivetta's "colleagues," such as Mary of Oignies and Eva of Liège.[90] The Church had little choice. Reformist clerics like James of Vitry, Thomas of Cantimpré and John of Lier had the same goals as the holy women: discipline of the clergy and more religious fervour among the laity. But unlike the inspired women, these clerics were unable to accomplish very much. In this period of "inner Christianization," when the Christian faith was just starting to penetrate into everyday life, the authority of priests and church dogma was not yet taken for granted. Nor were the power of the priesthood, the fear of hell and purgatory and the indispensability of the Church as mediator. People still had to be convinced. This was more difficult for priests than for the inspired women, who enjoyed the confidence of the people. The traditional clergy was not popular, but the well-meaning reformers were also unable to make much impact on believers who attached little importance to their admonishments. According to Church doctrine, ordained priests had at their disposal the power of the Word and the Sacrament, but this power was only effective for those who believed in it. Those who did not go to confession or who ignored the words of a priest, those who "ate judgment onto themselves," by taking communion with an unclean conscience, and did not lose a moment's sleep over it, were hard to deal with; the priests had no "earthly" sanctions for them. But someone like Ivetta, who had the gift of prophecy, did have sanctions. Ivetta could *see* which people were eating judgment onto themselves; she saw fire coming out of their nostrils. With her visions of hell and damnation she managed to bring these people to their knees. In this way she was of enormous support to the clergy.

But recluses went even further. They used the authority they had acquired through their saintly way of life and the charismatic power which was attributed to them to exact admission of guilt and contrition from the believers they summoned. Through prayer they procured forgiveness for these believers' sins.[91] This is why Hugh of Floreffe also calls Ivetta *mediatrix*, mediator. It is exactly the term used for the power of priests and for Mary's role: mediator of redemption.[92] Hugh used the term not because he thought that Ivetta could dispense grace in the same way as a priest, but because she was able to obtain forgiveness of sins by talking to believers and by praying to Christ on their behalf. The effect was the same.

We may conclude the following: women like Ivetta did not possess the clerical power and authority, based on an official function, to summon people to answer for themselves. But they did have the moral authority and the charismatic power. Men like James of Vitry did possess clerical power and authority but often lacked the moral authority to command obedience. The Church lacked accepted means of compulsion, unless they joined forces with the holy women; in that case they could gain the necessary means of pressure through them. James of Vitry recognized this: he admitted publicly that he was inspired and assisted by Mary of Oignies. He even discussed his sermons with her.[93] In the practice of daily life the clergy went quite a long way to meet ordinary believers.[94] They tried to justify this within the Church by appealing to the theologically well-founded role of Mary in the process of redemption.

A study of historical practice may enable us to add one more conclusion. It may be true that according to Church Law recluses had no official authority, based on an *officium* or function in the Church, but in practice, within the community of believers, there were other criteria than legal rights. If my interpretation of the sources is correct, and my conclusion is valid that recluses, on the basis of the socially recognized "function," *officium*, they exercised from their cells, were attributed with a sort of intermediary role, then in fact they did have an office-bound, a "functional" authority, based on this. If a priest had access to the Church's grace through his training and ordination, the recluse had access to God's grace through her experience and her isolation in a cell: Hugh often emphasizes that Ivetta *in libro experientiae didicerat*.[95] In the *Vita* of another recluse, Margaret the Lame of Magdeburg, this is stated in so many words.[96]

To summarize, Ivetta's physical motherhood (and subsequent widowhood) was no important factor in the construction of her sanctity as such; for her performance as a saint, however, it was of the utmost importance.

A MOTHER FOR ALL

So in fact Ivetta's role was similar to that of Mary, the mother of the Lord. It is hardly surprising that Hugh—whether prompted by Ivetta or not—used Mary to legitimize her activities and saw Ivetta as Mary's chosen handmaid, used by her to call sinners to account for themselves. It is worth noting that Mary is very clearly represented as Queen Mother and Ruler of Heaven. As mother of God she was raised above the stars and had become queen of heaven and earth, *Regina caeli, Domina terrae*.[97] She is the majestic queen, reigning over her heavenly palace and household from her throne, but also watching over her subjects and possessions on earth. She can demand in vengeance that her rights be honored, for example by the priest and the dean of the Notre Dame in Huy, the church dedicated to her. Usually we see only the actions of her handmaid, but at crucial moments the queen herself intervenes, acting with majestic authority from her elevated position, in shining garments and with royal dignity.

Mary was the heavenly mistress and housewife, shaped after the image of the earthly queens in feudal Europe. As Ivetta, as a *magistra* of the Beguines, was adorned with the qualities of a good housewife, she again mirrored her mistress Mary and is legitimized by her example: Mary is her theological justification, so to speak. Mary is portrayed as we often see her in twelfth-century texts and pictures. She is not the mild and gentle mother of the Gothic cathedrals, nor the humble Madonna who inspires inner devotion. Mary Magdalen, the second woman who played an important part in Ivetta's life, was more suited to this role. Mary Magdalen rather than Mary the mother of Jesus was the model for Ivetta's sainthood and the mother saint with whom the believers could identify her.

In Ivetta's time Mary Magdalen's cult had become part of popular devotional practice in the Low Countries.[98] From 1126 onward Bishop Adelbert of Liège had had her feast celebrated throughout the whole diocese. He spoke of believers who were devoted to Mary Magdalen, *Dei amatricis et converse devotus*; they venerated the woman who had "loved much" and wanted to wash the Lord's feet just as she had.[99] In 1226 Pope Gregory IX asked the clergy of the German Empire to celebrate the feast of Mary Magdalen, the model of true repentance.[100] As we have seen, Ivetta herself had obtained relics of Mary Magdalen for her own chapel and had had an altar dedicated to her. But what sort of figure did these believers have in mind when they venerated Mary Magdalen?

Quite a variety of images of Mary Magdalen exist, both in the medieval world and in scholarship today. She is now usually portrayed as the converted whore, the holy harlot, who, after a life of sin in the Jerusalem brothels, washed Jesus' feet with tears of repentance and from that moment onwards never left him. Sometimes certain French legends are added to the picture: after the Lord's death Mary sailed to France, preached the Gospel as a female apostle in southern France and ended her life as a hermit at Vezelay in Burgundy. But it is open to question whether this picture was the one familiar to the medieval religious community, at least in the Low Countries in Ivetta's time.

Since Pope Gregory the Great had preached about Mary Magdalen she had, in the Latin tradition, become an amalgamation of several New Testament women—and of several different ideals. She was Mary of Bethany, who according to Lk. 10:38–42 had sat at Jesus' feet, thereby personifying the *vita contemplativa*: this was how Hugh thought of her when, in describing how Ivetta was walled into her cell, he called her a second Mary, i.e., Mary Magdalen.[101] However, she is also identified with the anonymous woman in Lk. 7:36–50 who washed Jesus' feet with her tears and anointed them with precious ointment. This woman is called a sinner, *peccatrix*, just as Ivetta always called herself. Her sins were forgiven, "for she loved much": the same love, *caritas*, to which Caesarius of Heisterbach attached so much importance. So Mary Magdalen also represents the repentant sinner, or the *courtisane amoureuse*. Finally she was, of course, Mary of Magdala, from whom Jesus had cast out seven demons (Lk. 8:2), a devoted follower who had had the privilege of being the first to look upon the Lord after his Resurrection.[102] In Western tradition it was tacitly assumed that Mary Magdalen's sins were of a sexual nature; surely this was always women's weak point? In one of Odo of Cluny's sermons she calls herself "a sinner" and *immunda*: impure? unchaste?[103] We take this as a prostitute, a social outcast, but it is questionable whether this was understood in the same way in the Middle Ages. In moralistic literature all sex was regarded as sinful, and everyone who was married or in a love relationship was really a "fornicator"; so Mary Magdalen appears to be more of a symbol of married people in general.[104] Elsewhere we read that she came from a wealthy family and was married to the Lord of Magdala. James of Voragine did not believe, as some others did, that Mary Magdalen had been engaged to John the Evangelist and had been abandoned by her bridegroom at her wedding at Cana (!), after which, in desperation, she threw herself into a worldly life, until she too was called to the Lord.[105] Evidently this story, which presented Mary Magdalen as a married woman or a (grass) widow, was actually in circulation.

Caesarius of Heisterbach tells several *exempla* involving Mary Magdalen which may help us to understand how she was seen by ordinary believers, at least in that region. While certain pious women were being consecrated by a bishop, he tells us, a monk saw that the widows were assisted by Mary Magdalen and the virgins by Margaret.[106] So in this case Mary Magdalen is the patron saint of widows. Caesarius himself was converted when he was told of a vision in which the Virgin Mary, her mother Anne and Mary Magdalen appeared to Bernard of Clairvaux: three female saints, of whom two were certainly holy mothers, so that the impression is created that the third was also included for that reason.[107] A fellow monk was visited by *tres matronae mirae pulchritudinis*, Mary Magdalen, Mary the mother of God and Elizabeth, the mother of John the Baptist: again two holy mothers plus Mary Magdalen, thus a group of three matrons?[108] We may wonder not only whether Mary Magdalen was regarded as (a married woman or) a widow in the devotions of Caesarius and his circle, but also whether these threesomes of holy mothers were so popular because they provided the believers with an avenue to continue their old devotion to the three Mother goddesses, the three Matrons, in a Christianized form. In that case, it was chiefly the mother figure in Mary Magdalen who was venerated, the woman from the city, who loved so much,[109] the woman who had washed Jesus' feet and taken his head into her hands when the hour of his death was at hand; who had mourned at the grave and had continued to wait long after the disciples had gone home. This mother figure provided an excellent mirror for Ivetta.

In the Netherlands there was a different legend about Mary Magdalen in circulation, the so-called *Conversio beatae Mariae Magdalenae*. The oldest source is a fourteenth-century text from Utrecht, published by Hansel; De Vooys has traced four Middle Dutch versions.[110] The text is located in an urban setting which could easily be that of the Southern Netherlands in the twelfth or thirteenth century. Is that where the story originated? I recognize various motives in it to which Ivetta or her biographer may well have referred, if they knew this legend—or an earlier form of it. Mary Magdalen is portrayed as a frivolous young woman, pretty, elegant, from a good family and possessed of a considerable family fortune. She likes to go out dancing and to be courted by the young knights. She is the sort of town-dweller who is represented in Ivetta's *Vita* by her second son; they are both the antithesis of the model believer they are later to become. Good Christians reject this sort of life. In the legend, Mary Magdalen's sister Martha expresses this opinion, reproaching her when she comes home from yet another party. Like Lambert li Bègue in Liège, Martha abhors singing and dancing, and mundane pleasures in general.[111] She reminds Mary of Jesus and heavenly joy. She speaks so persuasively of the Lord that Mary feels herself being touched by God's hand and has a vision—just as Ivetta, as a young married woman, was drawn away from the road to hell by the Lord himself. Mary feels the hot tears welling up, tears her hair and asks herself in desperation how she could have thrown herself away like that: *publicam meretricem pro virgine me appellari procurasti*, a public whore instead of a virgin.[112] This is the only time the word "whore" crops up in the legend. She shuts herself up in her room and comes out only when Jesus comes to visit the neighbors;

then she washes his feet. Martha, who is serving the food there, happens to hear that Jesus has forgiven Mary's sins. She tells Mary, the Lord's mother, and it is Mary who tells Mary Magdalen! They embrace, and that is the beginning of an intimate relationship between them, just like Ivetta and Mary in the *Vita*.

CONCLUSION: IVETTA, A SECOND MARY MAGDALEN

Mary Magdalen had much to offer to the citizens of Liège and Huy and other urban centres of the Netherlands, and in her wake, so did women like Ivetta. As always, the believers needed religious models who were tailored to their own lifestyle. Their image of themselves was of people who had built up a good living and had developed a certain sophistication. They had discovered that God's world was not a bad place for those who knew how to use his gifts well, even though they also saw the harmful aspects of the new prosperity. Theirs was a society in which women, within the context of family and friends, were permitted to play an increasingly important part in social and economic life. This was the world in which the faithful were searching for models to inspire them, models with whom they could identify and in whom they could recognize elements of their own lives. Lambert li Bègue, whom pious people sought out to find inspiration round the middle of the twelfth century, was one of the first to realize this; another was the writer of the *Poème Moral*, who adapted a *Life* of the holy harlot, Thaïs. Before her conversion Thaïs was known as a woman who loved glamour and money. It is clear that in this environment Mary Magdalen was a suitable candidate to develop into an inspiring saint. She had been a worldly woman, had married young and been widowed young; she had a profound love of the Lord, but also a profound awareness of her own sins. It was mainly her love which appealed to people, the same love which was emphasized by contemporaries like Caesarius of Heisterbach: *caritas*, the love of God and solidarity with humanity. Like the holy mothers in Jesus' family, Mary, Anne, and Elizabeth, Mary Magdalen did not withdraw from life, but continued to fulfil an important role. Women like Ivetta, Mary of Oignies, and the other *mulieres sanctae* tried to live in the same way, felt they were "Mary Magdalens"; like the other holy mothers they assumed the spiritual tasks and functions which had previously been those of mother goddesses. Mary, Anne, and Mary Magdalen guided believers on their path through life, protected them and preserved them for eternal life. They could do this as if they were medieval widows who, after producing heirs and getting beyond the dangerous marriageable age, could serve the community as wise elderly matrons. Mary Magdalen even became a female preacher and apostle.

In their turn, Ivetta and the other pious women drew their inspiration from Mary Magdalen. Ivetta made the very most of the possibilities open to her. As a mother and widow she was respected in the community and had considerable freedom to play her part in society. However, what the Church permitted for holy women from the past—a public life, begging, preaching, etc.—it could not permit for contemporary women of flesh and blood. Reformist priests like James of Vitry presented male lust as an excuse for steering women into the convent. In Ivetta's *Vita* the uncontrollable appetites of men also play an important part. Ivetta chose (for that reason?) the role of the contemplative Mary Magdalen, who "chose the good part," and had herself walled up. From the keep of her cell she could continue to be a holy mother, a second Mary Magdalen, an apostle in her own town. Her motherhood was a prerequisite for this. It not only made it easier for her fellow-townspeople to accept her social activities, it also made it possible for theologians to compare her to Mary, thereby gaining a theological justification for her actions.

Ivetta *mediatrix*, or even better *mater et magistra*: who could have thought it possible for a woman in a period which is known to have been misogynous, and in a church which, also being misogynous, never wished to give women a place in the hierarchy.

NOTES

* I am grateful to Josine Blok and Liesbeth Brouwer for commenting on earlier drafts of this study.

1. Ivetta's *Life* by Hugh of Floreffe, *Vita B. Juettae Inclusae auctore Hugone Floreffiensi* was edited in the *Acta Sanctorum (AASS)*, 13 Januarii (3d ed. Brussels, 1863), vol. 2, 145–169; it is quoted here as Hugo, *Vita Juettae* with paragraph numbers and page in *AASS*. P.F.Chr. Henriquez, *Lilia Cistercii sive sacrarum virginum Cisterciensium Origo, Instituta et Res Gestae* (Douai, 1633), edited an abridged version. Little has been written about Ivetta (the French and Latin form of the name) or Jutta (Dutch form); see Alcantara Mens, *Oorsprong en betekenis van de Nederlandse Begijnen- en Begardenbeweging* (Antwerp: Standaardboekhandel, 1947), 384–402; Isabella Cochelin, "Sainteté laïque: l'exemple de Juette de Huy," *Le Moyen Age*, 95 (1989), 397–417; Anneke B. Mulder-Bakker, "In besloten kring? Het leven van de kluizenares Ivetta van Hoei," in *Vrouwen wegen wetenschap: Een keur van Vrouwenstudies Groningen*, ed. Ellen Offers et al. (Groningen: IWEV, 1991), 45–65. Scarcely anything is known about the author of the *Vita*. Formerly it was assumed that he also wrote the *Life of Ida of Nivelles* and the *Life of Ida of Zoutleeuw*; this is not the case, see Simone Roisin, *L' Hagiographie cistercienne dans le diocèse de Liège au xiiie siècle* (Louvain: Université de Louvain, 1947), 148.

2. From the *Apology* written by Lambert li Bègue in 1175 and published in Paul Fredericq, *Corpus Documentorum Inquisitionis haereticae pravitatis Neerlandicae* (The Hague: Nijhoff, 1896), 28f., it could be inferred that Liège did not have a very good reputation at this time.

3. Hugo, *Vita Juettae*, 56, ed. *AASS* 2, 156; Ivetta had the same sort of problems with her son as Bridget of Sweden was later to have with hers; see Nieuwland's

contribution to this volume: "Motherhood and Sanctity in the Life of Saint Birgitta of Sweden: An Insoluble Conflict?"

4. See n. 1 for edition.

5. André Joris, *La Ville de Huy au Moyen Age: Des Origines à la fin du xive siècle* (Paris, 1959).

6. This leprosarium had been built by the town council which also regarded itself as its administrator. A curate, appointed by the dean of Notre Dame, served there occasionally. Both the chapel and the convent remained in existence until the nineteenth century, when an earthenware factory and a distillery were set up in them. There are still a few remnants to be seen, in a garage. The convent was known as Sainte Marie Madeleine or Grands Malades, see Joseph Daris, "Notes historiques sur Huy," *Analectes pour servir à l'histoire ecclésiastique de la Belgique*, 14 (1877), 36–77.

7. Hugo, *Vita Juettae*, 60f., ed. *AASS* 2, 157; see Mens, *Oorsprong*, 384–402.

8. The term "mulieres sanctae" is coined by Brenda M. Bolton, "Mulieres Sanctae," in *Women in Medieval Society*, ed. Susan Mosher Stuard (Philadelphia: University of Pennsylvania Press, 1976), 141–159; idem, "*Vitae Matrum*: a Further Aspect of the *Frauenfrage*," in *Medieval Women: Dedicated and Presented to Rosalind M.T. Hill*, ed. Derek Baker (Studies in Church History: Subsidia, 1) (Oxford: Blackwell, 1978), 253–273; idem, "Some Thirteenth-Century Women in the Low Countries: A Special Case?" *Nederlands Archief voor Kerkgeschiedenis*, 61 (1981), 7–29. See also Brigitte Degler-Spengler, "Die religise Frauenbewegung des Mittelalters: Konversen–Nonnen–Beginen," *Rottenburger Jahrbuch für Kirchengeschichte*, (1984), 75–88, and idem, "Zahlreich wie die Sterne des Himmels: Zisterzienser, Dominikaner und Franziskaner vor dem Problem der Inkorporation von Frauenklöstern," *Rottenburger Jahrbuch für Kirchengeschichte*, (1985), 37–50, and Carol Neel, "The origins of the Beguines," *Signs: Journal of Women in Culture and Society*, 14 (1989), 321–341. A more general introduction to religious women in the later Middle Ages is Caroline Walker Bynum, *Holy Feast, Holy Fast: The Religious Significance of Food to Medieval Women* (Berkeley [etc.]: University of California Press, 1987).

9. Jacobus Vitriacus, *Vita Mariae Oigniacensis*, edited in the *AASS*, 23 Junii, (3d ed. Paris-Rome, 1867), vol. 25, 547–582; English translation: Margot H. King, *The Life of Marie d'Oignies by Jacques de Vitry* (Saskatoon: Peregrina, 1986); cf. Michel Lauwers, "Expérience béguinale et récit hagiographique: A propos de la *Vita Mariae Oigniacensis* de Jacques de Vitry (vers 1215)," *Journal des Savants*, (1989), 61–103 and his "Entre Béguinisme et Mysticisme: La Vie de Marie d'Oignies (d. 1213) de Jacques de Vitry ou la définition d'une sainteté féminine," *Ons Geestelijk Erf*, 66 (1992) 46–69.

10. Lamprecht von Regensburg, *Sanct Francisken Leben und Tochter Syon*, ed. Karl Weinhold (Paderborn, 1880), quoted by Mens, *Oorsprong*, 113, n. 35.

11. Thomas Cantipratanus, *Bonum Universale de Apibus*, 2.54, ed. Georgius Colvenerius (Douai: Bellerus, 1627), 522, quoted by Ernest W. McDonnell, *The Beguines and Beghards in Medieval Culture* (New Brunswick: Rutgers University Press, 1954), 64.

12. Quoted by Mens, *Oorsprong*, 270.

13. See the studies of Bolton and Degler-Spengler quoted above in n. 8.

14. In my opinion modern scholarship is led astray by a false hypothesis. Consciously or not, scholars try to define the Beguines as a sort of institution, a sort of order. They wonder if the Beguines were not essentially failed nuns, who would really have preferred to enter a Cistercian or Premonstratensian convent (Bolton, Degler-Spengler). Is it not possible that they deliberately chose a different way of life, a *via media*, as McDonnell and more recently Kaspar Elm, "Die Stellung der Frau in Ordenswesen, Semireligiosentum und Häresie zur Zeit der heiligen Elisabeth," in *Sankt Elisabeth, Fürstin, Dienerin, Heilige* (Sigmaringen, 1981), 7–28, held? In this context McDonnell, *The Beguines and Beghards*, 120, speaks of the Beguines's way of life as: "a spontaneous and popular movement; . . . a new way of penitential life, the very

essence of which remained its voluntary, temporary and informal character." Yet he too clings to a description of the Beguine movement as the (reformist) Church defined and modelled it: as a separate state of life for women, who for their own good had to be put into a separate organization which then gave them a right to protection by the Church; so again a clerical "status" rather than "a way of life."

15. Ursula Peters, *Religiöse Erfahrung als literarisches Faktum: Zur Vorgeschichte und Genese frauenmystischer Texte des 13. und 14. Jahrhunderts* (Hermaea: Germanistische Forschungen, NF. 56) (Tübingen: Niemeyer, 1988), passim.

16. Caesarius of Heisterbach, *Wundergeschichten*, 3, ed. Alfons Hilka (Bonn, 1933), 26f., quoted by McDonnell, *Beguines and Beghards*, 122.

17. Cf. Guibert of Tournai complaining about women in his home town: "Et apud nos mulieres aliae [others than nuns], de quibus nescimus, utrum debeamus eas vel saeculares vel moniales appellare. Partim enim utuntur ritu saeculari, partim etiam regulari," in A. Stroïc, "Collectio de Scandalis Ecclesiae: Nova editio," *Archivum Fratrum Historicum*, 24 (1931), 58.

18. *Chronica Villariensis Monasterii*, 23, ed. G. Waitz in *Monumenta Germaniae Historica. Scriptores (SS)*, vol. 25, 205.

19. Thomas, *Bonum Universale*, 2.57, ed. Colvenerius, 541ff.

20. Hugo, *Vita Juettae*, 35, ed. AASS 2, 152; 81, 161; 91, 162.

21. See the *Apology* of Lambert li Bègue in Fredericq, *Corpus Documentorum*, 28 and Chrétien Pfister, "La Vie de Sainte Odile," *Analecta Bollandiana*, 13 (1894), 5–32 and 197–287.

22. *Chronica Villariensis*, 23, ed. SS 25, 205.

23. Caesarius von Heisterbach, *Dialogus Miraculorum*, 8.8, ed. Joseph Strange, (Cologne [etc.], 1851), vol. 2, 87ff.

24. Ibid., 8.15f., ed. Strange, 2, 94.

25. Jacobus, *Vita Mariae Oigniacensis*, 21f.; trans. King, 21f.

26. Thomas Cantipratanus, *Vita Margarete de Ypris*, ed. G. Meersseman as an appendix to his "Les Frères Prêcheurs et le Mouvement Dévot en Flandre au xiiie siècle," *Archivum Fratrum Praedicatorum*, 18 (1948), 106–130.

27. See the contribution of Anja Petrakopoulos, "Sanctity and Motherhood: Elizabeth of Thuringia" to this volume and Norbert Ohler, *Elisabeth von Thüringen: Fürstin im Dienst der Niedrigsten* (Göttingen: Muster-Schmidt, 1984), 28.

28 Caesarius, *Dialogus*, 7.79, ed. Strange, 2, 148: "Attamen in ordine coniugatorum vel viduarum, multi sunt multis virginibus in merito multo maiores, quia penes carnis integritatem quae virtus non est, quam etiam infideles habent, meritum non consistit, sed penes caritatem."

29. Ibid., 148f.: "et hoc propter intentionem caritatis. Hinc est quod beatam Mariam Magdalenam Ecclesia in letaniis anteposuit virginibus, ne illis propter ruinam inferior videatur."

30. Quoted by Caroline Walker Bynum, "Women Mystics in the 13th Century: the case of the Nuns of Helfta," in her *Jesus as Mother: Studies in the Spirituality of the High Middle Ages* (Berkeley [etc.]: University of California Press, 1982), 215.

31. *Le Poème Moral*, ed. Alphonse Bayot (Brussels, 1929), 239, vs 3393–3400: "Cui li delis del siecle ne püent essaucier / Ne les aversiteit ne contraire abaissier, / Se dont ceaus qui desvoient seit la voie ensaignier, / Cil fait mult a amer, car il puet mult aidier. / Cui Deus done tel force, ne doit mie fuïr; / mies doit, entre les mauls del siecle, mal soffrir / Que, ceaus qui mestier ont d' aïde, relenquir, / Car plus en greit ne puent Nostre Signor servir."

32. In a sermon printed by Jean Baptiste Pitra, *Analecta Novissima Spicilegii Solesmensis* (Altera Continuatio, 2) (Tusculum, 1838), 435, Jacques de Vitry wrote: "Qui igitur in hac intentione laborant, ut poenitentiam a summo sacerdote sibi injunctam faciant, plerumque non minus merentur quam qui tota die in ecclesia cantant, vel de nocte ad matutinas vigilant."

33. "Propterea quedam prudentes et devote virgines, cum in domibus parentum

inter seculares et impudicas personas absque magno et gravi periculo non valeant commorari, maxime hiis diebus ad monasteria confugiunt, que Dominus in universo mundo multiplicavit," quoted in Joseph Greven, "Der Ursprung des Beginenwesens: Eine Auseinandersetzung mit Godefroid Kurth," *Historisches Jahrbuch*, 35 (1914), 46f.

34. James A. Brundage, *Law, Sex and Christian Society in Medieval Europe* (Chicago: University of Chicago Press, 1987), 403f.

35. Caesarius, *Dialogus*, 6.35, ed. Strange, 1, 387f.

36. *Chronica Villariensis*, 30, ed. SS 25, 202: "Apparet enim, eum fuisse virginem sanctum, immaculatum et incorruptum mente et corpore."

37. *Chronica Villariensis*, 9, ed. SS 25, 198.

38. *Dit is van der heiligher maghet croepel Margarite die seer heilich was van leuen*, in Royal Library, The Hague, MS 73 H 11, fols. 243–244: "Ende hoer dochte somtijt dat si also grote wijsheit had, al hadden alle die bedructe herten van der werelt voer hoer gheweest, si wolde se al wel ghetroest hebben ende een iegheliken nae sinen staet. Mitten luden sprac si alsoe waerlic ende mit also groter trouwicheit, dat si van rechter caritaten leuendich waert, ende van neersticheit hoer herte scoeren wolde."

39. Mens, *Oorsprong*, 65.

40 Jacobus, *Vita Mariae*, 69, trans. King, 68; Thomas, *Vita Margarete*, 57, ed. Meersseman, 130; cf. Thomas Cantipratanus, *Vita Lutgardis*, in *Acta Sanctorum (AASS)*, 16 Junii, (3d ed. Paris-Rome, 1867), vol. 24; trans. Margot H. King, *The Life of Lutgard of Aywières* (Saskatoon: Peregrina, 1987). It was in these circles that the *exempla*, the short stories from which I have quoted so often above, came into vogue in preaching and literature.

41. Jacobus, *Vita Mariae*, 82, trans. King, 80. Cf. André Vauchez, "Prosélytisme et action antihérétique en milieu feminin au xiiie siècle: la *Vie de Marie d'Oignies* (+ 1213) par Jacques de Vitry," *Problèmes d'histoire du Christianisme*, 17 (1987), 95–110.

42. Cf. McDonnell, *Beguines and Beghards*, and the above cited studies of Bolton and Degler-Spengler (see n. 8).

43. Lambert li Bègue in his *Apology* in Fredericq, *Corpus Documentorum*, 28f.

44. *Le Poeme Moral*, ed. Bayot, 42–134. Caesarius of Heisterbach speaks of an educated nun who had a deep admiration for John the Baptist. She wanted all boys to be named John or Zacharias (John's father's name) and all girls to be named Elizabeth, after John's mother: Caesarius, *Dialogus*, 8.50, ed. Strange, 2, 121f.

45. See below in: "The construction of sanctity."

46. Hugo, *Vita Juettae*, 9, ed. AASS 2, 147. Jack Goody, *The Development of the Family and Marriage in Europe* (Past and Present publications) (Cambridge: Cambridge University Press, 1983), 103–156 and cf. David Herlihy, *Medieval Households* (Cambridge, Mass.: Harvard University Press, 1985).

47. Goody, Development of the Family, 188f; see also Georges Duby, *Le Chevalier, la Femme et le Prêtre: Le Mariage dans la France féodale* (Paris: Hachette, 1981).

48. Brundage, *Law, Sex*, 333.

49. Hugo, *Vita Juettae*, 9, ed. AASS 2, 147.

50. Ibid., 10ff., 147.

51. Ibid., 12–17, 147f.

52. This is also demonstrated by her aversion to sexual intercourse within marriage, see Hugo, *Vita Juettae*, 10, ed. AASS 2, 147: "sed naturali quodam mentis impulsu agitabatur interius complexio munda cordis, quo dedignabatur foris caro carnis delectationi subesse." See also: Bolton, "Some Thirteenth-Century Women," esp. 18f.

53. With Ivetta we have a good example of a "mulier sancta" who was certainly not a failed nun. Considering that Ivetta's mother and father as well as both of her sons entered renowned Cistercian abbeys, we may assume that this would have been a possibility for Ivetta, too, and that she deliberately declined to make use of it. This is even more striking in light of the fact that she scarcely had any models: she

belonged to the very first generation of "Beguines."

54. Hugo, *Vita Juettae*, 15ff., ed. *AASS* 2, 148.

55. Brundage, *Law, Sex*, 343.

56. Hugo, *Vita Juettae*, 25f., ed. *AASS* 2, 150. Clarissa W. Atkinson, in her fine book *The Oldest Vocation: Christian Motherhood in the Middle Ages* (Ithaca [etc.]: Cornell University Press, 1991), 165, may not have read Ivetta's *Vita* herself, as she states that Ivetta abandoned her three children and left them with her father.

57. For the social position of married women and widows in the Netherlands, see Edith Ennen, *Frauen im Mittelalter* (3d revised ed. Munich: Beck, 1987), 134–193; and especially Martha C. Howell, *Women, Production and Patriarchy in Late Medieval Cities* (Chicago: University of Chicago Press, 1986).

58. Hugo, *Vita Juettae*, 25–32, ed. *AASS* 2, 150ff., of which 26–30 are devoted to Ivetta's sinfulness.

59. Hugo, *Vita Juettae*, 54, ed. *AASS* 2, 156: "laboratque denuo parturire gestiens ut pareret Deo, quem mundo pepererat prius, fieretque filius Dei per adoptionis gratia . . . ."

60. Hugo, *Vita Juettae*, 53, ed. *AASS* 2, 156.

61. *A Book of Showings to the Anchoress Julian of Norwich*, ed. Edmund Colledge and James Walsh (Toronto: Pontifical Institute of Mediaeval Studies, 1978), 57, quoted by Caroline Walker Bynum, "'. . . And woman his humanity': Female imagery in the religious writing of the Later Middle Ages," in her *Fragmentation and Redemption: Essays on Gender and the Human Body in Medieval Religion* (New York: Zone Books, 1992), 163.

62. At least, Hugh of Floreffe is saying so, see Hugo, *Vita Juettae*, 44–47, ed. *AASS* 2, 154. According to Bynum, *Holy Feast, Holy Fast*, 269, male biographers stressed the theme of women's imitation of Mary, whereas the women themselves were more pondering over the humanity of Christ and showed a "reverence for body." This might be true for Hugh and Ivetta as well.

63. Hugo, *Vita Juettae*, 88,ed. *AASS* 2, 161: "adolescens, qui specialiter sanctae huic ab infantia commendatus fuerat in filium spiritualem," and ibid., 72, 159: "specialem filiam ab annis eam infantiae jam dudum adoptaverat."

64. Ibid., 77–79, ed. *AASS* 2, 160, here 77.

65. Ibid., 88, 162.

66. Ibid., 115, 166 and 114, 166: "Intantum siquidem tenera in dilectione earum facta est, quia non diu se cum eis praesciebat esse mansuram, quod aliquantulum etiam orationibus et psalmis parcere videbatur ut frequentius eis colloqueretur et plenius disciplina instrueret Christi."

67. Ibid., 60f, 157f. Cf. Judas's 30 pieces of silver for which the potter's field was bought in which to bury strangers (Mt. 27:3–10).

68. Ibid., 16, 148: "tacita," and "cautius et sapientius respondens;" 24, 149; 62, 158: "occasionem vero scandali proximis dare nolebat."

69. Ibid., 33ff., 152. Hugh's portrait of Ivetta displays a number of the features which Roisin regarded as characteristic of Cistercian hagiography in the Southern Netherlands of that time: the emphasis on humility, the absence of miracles and an educated eye for style and composition. See Simone Roisin, "Réflections sur la culture intellectuelle en nos abbayes cisterciennes médiévales," *Miscellanea Historica in honorem Leonis van der Essen* (Brussels, 1947), 246f.

70. Ibid., 34, 152: "At illa quasi tunc primum vivere et esse inciperet, accinxit fortitudine lumbos suos, et roboravit brachium suum per omnia, et in omnibus viriliter agens . . . humiliavit se in oculis omnium;" 36, 152: "Vide, quaeso, feminam plusquam virum agentem." Bynum, ". . . And woman his humanity," 166f.

71. Elena Giannarelli, *La tipologia femminile nella biografia e nell' autobiografia cristiana del ivo secolo* (Rome, 1980), 66: the widow was "la tipologia più completa perché unisce in sé la vita di castità, la maternità e quella spirituale."

72. Hugo, *Vita Juettae*, 82, ed. *AASS* 2, 161: "Clericus, . . . vocatus a famula

Dei semel et iterum, venire contempsit;" 84, 161: "Decanum, ut sibi locuturus venire vellet, mandavit;" 93, 162 "accersiri mandavit Sacerdotem ad se." Others came to her of their own accord. The future saint Abundus, also from Huy, came to ask her advice on what to do with his life. Even reformist prelates like Thomas of Cantimpré, came to see her on their own initiative to receive a word of encouragement or even for advice on their sermons. All who came into contact with her had difficulty tearing themselves away: Ibid., 37, 152.

73. Luc F. Genicot, "Le Chapitre de Huy au tournant des xiie et xiiie siècles: Vie commune, domaine et prévôté," *Revue d'Histoire Ecclésiastique*, 59 (1964), 5–51.

74. Hugo, *Vita Juettae*, 83f., ed. *AASS* 2, 161.

75. Hugh is aware of the fact that he omits a lot. He explicitly says so in the introduction to the section about the dean: Ibid., 83, 161.

76. See on John of Huy: *Monasticon Belge*, ed. Ursmer Berlière (Abbaye de Maredsous, 1890–1897), vol. 1, 115f. and V. Barbier, *Histoire de l'Abbaye de Floreffe de l'Ordre de Prémontré* (Naumur, 1892), vol. 1, 112–121. I presume that the close relationship between Ivetta and the abbot of Floreffe dated from this time.

77. See the charter from 1226 in which bishop Hugh of Pierrepont takes the Nicholas-altar under his protection, in *Analectes pour servir à l'histoire ecclésiastique de la Belgique*, 12 (1875), 38; a charter from 1236 in which judges are appointed to settle the conflict about the altars in the leprosarium chapel, in Barbier, *Histoire de l' Abbaye de Floreffe*, 2, 90; and a charter from 1249 in which the dispute is settled, in *Analectes*, 12 (1875), 41ff.; and finally the well-informed Bartholomeus Fisen, *Historia Ecclesiastica Leodiensis* (Doornik, 1642), 398 and 480.

78. Hugo, *Vita Juettae*, 96, ed. *AASS* 2, 163.

79. Ibid., 112, 166; see below.

80. See Gabor Klaniczay, *The Uses of Supernatural Power: The Transformation of Popular Religion in Medieval and Early-Modern Europe* (Princeton: Princeton University Press, 1990), 7ff., and Aviad M. Kleinberg, "Proving Sanctity: Problems and solutions in the Later Middle Ages," *Viator*, 20 (1989), 183–205 as well as his *Prophets in their own Country: Living Saints and the Making of Sainthood in the Later Middle Ages* (Chicago: University of Chicago Press, 1992). Now also see Dieter von der Nahmer, *Die lateinische Heiligenvita: Eine Einführung in die lateinische Hagiographie* (Darmstadt: Wissenschaftliche Buchgesellschaft, 1994) and Arnold Angenendt, *Heilige und Reliquien: Die Geschichte ihres Kultes vom frühen Christentum bis zur Gegenwart* (Munich: Beck, 1994).

81. Hugo, *Vita Juettae*, 6, ed. *AASS* 2, 146 (Prologue).

82. Ibid., 42, 153: "haec mutatio," followed by her first vision: 44–47, 154.

83. Ibid., 42, 153. James of Vitry did exactly the same thing in his preface to the *Vita Mariae Oigniacensis*, 7, trans. King, 7, when he, supposedly, referred to Ivetta as someone "who, for almost thirty years, was kept with such zeal by the Bridegroom in the cloister of her heart, that even if a thousand men had tried to draw her out with their hands, no one could entice her out of her cloister."

84. Peter Dinzelbacher, "Heilige oder Hexen?" in *Religiöse Devianz: Untersuchungen zu sozialen, rechtlichen und theologischen Reaktionen auf religiöse Abweichung im westlichen und östlichen Mittelalter*, ed. Dieter Simon (Frankfurt, 1990), 46, refers to the mystic Sibilla, who seemingly lived on angelic nourishment, but in reality was provided with real food by a cleric at night. She was thrown into prison, in a small cell with only a very small window, by which little bread and water was given: she died subsequently.

85. Cf. the innovative study by Henry Mayr-Harting, "Functions of a Twelfth-Century Recluse," *History*, 60 (1975).

86. See n. 14.

87. See Kees Samplonius's contribution to this volume: "From Veleda to the *Völva*: Aspects of female Divination in Germanic Europe."

88. Ludo Milis, "Pureté et sexualité," in *Villes et Campagnes au Moyen Age: Mélanges Georges Despy*, ed. Jean Marie Duvosquel and Alain Dierkens (Liège: Perron, 1991), 504.

89. They could feel legitimized by synodal canons like the *Statutes of Cambrai*, where the faithful were exhorted to teach each other the "Symbolum" and the prayers, "et d'exhorter à vivre avec piété et justice," see P.C. Boeren, "Les plus anciens Statuts du diocèse de Cambrai," *Revue de droit canonique*, 4 (1954), 157.

90. See, again, the studies by Bolton, "*Mulieres Sanctae*," and "*Vitae Matrum*," as well as McDonnell, *Beguines and Beghards*.

91. See the example of a Brabant recluse given by Thomas of Cantimpré in his *Bonum Universale*, 1.23, ed. Colvenerius, 92ff.

92. Hugo, *Vita Juettae*, 107, ed. *AASS* 2, 165: "mediatrix quodammodo haberetur ad correctionem multorum, inter caelestia et terrestia, visibilia et invisibilia, inter Deum et homines."

93. Jacobus, *Vita Mariae*, 69, trans. King, 68.

94. Since they are our only source of information, we know only of matters of which they approved or which they thought merited written disapproval.

95. Hugo, *Vita Juettae*, 14, ed. *AASS* 2, 148.

96. See Anneke B. Mulder-Bakker, "Lame Margaret of Magdeburg: The social function of a medieval Recluse" (forthcoming).

97. Hugo, *Vita Juettae*, 24, ed. *AASS* 2, 150; cf. 45, 154: "Regina caelorum, Angelorum Domina, mater Dei, gloriosa virgo Maria. Cuius ad imperium . . . caelestis regia pendet."

98. Hans Hansel, *Die Maria-Magdalena-Legende: Eine Quellenuntersuchung* (Greifswald, 1937); idem, "Zur Geschichte der Magdalenenverehrung in Deutschland," *Volk und Volkstum: Jahrbuch für Volkskunde*, (1936), 269–277; Victor Saxer, *Le Culte de Marie Madeleine en Occident des origines à la fin du Moyen Age*, 2 vols. (Paris, 1959); Baudouin de Gaiffier, "Notes sur la Culte de Sainte Marie Madeleine," *Analecta Bollandiana*, 78 (1960), 161–168 and Susan Haskins, *Mary Magdalen: Myth and Metaphor* (London: HarperCollins, 1993).

99. Cf. Lk. 7:36–50. In 1126 Adelbert confirms the construction of an oratory for Mary Magdalen where the founder: "cum aliis, si quos sibi vellet Deus adiungere, pro peccatis suis et nostris, sancte penitentis exemplo, pedes Domini lacrimis rigare, capillis mereretur extergere et deosculari cotidie," quoted by De Gaiffier, "Notes sur la Culte," 166.

100. Hansel, "Zur Geschichte der Magdalenenverehrung," 274f.: "penitencie . . . exemplar insigne."

101. Hugo, *Vita Juettae*, 42, ed. *AASS* 2, 153: "omissoque ministerio Marthae, in partem Mariae, quae optima est, totam se contulit atque in cellula . . . se fecit includi." He adds the image of the dove: "in foramine petrae et in caverna maceriae," the image from the *Song of Songs* 2:14, which Bernard of Clairvaux had used in his *Sermones super Cantica Canticorum* to characterize the monk's seclusion. See the edition by Jean Leclercq et al., *S. Bernardi Opera* (Rome, 1958), vol. 2, 26f.

102. Mk. 16:9 and, in a different version, Jn 20:1–18.

103. Odo of Cluny, "Sermo de S. Maria Magdalena," in *Acta Sanctorum (AASS)*, 22 Julii (3d ed. Paris-Rome 1868), vol. 32, 218: "Peccatris sum et immunda," and 221: "per beatam Mariam Magdalenam, opprobrium feminei sexus deletum est."

104. Sarah Wilk, "The cult of Mary Magdalen in fifteenth century Florence and its iconography," *Studi Medievali*, 3d ser. 26 (1985), 694, refers to the influential Tuscan theologian Antoninus, who, in the fifteenth century as yet: "seems to have downplayed the sins attributed to the Magdalen. He defended her against allegations of sexual impropriety, and cited her merely as an example of feminine immodesty."

105. *Die Legenda Aurea des Jacobus de Voragine*, trans. Richard Benz (Heidelberg, 1984), 481: "Da nun Magdalena überflüssig reich war, und die Wollust allezeit eine Gesellin ist des Reichtums, sah sie ihre Schönheit und ihren Reichtum an und gab

sich gänzlich den leiblichen Wollüsten, also dass sie ihren eigenen Namen verlor und allein die Sünderin wurde genannt."

106. Caesarius, *Dialogus*, 8.80, ed. Strange, 2, 149.

107. Ibid., 1.17, ed. Strange, 1, 24.

108. Ibid., 7.15, ed. Strange, 2, 17.

109. Odo of Cluny, *Sermo*, ed. *AASS* 32, 218: "erat quaedam mulier in civitate peccatrix, quae quia dilexit multum, dimissa sunt ei peccata." Cf. Hugo, *Vita Juettae*, 112, ed. *AASS* 2, 166: "Dimissa sunt tibi peccata tua, quoniam dilexisti multum."

110. Hansel, *Maria-Magdalena-Legende*, 115–119; C.G.N. de Vooys, "De legende 'Van Sunte Maria Magdalena Bekeringhe,'" *Tijdschrift voor Nederlandse Taal-en Letterkunde*, 24 (1905), 16–44.

111. Lambert li Bègue wrote in his *Apology* in Fredericq, *Corpus Documentorum*, 29: "sollempnibus etenim diebus a labore manuum tantum abstinentes, ad mimos, saltatrices, histriones intendebant, ebrietatibus et aleis vacabant, choreis mulierum illecebrosis aut ducendis aut spectandis insistebant, obscenis cantibus et gestibus impudicis pro foribus ecclesiarum et super tumulos parentum et affinium suorum." Presumably he is referring to heathen and therefore reprehensible rituals.

112. Hansel, *Maria-Magdalena-Legende*, 117.

8. SANCTITY AND MOTHERHOOD

ELIZABETH OF THURINGIA*

Anja Petrakopoulos

Medieval saints are sometimes so undistinguished it seems a miracle that they ever earned sainthood. In the case of Saint Elizabeth of Thuringia it seems strange that not everybody who knew her noticed she was holy. When she suffered an unjust beating, she smiled and murmured sweetly that the grass bends under the flood's flow, but afterwards grows better for its nourishing effects. Ordered to dismiss her beloved lady companions, she obeyed without delay. Bare feet and woollen cloth she preferred to the costly raiment of the court; instead of being served she preferred to serve. The blood she shed in her penitentiary practice gave her the name of a martyr and her way of life was held up as an example for all. Such measure of sanctity was rewarded by a widespread devotion throughout the Middle Ages, and even today Elizabeth is commemorated in the Roman Catholic Church. But behind this paragon of virtue, this follow-the-book pattern of perfection, is a flesh-and-blood presence. The figure of Elizabeth has become an icon, yet she had enough force to change the icon to fit her own shaping of piety, which she expressed in the *imitatio Christi* as well as in the earthly endeavours of marriage and motherhood. In addition to being a near personification of charity, poverty, fortitude, temperance, chastity, justice, humility, compassion, patience, obedience, continence and discretion, Elizabeth was a happily married woman and an unvirginal mother of three children. This saint is furthermore unusual for the quality of historical sources about her. They provide an exceptional opportunity to study not only the image of the saint but also the historical person.[1]

How did Elizabeth reconcile her life in the world to the traditional standards of divine commitment? How did the saint's motherhood, and the related themes of dynasty, marriage and sexuality impact the tradition of sacred biography? How did Elizabeth's hagiographers give pious meaning to the more profane aspects of her life? A synchronic and diachronic comparison of versions of her story show the richness and elasticity of the hagiographical genre, as well as the diversity of meanings and interpretations possible in medieval religious culture. In the role of intercessor and model, Saint Elizabeth, both in her life on earth and in her life in the communion of saints, has remained through centuries a vital source of inspiration, comfort and hope to men and women. Did gender construct her life story and did gendered symbolization make a difference to the men and women believers who worshipped her and celebrated her memory? By engaging a long-term view of Elizabeth's legend as model and ideal, peeking over the confines of the medieval period, more understanding can be gained of the dynamic interplay of remembering and forgetting in the collective effort of human memory and the making of meaning. The tension between tradition and innovation in a profoundly memorial Western culture will be a central focus of this thematic study of sanctity and motherhood in the life and legend of Saint Elizabeth of Thuringia.

HANDMAID OF CHRIST AND PRINCESS OF THE COURT

Elizabeth of Thuringia's departure from traditional models of sanctity will have something to do with the times of transition into which she was born, in 1207, the beginning of the thirteenth century, and the place which she took in that time, daughter of King Andrew of Hungary and his consort Gertrude.[2] The royal princess was immersed in a world of political intrigue, cutthroat leadership, and the glow of the Lord's especial grace. Through her father's line she is one of the Arpades, known since the canonisation in 1192 of the Knight-King Ladislaus I as the dynasty (*Geschlecht*) of holy kings.[3] Through her mother she is one of the line of the Andechs, which between 1150 and 1500 could show for itself a total of twenty-one saints and *beati*.[4] By virtue of birth, Elizabeth is implicated in the exercise of political authority strengthened by the lustre of divine will. By way of marriage, she brings this piety into the Ludowinger family of the landgraves of Thuringia and Hesse, joining with the good and just Louis IV to rule well in the bond of holy wedlock. This bond was turned to imperial advantage by Frederick II, who appropriated Elizabeth as a "house saint" of the Holy Roman Empire through his familial tie to the Ludowingers.[5] While today this saint is celebrated as Elizabeth of Hungary, in the Middle Ages she was a national saint of both Hungary and Germany, as testified by liturgical texts commemorating her, beginning with *Laetare Germania*, *Gaudeat Hungaria*, *Felix gaude Germania*, *Ave, rosa Ungarorum* or *Laeta stupet Thuringia*.[6] Dynastic ties lead to her close association with Hesse and Brabant as well.

The betrothal of Elizabeth and the crown prince of Thuringia was arranged early by two families astute in the politics of marriage.[7] The bride was brought to the court of the Ludowingers, a center of middle-high Ger-

Figure 8.1. Elizabeth, heavy with her third child, bids her husband Landgrave Louis farewell. Panel 19 in the Saint Elizabeth cycle in the Heiligen-Geist-Hospital in Lübeck, Germany (Heiligen-Geist-Hospital)

man culture under the rule of that lover of arts and literature, Hermann I of Thuringia, in 1211, at the age of four. Her education and upbringing took place under the direction of the pious Landgravina Sophia. In 1221 Elizabeth's foster-mother/mother-in-law retreated to the Saint Catherine convent at Eisenach, four years after the death of her husband the Landgrave Hermann and in the same year that the marriage between Louis and Elizabeth took place. By her withdrawal from the Ludowinger court Sophia made way for the new landgravina: it seems she waited for Elizabeth to reach an age appropriate to take her place at the pinnacle of power next to Louis, who had begun service as landgrave at the age of seventeen, immediately following his father's decease.[8] Louis, who has gone down in the history books a pragmatic politician, seems to have found a good match in his landgravina: the Hungarian princess arraigned herself in magnificent dress appropriate to the ritual of the court; she attended the court-feasts, often accompanied Louis on his travels, and fulfilled her duties as hostess to illustrious guests.[9] Furthermore she ensured the continuance of the princely line: three children were born, Hermann in 1222, Sophie in 1224, and Gertrude in 1227. Aside from the success of the match in terms of ruling capability and progeny, it seems that Louis and Elizabeth were much pleased with each other in terms of love and passion. One biographer has characterized their personal relationship as "wild love." Indeed, the sources unanimously declare their mutual happiness in the marriage. Louis even neglected to follow the adulterous custom of princes and nobility and remained faithful to his landgravina; for Elizabeth it was a form of castigation *not* to sleep next to the landgrave.[10] Elizabeth's increasing religiosity was tolerated by Louis; they appear to be in agreement with each other in religious matters. Elizabeth's confessor Conrad of Marburg, for instance, was also Louis's advisor in spiritual questions. Conrad[11] took his place at the Ludowinger court in 1226–27. He had already done years of service to the Pope as Preacher of the Cross and belonged to the elect religious circle made up of men whose lives stood for far-going asceticism, radical poverty and persecution of heresy. Elizabeth chose this harsh man, whom she came to hold in fear, above abbots or bishops precisely because he owned no property. In 1226—at the Saint Catherine monastery in Eisenach, in the presence of high-ranking witnesses—Elizabeth vowed obedience to Conrad of Marburg, and continence, should she outlive her husband. Under Conrad of Marburg's direction and discipline Elizabeth brought the principles of religious reformers into the heart of one of the most powerful princedoms of Germany. Her gain in worldly power through marriage gave her a wide scope of influence and action in which she was able to express her piety.

As a ruler of the realm, Elizabeth fulfilled the ritual requirements for charity to the poor and sick. André Vauchez has compared her performance during the famine of 1226, in the absence of Louis, to that of Charles the Good during the Flanders famine of 1125; her charity is traditional and fulfills the moral obligations of a lord to his subject. However, as Vauchez argues, in certain aspects her charity extends beyond the theatre of ritual; she personalizes the practice of this virtue and seeks direct contact with the poor. This level of engagement is again neither new nor original; in the twelfth century Thibaut of Champagne, and later, Saint Francis and Saint Louis are comparable. Yet she stands out, surpassing traditional forms of charity by her extraordinarily close attention to the needy. When she managed the crisis of famine in 1226 by herself, she did not stop at opening the grain stores to the subjects of Thuringia. She established a house at the foot of the Wartburg in order to minister to those who had not received from the *generalis elemosina*, being too sick, crippled or elderly to make the climb up and down to the Wartburg, and she sold from her personal belongings for their benefit.[12] Aside from her efforts to relieve human misery, Elizabeth often shows a keen grasp of the conditions behind misery. She provided tools in order that people would be able to work, and in obedience to her confessor Conrad she abstained from ill-gotten food. This abstinence caused real problems for Elizabeth and her companions—when travelling for instance— and it caused equally real discomfiture for the noble hosts receiving the landgravina and the landgrave as guests. Elizabeth's companions reported that Louis approved and would have abstained himself if not prevented by duties of state. That Elizabeth succeeded seems indicative of her dedication to a holy life. Indeed, her court duties did sometimes stand in the way of her meeting the demands of Conrad of Marburg. When the markgravina of Meissen, for instance, was received at the Ludowinger court, Elizabeth disregarded Conrad of Marburg's call for her presence at a sermon.[13]

The sources show that Elizabeth is a devout "religious" within the state of marriage, combining elements of the *vita activa* and the *vita contemplativa*. The social status of widowhood allowed her to undertake more steps in religious life, as it did other medieval women.[14] After Louis died on the way to the Holy Land, on crusade with Frederick II in 1227, Elizabeth left behind her dowry and the court and wandered penniless, ejected, so recounts the *Golden Legend*, as a *dissipatrix* and *prodiga*.[15] It now appears to historians that Elizabeth left the court and her fortune by choice; the legends prefer to show Elizabeth an outcast.[16] When Louis's brother Heinrich Raspe took his place at the head of the princedom, he illegally deprived Elizabeth of her *witwengut*, the lands and revenues which Louis had granted her. Heinrich Raspe stipulated that she be supported at the court, which would have made it impossible for Elizabeth not to eat food obtained by oppression and injustice.[17] The widow left the court in penury, finally able to fulfill her desire to become one with the poor. In early 1228, however, her maternal relative the abbess of Kitzingen put a stop to her poverty, and led her to her maternal uncle the bishop of Bamberg, whose attempts to remarry her against her will failed. When Louis's men returned from crusade, bringing Louis's bones to the monastery at Reinhardsbrunn, Elizabeth, Conrad of Marburg, since 1228 Elizabeth's protector by papal appointment, and the Ludowingers met over the tomb and an arrangement was made. Elizabeth was settled with an amount of money—2000 mark—and residence at Marburg, in the landgrave's territory in Hesse.

Once at Marburg Elizabeth was robed in the "grey cloth" by Conrad, neither she nor he tied to any particular order, and in the summer of 1228 Elizabeth founded a hospital for the care of the sick and the poor. There she served as nurse and did manual labor to earn money for the poor. Fittingly for this female lover of Lady Poverty, the chapel along with the hospital Elizabeth founded was dedicated to Saint Francis, who had just been canonized in July of 1228.[18] From 1228 to her death in November 1231 she proved herself righteous in the terms of the Gospel (Mt. 25:31–46), feeding the poor, clothing the naked, and caring for the sick.

HAGIOGRAPHICAL REPRESENTATIONS

The life and works of the widowed Elizabeth cause no tension for hagiographers. Her vow of chastity, her generous almsgiving, her humble willingness to do manual labors, and her renunciation of her children and friends, all these work together for an uncomplicated holy image. At Marburg she engaged in the last steps of the work of spiritual perfection, free from the demands of court-life, supervised and supported by her confessor and protector Conrad of Marburg. And immediately after she died, people began to venerate her. In the days before she was buried, bits of her clothes, her hair and nails, even her ears and the tips of her breast were taken to be used as relics.[19] In 1235 she was canonized by Pope Gregory IX.

While Elizabeth's widowhood and girlhood fit into conventional ideals, her wifehood did not. There were more married saints in the medieval canon, too numerous to mention. Some were even direct kin to Elizabeth, such as Elizabeth's aunt Saint Hedwig of Silesia and her niece and namesake Elizabeth of Portugal. But their marriages were unhappy, their payment of the marriage debt unwilling.[20] The husbands were often part of these saints' tribulations, by trying their patience with unfaithfulness, or objecting to the saints' religious activity.[21] The saints' husbands formed an opportunity for evangelizing and an occasion for the display of virtue. In other cases, the yearning for holiness is manifested after the death of the husband, as in the example of Rictrude.[22] Elizabeth, on the other hand, is devout from early childhood and Louis was an exemplary Christian husband. In her harmonious relation with him, her marriage is more like unto the earlier—but rare—examples of Empress Mathilda (d. 968) and Saint Margaret, Queen of Scotland (d. 1093).[23] Furthermore, unlike the marriages of the Empress Cunegund (d. 1033) and Edward the Confessor (d. 1066), there is no suggestion that the marriage was continent. There is just one jarring note to the records of marital satisfaction, and that is found in a letter written by Conrad of Marburg: "Two years before she was commended to me, while her husband was still alive and I was her confessor, I discovered her full of regret that she had ever been united in wedlock and that she would not be able to end her present life in the flower of virginity."[24] This anxiety seems more directed at the desire for pious perfection than discord with the landgrave. The testimony of Ysentrude gives a picture of praiseworthy and pious matrimony: "[Elizabeth and Louis] cherished each other with extraordinary love and by turns they sweetly urged and supported each other in the praise and service of God." Furthermore, although Louis attended to the business of his princedom, "in private he always had the fear of God foremost in his thoughts and he granted the blessed Elizabeth generous possibilities to do all things which refer honor to God, urging her on to the salvation of the soul."[25]

How did hagiographers deal with Elizabeth's marital bliss? To overlook it was nigh impossible. The historical sources, sworn testimonies of those who knew the landgravina best and handed over to the Pope for the canonization trial, bear witness to not only the felicity of her marriage, but also to the early signs of divine virtues in Elizabeth. The tale of her life would not be made into a story of conversion.[26] Furthermore, the hagiographical trend in the thirteenth century was to emphasize the saint's earthly life instead of focussing on the miracles of the saint after death as evidences of divine power.[27]

Caesarius of Heisterbach's *Vita*

The first hagiographer to attempt a full-scale life of Elizabeth was the Cistercian abbot Caesarius of Heisterbach, best known for his *Dialogus Miraculorum*.[28] His *Vita sancte Elyzabeth Lantgravie* was commissioned by the Marburg House of Teutonic Knights, i.e., the *Ordo domus Sanctae Mariae Theutonicorum Jerosolimitani*, a brotherhood organized to the models of the Knights Templar and the Hospitalers of Saint John. The hospital founded by Elizabeth was transferred to the Teutonic Knights at the request of Elizabeth's in-laws, the Landgraves Heinrich and Konrad, after Conrad of Marburg, caretaker from Elizabeth's death in 1231, was murdered on the thirtieth of July 1233. The connections between Elizabeth and the Ludowinger landgraves were not severed by this transfer; this order of knights was much patronized by the landgraves, and the favor in which the Teutonic Knights were held was only affirmed in 1234 when Landgrave Konrad became a member of the Order. After Conrad of Marburg's death, these Knights took over the canonization campaign for Elizabeth, which was successful in 1235. They approached Caesarius of Heisterbach for a biography of Elizabeth, useful for widespread dissemination and the promotion of her cult. Caesarius completed the *Life* in 1236–37. Although there is little manuscript evidence that this biography actually did the "public relations" work it was intended for, it had other means of reaching a wide audience. The glass windows of the Elizabeth church, on which building began under the Teutonic Knights on August 14, 1235, are based on Caesarius's *Life*. Thousands of pilgrims will have looked upon and pondered these images from the saint's life.[29]

How does Caesarius manage the phenomenon of marriage in Elizabeth's life? Basing himself on the testimony of Guda, he tells that in the time of Elizabeth's youth, it was the practice of all ladies (*domina[e]*) to cast and draw lots to obtain an apostle for special devotion. When it came time for Elizabeth to come by an apostle in this way, she wished for and so it happened that she thrice drew the blessed John, the guardian of chastity.[30] She desired to imitate the apostle who, according to popular apocrypha, remained a virgin throughout his life, after Jesus called him away from his wedding.[31] In the *Golden Legend* this event in Elizabeth's life is drastically changed. There we read that Elizabeth chose the blessed Virgin Mother of God as her patron and advocate and the blessed John the Evangelist as the guardian of her chastity. When it came time to draw lots, she thrice drew the lot with the name of Saint Peter, as she desired![32] (Saint Peter in the *Golden Legend* is portrayed as a stern father and spiritual guide to his daughter, Saint Petronella, and an encouraging bystander at his wife's *Passio*, calling out to her O *conjux, memento domini!*) The amendation in the *Golden Legend* is a sign of a hagiographical problem, and Caesarius seems aware of it himself. He solves it with a different tactic. Instead of disregarding or changing the evidence that despite John the Evangelist's patronage of chastity Elizabeth married against the desire of her heart, Caesarius intervenes with his own commentary on the lost flower of saintly virginity, saying: "God ordained otherwise in his wonderful dispensation."[33]

Let us move away from the text for a moment to consider these words. A medieval audience could only be astonished and perhaps even astounded at the Lord's wonderful dispensation, contrary as it is to all expectations. Virgins who desire virginity and long for the heavenly Bridegroom, as a medieval person would know from the widely popular stories of the virgin martyrs, withstand tortures and death gladly in order to avoid losing the integrity of the body. For instance Saint Catherine, who enjoyed special veneration at the Ludowinger court under Hermann I,[34] suffered the wheel and decapitation to keep her bridal vow to Christ. From a maiden destined for sanctity is expected the resistance of a lion, to marriage, and if not to marriage, then to consequent copulation.

At this point in the *Vita*, Caesarius withholds explicit explanations, providing only a short statement: "When the blessed and venerable virgin Elizabeth reached marriageable age, against the desire of her heart she was betrothed and joined in marriage to the most noble prince the Landgrave Louis."[35] What follows this statement may be read as Caesarius's attempt to clear up his audience's possible questions about divine dispensation. He uses the loophole in the virgin martyrs' stories, namely that the marriages they resist are generally to *pagan* princes. He introduces Louis. Speedily it becomes apparent that a Christian like Louis is hard to find: "In his adolescence he showed wonderful integrity; he was ornamented with virtues, an enemy of vices, and," (here Caesarius underlines his point) "this is truly commendable in a lay person of such [young] age, he feared God, which [virtue], proven by experience, was manifested in all his decisions and his actions."[36] Thus the divine power, who knows everything, provided. For Louis, a good woman, Elizabeth. Caesarius supports his explication of the good wife theme with biblical quotes.[37]

The combination of the traditional *topos* of the virgin lover of chastity with the upcoming ideal of the Christian wife seems another sign of the transitional period in which Elizabeth's life was lived and in which the life story was written. On the one hand, the hagiography answers to the force of traditional *topos*: the virgin saint who is happily chaste experiences sexual conflict and escapes sexual violation. But Elizabeth did not die in "the flower of virginity" and another religious ideal could be served by her sanctity. The marriage of Louis and Elizabeth was turned to good use in the propagation of the Christian ideal of marriage, developed by the Church in the late Middle Ages.[38] Caesarius of Heisterbach shows that the marriage increased piety of husband and wife and that the marriage was "good," that is, the noble prince is faithful: for this conjugal fidelity Louis is described as *amator castitatis*; the marital bond is based on *dilectio*.[39] Caesarius elaborates the theme and the later legends we will examine below also give a prominent place to the "good Christian marriage." In Caesarius of Heisterbach's *Vita*, Elizabeth in her obedience, and Louis in his patience with her obedience, are portrayed a very saintly pair.

The implicit parallel between them and Maria and Joseph—she obedient to the divine will, he a loyal standby—is made explicit in other hagiography. In later *Lives* of Elizabeth as well as in his own *Lives*, Louis is dubbed a new Joseph.[40] Caesarius passes over this parallel in silence, as he does the theme of marital sexuality. This silence is striking, and can be read neither as a sign of the times nor necessarily resulting from the nature of the princely couple's marital love. His avoidance of Elizabeth's marital sexuality stands out in contrast to the text which forms the prologue to the *Libellus*, the sermon *Ad Decus et Honorem*. There Elizabeth is held up as a mirror of innocence to married women, widows and virgins. These women are admonished to read "in the book of this mirror" and to learn about whatever is respectively appropriate to their status. The "married women of our time" are enjoined to "read and learn . . . to tame the wantonness of the flesh . . . to bridle the impudence of the body's movements, to show the constancy of modesty with matrimonial voluntarity. Apply yourselves . . . to adorn such sacred matrimony with pure procreation."[41]

The legacy of centuries that hallowed virginity was not easily discarded, and when the question of marriage comes up again in Caesarius's *Life of Elizabeth*, chastity wins. The narrative tension around the transition from virgin to wife reappears in another episode with a sexual dimension, when Elizabeth's status as widow is the crux of the matter. The episode occurs while Elizabeth is under the protection of the bishop of Bamberg after Louis's death. "Elizabeth, lover of chastity, while her husband was still alive, made the promise of continence to God in the hand of magister Conrad, if she should outlive her husband."[42] But her powerful maternal uncle wants her to remarry. To keep the vow of continence, the widowed woman—again described as *castitatis amatrix*—employs the tactic of virgin martyrs.[43] She announced to her timorous lady companions, awed by the bishop, that she would cut off her nose and make herself so unattractive no man on earth would want her, should her uncle persist with plans of a second marriage.[44] At last Elizabeth displays the "heroics of virginity" commemorated in the *Lives* of female saints. Hers was no empty threat, for women before her, like Oda of Hainault (d. 1158), had cut off their own noses to avoid marriage and to enter religious life. This self-mutilation also worked: Oda became prioress of a Praemonstratensian monastery.[45] If the threat of self-disfigurement were not effective, the mutilation seems to have been a certain defense against the sexual touch whether in rape or in marriage.[46] Elizabeth's threat can be placed in a well-documented tradition of medieval religious women. For Caesarius her vow of continence and her return to chastity in widowhood are central to his evaluation of her sanctity. He suggests that virginity is measured not only by integrity of the flesh, but also by the intention of the spirit. He points out that not all virgins win the crown, for instance those young women who wish to marry but die before they can make their marriage vows. Calling upon the testimony of the blessed Lucy to strengthen his case, he closes with: "I trust that someone, who had the vow and intention of virginity, but who—having suffered violence—was corrupted, and thereafter again lives in chastity, mourning the corruption of the flesh, has squandered none of the heavenly reward for virginity."[47]

The paradox in Elizabeth's story as the sources reveal it to us—that of the virgin who loves chastity, the excellent wife who loves Louis, the continent widow dedicated to divine service—indicates that the lines of narrative concerning her status as "wife, widow, virgin" might be untangled by a theological interpretion.[48] Not only physical changes accompany the status shift from virgin to wife to widow, theological changes are also inherent in that same shift. Theologically, the virgin, the widow, and the wife are arranged hierarchically, with the virgin most valued, next the widow, then the wife. Jerome drew the later well-known comparison with the evangelical parable about the sower who went forth to sow, and "some seeds fell into good ground, and brought forth fruit, some an hundredfold (ap: the virgins), some sixtyfold (the widows), some thirtyfold (the wives)."[49] Elizabeth's responses to her status shifts might be theologically oriented rather than sexual. Her concerns about physical integrity and even her refusal of a second marriage might be in response to received learning from the Church about the value of virgins, widows, and wives. It should be noted that the "ground" of these three categories of womanhood has already been valued as good, it is a matter of how good. Having said that, copulation remains a thorny theological problem for the married, and in the following we see how this is resolved in the narrative of Elizabeth's life.

As a married woman Elizabeth transgresses the bounds of human comfort for the divine service, as do so many saints while in a secular setting. The running commentary the saints receive stresses their differences from the behavior and the ideas of other humans. Nightly vigils, which tax the human body with lack of sleep, testify to how willingly the saint undergoes deprivations, while the bystanders are anxious about such an onslaught to health.

It might be that the commonplace of vigils in Elizabeth's legend has its antecedents in earlier *Lives* of married women. The *Life of Radegund* seems in many respects similar to Elizabeth's, and one of the similarities is found in their nocturnal activities. This sixth century princess from Thuringia was kidnapped by the King Clothar I, to whom she was married, albeit unhappily, until she was able to beat a religious retreat to Poitiers.[50] In the illumination of an eleventh-century manuscript of her life she is shown in situations before her entry into the convent which reappear in the hagiography of Elizabeth: at the table of the King, praying before an altar, and praying on the floor in front of her husband's bed, while the husband sleeps on.[51] Were Elizabeth's nightly prayers modelled to this saintly predecessor? The *topoi* of saints' *Lives* are part and parcel of hagiographical genre, but they also result from the influence of holy examples. The hagiographies were used as pedagogic devices to train the pious and many medieval saints will have followed the example of forebears in the course of their holy conversion.

Elizabeth's nightly vigils show up some more intimate details of the marriage. Louis was the one person who would notice her freqent absences from the bedroom. Although he asked her to leave off with these vigils, he does not seem unduly disturbed when he discovers she has been going on with them in secret. But it is when he is away from court, which he was frequently, that Elizabeth is able to spend the nights in vigils, scourgings and castigations to her heart's content (and in obedience to Conrad of Marburg).[52] Caesarius, in recounting the vigils, follows the testimony of the eye-witnesses carefully. He seems to miss out on another chance to refer to marital sexuality. In the anonymous *Vita S. Elisabeth, Landgraviae Thuringiae*, an early *Life* which in the following respect anticipates the very popular version of Elizabeth's *Life* considered below, the landgravina's juggling of marital sexuality and the epithalamic bond to Christ are dealt with in one sentence:

> Indeed she, faithful as she was and devoted to prayer, and preferring the company of the eternal spouse to the temporal, consistently—whenever possible without violating the marriage debt—rose from the side of her husband to pray, he all the while asleep or pretending to be. After her prayers she was scourged in some room by her handmaidens, whereupon she would joyfully return to the bed of her husband, or fall asleep on the carpet in front of the bed while in the sweetness of prayer.[53]

For Caesarius the vigils provide an opportunity to cast Elizabeth, not as temporal wife doing service as Bride of Christ, but as a martyr.[54]

Elizabeth's three children, Hermann, Sophie, and Gertrude have no roles as independent personalities in the *Vita* written by Caesarius. They are not even mentioned by name. We catch only glimpses of them, once at the ritual of purification which takes place after the birth of a child. Elizabeth and her infants are central figures in this ritual procession to the church, re-enacting the presentation of the child Jesus to the Lord after the days of Mary's purification were completed, according to the laws of Moses. Mary took part in this ritual not because she was polluted from childbirth, but because she was obedient. It is Mary's obedience which women in the Roman Catholic Church emulate when they take part in this rite. The ritual was customary after children were born in Elizabeth's day, but Elizabeth more thoroughly imitates the Mother of God. Instead of donning sumptous apparel as do other matrons, she wears wool and goes barefoot into the church, carrying her infant in her own arms. With her own hands, she makes the offer of the child, the candle and the lamb. Caesarius of Heisterbach closes this episode with a sharp reproach to the ladies who put a well-shod and worldly foot forward when they participate in the ceremony: "Heed this, you matrons, you who in great ostentation make this type of procession wearing rich garments, you who do not imitate the humility of the Mother of God, as did Elizabeth, a most blessed woman and daughter of a rich king."[55]

The hagiographer does not minimize the children's importance in Elizabeth's life, although the greatest role they play on her path to perfection is one of absence and transference. Again we find he maintains silence where elsewhere, as in the prologue to the *Libellus*, Elizabeth's motherhood provides opportunities to recommend the pious work of educating one's children in the service of god.[56] In his *Vita*, one of the major spiritual endeavours of the saint seems to be extending or even transferring the love of a mother for her children to all children. When the aim is to show how caring Elizabeth was to the poor, he repeats maternal and filial metaphor used to the same end in the eyewitness testimonies: "Elizabeth gathered them to her as if they were her own children."[57] Interestingly, in the practice of charity it is documented that Elizabeth often showed especial concern for poor and sick infants and children, and an even more fascinating concern for pregnant paupers. She took part in their pains, both spiritual and physical, and became a "godmother" at the baptism of the child.[58] At Elizabeth's death, the laments are of a filial tone: "they cried as if she had been a mother to them all."[59] It is, by the way, precisely this facet of motherhood, this positive appraisal of a mother's bond to her children, of Elizabeth's love for Hermann and Sophie and Gertrude, that provided Conrad of Marburg a formidable test to try Elizabeth's constancy.

The saint's ordeal of renunciation had already begun. The words Elizabeth spoke upon the return of her husband's bones are recorded:

> Lord I give thanks to you, that you in your mercy have consoled me with my husband's bones, which I have so much desired. You know that, however much I loved him, still I did not envy you him, the most dearly beloved, offered to you by him and by me in service to the Holy Land. If I could have his company, I would give all the riches of the world to be with him always a beggar, but against your will, as you have shown, I would not wish to redeem his life with a single hair. Now I recommend to your grace his soul and myself, let your will be done unto us.[60]

Caesarius exclaims after this speech of the young widow: "This is true love, when loved ones are loved so much, but not preferred above divine love!"[61] But Elizabeth's trials are not over yet, for she will be afflicted, not by the will of God this time, but Conrad of Marburg, "a man," writes Caesarius of Heisterbach, who "as we all knew was *rigidus et austerus* whence many feared him, also because of the authority vested in him by the highest episcopate, which he did not neglect to exercise."[62] Nor did he neglect to use his authority over Elizabeth. He required of her that she send away her companions Guda and Ysentrude; he also required that she relinquish her own children. Again, Elizabeth speaks:

> The Lord has heard my prayers and lo, all of my earthly possession, which I once loved, now I reckon as so much dung. My children, whom the Lord gave me, ipso teste I reckon strangers. When injured, slandered and scorned, yet do I delight and rejoice. (cf. 2 Cor. 12:10) Absolutely nothing do I love, except for God, who gave all.[63]

All bonds with family and fortune must be broken for the last steps of perfection. Caesarius praises Elizabeth's obedience, her doing of Conrad's, that is God's will, for in this she was like Christ, who did not do his own will, but his father's will.[64]

This far-going obedience to the preacher of God seems in its extremity much like the tale of the patient Griselda, who also was ordered to relinquish her young child in a test of obedience. And the patient Griselda, like Elizabeth before her, was held up as an example to all women.[65] Yet it is not only in this fairy tale and Elizabeth's *Life* that renunciation of children is a sign of true love for the Father. The Church Fathers agree that a mother's love for her children weakens the strength of her passion for the divine. A martyr like Perpetua, who dies for Christ and thus orphans her baby, is praised by Augustine; Jerome praises Paula and another renouncing widow, Melania, for "deserting their children [as they] lifted up the Lord's cross."[66]

CAESARIUS'S SERMON

In the making of his *Vita*, Caesarius of Heisterbach seems to have functioned not primarily as a writer, compiling information from various sources into a narrative, but as an editor, adding notes here and there. He reproduces passage upon passage from the testimonies of the four companions, interspersing words to heighten dramatic effect or adding religious commentary and biblical citations. He asks no questions and he raises none. His hand as writer in this *Life* is found in the passages explaining the significance of Elizabeth's name, about Louis IV of Thuringia, Conrad of Marburg, and about the Ludowinger Konrad who joined the Teutonic Knights. It is in his sermon for the second feast of the translation of the *sanctissimus corpus* that Caesarius composes and shapes. Here, the conflict between the life story of the holy Elizabeth and monastic ideals of sanctity come sharply to the fore. In this sermon, given on the second of May 1237 at Heisterbach,[67] he stresses the wonder of miracles by which the celestial privilege of the saint is declared in the world. He relates that, in preparation for the translation ceremony, the Teutonic brothers find the body of the saint *integrum et incorruptum*, and "from the opened tomb lo! such fragrance rose from the sacred body, that all, revived by the sweetness of the odor, turned to God in admiration and joined in praise."[68] And then, after the translation, the brothers tending Elizabeth's body find it exudes oil, oil which is collected into vases, oil which heals the frail and weak. Brothers, Caesarius demands, consider the privileges which the Lord grants the saint. In the Old Testament, peopled with the just, the elect, patriarchs and prophets, there is not one mention of a body which exudes oil after death. John the Baptist is the first to whom this wonder is conceded, Demetrius the martyr is so honored, as are the virgin and martyr Saint Catherine and the Bishop Nicholas, and now Saint Elizabeth, widow. Caesarius explains: "And so God deemed worthy to honor all orders of the church. In the order of martyrs even apostles and the married are included."[69]

The sanctity and divine grace of the body is emphasized in the sermon; the fact that Elizabeth had married and had known a man, comes up again and again. The Lord may be wonderful in divine dispensation, but also amazing and even disturbing. How to understand that the body corrupt, the body bereft of the integrity of virginity, was the body that was gloried by miracle upon miracle? Caesarius feels it necessary to break the flow of his sermon to reason with his listeners: "Many of you," he preaches, "will wonder that this woman is graced with such a number of miracles, while there were and are so many virgins, in monasteries as well as in secular habit, to whom it is not given to shine forth in miracles."[70] But there is a reason in all God's doings, and Caesarius does not neglect to inform his wondering brothers about them. It is the virtue of charity which distinguishes Elizabeth, and he then refers his listeners to the parable of the Wise Virgins, the Foolish Virgins, and the oil-lamps. Bringing the sermon to a close, Caesarius implicitly dismisses the arguments of the divine providence of a good marriage used in his *Vita*, the religiosity of Elizabeth's life as a married woman, the pious works of the landgravina, her vigils and her obedience. He has found the key to the divine riddle:

> The weightiest reason for these miracles appears to have been that the blessed Elizabeth, who was the daughter of a king and the wife of a great prince, humbled herself to such a degree after the death of her husband, that she—scorning a (new) spouse, riches and honors—served the poor of Christ in much poverty and humility; she did the works of mercy and sustained the many tribulations and persecutions on account of all this cheerfully and thankfully, so that she made an example of herself for other noble matrons to do the same. (Thus) the good lord deemed worthy to honor his servant after death with miracles.[71]

Sanctity is thus achieved—in the view of the monk Caesarius, the view he presented for an audience of fellow brothers—by removal, renunciation, and alteration. In this sermon we see Caesarius remodelling the memory of sanctity along the same lines of holiness magister Conrad of Marburg used to direct Elizabeth's religious life as widow. Perhaps it is in the testimony of the *ancillae* that Elizabeth's own expression of piety and the path to perfection is best preserved. There we see the sanctity of Elizabeth manifested in the world peopled by friends and family: as a young girl genuflecting before the altar, her lips pressed to the ground; as landgravina walking among the women paupers, tending them in childbirth and becoming godmother to their children; distributing care, food, drink and discipline. In these aspects her own shaping of religiosity is in line with the upcoming mode of lay spirituality, in which the expression of piety is embedded in the rhythms and surroundings of everyday life. Perhaps for Elizabeth herself this holy life was most in line with the model of royal sainthood with which she was connected by right of birth.

The stories told about Elizabeth, it seems, negotiate between historical events and point of view, generic form, religious ideals, and audience. In the following versions of Elizabeth's *Life* to be considered, these dynamics of storytelling are no less discernible.

A CHARMED *Life*: THEODORIC OF APOLDA'S *Vita*

The next version of Elizabeth's life was written by the Dominican Theodoric of Apolda (c.1228–after 1297), who joined the *Ordo Praedicatorum* at Erfurt in 1247. He worked on this *Life* from 1289 to 1297. It is one of the lengthiest and one of the most popular *Lives* of Elizabeth, widespread throughout the Dominican Order but also beyond the order in later centuries. According to Ortrud Reber: "Das 14. und das 15. Jhdt. sind von Dietrichs Lebensbeschreibung beherrscht."[72] Its influence must have been enormous: the Dominicans played an important role in the late medieval enterprise to edify women,[73] and Elizabeth's exemplaric portrait in this hagiography will have served as a useful pedagogic device. The narrative is geared to a wide audience, not only the monastery, but the court and the city is reached by the example of the saint's cheerfulness in adversity, her pure heart, her good conscience, and her true faith. The hagiography concentrates more on elements of lay spirituality, offering examples to fill in daily life in the world with the service of God. In this sense, it prepares the way for the message of the late-medieval *Life of Anne*. In the following I will consider not only the Latin but also a vernacular translation, namely the middle-Dutch *Sunte Elizabetten Legende* preserved in manuscripts from the fifteenth and early sixteenth centuries.

With the *Vita Sancte Elyzabeth* by Theodoric of Apolda, the fairy tale seems to compete with hagiography in the narrative. Perhaps the fairy-tale quality is the reason Apolda's version was so overwhelmingly successful in the fourteenth and fifteenth centuries. Even today, this *Life of Elizabeth* is as captivating and as charming as any Walt Disney production of *Beauty and the Beast* or *Cinderella*. It is also as sugary-sweet. This is strange, considering the intentions of the Dominican monk who wrote this *Vita*. He decided to work on this *Life*, so that Elizabeth's story would be "written into history." The historical sources, namely the testimony of the *ancillae* and the *Life* written by Conrad of Marburg, Theodoric of Apolda explains, are incomplete because much was taken to be common knowledge and thus omitted from written record. His aim is to fill in the names and the places. Also, the arrangement of the material is not orderly. After all, the *Libellus* is a transcript of sworn testimony, and memories do not arrange themselves into pleasing narratives. Thus matters pertaining to one topic are scattered throughout the whole just as they were remembered.[74] In his aim of providing an artful narrative, Theodoric of Apolda has succeeded. In his aim of providing a better history, one cannot be sure. Apolda's *Life of Elizabeth* wavers between historical hagiography and hagiographical legend. Or hagiographical romance, one cannot help adding.

The middle-Dutch edition based on Theodoric of Apolda's *Vita* matches its style to the light tone of happy lovers in springtime.[75] Not that Elizabeth does not have her share of problems. For instance, when she reaches marriageable age, everybody turns against her. The rumor runs that Louis will choose another bride, or at least that he should choose another. Her future mother-in-law, Sophie, is especially industrious about getting Elizabeth into a convent instead of to the marriage altar with Louis. But God intervenes, like the good godmother in fairy tales. In Louis's heart the Heavenly Power instills such a love for Elizabeth that, as Louis assures one of his vassals, he would sooner scorn a mountain of gold than he would this maiden. There is no suggestion that Elizabeth married against the desire of her heart, although the story about casting lots for the virgin apostle John the Evangelist is retold. Instead it seems it is the desire of her heart to marry Louis, and when one of the vassals reassures her about the landgrave's good intentions, her reaction is one of great relief. The audience too is instructed about Louis's good intentions, which are manifested in his choice of gifts by which to please his bride: "Consider this pure young man's intentions! He did not want to pull his bride to the pleasures of the flesh but rather to the grace of God—he sent her a precious gift, an image of the Crucifix."[76]

A motive for God to act as Cupid is to provide some *aanzien* for Elizabeth: her marriage ensures her social status, just as it did for many medieval women in actuality. God has a similar motive in providing Elizabeth with three children: "nor did she lack the principal good of lawful wedlock, for the divine blessing of children came upon her."[77] Children here become another sign of God's grace, much as the wonders and miracles function to show especial favor with the divine. It seems standards of sanctity have changed to accomodate the possibilities of a lay person in the divine service.

This lack of tension in the *Vita Sancte Elyzabeth* about the saint's marriage could be attributed to Elizabeth's personal success as a saint as well as to the historical climate of the later Middle Ages which made this success possible. Her miracles, for instance, have widely and thoroughly attested to her power. She is able to do that most wonderful and unusual miracle, bestowing the gift of sight upon the blind.[78] Her doings in life were such that the Franciscans appropriated her for themselves and saw in her the mother of the Franciscan Order.[79] Like Francis and like Dominic, Elizabeth makes it into the "big time."[80] It can be argued that her fame, spread widely by virtue of her miracles and her exemplary works of mercy, fostered acceptance of her life before widowhood as pious and a logical part of God's plan. When Theodoric of Apolda began writing, there may no longer have been any need for an apologetic strain about Elizabeth's married life. Elizabeth's by now well-known story would have changed the expectations of the audience. Argumentation, as in Caesarius of Heisterbach's sermon, seems no longer necessary.

Purposes of authors also structure narratives. In the tale about Elizabeth taken up in the *Golden Legend*, no less popular as a whole than Apolda's *Life of Elizabeth*, and its near contemporary, a different twist is given to her marriage. There she enters the state of marriage not for pleasure but in obedience to her father and in order to raise Christian children. With the *Golden Legend* in mind as comparison, Apolda's romantic passages cannot be reduced to a general "sign of the times" explanation. A more detailed background study than I have undertaken is needed to better understand the text and its reception.

Apolda's *Vita* stands out because it succeeds most in weaving the love of God into the everyday life of the landgravina. Instead of lessons drawn *out* from her example, in his narration everything the saint does is suffused with moral significance. Religious ideals permeate his narrative; the conjunction between Saint Elizabeth and God is seamless; the fissures noted in earlier representations have disappeared.

In Apolda's rendition of Elizabeth's life, instead of a physical conception of purity in virginity, there is a spiritual conception of purity in love. Physicality is a measure not absolute. This *Vita* spans a bridge between strict religious and secular divisions, with its sliding rule suitable for pious laity who do not benefit from monastic enclosure. Elizabeth's simplicity in clothing (except when for reasons of state she had to be grand), and above all, her choice of simple food and her love for Louis while she scorned the pleasures of the flesh, make her a saintly model for those who live in the world. And so the hagiographer recommends: "People of all conditions, young and old, note and wonder and follow the example of the king's daughter, who at the table of the prince, loaded with delicious dishes, scorned such luxurious pleasure, and in the bedroom of her beloved husband, scorned the delights of the flesh."[81]

One does not have to withdraw from the world in order to attain a standard of piety, yet neither does intention or will suffice in the service of

God. Chastisement of the flesh is an exterior sign of interior direction. We see a line of causality is drawn between the events of the marriage bed and the nightly vigils of Elizabeth. The temporal sequence built into the narrative—the series of marriage, bed, chastisement of the flesh—gives a suggestion of direct cause and effect:

> Between them was honorable marriage and undefiled bed, not in carnal love but in the holy purity of matrimony. For this young virgin, shortly after marrying her husband, chastised her flesh with many vigils. For in the night she would get up to pray while her husband slept. . . . she sought the true husband of her soul.[82]

In many ways, then, Elizabeth as a bride-to-be and as a wife in the widely popular version of Theodoric of Apolda was very close to the life that could be had, or at least dreamed of, by a virtuous young woman of one of the more prosperous classes. It is a story in which Elizabeth is granted, by the grace of God, the gifts of a good husband and three children. Indeed, she is able to be bride of her husband and bride of Christ simultaneously. In the state of matrimony both Louis and Elizabeth are depicted as holy, joined together as *sanctus cum sancta*.[83]

In one peculiar way, the saint comes down from her pedestal, as it were, to behave in an unsaintly fashion when her husband takes the Cross, and prepares to venture to the Holy Land. This would seem to magnify the possibility of identification and emulation for a woman of a more ordinary sort. In Apolda's story, Elizabeth is desolate that Louis has promised to undertake the perilous journey in the service of God. When Louis sees her distress, this "sweetest prince" comforts her with pious admonitions and many soft words. Her initial desolation is strange on the part of a future saint, but a commonplace reaction on the part of wives whose husbands signed the Cross, at least as recorded in historical documents. These sources record the wonders which taught many medieval wives that they should not stand in the way of husbands taking the Cross.[84]

Elizabeth as a wife becomes an accessible model, someone to wonder at, someone to admire, but also someone to imitate in the endeavours of marriage.[85] Elizabeth's widowhood as model might have influenced the history of many a medieval community and a medieval woman in a concrete way. One instance of a queen who seems to have followed in Elizabeth's footsteps is Margaretha of Burgundy, Queen of Sicily and sister-in-law to King Louis of France. She founded a hospital dedicated to the Holy Ghost (the most common patron of medieval hospitals) in 1293. The queen herself set up residence next to the hospital and spent the rest of her life working there.[86] In the fifteenth century groups of religious women, under the name "Elisabettinen" did the works of mercy as "nurses" in hospitals.[87] The miniature and lesson for Saint Elizabeth in the fifteenth-century *Festal Evangelistary* by the Masters of Otto van Moerdrecht juxtapose widows, their offers, and their nursing through the Biblical text and illumination of Elizabeth's work in Marburg. The miniature shows Elizabeth in one of the hospital rooms, tending to the bath of two beggars. The lesson from the Gospel (Mk. 12:41–44) is about the poor widow who gave all she had, and thus gave more than the rich who had given of their abundance.[88] Elizabeth's works in widowhood may have been a model accessible not only for nurses, but also for widows with inheritances.

VISUAL REPRESENTATION: THE LÜBECK CYCLE

The next story of Elizabeth's life is told in twenty-three painted panels displayed at the *Heiligen-Geist-Kirche* in Lübeck.[89] They were painted between 1420–30 by an artist of the school of Conrad of Soest. The vagaries of time cannot account for the discrepancies this version has with the earlier versions of Elizabeth's life; one begins to empathize with Protestant objectors to the cult of the saints. The panels incorporate elements from Apolda's *Life*, but another *Legend* (or group of legends) has been drawn upon. Themes of mothers and mothering run through the images, and because the panels give a heightened significance to these scenes, lifted out from the full web of written narrative into the outline of paint, they suggest that these are more significant parts of the *Lives of Elizabeth* than a quantitative analysis of the words spent on these scenes in hagiography indicates.

The panels show the following: the prophecy of Clingsor, the necromancer from Hungary who travels to the Ludowinger court to judge a knights' singing contest. He reads the stars, which announce that a princess has been born who will be a saint and a Ludowinger landgravina. Then Gertrude, Queen of Hungary, in the birth bed, nursing Elizabeth; King Andrew and retinue look on (fig. 8.2). A sumptuous silver cradle stands ready for the holy princess. Follows the betrothal negotiations between Thuringia and Hungary. Panels five to seven show the journey of four-year old Elizabeth to Thuringia in 1211, the transport of dowry, the two engaged children together, with entourage. Panel eight has Elizabeth playing with her childhood friends, snatching a moment to run into the church in early attendance to the divine. The next one depicts the murder of Gertrude, Queen of Hungary, which took place at the *Jagd Opfer* 28 September 1213, when Elizabeth was six years old, only two years after her journey to Thuringia.

In panel ten Elizabeth is full-grown and dressed in alms-giving garb, her two lady companions similarly clad. Panel eleven shows Elizabeth making her vow of obedience to her confessor Conrad, the *magister* and *predicator verbis Dei*, while Louis and a maidservant watch. The next has Elizabeth at the table of the landgrave, a feast in process, followed by a scene of three beautiful and beautifully dressed court ladies, astonished at the simple tunic Elizabeth wears under her mantle. Panel fourteen is another study in the saint's humility, as Elizabeth kneels before the Christ on the Crucifix. She has removed her crown from her head and placed it beside her. Then a juxtaposition: in the foreground Elizabeth in simple garb bids an equestrian and armoured Louis farewell. Behind the scene of the parting landgrave and landgravina, Elizabeth is in bed, propped up on cushions, nursing one of the two children shown with her. In panel sixteen she is combing the hair of a leper, with bystanders closely watching this act which does not correspond to the status of landgravina. On the next her works of mercy during the famine of 1226 are shown. Louis is at the court of Frederick II when the greatest crisis of his rule hits Thuringia. Elizabeth, who rules in his stead, opens the granaries of the *lantgravium* to the starving subjects. In panel eighteen the landgrave has returned to find that Elizabeth's charity has brought a leper to the bridal bed; a wonder occurs, and the wonder is what the painting shows: the leper has become the crucified Christ. Elizabeth kneels before Louis. Three amazed onlookers complete the scene. In panel nineteen the landgrave and the landgravina again must part: this time Louis is off to crusade. Elizabeth, heavy with child, stitches the cross on his cloak. She wears the simple clothes denoting the saint's humility; Louis, by taking the Cross, has become a *gotes helt*, off to do his *officium*.[90] The scene resonates with holy meaning. The third to last panel shows Louis's brothers Heinrich and Konrad literally throwing Elizabeth out of the castle, two of her little children with her (fig. 8.3). Then follows an old woman who once had received charity from Elizabeth rudely shoves her into a ditch. The last scenes show Elizabeth "leaving the world" at the altar, and then on her deathbed.

There are some striking elements to this cycle. Almost all the panels show scenes from Elizabeth's life before she was widowed. It seems odd that Elizabeth's three years of service at the Marburg hospital were not chosen by the painter as subject of the panels, since they were commissioned for a hospital church.

Elizabeth's differences are highlighted: she is dressed humbly, she touches lepers, she is haloed. The looks of bystanders direct our gaze to the saint: she is marked by the medium of amazed vision. Yet the holiness does

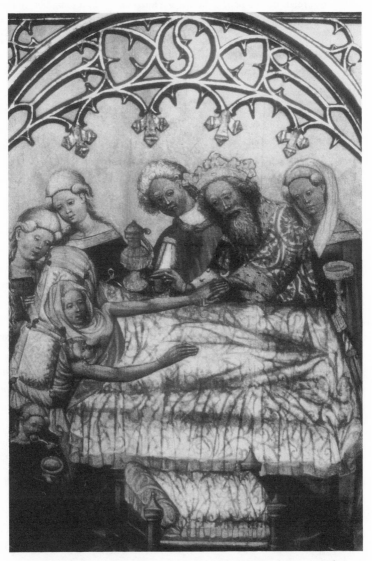

*Figure 8.2. Gertrude, Queen of Hungary, in the birth bed, nursing Eliza-
beth. Panel 2 in the same cycle*

not create distance between the saint and surroundings. Her sanctity is embedded in her royal parentage, her princely marriage, her progeny. Elizabeth
is a saint; she is also daughter, wife and mother.

Elizabeth's mother Gertrude, Queen of Hungary by marriage, by birth
member of the Andechs-Meranien family, a noble German clan, is the cen-

tral focus of two panels. In one she nurses her infant daughter; in the other she is murdered. Why is Gertrude prominent in this sequence of panels? What does her motherhood mean to Elizabeth's sanctity? In the *Golden Legend*, Gertrude is not mentioned, only the paternal line is designated: Elizabeth is "daughter of the famous king of Hungary, of noble birth."[91] Theodoric of Apolda's *Vita Sancte Elyzabeth* introduces Gertrude as the wife of King Andrew, daughter of the noble Duke of *Carinthia*, who bore a daughter (Elizabeth) "who did honor to her clan."[92] In book II Gertrude's character is sketched and her role as mother amplified: she is virtuous and strong, with the temper of a man.[93] It is she who prepares Elizabeth's dowry, and it is she who bids the rulers of Thuringia to take good care of her daughter, and in return she promises to gather great riches for her daughter, as long as God grants her life.[94] Then is told of the riches Gertrude sent with her daughter, gold, silver, silks, and many other precious goods. The book closes with the message that Gertrude was murdered three years after Elizabeth's journey to Thuringia. Later Gertrude reappears in the story, asking Elizabeth to intercede for her. "Her mother who long ago had been murdered in Hungary, appeared in her sleep, and kneeled, and said to her: 'My dear daughter, pray for me. I am still in pain, for I lived carelessly.'"[95] Elizabeth awoke, prayed amidst tears, and returned to sleep. Her mother reappeared and thanked her, saying that she had been saved.[96]

Caesarius of Heisterbach gives a very different assessment of Gertrude's moral quality, and thereby represents a strong and determining bond between mother and daughter beyond the maternal provision of material goods. The political murder of Gertrude was, in Caesarius's view, a martyrdom. She was forewarned of murderous intent, "but she committed herself to the grace of God and won the martyrs crown from the Hungarians in her innocence."[97] Thus Gertrude suffered in the way that Abel did, who, innocent as he was, was killed on account of the jealousy of his brother. "Lo and Behold!" cries Caesarius, "from such noble and devout stock the blessed Elizabeth drew her origins. For if from the flesh of the mother [Elizabeth] drew forth nobility, it is not to be wondered at if from the spirit of the mother, just as from a fountain of piety, she was able to draw forth sanctity, supported both by the merits of her mother and by her prayers."[98]

This vision of spiritual and physiological motherhood added to the holy fame of Elizabeth's youngest daughter Gertrude (1227–1297), a Praemonstratensian abbess of the Altenberg convent, who in 1348 was canonized by Pope Clemens VI.[99] Landgrave Herman II already identifies himself the son of the saint in his very first charters;[100] Sophie (1224–1284),

Elizabeth's second child, who in 1240 became the second wife of Hendrik II (de Edelmoedige) Duke of Brabant, also stressed her holy parentage to her political advantage. She was the founding mother of the Landgraves of Hesse, having successfully fought for her son's right to inherit against powers like

Figure 8.3. After Louis's death Elizabeth is thrown out of the Landgrave's castle, two of her little children with her. Panel 20 in the same cycle

the archbishop of Mainz and the markgrave Heinrich von Meissen. In the thick of the fight, her seals announced her *Sophie Filie Sancte Elizabet Duccisse Brabancie et Domine Hassye.*[101]

The sources by which we reconstruct the parameters of Elizabeth's sanctity and motherhood are all part and parcel of Church and State politics: within each story interests are being served, sometimes escaping the eye of the modern reader, sometimes clear, the nature of the sources always urging us to treat with caution the histories they serve us. Sometimes the carefully constructed veil of the story will "slip," showing us perhaps a ruler out of character, or a saint out of iconic frame. Although what is unsaid can only be surmised, the following story about Elizabeth puts her sanctity and motherhood into a light other than the teller perhaps intended. It is the tale of the unjust punishment mentioned at the beginning of this article. Elizabeth and her maidservant have been beaten so hard that the marks are still clearly visible three weeks later. Why? The sisters of the convent Altenberg, for whom Elizabeth spins wool, had requested of Conrad that Elizabeth be given permission to visit inside the monastic enclosure. His answer was no—albeit a cryptic no, Elizabeth understood yes. She did visit the nuns and was—unwittingly—disobedient.[102] There is something implausible about this story, but the dynamics appear less odd when it is taken into account that Elizabeth's youngest child, Gertrude, is in the convent. It was to Altenberg that she was brought after her mother renounced her, at the age of one and a half.[103] This extra dimension makes the austere Conrad more of a frustrated man of God; it also makes the humble Elizabeth a bit more worldly-wise, her disobedience cloaked in misunderstanding, her visit to her child masquerading as a visit to the sisters.

The above must remain conjecture; the sources do sometimes show that the shaping of Elizabeth's piety was not always in accordance with her own sense of religious direction. How would Elizabeth herself have modeled her experience of religious life? How would the dynamics of storytelling have functioned in her remembrance? The fissures between her life story, in which she acted according to religious precepts while in the state of matrimony, surrounded by kith and kin, and the still dominant ideal of religious life as withdrawal from the world and renunciation, seems to have been resolved in the passages of time. It became possible to "forget" what was difficult to fit into religious models; these same passages of time made it possible that the memory of Saint Elizabeth could bring renewal and change in the models. These processes seem essential for the plenitude of understandings possible in the reading of symbols.

Processes of remembering and forgetting are well-illustrated by the long "lives" of saints, for saints have a tendency to live on in history. This tendency seems part of the nature of sanctity, since the life of the saint begins with their physical death. And after all, when saints are revered they are also called upon to interfere in the affairs of this world. The image of Saint Elizabeth, whether as widow or wife, so often invoked as an example for women to follow or chosen by women to follow and to authorize their own *vita activa* and *vita contemplativa*, continued to have its use in later ages. Saint Elizabeth's "potency as cultural symbol," like Saint Anne's in the late Middle Ages, "was a function of her usefulness in triggering or activating ideological formations." As in the case of Saint Anne, "we may see her gender as a metaphor with functions that varied according to social and ideological situation."[104] While Elizabeth's many virtues were held up for imitation to a wide variety of medieval orders of people, Elizabeth's example of chastity and humility was specifically deployed or employed in her function as an ideal for women, especially rich aristocratic and later rich urban women.[105] In her supernatural power of working miracles, Saint Elizabeth was available to men and women and children; in her name rich burghers as well as rich burghesses founded hospitals; she patronized the Teutonic Knights; her male descendants could invoke her sanctity and motherhood as well as her female descendants.[106] Thus one may speculate that her holiness and symbolic power as intervention or genealogical legitimation of authority was significant to both men and women. But it seems that her life as an example to follow, especially in certain aspects, was more important to women. We see this already in her own lifetime, for it is *matron[ae]* she teaches about religion,[107] in her cult in medieval times as shown above, and even after her relics were moved from Marburg by her reforming sixteenth-century descendant Philip of Hesse. In the fifteenth century Elizabeth was included in the group of the Nine Female Worthies which replaced the *neuf preuses* who embodied the chivalric ideal of *prouesse*. These new Nine Worthies were historical women who embodied the Christian-humanist ideal feminine, characterized by *castitas*, *virtus*, and *sanctitas*.[108] These images of the most virtuous women from the ancient, biblical and medieval period were divided up into the categories of virgin, wife and widow in the series of engravings (1600–02) by Crispijn de Passe de Oude: here Elizabeth is the medieval representative of the ideal wife. Her image formed a pedagogic instrument; her charity, the predominant theme of the illustration and accompanying text, is to be emulated.[109] The most striking instances of women in the mold of "Elizabeth" occur when historical women are depicted as Saint Elizabeth. In these images we clearly recognize the icon of the saint, but upon closer examination, we see that her face is filled in with the features of another woman. In the museum of the Catharijneconvent in Utrecht, a 1640 painting by Christiaen van Couwenbergh portrays (an unfortunately nameless) Delft Beguine as Elizabeth, leading a sick beggar to the angel of healing, Rafaël. In eighteenth-century Germany it was customary for contemporary female rulers to have their portrait done in the figure of a saint. In one miniature reproduced in a catalogue dedicated to the figure of Elizabeth, the Gräfin Freyberg's face peers out from the form of Saint Elizabeth.[110] The confluence of icon and personal portrait creates a disturbing confusion of identity. When in the nineteenth century the Catholic Church promoted the virtue of charity Elizabeth again became an important example,[111] and again she left her mark on charitable societies as the St. Elisabeth Vereniging, founded to help the sick and women in childbed.[112] It is precisely Saint Elizabeth's "after-life," in the medieval as well as the modern period, that seems to cry out for more concerted effort on the part of researchers. The biography of her legend deserves as masterful a study as Charles W. Jones gave to Saint Nicholas.[113] It seems that her widespread popularity and her lack of affiliation to any particular order (and the failure of the fifteenth century *Elizabettinen* to found a long-lasting order) has created a hiatus in history writing. Unlike her contemporaries Francis and Dominic, who were as speedily canonized as Elizabeth herself, she instituted no Order in which historians could locate her influence as example. In the same oblique way, Elizabeth has provided a model for pious wives and pious mothers, herself—we assume—drawing on early medieval models of saintly queens. As a historical person and as icon, she seems to bely the message of the Catholic Church about the Virgin Mary and her relation to women, as succintly formulated by Marina Warner in the title of her work about the cult of the Virgin Mary, *Alone of All her Sex*.[114] For mothers, nurses, rulers, wives and widows, Saint Elizabeth has functioned as a means of religious empowerment.

NOTES

* At the beginning of this project, Dimphéna Groffen gave freely of her research experience with helpful advice and suggestions. She was my beginner's luck. Towards the end, Karl Lutterkort shared generously of his erudition, giving my Latin translations and references a vigorous critical reading. Our conversations were invaluable. My greatest debt is to Anneke Mulder-Bakker, who provided unfailing and excellent guidance from beginning to end. To all of them my heartfelt thanks.

1. Primary sources have been edited by Albert Huyskens, *Quellenstudien zur Geschichte der hl. Elisabeth: Landgräfin von Thüringen* (Marburg, 1908) and *Der sog. Libellus de Dictis Quatuor Ancillarum s. Elisabeth confectus* (Kempten and Munich: Verlag der. Jos. Kösel'schen Buchhandlung, 1911), 1–86 (BHL 2493d–h). The depositions of the four companions of the saint, known as the *Dicta Quatuor Ancillarum*

(BHL 2493m), is found in Huyskens' *Quellenstudien*, 112–140. For an extensive inventory of medieval sources about the cult of Saint Elizabeth see Ortrud Reber, *Die Gestaltung des Kultes weiblicher Heiliger im Spätmittelalter: Die Verehrung der Heiligen Elisabeth, Klara, Hedwig und Birgitta* (Hersbruck, 1963), 5–14. Central to this study will be the *Life of Elizabeth* by Caesarius of Heisterbach, *Vita Sancte Elyzabeth Lantgravie* (BHL 2494), in: "Des Cäsarius von Heisterbach Schriften über die hl. Elisabeth," ed. Albert Huyskens, *Annalen des Historischen Vereins für den Niederrhein*, 86 (1908), 17–50 and the *Vita Sancte Elyzabeth* by Theodoric of Apolda (BHL 2496) in Monika Rener, *Die Vita der heiligen Elisabeth des Dietrich von Apolda* (Veröffentlichungen der Historischen Kommission für Hessen, 53) (Marburg: Elwert Verlag, 1993). The middle Dutch translation was consulted in the edition by Lodewijk Scharpé, "Sunte Elisabetten Legende," *Leuvensche Bijdragen*, 5 (1903–1904), 1–140. The "Elisabeth-Zyklus" is on display at the Heiligen-Geist-Hospital am Koberg in Lübeck, Germany; for literature on the panels see note 89 below. A useful short biography of Elizabeth is: Norbert Ohler, *Elisabeth von Thüringen: Fürstin im Dienst der Niedrigsten* (Göttingen: Muster-Schmidt Verlag, 1984). Also see *Sankt Elisabeth: Fürstin, Dienerin, Heilige: Aufsätze, Dokumentation, Katalog* (Sigmaringen: Thorbecke, 1981).

2. André Vauchez, "Lay People's Sanctity in Western Europe: Evolution of a Pattern (twelfth and thirteenth centuries)," in *Images of Sainthood in Medieval Europe*, ed. Renate Blumenfeld-Kosinski and Timea Szell (Ithaca, N.Y.: Cornell University Press, 1991), 30f.

3. Thomas von Bogyay, "Die ungarischen Vorfahren der hl. Elisabeth," in *Sankt Elisabeth: Fürstin, Dienerin, Heilige*, 319–322; cf. Gábor Klaniczay, "From Sacral Kingship to Self-Representation: Hungarian and European Royal Saints," in his *The Uses of Supernatural Power: The Transformation of Popular Religion in Medieval and Early-Modern Europe* (Cambridge: Polity Press, 1990), 79–94.

4. Michael Goodich, "The Politics of Canonization in the Thirteenth Century: Lay and Mendicant Saints," in *Saints and Their Cults: Studies in Religious Sociology, Folklore and History*, ed. Stephen Wilson (Cambridge: Cambridge University Press, 1983), 170.

5. See Helmut Beumann, "Friedrich II. und die heilige Elisabeth: Zum Besuch des Kaisers in Marburg am 1. Mai 1236," in *Sankt Elisabeth: Fürstin, Dienerin, Heilige*, 151–165, here 163, n. 36: on kinship: "Landgraf Ludwig IV., Elisabeths Gemahl, war ein Vetter zweiten Grades Kaiser Friedrichs II. wegen der Ehe seines Grossvaters, Landgraf Ludwigs II., mit Jutta, einer Stiefschwester Friedrich Barbarossas. Von einer Verwandtschaft des Kaisers mit Elisabeth konnte allenfalls insofern gesprochen werden, als ihr Oheim, König Emrich von Ungarn (1196–1204), der erste Gemahl Konstanzes von Aragon, der späteren Kaiserin und Mutter Heinrichs (VII.), gewesen war."

6. Reber, *Die Gestaltung des Kultes*, 7, 12f., 117.

7. Fred Schwind, "Die Landgrafschaft Thüringen und der landgräfliche Hof zur Zeit der Elisabeth . . .," in *Sankt Elisabeth: Fürstin, Dienerin, Heilige*, 30; Ursula Braasch, "Die Eltern der hl. Elisabeth," in the same volume, 317ff.

8. Werner Rösener, "Die höfische Frau im Hochmittelalter," in *Curialitas: Studien zu Grundfragen der höfisch-ritterlichen Kultur*, ed. Josef Fleckenstein (Veröffentlichungen des Max-Planck-Instituts für Geschichte, 100) (Göttingen: Vandenhoeck & Ruprecht, 1990), 203.

9. Ibid., 204f.

10. *Dicta Quatuor Ancillarum*, ed. Huyskens, 116f.: "Item propter prolixitatem orationis sepe ante lectum obdormivit super tapete. Unde cum argueretur ab ancillis, quare non libentius dormiret cum marito, respondit: 'Licet non possim semper orare, tamen hanc vim faciam carni mee, quod avellor a predilecto marito meo.'"

11. Matthias Werner, "Die heilige Elisabeth und Konrad von Marburg," in *Sankt Elisabeth: Fürstin, Dienerin, Heilige*, 45–69.

12. André Vauchez, "Charité et pauvreté chez sainte Elisabeth de Thuringe, d'apres les actes des procès de canonisation," in *Études sur l'histoire de la pauvreté (Moyen Age—XVIe siècle)*, ed. Michel Mollat (Paris: Sorbonne, 1974), 165f.

13. *Dicta Quatuor Ancillarum*, ed. Huyskens, 118.

14. See Margaret Wade Labarge, "Three Medieval Widows and a Second Career," in *Aging and the Aged in Medieval Europe*, ed. Michael M. Sheehan (Papers in Mediaeval Studies, 11) (Toronto: Pontifical Institute of Mediaeval Studies, 1990), 159–172.

15. *Jacobus a Voragine Legenda Aurea vulgo Historia Lombardica dicta*, ed. Th. Graesse (1890; rpt Osnabrück: Otto Zeller Verlag, 1969), 758.

16. The legends follow the *Dicta Quatuor Ancillarum*, ed. Huyskens, 121: "Post mortem vero mariti eiecta fuit de castro et omnibus possessionibus sui dotalicii a quibusdam vasallis mariti sui, fratre ipsius mariti adhuc iuvene existente."

17. Werner, "Die heilige Elisabeth," 53.

18. Thomas Franke, "Ablassurkunde Papst Gregors IX. fur das Franziskushospital in Marburg," in *Sankt Elisabeth: Fürstin, Dienerin, Heilige*, 429.

19. *Dicta Quatuor Ancillarum*, ed. Huyskens, 139: "Indutum autem tunica grisea corpus eius et faciem eius pannis circumligatam plurimi devotione accensi particulas pannorum incidebant, alii rumpebant, alii pilos capitis incidebant et ungues. Quedam autem etiam aures illius truncabant. Etiam summitatem mamillarum eius quidam precidebant et pro reliquiis huiusmodi sibi servabant."

20. Donald Weinstein and Rudolph M. Bell, *Saints and Society: The Two Worlds of Western Christendom, 1000–1700* (Chicago: University of Chicago Press, 1982), 87–97.

21. Richard Kieckhefer, *Unquiet Souls: Fourteenth-Century Saints and Their Religious Milieu* (Chicago: University of Chicago Press, 1984), 54.

22. See the contribution of Ineke van't Spijker, "Family Ties: Mothers and Virgins in the Ninth Century" to this volume.

23. Vauchez, "Lay people's sanctity," 22; for an extensive treatment of Saint Mathilda see Patrick Corbet, *Les Saints Ottoniens: Sainteté dynastique, sainteté royale et sainteté féminine autour de l'an Mil* (Sigmaringen: Thorbecke, 1986).

24. *Epistola magistri Cunradi de Marburch ad Papam de Vita Beate Elyzabet* (BHL 2491b), ed. Huyskens, in his *Quellenstudien*, 156: "Duobus annis antequam michi commendaretur, adhuc vivente marito suo, confessor eius extiti, ipsam querelosam reperiens, quod aliquando fuerit coniugio copulata et quod in virginali flore non poterat presentem vitam terminare."

25. *Dicta Quatuor Ancillarum*, ed. Huyskens, 121: "[M]iro se affectu diligentes et se invicem ad Dei laudem et servitium dulciter invitantes et confortantes. Maritus enim eius cum circa temporalia necessitate suorum principatuum intendere et necessare, in secreto tamen Dei timorem semper habens pre oculis, beate Elizabet ad omnia exercenda, que ad Dei spectant honorem, liberam concessit facultatem eam ad anime salutem promovendo."

26. Cf. Caroline Walker Bynum on the lack of turning points in medieval women's stories, "Women's Stories, Women's Symbols: A Critique of Victor Turner's Theory of Liminality," in her *Fragmentation and Redemption: Essays on Gender and the Human Body in Medieval Religion* (New York: Zone Books, 1991), 27–51.

27. Michael Goodich, *Vita Perfecta: The Ideal of Sainthood in the Thirteenth Century* (Stuttgart: Hiersemann, 1982), 4.

28. See Anneke B. Mulder-Bakker, "Ivetta of Huy: *Mater et Magistra*," in this volume.

29. Reber, *Die Gestaltung des Kultes*, 36; also see Renate Kroos, "Zu fruhun Schrift- und Bildzeugnissen über die heilige Elisabeth als Quellen zur Kunst- und Kulturgeschichte," in *Sankt Elisabeth: Fürstin, Dienerin, Heilige*, 222.

30. *Dicta Quatuor Ancillarum*, ed. Huyskens, 112f.: "Item aliquantulum adulta beatam Johannem evangelistam, tamquam castitatis custodem, diu affectabat habere apostolum. Unde cum secundum consuetudinem dominarum omnium aposto-

lorum nominibus vel in candelis vel in carta scriptis singulariter simulque super altare mixtim compositis, singulis sibi apostolos sorte eligentibus, ipsa oratione fusa secundum suum votum tribus vicibus sorte beatum Johannem recepit apostolum, in cuius honore quicquid petebatur vel muneris vel offense relaxando, vel de quocumque faciendo vel dimittendo numquam negabat" and Caesarius of Heisterbach, *Vita sancte Elyzabeth Lantgravie*, ed. Huyskens, 22: "Future perfectionis et sanctitatis inicia atque indicia hec in tali fuere infante necnon et illa, que sequuntur. Cumque aliquantulum adulta esset, beatum Iohannem ewangelistam tamquam castitatis amatorem habere apostolum affectabat eumque imitari, quamquam deus mira sua dispensacione aliter ordinasset."

31. Later in the same century, at the Saxon monastery of Helfta served by nuns recruited from Thuringia and Saxony, the nun Gertrude of Helfta recorded in *The Herald of Divine Love* (1289) a lengthy conversation with this popular apostle, with much attention for the subject of "integritas virginitatis" and its complexities. A vision about the virgin Saint John the Evangelist and the also virgin Saint John the Baptist instructs the mystic and the reader about the differences between virginities, and why it is not the blessed John the Baptist, wholly free of all carnality ("omnino immunis ab omni carnalitate") but the blessed John the Evangelist, chosen by the Lord and called away from the wedding ("legatur a Domino de nuptiis vocatus"), who is glorified for virginity. The vision shows John the Baptist, as if seated on a throne over the sea, raised and far from all things, while John the Evangelist is seen standing in the middle of a raging furnace, dreadfully inflamed, fire on all sides, above and below. She continues: "Hinc intellexit quod valde dissimilis est praemii virtus impugnata (ap: as in John the Evangelist) et virtus in pace servata (ap: as in John the Baptist)." Loving chastity is not necessarily a matter of easy infatuation. Gertrude of Helfta, *Oeuvres spirituelles 4: Le Heraut*, 4.9, ed. Jean-Marie Clement et al. (Sources Chretiennes, 255) (Paris: Cerf, 1978), 76f.

32. Jacobus a Voragine, *Legenda Aurea*, ed. Graesse, 753: "Crescens vero per aetatem temporis et crescebat amplius per affectum devotionis, nam beatam virginem Dei genitricem in sui patronam et advocatam et beatum Johannem evangelistam in suae castitatis custodem elegit. Cum enim singulae schedulae singulorum apostolorum nominibus inscriptae altari imponerentur et quaelibet aliarum puellarum casu sibi schedulam contingentem acciperet, ista oratione fusa tribus vicibus schedulam, ubi nomen sancti Petri erat inscriptum, ut desiderabat, accepit, ad quem tanto devotionis ferebatur affectu, ut nihil in ejus nomine petentibus denegaret."

33. See n. 30 above.

34. Renate Kroos, "Sog. Elisabethpsalter," in *Sankt Elisabeth: Fürstin, Dienerin, Heilige*, 348.

35. Caesarius von Heisterbach, *Vita*, ed. Huyskens, 24: "Cumque beata et venerabilis virgo Elyzabeth ad nubiles annos pervenisset, contra cordis sui desiderium nobilissimo principi Ludewico lantgravio desponsata est et matrimonio iuncta."

36. Ibid., 24: "Erat autem idem Ludewicus adolescens mire probitatis, virtutibus ornatus, viciorum hostis, et, quod in tali etate et persona laica valde commendandum est, deum timens, sicut in eius iudiciis et actibus experte declaratum est." The connotations of "probitas" might incorporate to Louis' sexuality. The *Oxford Latin Dictionary*, ed. P.G.W. Glare (Oxford: Oxford University Press, 1982), defines "probitas" as a) moral integrity, uprightness, honesty, probity, b) sexual purity, virtue, c) decorous behaviour.

37. Caesarius von Heisterbach, *Vita*, ed. Huyskens, 25: "Deus, cui omnia presencia sunt, huiusmodi opera iusticie necnon et pietatis, que timore eius exercuit, in eo previdens mulierem bonam, sanctam et pudoratam illi sociavit secundum illud ecclesiastici: Pars bona mulier bona in parte bona timencium deum dabitur viro pro bonis factis (Sir 26:3). Nam dicit idem: Gratia super gratiam mulier sancta et pudorata (Sir 26:19). 'Domus et divicie dantur a patribus, a domino autem proprie uxor prudens' verba sunt Salomonis (Prov. 19:14)."

38. Silvana Vecchio, "La buona moglie," in *Storia delle donne in occidente: Il medioevo*, ed. Christiane Klapisch-Zuber (Rome: Editori Laterza, 1990), 129–165; trans. *A History of Women in the West 2: Silences of the Middle Ages* (Cambridge, Mass: Belknap Press, 1992).

39. Claudia Opitz, "La vita quotidiana delle donne nel tardo Medioevo (1250–1500)," in *Storia delle donne*, 2, 348, also trans. in *Silences of the Middle Ages*.

40. Reber, *Die Gestaltung des Kultes*, 200; *Sente Elsebede Leben: Das Leben der hl. Elisabeth vom Verfasser der Erlösung*, ed. Max Rieger (Bibliothek des litterarischen Vereins, 90) (Stuttgart, 1868); *Das Leben des hl. Ludwig, Landgrafen von Thüringen, Gemahls der hl. Elisabeth*, trans. Friedrich Ködiz von Saalfeld, ed. Heinrich Rückert (Leipzig, 1851); and Theodoric of Apolda, *Vita Sancte Elyzabeth*, ed. Rener, 53.

41. *Der sogenannte Libellus*, Prologue, ed. Huyskens, 7: "In huius itaque speculi libro sancti coniugii regulam lineariter exemplante legant, legant, inquam, et discant nostri temporis coniugate, carnis petulantiam edomare, . . . gestuum lasciviam refrenare, matronali gratuitate pudicitie constantiam declarare. . . . Studeant . . . casta generatione sancti tantum matrimonii adornare."

42. Caesarius von Heisterbach, *Vita*, ed. Huyskens, 29f.: "Sicut beata Elyzabeth amatrix castitatis, adhuc marito vivente, si ipsum superviveret, in manus magistri Cunradi continenciam deo promisit."

43. See also Clarissa W. Atkinson, *The Oldest Vocation: Christian Motherhood in the Middle Ages* (Ithaca, N.Y.: Cornell University Press, 1991), 166.

44. Caesarius von Heisterbach, *Vita*, ed. Huyskens, 37: "Et hoc fixum teneatis, si avunculus meus dominus episcopus me invitam alicui matrimonio coniunxerit, corde et ore contradicam. Quod si aliam viam evadendi non haberem, in secreto proprium mihi nasum preciderem et sic nullus ducere me curaret tam deformiter mutilatam."

45. Jane Tibbetts Schulenburg, "The Heroics of Virginity: Brides of Christ and Sacrificial Mutilation," in *Women in the Middle Ages and the Renaissance: Literary and Historical Perspectives*, ed. Mary Beth Rose (Syracuse, N.Y.: Syracuse University Press, 1986), 48f.

46. Ibid., 29–72.

47. Caesarius von Heisterbach, *Vita*, ed. Huyskens, 29: "Non enim omnes virgines carne habebunt aureolam, veluti ille, que nubere desiderant et in illa voluntate decedunt. Sic a simili secundum testimonium beate Lucie virginis et martyris, si aliqua votum et propositum habens virginitatis vim passa corrumperetur et sic deinceps caste vivendo de eadem corrupcione finaliter doleret, spero, quod de premio virginitatis nichil perderet."

48. This reading of "cultural symbols" (in my case: virgin, wife, widow, in Ashley's case the figure of Saint Anne) in an attempt to better understand medieval people is argued for by Kathleen Ashley, "Image and Ideology: Saint Anne in Late Medieval Drama and Narrative," in *Interpreting Cultural Symbols: Saint Anne in Late Medieval Society*, ed. Kathleen Ashley and Pamela Sheingorn, (Athens [etc.]: University of Georgia Press, 1990), 126.

49. Eusebius Hieronymus, *Commentarium in Evangelium Mattaei*, 1.2.13, in Migne, *Patrologia Latina*, vol. 26, 92; see Chiara Frugoni, "La donna nelle immagini, la donna immaginata," in *Storia delle donne*, 425, also trans. in *Silences of the Middle Ages*.

50. See Giselle de Nie's contribution, "Consciousness Fecund through God: From Male Fighter to Spiritual Bride-Mother in Late Antique Female Sanctity," in this volume.

51. From an eleventh century manuscript of the *Vita Radegundi* by Venantius Fortunatus, see Maaike van Rossem, "De poort in de muur: Vrouwenkloosters onder de Regel van Caesarius," *Vrouwen in de Geschiedenis van het Christendom* (Jaarboek voor Vrouwengeschiedenis, 4) (Nijmegen: SUN, 1983), 73; Renate Kroos also argues that Radegond could well have been an example for Elizabeth, as they both cared for

the poor and the sick, nursed lepers, did humble labor in kitchen and hospital, and did not neglect the "vita contemplativa," prayers, and psalms. R. Kroos, "Darbringung von Votivgaben in einer Wallfarhtskirche," in *Sankt Elisabeth: Fürstin, Dienerin, Heilige*, 462.

52. *Dicta Quatuor Ancillarum*, ed. Huyskens, 117: "Item surgens a viro in secreta camera fecit se fortiter verberari per manus ancillarum et post orationum rediit letanter in lectum mariti et hoc fecit frequenter, postquam fecit obedientiam magistro Cunrado. . . . Absente autem marito in vigiliis, genuflexionibus, verberibus et orationibus multas noctes deducebat."

53. Anonymus, *Vita Sanctae Elisabeth Landgraviae Thuringia*, ed. Diodorus Henniges in *Archivum Franciscanum Historicum*, 2 (1909), 253: "Orationibus etenim, quantumcumque sine debiti maritalis offensa poterat, constanter instabat et eterni sponsi consortium preferens temporali, ad orationem frequenter dormientis aut dissimulantis interdum viri latere devota surrexit ac post orationem in aliqua camera per manus ancillarum aliquando verberata, ad mariti lectum letanter rediit, aut in tapeto coram lecto sub orationum suavitate dormivit." The editor maintains this *Life* was written sometime between 1 May 1236–20 March 1239.

54. Caesarius von Heisterbach, *Vita*, ed. Huyskens, 28f.: "Ecce in tali martyrio sancta Elyzabeth passionibus Christi conformare se studuit, cum tria sint genera martirii, sicut scribit beatus Gregorius, videlicet in sanguinis effusione, in assidua carnis maceracione et in proximorum compassione, nullius horum expers exstitit Elyzabeth. Sicut dictum est, usque ad sanguinem virgis acutissimis se verberavit, vigiliis, ieiuniis, oracionibus et multis aliis incommodis corpus suum cotidie mortificavit. . . . Quam pleno corde proximis egentibus infirmantibus sive aliam quamcunque necessitatem pacientibus compassa sit et in eorum miseriis passa, satis declarant exempla precedencia, sed et subsequencia in hoc eius martirium non tacebunt, cum tempore suo fuerint recitata."

55. Ibid., 30: "Habebat hanc consuetudinem beata Elyzabeth ut, quociens peperisset puerum, completis diebus purgacionis sue contra gentis consuetudinem laneis induta et pedibus nudis tam humiliter quam familiariter veniens ad ecclesiam et propriis ulnis exemplo beate virginis Marie infantem suum gestans cum candela et agno super altare illum obtulit. . . . Attendant hoc matrone, que multum pompatice in vestibus preciosis huiusmodi processiones faciunt, humilitatem dei genitricis non imitantes, quam Elyzabeth beatissima et divitis regis filia secuta est."

56. *Der sogenannte Libellus*, Prologue, ed. Huyskens, 7.

57. But sometimes the hagiographers add maternal metaphor; compare this passage from the testimony of Irmingard in *Dicta Quatuor Ancillarum*, ed. Huyskens, 128: "Dixit etiam, quod quendam puerulum scabiosum et monoculum una nocte sex vicibus ad requisita nature deportabat. Ad lectum portans frequenter ipsum tegebat, pannos etiam ipsius pueri defedatos ipsa lavabat et iocundissime eidem blandiendo loquebatur," to Caesarius von Heisterbach, *Vita*, ed. Huyskens, 40: "Dixit enim, [quod] quendam puerulum scabiosum monoculum uno die sex vicibus ad requisita nature deportabat. Pannos eciam ipsius pueri defedatos ipsa lavabat et iocundissime eidem blandiendo *more materno* loquebatur" (emphases mine).

58. Ibid., 30; see also Vauchez, "Charité et pauvreté," 166.

59. Caesarius von Heisterbach, *Vita*, ed. Huyskens, 50: "Quantus autem dolor pauperum atque infirmorum illic concurrencium et de tante matris morte vociferancium sit auditus, paucis explicari non potest. Ac, si omnium mater carissima fuisset et omnes in carne genuisset, ita illam querulosis vocibus plangebant" and *Dicta Quatuor Ancillarum*, ed. Huyskens, 139: "Quantus autem dolor concurrentium pauperum sit auditus de morte eius quasi mater omnium exstitisset."

60. Caesarius von Heisterbach, *Vita*, ed. Huyskens, 37: "Domine gracias ago tibi, quia in ossibus mariti mei multum desideratis misericorditer es me consolatus. Tu scis quod, quantumlibet eum dilexerim, tamen ipsum dilectissimum tibi a se ipso et a me in subsidium terre sancte oblatum non invideo. Cuius si liceret uti concorcio,

omnibus mundi deliciis illum anteferrem semper secum mendicatura, sed contra voluntatem tuam te teste nollem vitam eius uno capillo redimere. Nunc ipsius animam et me ipsam tue gratie recommendo, de nobis fiat tua voluntas."

61. Ibid., 37: "Vera dilectio hec, ubi proximis sic diligitur, ut divine dilectioni non preferatur!"

62. Ibid., 31: "Erat idem Cunradus, sicut omnes novimus, homo rigidus et austerus, unde a multis timebatur, maxime propter auctoritatem a summo apostolico sibi concessam, quam exercere non neglexit."

63. Ibid., 38: "Dominus exaudivit oraciones meas et ecce omnes mundanas possessiones, quas aliquando dilexi, nunc ut stercora reputo, pueros meos, quos dominus dedit mihi, ipso teste tamquam extraneos reputo, in dampnis, in detractionibus et mei contemptu delector et gaudeo. Nichil pure diligo, nisi deum, qui dedit omnia."

64. Ibid., 39: "Sciens mulier illa fortis, quia manum suam miserat ad forcia (Prov. 31:19), Christum, qui est fortitudo dei, dixisse, non veni facere voluntatem meam, sed voluntatem eius, qui misit me (Jn 4:34), patris, sine murmure cordis et contradictione responsionis universa hec sustinuit."

65. See Atkinson, *The Oldest Vocation*, 166.

66. Atkinson, *The Oldest Vocation*, 20; 68f and see De Nie's contribution, "Consciousness Fecund through God."

67. Matthias Werner, "Bericht des Caesarius von Heisterbach über die Erhebung der hl. Elisabeth," in *Sankt Elisabeth: Fürstin, Dienerin, Heilige*, 504.

68. Caesarius von Heisterbach, *Sermo de Translacione Beate Elyzabeth* (BHL 2495), ed. Albert Huyskens, *Annalen des Historischen Vereins für den Niederrhein*, 86 (1908), 55: "[E]cce tanta frangrancia lapide amoto de sacro corpore efferbuit, ut omnes odores illius suavitate recreati in ammiracionem versi deum collauderent."

69. Ibid., 57: "Sicque deus universos ordines ecclesie honorare dignatus est. In martyrum ordine eciam apostoli et coniugati comprehenduntur."

70. Ibid., 58: "Cum beata Elyzabeth non fuerit corpore virgo, sed vidua et viro cognita, plurimi tantam miraculorum gloriam in ea mirantur et hoc ideo maxime, quia sciunt infinitas fuisse et esse sacras virgines tam in cenobiis quam in habitu seculari, quibus coruscare miraculis concessum non est. Ad quod primo loco respondetur: neque meritum neque premium consistere penes carnis integritatem, sed penes caritatem."

71. Ibid., 59: "Causa vero miraculorum eius hec maxima fuisse videtur, quia beata Elyzabeth filia fuerat regis et uxor principis magni et in tantum se humiliavit, ut post mortem mariti contempto sponso, contemptis diviciis et honoribus in multa paupertate et humilitate Christi pauperibus serviret, opera misericordie exerceret et multas tribulaciones et persecuciones propter hoc libenter et gratanter sustineret, ut eius exemplo cetere nobiles matrone similia facerent, pius dominus famulam suam post mortem miraculis honorare dignatus est."

72. Reber, *Die Gestaltung des Kultes*, 66.

73. Carla Casagrande, "La donna custodita," in *Storia delle donne*, 88–128, also trans. in *Silences of the Middle Ages*.

74. Theodoric of Apolda, *Vita sancte Elyzabeth*, ed. Rener, 21: "Non enim in eis persone et personarum genus, nomina, dignitates, et officia exprimuntur, sed nec provinciarum, locorum temporumque varietates et vocabula ad hystoriam pertinencium sunt descripta. Que illi, licet nobis necessaria forent nunc, tunc sibi tamquam notissima omiserunt. Quomodo ergo legenti satisfacient incompleta? Sed nec materie ad eandem rem pertinentis coniunccio ibi est sparsim positis cunctis prout occurrerunt memorie referentis. Sub iuramento enim narrancium conscripta sunt, sicut dicta testium recipi consueverunt."

75. The editor remarks: "De taal boeide mij, en niet minder het verhaalde, zoo vriendelijk vroom, en argeloos, en kinderlijk frisch en rein." For him as well as for me, the "vloeiende middelnederlandsche proza" is a reason to share this vernacular version with readers, despite the fact that it is but a translation of a Latin life.

76. *Sunte Elizabetten Legende,* ed. Scharpé, 25: "Denke wel neerstelic om des suveren jongelinx ghemoede, die sine bruut niet en woude trecken tot des vleisches ghenoechte mer totten gracien Godes, die haer sende die duerbaer gave als een beelde des crucifixes" and Theodoric of Apolda, *Vita,* ed. Rener, 32: "Perpende propensius casti adolescentis animum, qui sponse sue, non ad petulancium alliciens sed pocius ad graciam afficiens donum transmisit preciosissimum, ymaginem crucifixi."

77. *Sunte Elizabetten Legende,* ed. Scharpé, 33: "Noch hoer en ontbrac niet dat principael guet witlikes hilikes, daer die benedixie nae volghet als kijnder te krighen. Want onse Here begavede se mit eenre gueder gave in dien dat Hi se drachtich maecte mit edelre vruchten, op dat se den laster der onvruchtbarheit ontgaen soude ende ghebruken troest van den kijnderen" and Theodoric of Apolda, *Vita,* ed. Rener, 39: "Nec defuit ei bonum illud principale matrimonii, quo benedictionem in liberis consecuta est. Dotavit enim Deus eam dote bona fecundans uterum eius sobole nobilissima, ut et sterilitatis careret obprobrio et liberorum frueretur solacio."

78. Reber, *Die Gestaltung des Kultes,* 133f.

79. Kaspar Elm, "Die Stellung der Frau in Ordenswesen, Semireligiosentum und Häresie zur Zeit der heiligen Elisabeth," in *Sankt Elisabeth: Fürstin, Dienerin, Heilige,* 7, 24 n. 1.

80. Reber, *Die Gestaltung des Kultes,* 91ff, 101.

81. *Sunte Elizabetten Legende,* ed. Scharpé, 30: "Alle staet van menschen, jonc ende out, merc ende verwonder ende nae volge des coninges dochter, die tot des princen tafel onder vele lecker gherechten versmade die weelden, ende in die slaepcamer hoers geminden mans de vleischelike ghenuechte versmade" and Theodoric of Apolda, *Vita,* ed. Rener, 36f.: "Attendat et miretur et imitetur omnis sexus et etas, quomodo hec regis filia in mensa principis inter tot epulas abstinens delicias respuit et in thalamo tam amati coniugis illecebras carnales non quaesiuit."

82. *Sunte Elizabetten Legende,* ed. Scharpé, 26: "Onder hem was witlic huwelic, niet in vleischeliker lieften mer in heilicheit der suverheit witlikes huwelics. Want dese jonghe maghet, cortelic daer nae dat se horen man getruwet hadde, castide se hoer vleische mit vele te waken. Want inder nacht soe plach se dicwile op te staen om te beden als hoer man sliep, oft als hi baerde of hi gheslapen hadde. . . . Waerlike dexer jonger maghet devocie was groet, die aldus van haren slaep des nachtes opstont ende sochte Christum den se mynnede, ende sochte den waren man hoerre sielen" and Theodoric of Apolda, *Vita,* ed. Rener, 34: "Erat inter eos honorabile connubium et thorus immaculatus (cf. Hebr. 13:4), non in ardore libidinis, sed in coniugalis sanctimonia castitatis. Etenim macerabat adolescentula sancta, recenter nupta, carnem suam multis vigiliis singulis noctibus consurgens ad orandum, marito quandoque dormiente vel eciam dissimulante. . . . Magna revera huius iuvencule devocio, que carnalis mariti surgens per noctem a lectulo, quesivit Christum, quem dilexit verum anime (cf. Cant. 3:1–2) sue virum."

83. *Sunte Elizabetten Legende,* ed. Scharpé, 25: "Ende aldus wert versament die guede man mit den gueden wive, die heilighe man mit den heilighen wive. Ende daer was meer gheestelic huwelic tusschen hem tween dan vleischlic, daer se malcanderen om minden" and Theodoric of Apolda, *Vita,* ed. Rener, 33: "Coniunctusque est dei nutu vir fidelis cum muliere fideli, sanctus cum sancta, innocens cum innocente (cf. Ps. 17:26). Et non tam carnale quam spirituale connubium sortiti invicem se in caritate domini, supra quam credi valeat, dilexerunt."

84. See Gerald of Wales, *The Journey Through Wales: The Description of Wales,* trans. Lewis Thorpe (Harmondsworth: Penguin, 1984 [1978]), 80, 172; see also Caesarius von Heisterbach, *Dialogus Miraculorum,* 2.22, ed. Josephus Strange (Cologne, 1851; rpt Ridgewood, N.J.: The Gregg Press, 1966), 234: "De matrona quae sine dolore peperit, cum convenisset in mariti signatione," cited in James M. Powell, *Anatomy of a Crusade 1213–1221* (Philadelphia: University of Pennsylvania Press, 1990 [1986]), 61, n. 43.

85. See for a discussion of admiration and imitation of saints and hagiography, André Vauchez, "Saints Admirables et Saints Imitables: Les Fonctions de l'Hagiographie ont-elles changé aux derniers siècles du moyen âge?" in *Les Fonctions des saints dans le monde occidental (IIIe–XIIIe siècle)* (Collection de l'École Française de Rome, 149) (Rome: École Française, 1991), 161–172.

86. Werner Moritz, *Das Hospital im späten Mittelalter* (700 Jahre Elisabethkirche in Marburg 1283–1983, 6) (Marburg, 1983), 84.

87. Louis Goosen, *Van Afra tot de Zevenslapers: Heiligen in religie en kunsten* (Nijmegen: SUN, 1992), 132.

88. *Festal Evangelistary* by the Masters of Otto van Moerdrecht (c. 1430–40) in Koninklijk Huisarchief, The Hague, MS unnumbered; for Elizabeth as patron of medieval hospitals, see Reber, *Die Gestaltung des Kultes*, 92. Moritz, "Das Hospital," 113, argues that Elizabeth's patronage is due to the fact that patrons chosen were always well-known saints and that the choice for her patronage specifically did not materially have any effect on hospital foundations. Moreover, other patrons were available, for instance Saint Nicholas, Saint George and Saint Catherine. It does seem indisputable that the great wave of hospital building in the thirteenth and fourteenth century would have happened even without Elizabeth. But on the level of micro-history (the case of Margaret of Burgundy is suggestive) Elizabeth may well have had a discernible influence.

89. See Brigitte Rechberg, *Die heilige Elisabeth in der Kunst—Abbild, Vorbild, Wunschbild* (700 Jahre Elisabethkirche in Marburg 1283–1983, 2) (Marburg, 1983), 16f.; Moritz, *Das Hospital*, 25f.

90. For this medieval designation of Louis as Crusader: Jeffrey Ashcroft, "Miles Dei—Gotes Ritter: Konrad's Rolandslied and the Evolution of the Concept of Christian Chivalry," in *Knighthood in Medieval Literature*, ed. W.T.H. Jackson, (Bury St. Edmunds: St. Edmundsbury Press, 1981), 70.

91. Jacobus a Voragine, *Legenda Aurea*, ed. Graesse, 753: ". . . illustris Ungariae regis filia, genere nobilis."

92. *Sunte Elizabetten Legende*, ed. Scharpé, 12: ". . . wes wijf Ghe[r]truut hete ende was dochter des alre edelsten princen ende hertoghen van Carinthien. Ende dese wan ene dochter die eere was haers geslachtes" and Theodoric of Apolda, *Vita*, ed. Rener, 25: "Cuius uxor Ghertrudis nomine, nobilissimi ducis Carinthie filia, ut premonstratum fuerat a domino, peperit filiam (cf. Luc. 1:57), generis sui decus."

93. *Sunte Elizabetten Legende*, ed. Scharpé, 13: ". . . die een manlic ghemoet hadde" and Theodoric of Apolda, *Vita*, ed. Rener, 25: Que feminee cogitacioni virilem animum inserens (cf. 2. Macc. 7:21) . . ."

94. *Sunte Elizabetten Legende*, ed. Scharpé, 14: "[E]nde ic sel mijnre dochter groete rijcheiden gaderen, ist dat mij God leven laet" and Theodoric of Apolda, *Vita*, ed. Rener, 26: "[E]go eum (in the Latin eum refers to the landgrave, the other party in the marriage negotiations between Thuringia and Hungary) maximis diviciis, si dominus michi vitam dederit, cumulabo."

95. *Sunte Elizabetten Legende*, ed. Scharpé, 84f.: "Hoer moeder die lange tijt van dien van Ungarien gedoet was, die openbaerde hoer inden slape, ende knielde, ende seide tot haer: 'Mijn lieve dochter, bidde voer mi want ic noch in pinen bin om dat ic versumelic geleeft hebbe, wantuut wel vermoghest'" and Theodoric of Apolda, *Vita*, ed. Rener, 95: "Mater quoque eius iam dudum miserabiliter ab Ungaris interempta, in sompnis ei apparens flexis genibus dixit: 'Mi dilecta filia, ora pro doloribus meis, quos adhuc patior, quia negligenter vixi: potes enim.'"

96. *Sunte Elizabetten Legende*, ed. Scharpé, 85: "Doe wert Elizabeth ontwaken ende stont op, ende sprac hoer ghebet mit tranen, ende sliep weder. Ende doe openbaerde hoer weder hoer moeder ende dankede hoer, ende seide dat si verloset was" and Theodoric of Apolda, *Vita*, ed. Rener, 95: "Evigilans Elyzabeth, surgit cum fletu, oravit devote et iterim obdormivit. Adest mater denuo et gracias agens se asseruit liberatam dicens oraciones eius cunctis eam invocantibus profuturas."

97. Caesarius von Heisterbach, *Vita*, ed. Huyskens, 19: "[I]psa vero se gracie dei committens ab Ungaris coronam martirii innocencia sua promeruit."

98. Ibid., 19: "Ecce de tam nobili et tam religiosa prosapia beata Elyzabeth duxit originem. Quod si de carne materna carnis traxit nobilitatem, non mirum si de spiritu matris, tamquam de fonte pietatis, ipsius matris meritis simul et precibus suffragantibus, ducere potuit sanctitatem."

99. Reber, *Die Gestaltung des Kultes*, 148.

100. Thomas Franke, "Urkunde Landgraf Hermanns II. für Haina mit Siegel," in *Sankt Elisabeth: Fürstin, Dienerin, Heilige*, 372.

101. Thomas Franke, "Reitersiegel der Herzogin Sophie von Brabant," ibid., 373.

102 *Dicta Quatuor Ancillarum*, ed. Huyskens, 135f.: "Item dixit Irmingardis, quod magister Cunradus quandoque mandavit beate Elizabet, ut veniret Altinburch, ut consilium haberet, si eam in reclusorio poneret, et petebant domine claustrales hoc a magistro Cunrado, ut in adventu beate Elizabet daret licentiam ei, ut claustrum intraret et ipsam viderent. Et respondit magister Cunradus, 'Intret, si vult,' bene credens, quod non intraret. Intrabat nichilominus credens se habere licentiam, confisa verbis prioribus magistri Cunradi. Quod intelligens magister Cunradus evocatam beatam Elizabet arguens librum preparatum exhibuit, ut iuraret stare mandatis eius propter excommunicationem, quam incurrit intrando claustrum. Et licet soror Irmingardis foris stetisset, quia tantum foris accepta clave ostium aperuerat claustri, dixit ei, ut se prosterneret cum beata Elizabet et precepit fratri Gerhardo, ut bene verberaret illas cum quadam virga grossa satis et longa. Interim autem magister Cunradus 'Miserere mei Deus' decantabat. Et dixit prefata Irmingardis, quod post tres ebdomadas habuit vestigia verberum et amplius beata Elizabet, que acrius fuerat verberata. Et dixit Irmingardis, postquam talia sustinueret beata Elizabet, quod audivit ab ipsa: 'Oportet nos talia sustinere libenter, quia sic est de nobis, ut de gramine, quod crescit in flumine, fluvio inundante gramen inclinatur et deprimitur et sine lesione ipsius aqua inundans pertransit. Inundatione cessante gramen erigitur et crescit in vigore suo iocunde et delectabiliter.'"

103. Ulrich Reuling, "Kloster Altenberg bei Wetzlar: Grabmal der sel. Gertrud," in *Sankt Elisabeth: Fürstin, Dienerin, Heilige*, 375.

104. Ashley, "Image and ideology," 125.

105. Reber, *Die Gestaltung des Kultes*, 113; Gábor Klaniczay, "Legends as Life-strategies for Aspirant Saints in the Later Middle Ages," *The Uses of Supernatural Power*, 95–110.

106. For a royal's use of all, male and female, saintly ancestors (among whom Saint Elizabeth) to legitimate intervention in religious affairs see: Ronald G. Musto, "Queen Sancia of Naples (1286–1345) and the Spiritual Franciscans," in *Women of the Medieval World: Essays in Honor of John H. Mundy*, ed. Julius Kirshner and Suzanne F. Wemple (Oxford: Blackwell, 1985), 179–214.

107. *Dicta Quatuor Ancillarum*, ed. Huyskens, 117: "Item secularibus matronis ad se venientibus quasi predicans cum eis de Deo conferebat, frequenter inducens eas et precum instantia voto astringens ad abstinendum saltem ab aliquo uno ad seculi vanitatem tendente, si ad plura vitanda eos non poterat inducere, velud de choreis et manicis consuticiis, nimis strictis, aut zonis sericis pro ornatu crinibus implicatis et crinalibus et aliis superfluitatis vitandis, manicas decentes bonis moribus convenientes in ipsis nitendo, postea inducens eas ad votum continentie post mortem maritorum."

108. Horst Schroeder, *Der Topos der Nine Worthies in Literatur und bildender Kunst* (Göttingen: Vandenhoeck & Ruprecht, 1971), 174.

109. Ilja M. Veldman, "Vroom en ongeschonden: Deugdzame vrouwen als morele exempla bij Crispijn de Passe de Oude," *Deugd en Ondeugd*, ed. Josine Blok et al. (Jaarboek voor Vrouwengeschiedenis, 13) (Amsterdam: Stichting Beheer IISG, 1993), 39–60.

110. Anonymous (c. 1735), "Gräfin Freyberg als hl. Elisabeth," see Brigitte Rechberg, *Die heilige Elisabeth in der Kunst*, 106.

111. Jan van Laarhoven, *De Beeldtaal van de Christelijke Kunst: Geschiedenis van de iconografie* (Nijmegen: SUN, 1992). 297.

112. "St. Elisabeth-Vereeniging," in *De Katholieke Encyclopaedie*, 10 (Amsterdam: Joost v.d. Vondel, 1935), 122.

113. Charles W. Jones, *Saint Nicholas of Myra, Bari, and Manhattan: Biography of a Legend* (Chicago: University of Chicago Press, 1978).

114. Marina Warner, *Alone of All Her Sex: The Myth and Cult of the Virgin Mary* (London: Weidenfeld and Nicholson, 1976).

9. MOTHERHOOD AND SANCTITY IN THE LIFE OF SAINT BIRGITTA OF SWEDEN

AN INSOLUBLE CONFLICT?

Jeannette Nieuwland *

One of the most fascinating women of the fourteenth century was certainly Saint Birgitta of Sweden. Born at the beginning of the century (1302 or 1303), Birgitta soon manifested an inclination towards the religious, if we may believe her two confessors who recorded the story of her life. This youthful religious bent was possibly related to the early death of her mother, in 1314. At the age of thirteen Birgitta was married to Ulf Gudmarsson, who in the *Vita*[1] is described as "rich, young, noble and prudent." The marriage was blessed with eight children, born approximately between 1319 and 1334. As a married noblewoman Birgitta was responsible for heading a large household and keeping an eye on the education of the children. Besides, she found time to run a small hospital in the neighborhood of her residence, to help the sick and poor wherever she could, and to stay for longer periods at the royal court, acting as a lady in waiting to the queen.[2]

Then, in 1344, her husband died. Before his death, the couple had already decided to join a monastic order, but now Birgitta found the last barriers to a religious way of life dissolved. She began to receive heavenly revelations, in which Christ and Mary appeared and convinced her of her very special religious calling. She gave up most of her possessions and began to lead a life of religious contemplation and asceticism.

The Swedish bishops recognized the revelations as genuine and that helped her to win influence with the Swedish king. In one of the revelations Christ ordered Birgitta to establish a new monastic order, for which he himself would dictate the rule. Birgitta convinced the king to bestow Vadstena, an old royal castle, on her, in order to have it reshaped into the first Birgittine convent. A mission of Swedish bishops went to the Pope in Avignon carrying emphatic warnings from Birgitta that he should return to Rome and act as an intermediary in the Hundred Years' War. Probably, they also took with them a copy of the new rule in order to obtain papal approval. However, this embassy did not receive a warm welcome in Avignon. Things changed for the worse. After an unsuccessful crusade to the pagans living to the southeast of Sweden and started at Birgitta's instigation, she lost the support of both the king and her confessor at the time, Saint Mattias of Linköping. This must have been a great blow for her. Christ consoled her in a vision and advised her to go to Rome, where she should await the return of the Pope, who would then ratify the new rule.

So Birgitta undertook the long journey to Rome (1349–50), crossing a continent ravaged by war and pestilence and leaving behind her children, fatherland, and possessions. She never returned to Sweden. The rest of her life she acted as an offended God's messenger in a sinful world, tirelessly reminding those she met of God's wrath. She became famous for the courageous way in which she dared to criticize the secular and ecclesiastical rulers of her time. Pope after Pope received her messages, in which Christ summoned the leader of his Church back to Rome. Meanwhile, Birgitta herself led a very sober life of praying, visiting churches, studying—she undertook to learn Latin—and practicing charity.

In 1367 Pope Urbanus V returned to Rome. Birgitta was given an audience and finally, in 1370, received papal sanction for her new order. It would not be recognized as an entirely new order, but was to be placed under the umbrella of the Rule of Augustine. The Pope did not stay long in Italy, but returned to Avignon in 1370, to Birgitta's great distress and anger. But at least one of her life's goals had been fulfilled: the founding of the order could be started, even though the foundress herself was never to witness its inauguration.

Birgitta had become an old woman when she finally embarked upon the journey she had been longing to make for over thirty years: a pilgrimage to the Holy Land. The voyage was a long and harsh one. Back in Rome she found her strength failing and not long afterwards, in 1373, she died.

Birgitta left us an incredible pile of writings. After her calling as Christ's mouthpiece, she continued to receive revelation after revelation, of which about 600 have been preserved. These heavenly messages were translated into Latin and written down by her confessors, and later on divided over eight books plus a rest-collection, the *Revelaciones Extrauagantes*.[3] It remains a matter of dispute how much the confessors have altered in the original dictation from Birgitta, but the *Vita* strives to assure us that she always checked what had been written, to make sure everything was in agreement with what she had heard and/or seen. After her death the revelations were, as had been ordered by Christ,[4] sorted and edited by her friend and confessor Alfons of Jaén. There is a general consensus among scholars that

Figure 9.1. The young Birgitta of Sweden. Reredos in Ög Appuna Kyrka (Riksantikvarieämbetet Sweden)

the revelations mirror if not the actual words of Birgitta in any case her spirit.[5] Apart from the revelations, Birgitta also wrote a comprehensive rule for her new order and, together with her confessor Master Petrus Olovsson from Skänninge, the so-called *Sermo Angelicus*, that was to provide the texts for the daily readings of the sisters in the Birgittine convents. Apart from these, quite a few sources have been handed down telling us *about* Birgitta. Most of these have been compiled for the canonization process, including the *Vita*, testimonies and miracle stories.[6]

Because of the abundance of the sources, it will in Birgitta's case not be possible to deal with all the issues of this book. Therefore, I have chosen to concentrate upon just one topic, i.e., Birgitta's motherhood, using mainly the revelations and the *Vita* as sources.

It can be said that Birgitta was outstanding, though not unique, amongst her female contemporaries in that she had followed both a secular and a spiritual way of life. Experiences from her secular period can be traced in the expressions of her spiritual world-view, the revelations. Among those, experiences connected to Birgitta's motherhood stand out. Therefore, the revelations offer a unique possibility to investigate how Birgitta felt about being a mother and what her general attitude was towards motherhood.

Most intriguing is the question of how Birgitta in her life and work managed to combine motherhood and a religious way of life. What follows is an attempt to answer this question, concentrating upon three facets of Birgitta's life and work: first, the picture we get of motherhood and mother-child relationships in the sources; second, Birgitta's relationship with her own children, both before and after her religious breakthrough; and third, the way in which Birgitta tried to combine the secular and the spiritual way by aspiring to a universal, spiritual motherhood.[7]

IMAGES OF MOTHERHOOD AND MOTHER-CHILD RELATIONSHIPS IN THE BIRGITTINE SOURCES

The revelations abound in images connected with motherhood. It is interesting to see what was Birgitta's own view of matters like the procreative process and the relationship between mother and child. The section will be concluded with some reflections upon the deeper meanings of these images.

Conception, Pregnancy, and Childbirth

For Birgitta, procreation should be the primary aim of marriage and sexual intercourse.[8] She seems to be aware of the fact that the contribution of the mother to the conception is equal to that of the father:

> Indeed, all the strength of a child's body is derived from the seed of the father and the mother, but because the embryo does not have the necessary strength owing to some weakness of the father or the mother, it soon dies.[9]

This was, however, not the most generally accepted view in Birgitta's times. More common was the theory of Thomas Aquinas, who, following Aristotle, held that the mother only contributed "matter," whereas the father donated "form" and "movement." Diverging as these views on the very first step in a child's life might be, there was general consensus that after the conception itself women carried the full responsibility for the growth and the health of the fruit.[10]

Childlessness was something else for which primarily women were held responsible. People often suspected a childless woman of some hidden sin or a lack of religious fervor. Therefore, childlessness was felt to be a disgrace. The stories about the immense joy of childless couples receiving after all, as a gift from heaven, a child, indicate how important it was to have children.[11] For Birgitta, having children was both a blessing and a duty. She sharply criticized the Swedish Queen Blanka for practicing continence because she suspected her to do so only in order to avoid painful deliveries. Abortion also was something she strongly condemned.[12]

Birgitta seems to have had some idea of how long an unborn child stayed in the womb, for she said about Christ that "he remained just as long in the virgin, as it is necessary for other infants before their birth to stay in the mother's womb."[13] During that time, Birgitta repeatedly tells us, the mother prepares everything for the new child and makes sure there will be little clothes waiting upon its arrival.[14]

> "Don't you know," Christ asks in a revelation, "what is the heaviest to bear of the things that grow? It is certainly the infant, that reaches the day of birth but cannot be born and dies in the mother's womb, for which reason also the mother is torn apart and dies, who is then together with the child borne to the grave by the father."[15]

This, I think, sums up the tragedy of many a medieval woman's life. Birgitta has given the problems surrounding pregnancy and childbirth much thought. "Why," she asks, "does one child come from the mother's womb alive, while the other dies inside? . . . And why is everyone born with pain?"[16] It is a well-known fact that childbearing was a dangerous endeavor in the Middle Ages. Many women died. Birgitta found it unfair that although some infants were born dead, the mothers suffered quite as much as if they had been alive. She also felt compassion for the child, because it would never receive mother's milk or motherly warmth and never hear the mother's voice.[17]

We should not overestimate the help that midwives and matrons could offer at childbirth. Men, including doctors, were not admitted into the room.

Women, however, were supposed to support each other, so often neighbors, relatives, and friends gathered around the bed. Birgitta, experienced as she is, tells us that it often happens that a child in the womb is so closely bound to the mother, that it cannot separate itself from there in any possible way. In that case the midwife will separate the child from the mother, even though that can cost the mother her life.[18] Utterly helpless, a woman in that situation could only pray and ask for the assistance of saints like Mary, Elizabeth, and Anne, who during their life had been mothers themselves.[19]

Birgitta also had once feared for her life at childbirth:

> Once upon a time Lady Birgitta was in danger during childbirth and her life was despaired of. Suddenly, plainly visible for the women who were waking at her side during the night, keeping the watch over her, some person dressed in white silk was seen to enter and stand before the bed and handle each of Lady Birgitta's members as she lay there— and all present were afraid. Then when this person had left, Lady Birgitta gave birth so easily that it was astonishing, and there is no doubt that the Blessed Virgin, who gave birth without pain, was that person who allayed the labors, pains and danger of her handmaid . . .[20]

Later on, Birgitta is convinced that she would not have survived but for the help of Mary. This was one of the reasons for Birgitta's very special adoration of the Virgin, about which I shall speak later. However, sometimes suffering and even death caused by delivery seem to have moral causes in the revelations, for instance when Birgitta witnesses the judgment over the soul of a woman who died in childbirth: the soul will be punished in purgatory because the woman got married after she had first made a vow of virginity.[21]

According to Claudia Opitz, who has investigated what can be learned from saints' lives about the daily life of women in the thirteenth and fourteenth century, childbirth was, after all, not the unanimously negative experience we perhaps expect it to have been. If one succeeded in surviving the ordeal, there was reason for pride and happiness. In Opitz's sources it seems that in that case the importance of the child was secondary, all attention going to the mother. No special care was shown for the welfare of the child's soul.[22] That is, however, not what we read in Birgitta's revelations. There it is stated that a mother during childbirth is only hoping that the child will be born alive, so that it can be baptized. Compared to that, the possibility of her own death is looked upon with indifference by the mother. If all goes well, the mother is happy, notwithstanding her sufferings, that the child will never return to the misery from which it has just been delivered.[23]

It seems to go without saying that not only bearing and giving birth, but also feeding of children was considered to belong to the tasks of a dutiful wife. In practice, however, this was often left to a wet nurse, especially in the upper classes. It is said that Birgitta's daughter Katarina, who herself became a saint, refused to drink the wet nurse's milk. She would only accept her mother's milk or that of another continent woman.[24] This perhaps legendary story aims at convincing us of Katarina's sanctity while she refused to be in touch with a sinful wet nurse. There was a widespread belief that sexual intercourse contaminated the purity of the milk and reduced its flow. Also, as can be seen from the motives of Ida of Boulogne for feeding her own children, the qualities of the milk were thought to influence the shaping of the child's character and behavior. No wonder Katarina became a saint, having drunk from such a holy source! Even theologians, preachers and medical writers recommended breast feeding by the mother, because it would strengthen the bond between mother and child.[25] We will, of course, never know whether Birgitta really fed her own children, but we do seem to hear an experienced mother's advice, when Birgitta tells us that in order to wean a child, the breasts should be smeared with ash or something with a bitter taste.[26] Of images connected with childbearing many more examples could be given, but we will now move on to the next topic, i.e., the relationship between mother and child.

The Relationship between Mother and Child

For some time now a discussion has been going on amongst scholars about the question of whether people in the Middle Ages acknowledged the child as child, that is as someone different from an adult. The discussion was started by Philippe Ariès, who in his famous study of the history of childhood maintained that the child was treated as a little adult in the Middle Ages and that feelings of affection between parents and children were mostly lacking. Careful source-studies have, in the meantime, largely contradicted this view. Both the descriptions of the youth of saints and miracle stories—mostly healings—in which children are involved, indicate that, on the one hand, childhood was certainly recognized as a special period and that, on the other, both mothers and fathers showed great love and care for a sick or infirm child, going to any length to try and find healing and grieving bitterly when the child died.[27] The concepts "mother" and "love" were often closely connected. In hagiographical sources, for instance, it is a frequent theme that the saint cared for the poor and the sick "as a mother," meaning "with tender charity." This is also said of Birgitta in the Vita.[28]

Birgitta herself tells us that a mother treats different children in different ways: apparently even the individual child's needs are recognized by the mother. And she will also continue to help those for whom there is no hope, as best she can.[29]

In the revelations the image of the caring mother appears frequently:

> Like when a devoted mother, when she sees her beloved child lying naked and cold on the ground, without the physical force to get up, weeping with wailing sounds and lamentation out of longing for maternal attention and mother's milk, quickly runs towards her child with compassion and tender love, and then, lest he succumbs through the cold, picks him up from the ground with a devoted maternal hand and instantly cuddles him softly and tenderly warms him with the motherly warmth of her breast and sweetly feeds him with the milk from her nipples, . . .[30]

Other examples are the joy of a mother who hears the voice of her son and the indifference of a woman in labor about her own life, as long as her child will survive to be baptized.[31] The best example, however, might be Birgitta herself. Of other holy women, like Saint Elizabeth of Thuringen, we know that it cost them a lot to leave their children behind and follow the religious path. Later, we will see how Birgitta experienced deserting her children. But first, the ways in which the images recounted here should be interpreted need to be considered.

Metaphors or Reality?

Above, the images of motherhood and mother-child relationships have been taken at face value. However, most of them are embedded in the Latin construction *sicut . . . sic*, like . . . so, meaning that they are, in fact, metaphors, used in order to grasp spiritual truths. In many cases Christ turns out to be the caring mother, urging sinners—the children—to seek a safe haven in his embrace. Does this mean that these images cannot be used to enhance our knowledge about real life in Birgitta's time and Birgitta's own ideas of motherhood? I think they can, firstly, because these images had an explanatory function which would be lost if contemporaries did not see instances of them in real life; and secondly, because, as we will see later, Birgitta herself was living proof of the image of the loving mother. On the other hand, taking these images at face value naturally does not mean that reality was like this. We know enough about late medieval life to realize that it was not. Instead, these images represented ideals about how a mother should feel and behave and it can be expected that at least some mothers did indeed (try to) love their children in this way. The ideal of a loving mother was not an original concept of Birgitta's time. In fact, it can be traced back to the Bible, where the loving mother is a prominent image. Because of her intensive studies of the Holy Scripture, Birgitta's work carries a very strong biblical mark. Apart from her own experience, it must have been the Bible which taught her the characteristics of a good mother.[32]

Now, let us see what can be learned from taking these images for what they are, i.e., as metaphors. In a very interesting essay, Caroline Walker Bynum reviewed the growing use of just such female imagery in the religious writings of the Later Middle Ages.[33] According to her the image of the motherhood of Christ expressed three aspects of the belief in Christ's role in the redemption: firstly, Christ's sacrificial death, which generated redemption, is compared to a woman in labor; secondly, Christ's love for the soul is compared to a mother's love for her child; and thirdly, Christ's feeding the soul with his own body and blood in the eucharist is compared to a breast feeding mother. Of all three we find examples in Birgitta's revelations.[34] Besides, Birgitta also uses the image of the divinity as mother to visualize quite different events, like when she compares God in his preparation of the law of the Old Testament to a pregnant woman laying ready the little clothes needed for the baby.[35]

Bynum finds that there are important differences between male and female writers using the image of the mother. Men, in contrast to women, often clearly associate motherhood with nurture, security and affection and oppose it as such to the leading, instructing and disciplining role of the father. Women, however, simply tend to see themselves as children of mother Jesus, and if they use dichotomous gender images at all, they speak of biological, not of social roles.[36]

Birgitta's writings do not fit very well into this picture. As may become clear from the examples given above, the outstanding characteristics of motherhood in the revelations are love and instruction.[37] Time and again the selfless, loving care of the mother is stressed. This is not only true for those images in which the mother stands for Christ, but also where someone else is meant, for instance Mary.[38] Mothers are also ascribed an instructing and disciplining role. We hear for instance that out of love, for the goodwill of her child, the mother sometimes decides to punish it or act against its will.[39] When Birgitta uses a dichotomous gender image in describing the tasks of a bishop, his divine authority over his domestics is associated with that of a father, but his benevolent teaching is seen as a maternal attribute.[40]

As antipole of the good, loving, and caring mother, we find the image of the "bad" mother in Birgitta's writings: in one of her *Revelaciones* we find a family where the devil is the father who fecundates the soul (the mother) with sin (the child), whereupon the unborn child dies in the womb, so that the mother, too, dies.[41] Most of the "bad" mothers, however, were, perhaps not surprisingly, real-life women that Birgitta strongly disapproved of, for instance the mother of King Magnus Erikson.[42]

An explanation for the fact that Birgitta tends towards the "male" approach in her use of the image of motherhood might be the fact that she was deeply influenced by the Bible and by traditional, i.e., male, writing. We also need to consider a directing role by her confessors. Moreover, Birgitta was not primarily a mystic; although she received the heavenly messages as revelations, most of them seem to be more the result of careful meditation than of spontaneous mystical outbursts. Thus, mystical union with the Godhead was not her main religious experience, as it was for so many of her religiously oriented female contemporaries. Most important, however, we have to bear in mind that Birgitta speaks from real-life experience. She knew what it meant to be a mother. The question then arises of what we know of Birgitta's own motherhood. Could it be that that is the basis of her use of the image of the mother in the revelations?

Birgitta's Relationship with Her Own Children
Birgitta as Aristocratic Wife and Mother

At the age of thirteen, Birgitta married Ulf Gudmarsson. Scholars disagree about the question whether Birgitta did so of her own free will.[43] This question is important in this study, because it can shed light on Birgitta's attitude towards motherhood, for rejecting marriage meant in those days also rejecting motherhood. The discussion is founded upon the divergence between, on the one hand, the testimony of Birgitta's daughter Katarina that Birgitta as a girl had cherished the wish to remain a virgin and give herself to Christ but was forced by her father to marry[44] and, on the other hand, the simple statement of the confessors in the *Vita* that Birgitta was betrothed to Ulf (*desponsatur*) and then lived in matrimony with him (*inter se coniugium habuerunt*). Katarina's testimony forms part of the records of the canonization process, and that is why the suspicion has arisen that she made up the story in order to strengthen her mother's claim to holiness. No other witnesses, for that matter, speak of Birgitta's aversion of matrimony. The confessors, also writing with the canonization process in mind, apparently did not consider the rejection of matrimony as an absolutely indispensable argument—in contrast, for that matter, to an impeccable matrimonial lifestyle. Maybe they simply did not know about it? Or did Katarina make it all up? Could it be that Birgitta told only her?

I fear we will never have the final answer. But maybe we should, as far as we can, try to imagine ourselves in the position of Birgitta at the age of thirteen. A few years earlier she had lost her mother, shortly after the birth of her youngest brother. Altogether, her mother must have borne at least seven children, of which only three survived into adulthood. Perhaps the fate of her mother did not enhance the appeal of marriage to Birgitta.[45] Moreover, the loss of her mother can have led Birgitta to find substitutes in Christ and Mary—according to the *Vita* both appeared to her already in childhood—whereafter the wish to spend her life in their service came up quite naturally.[46] And next, might not also the fear for the unknown, of which even today women witness who enter marriage as virgins, have played a role? If we add these suggestions to the fact that Birgitta in church must have heard rather disapproving lectures about the "lusts of the flesh," then I find it hard to believe that Birgitta did look upon marriage with unambiguous enthusiasm. Later on, in the revelations, she confessed to having enjoyed the physical contacts with her husband, but that does not automatically mean that she looked forward to that aspect of matrimonial life even before she got married. Perhaps she was rather more attracted by the power and prestige she could expect to have as Ulf's wife.[47]

It is probably best, then, to conclude that Birgitta's attitude towards marriage was ambivalent.[48] We do not know whether she got married out of her own free will, but we can suspect that a tiny voice in the corner of her conscience kept reminding her all through her married life that she should, in fact, have devoted herself to Christ and Mary.

According to the *Vita*, Birgitta and Ulf lived in abstinence for some time after their wedding. The confessors claim this was for religious reasons, but it might also have been that Birgitta was not yet physically mature. Circa 1319 the eldest child, a daughter named Margareta, was born. Seven other children followed. The delivery of the last child, a girl named Cecilia, was especially difficult, as we have seen. This can have been a (subconscious) motive for Birgitta to leave home, thus avoiding future pregnancies, for one year after the birth of Cecilia, Birgitta went to the royal court to be a lady in waiting to the queen.[49]

What kind of a mother was Birgitta? The *Vita* does not tell us much, just repeating the traditional ideal that she carefully educated her sons and daughters in virtue, and that she left them to the care of teachers in order to learn discipline and good behavior. Moreover, she cried daily over their sins, out of fear they would offend God.[50] We can, however, doubt if this is the whole truth, for there are traces in the sources that point in another direction. How, for instance, can this picture of the virtuous and pious mother be reconciled with the fact that Birgitta in the revelations repeatedly expresses fear at having failed at her children's education?[51] The *Vita* mentions similar feelings, which Birgitta is said to have had at the death of her sons Gudmar and Bengt, who both passed away in childhood. Here is the story of Bengt's death:

> When Lady Birgitta returned from the [court of the] king of Sweden to the monastery of Alvastra, she found one of her sons at the point of death, who had long been ill when she departed. Crying a lot about such a long infirmity, she ascribed it to the sins of his parents. Then the devil appeared to her and said: "Why, woman, do you weaken your sight with so much water of tears and why do you labor in vain? Water cannot ascend to heaven, can it?" At the same hour Christ appeared to his bride in his human body and said: "This boy's illness is not because of the constellations of the stars, as fools say, nor because of his sins, but caused by his natural condition and in order to enlarge his crown. And so, if he has hitherto been called by his own name Bengt, son of Ulf, he will from now on be called son of tears and prayers and I will end his distress." On the fifth day thereafter a very sweet singing was heard, as of birds, between the boy's bed and the wall, and see then the boy's soul left the body; and the Holy Ghost said to Lady Birgitta: "See what tears can do, for the son of waters has traversed to rest. Therefore the tears of good people, which come forth out of love of God, are hateful to the devil."[52]

This episode shows that Birgitta was not at all sure that she had educated her children according to God's will. That is even more clear in the case of her eldest surviving son, named Karl. In a famous vision, Birgitta observes how a serpent-mother educates her young in pride, worldly honor, greed and all sorts of venom. At first sight, the pair is identified with a Swedish nobleman, who aspired to the Swedish crown, and his mother. But Hjalmar Sundén, a psychologist of religion who has studied Birgitta's revelations from a psychological point of view, thinks that on a deeper level Birgitta is here attacking herself and the aspirations she once had for her own son Karl. That explains the razor-sharp vehemence of her criticism.[53] As we will see later, Karl was the son who best learned the early, worldly lessons of his mother and rebelled most fiercely against her conversion.

One more example should suffice. In front of Saint Mary, Birgitta is ashamed to tell about the proud women of Sweden, "for I am one of them." These women think:

> "Even our mother sat among the most prominent, dressed nobly, had many servants and educated us with honor. Why shouldn't I pass on to my daughter the things, that I learned, like behaving aristocratically and living with physical pleasure, and even dying with great worldly honor?"[54]

Crisis and Conversion

It can be concluded that Birgitta in the first stage of her marriage lived the life of pride, power, abundance, and pleasure usual for her class. Gradually, the tiny voice in her conscience mentioned earlier must have become louder, strengthened by Birgitta's sense of guilt about the death of her sons. Conflicting tendencies contended in her for mastery. The attraction of spiritual things slowly took the place of her leaning toward worldly pleasures, no doubt supported by her susceptibility for the lessons of the Church.[55] Still, her love for Ulf and her children stood in the way for following Christ, but soon her maternal love would be lifted up onto a spiritual plane, in that she started to seek a religious life even for her children.

After the hazardous birth of Cecilia, Birgitta perhaps decided that she could not cope with another pregnancy. To avoid that, and maybe also to take revenge on Ulf, who against her will had married off their eldest daughter to a scoundrel (in Birgitta's eyes), she departed for the royal court, leaving husband and children behind. The time at the court must have been a period of internal conflicts, that can have contributed to Birgitta's spiritual development. Her new position, however satisfying for her hunger for esteem and power, was contradictory to Christ's calling. Moreover, she must have felt guilty about the impact of her absence upon her children.[56]

It seems that Birgitta returned home just before the death of Bengt and started to live the pious life the *Vita* reports of. She succeeded in converting even Ulf, and together they went on a pilgrimage to Santiago in Spain in 1341–42. The situation on the continent, where the Hundred Years' War was raging, must have impressed Birgitta deeply. As a result, she became intensely aware of the gap between Christian theory and Christian practice.[57] This was probably the time when she started to feel responsible for all humankind, a feeling which she later on testified to so intensively in her revelations. Another event on this journey that was crucial to Birgitta's religious development was a revelation she received from Saint Denis in Arras, where

Ulf had become so seriously ill that his life was feared for. Saint Denis told her that she was to become Christ's special messenger, and as a proof of the truth thereof Ulf would recover. Thus it happened, and both returned to Sweden. Shortly afterwards Ulf died, and Birgitta changed her lifestyle completely.

Love of God versus Love of Children

It seems that Birgitta's eventual religious and revelatory breakthrough was the result of a long process of inner maturation, as outlined above. Ulf's death was a decisive moment, because it liberated her of her husband's objections and enabled her to free herself from all worldly duties. Soon, she was called to new tasks in revelations by Christ and Mary. Like Christ had done during his lifetime with his disciples, they made an absolute claim on her: she wasn't to love anyone but them, and she should leave all carnal love behind.[58] To Birgitta, that meant in the first place the love for her children. It must have been very difficult for her to go to Rome and leave them behind, as is shown by the following revelation:

> It happened once in the monastery of Alvastra that the heart of the blessed Birgitta, when she was about to set off for Rome, was inflamed with the love for her children, feeling pity to leave them bereft of maternal consolation and even fearing that they after her departure would more recklessly offend God in some matter, for they were young, rich and powerful. Then she saw in a vision a cauldron set over a fire and some boy blowing at the coals to make the cauldron boil. The blessed Birgitta said to him: "Why are you making such an effort at blowing in order to make the cauldron boil?" The boy answered: "To kindle and fan the love for your children even more in you." The blessed Birgitta then asked: "Who are you?" "I am the salesman," he said. Then Birgitta, understanding that there was an improper love for her children in her heart, immediately mended her ways, so that she would not put anything before the love for Christ.[59]

Christ and Mary demanded something that was almost impossible for Birgitta, but they also supported her in this by promising to share in the responsibility for her children. In exchange, Birgitta was convinced that she succeeded in loving them above her children.[60] Perhaps Birgitta consciously imitated the example of Paula, whose story she very likely must have known. She seems, however, to have succeeded even less than Paula in banishing her children from her heart. She remained much more involved in their lives and even forced, as we will see, one daughter to stay with her in Rome. But she also, in a way unknown to Paula, managed to transform her grief about having to give up her motherly love "into a warm, liberating, and generative spiritual motherhood of all."[61]

It seems that not all of Birgitta's children were very happy with their mother's conversion, which also had radical consequences for their own lives, since they were being pushed in a religious direction. The youngest, Cecilia, for instance, had been sent at the age of seven to the Dominican convent at Skänninge. But later on, when Birgitta was already in Rome, she left the convent and got married with the help of her brother Karl, much to her mother's distress. Then Christ appeared to Birgitta and gave her the consolation that he preferred a married woman over a virgin who was not a virgin at heart. Intriguing, however, is that Christ proceeded to explain why Cecilia did not get the husband Birgitta had hoped for.[62] On one level, Birgitta seems to have wished a religious course for her daughter, but on another, she also considered the possibility of a marriage! This shows that at that time Birgitta had not completely given up worrying about worldly interests, and, more importantly, that Birgitta's thoughts were still with her children.

Even Birgitta's second daughter, named Ingeborg, had been sent to a convent. When she died young, Birgitta cried bitterly, because she felt she had failed in this daughter's education. But she also rejoiced that Ingeborg had died young, so that she had not had so much opportunity to sin. Later on, in a vision, she witnessed Ingeborg being punished in purgatory.[63] She seems to have consoled herself with the thought that the final destination of her daughter was more important than her own wish to keep her on earth a while longer. Thus she tried to give spiritual love the primacy over worldly love, but one can of course doubt whether she only cried out of regret over the kind of education she gave her daughter. Striking is that Ingeborg is promised a crown of honor, because of the love and good will of her mother. That means that the mother's role in the spiritual welfare of her child is considered very important here. The fact that Ingeborg herself spent the greatest part of her life in a convent, apparently was worth less than her mother's religious ardor![64]

Birgitta expected her children to do as she wished, both in worldly and in spiritual matters. Contrary to Cecilia, Katarina, another daughter, did not succeed in breaking away from her mother's influence. True enough, in the end it made her reach the status of abbess and even saint, but the price was high. When Birgitta had been in Rome for some time, Katarina felt such longing for her that she left her husband in Sweden and went to visit her. Once in Rome, Birgitta saw in her the help that had been promised her in a vision. However much Katarina desired to return to Sweden and her husband, Christ insisted in a revelation that she should stay, the more so because her husband had died in the meantime. Still, Katarina found it difficult to give up her previous freedom. According to Katarina's *Vita*, Birgitta advised her to use the rod to beat out the longing.[65] Katarina stayed with her mother until Birgitta's death and then returned to Sweden to work on the founding of the monastery in Vadstena.

I cannot agree with Sven Stolpe's interpretation of the conflict between Birgitta and Katarina. Katarina is described by him as very young and immature—even though she must have been around twenty years of age, and was certainly considered an adult in the eyes of her contemporaries—as irresolute and easily influenced. Therefore, he thinks that Birgitta acted very prudently in a delicate situation, trying as she did to keep her daughter, whom she felt to be unable to look after herself, with her. But there is nowhere any real sign of Katarina being the immature person he describes. Her ambivalence is quite understandable and must have sprung from an insoluble conflict of desires: on the one hand she wanted to be with her mother, on the other hand she longed to return to her husband and friends in Sweden; after all, she must have been away from home for quite some time already. And how can he be so sure that Birgitta's motives were purely practical and sensible? She needed someone trustworthy to help her, and her daughter seemed to be just that. Perhaps she also had in mind the example of Paula, who had also allowed herself the joy of one daughter's company.[66]

It can be concluded that Birgitta after her breakthrough did not succeed very well in giving up worrying about and interfering in her children's fate. It goes without saying that she from that moment onwards tried to push them in the direction whither she was going herself. She succeeded quite well with Katarina, and also with her youngest son Birger,[67] less well with Ingeborg and Cecilia, and the least with her eldest surviving son, Karl. Above, I have already indicated that Birgitta had cherished ambitious worldly plans for Karl. Disappointment in that respect might have pushed her further onto the religious path. Gradually she adjusted her expectations for her favorite son. After her breakthrough, she wanted Karl to become the prototype of her new ideal of knighthood. The knight, according to Birgitta, had to stand in God's service, help the poor and suppressed, support the Church, and contribute to the conversion of pagans. Christ even dictated her a new ritual for the accolade, in which her idealistic view of the knight's duties found expression.[68] Exemplifying in this context is also the *Revelation* in which a poorly armed Karl is equipped by various saints with all kinds of armor symbolizing virtues, also because of the merits of his parents![69]

But to what extent did Karl fulfil the expectations of his mother? It has already been mentioned that he helped his sister Cecilia to flee the convent. That is a small sign of filial aberration from a mother's designs. Much clearer and more extensive proof thereof is given in a long revelation, which Birgitta received after Karl's death and in which she witnessed the judgment over his soul:

> At the same hour Lady Birgitta saw herself transferred to some huge and beautiful palace and there she saw the Lord Jesus Christ sitting on the judgment-seat as if crowned as an emperor, with an endless host of serving angels and saints, and next to him she saw his most worthy mother standing, intently listening to the jurisdiction. Also in the presence of the judge some soul was seen standing in great fear and distress, naked as a newborn infant, and, as it were, completely blind, so that it did not see anything; however, in its conscience it understood what was said and done in the palace. On the right side of the judge, next to the soul, stood an angel, and on his left a devil, but neither of them touched the soul or pulled him towards himself.

The devil starts with exclaiming that it is not fair that Mary was allowed to accompany this soul, as soon as he died, to the divine judge. For the soul belongs to himself. Mary defends her action by ascertaining that the soul did love and honor her above all else. Then the devil addresses the judge:

> "I know, that you are justice and power itself. You do not judge less justly for the devil than for an angel. Adjudge therefore that soul to me. For in the same wisdom, as I had when you created me, I had recorded all its sins. . . . For once that soul had reached that state of discretion, that made it understand that what it was doing was sinful, then its own will drew it towards living in worldly pride and carnal lust, instead of resisting such things."

And the angel answered: "As soon as his mother understood that his will tended towards sin, she immediately came to his succor with works of mercy and daily prayers, that God might deign to have mercy on him, and would not move away from him. Because of these works of his mother he obtained divine fear, so that he immediately hurried to do confession, whenever he fell into sin."

The devil answered: "I must tell his sins." Intending to start immediately, he at the same time started to cry out and lament and thoroughly to search himself in his head and all his members, that he was seen to have, and he seemed to be trembling all over and exclaimed in great confusion: "Woe to me in my misery, how could I lose the result of such long work, for not only is the text forgotten and wiped out, but also the material, on which everything was written, has completely burnt. . . ."

The angel answered: "The tears, the long labors and the many prayers of his mother did that, so that God, out of compassion for her sighs, gave her son such grace, that he repented of whatever sin he committed, humbly making confession out of love of God, and it is thus that those sins are forgotten and neglected in your memory."

The devil protests that he knows of more sins, which he has assembled in a large sack. But even these have disappeared. Once more, the angel confirms:

His mother did this with her assiduous prayers and labors, because she loved his soul of all her heart. Thus it pleased God, because of her love, to forgive him all his venial sins, that he committed from childhood onwards until his death.

Insisting, the devil now comes with the fact that Karl neglected to practice good deeds and charity. So the angel explains once more:

"Listen then, you devil! With her loving prayers and pious works his mother has perseveringly knocked at the gate of mercy on his behalf; over more than thirty years she has shed many thousands of tears that God might deign to pour the Holy Spirit into his heart, so that this son of hers would of his own will offer his goods, his body and his soul to God's service. And God did so. . . . And the virgin, God's mother, has given him, out of her own virtue, whatever he lacks in spiritual weapons and garments, that befit knights, who must enter into the heavenly kingdom unto the highest emperor. . . . Know that now, in heaven, he is called 'son of tears.'"

The devil answered, crying out: "O, what a cursed sow his mother is, that pig, who had such an enormous belly, that so much water was poured into her, that all space of her belly was filled with liquid for tears!"[70]

This is not the only time Birgitta witnesses the judgment over a soul. In fact, there is a whole group of visions in which Birgitta is shown a soul—not necessarily of someone already deceased!—standing in front of the divine judge, or being punished in hell or purgatory. Maybe not surprisingly, most of the souls are adjudged severe penitence in purgatory, or directed towards hell. As in the revelation cited above, the devil acts as prosecutor and Mary and/or an angel as advocate. Remorse, even at the last moment before death, always helps, as does having honored Mary. In fact, if Mary speaks up for a soul, Christ cannot refuse its salvation. Nevertheless, an often-repeated theme in the revelations is Christ's justice. If punishment is deserved, he will certainly punish. Souls that go to purgatory have to do penance for the sins they committed; often an explanation follows of which chastisements are given for which sins.[71]

But in Karl's case, all his misdeeds have been wiped out and Christ invites him to come as one of the elected.[72] This makes us wonder if justice, in this particular case concerning Birgitta's favorite son, has not been put aside. Of course, Birgitta's tears have prompted God to pour contrition and a wish for good deeds into Karl's heart, but we can wonder if it were not those tears that turned the scale of justice. Herself guilty of his worldly lifestyle, Birgitta has redeemed her guilt in long years of tears and prayer.[73] We see here, as with Bengt and Ingeborg above, that Birgitta is placed in the tradition of "mothers weeping about their children's sins" with Monica, Augustine's mother, as prototype. However, Karl's case for salvation through conversion and penitence seems to be much weaker than Augustine's![74]

Atkinson uses this episode to underline Birgitta's awareness of the enormous responsibility of mothers for their children's spiritual welfare. She finds further support for her view that this responsibility is an essential trait of motherhood to late medieval mother-saints in quoting from a *Revelation*, where a mother and grandmother are strongly reprimanded for their failure in their respective daughters' spiritual education.[75] Atkinson seems to be unaware, however, of the fact that the mother in this revelation has been identified with Birgitta herself. The grandmother, then, is Birgitta's own mother, being punished in a terrible way in hell, because of her sins and her bad example. All this turns the revelation into a much more personal testimony. Certainly, Birgitta's mother seems to have fostered her daughter in worldly ways, but we can wonder whether that is the main reason for seeing her in hell. Psychological examination has suggested that the description of the punishment is not free of grudge against the victim. At the surface is certainly the blame of a wrongly oriented upbringing, but maybe at a deeper level Birgitta is reproaching her mother for a lack of love and attention, thus expressing the feelings of a forsaken child.[76]

The vision of the judgment of Karl also needs to be considered primarily as a very personal document, as a testimony of a loving mother's agony. Love, not responsibility, seems to be at the core of this revelation. Because of her great love for him, and albeit the fact that Mary promised to take care of her children, Birgitta was unable to give up praying and crying for Karl. Within the framework of her new orientation, it is natural that her love is now focused on saving her children's souls. It seems that she found it unbearable to see him condemned, even though she, in a corner of her mind, might have had doubts about the justice of his salvation.

Atkinson does not mention Birgitta's personal development from a worldly oriented to a deeply religious person of which both this and the above-mentioned revelation testify.[77] Both before and after her conversion, however, the love for her children seems to have been one of the great moving forces of her life.

Returning to the questions posed at the end of the previous section, i.e., what kind of a mother Birgitta was and whether her own motherhood was the basis of her use of the image of the mother in the revelations, it can be concluded that Birgitta herself must have been the loving mother she so often describes. Even the second important motherly characteristic, the pedagogical involvement of the mother, can clearly be traced back to Birgitta's own life, although it seems to have switched from a more secular to a religious direction.

Even though Birgitta's attitude towards marriage, and motherhood as a result of that, might have been rather ambivalent at first, once she was in the middle of it all, she seems to have enjoyed her role as wife, mother, and prominent noblewoman. Only gradually the longing for a religious way of life grew. To this might have contributed doubts whether she could justify such a worldly lifestyle, strong ties with Christ and Mary, originating in her childhood, and the death of her sons, making her painfully aware of the vanity of life on earth. Ulf's death was the decisive moment for the great breakthrough.

She found it hard to part with her life of wealth, power and esteem, but much harder still to part with her children, and, as a poor pilgrim, follow Christ to Rome. She reached the point where she could tell Mary that she loved her above her children. But we can wonder whether Birgitta really succeeded in banishing her children from her heart. What she did succeed in was setting out a religious path for each of them. But to her distress, not all of them wished to go that way.

Designing a spiritually oriented career for her children was one way for Birgitta to continue her unfinished motherhood; another way, more wide-ranging and ambitious, was her striving for universal, spiritual motherhood.

SPIRITUAL MOTHERHOOD

There is a striking resemblance between the life of Paula and the life of Birgitta. Both started off as ordinary wives and mothers, loving their husbands and their children. When Paula lost her husband, she turned to a religious way of life. If we may believe the *Vita*, Birgitta's religious inclinations started already before Ulf's death, but even for her this was a decisive event. Both felt obliged to forsake their children. Although Birgitta's asceticism seems to have been a little less stringent than Paula's, perhaps it was even for her a means to cope with her feelings of loss and longing. The crucial question, however, is whether Birgitta, in contrast to Paula, did succeed in "widening and transforming her grief into a warm, liberating, and generative spiritual motherhood of all."[78] In what follows, it shall be argued that she did, practicing a motherly charity in daily life and claiming a universal, spiritual motherhood in her writings.

The *Vita* tells us that Birgitta had set up a house for the poor in Sweden, helping and serving them "with tender compassion and the greatest of maternal charity."[79] Clearly, Birgitta's motherly care was already in Sweden offered to others than her own children. This care was not restricted to physical service alone,[80] but involved a mother's pedagogical obligations, i.e., trying to improve a person's spiritual well-being; for instance, converting a prostitute. Soon Birgitta's interest in other people's welfare could no longer be confined within the Swedish borders, and she started addressing the world's great with the warnings and advice she received from Christ and Mary. As we shall see, she felt others to be her spiritual children.

The *Vita* expresses admiration about her unusual—motherly?—insight into people, shown by her knowledge of their innermost thoughts and motives. Many came to her for advice, help, or healing, whereupon she would pray for them and come back with a heavenly answer. Even in the group that lived with her in Rome, she seems to have played the self-sacrificing role of a mother, always putting other people's interests before her own. As appears from the testimonies in the canonization process, the people around her must have recognized her motherly qualities, must have experienced her as a mother-saint. Just before her death, Christ confirmed this by promising her that henceforth she would be counted as a mother in Vadstena.

As has been pointed out in previous contributions in this book, the concept of spiritual motherhood had already been developed in late antiquity. When physical maternity, i.e., being sexually active, became unacceptable for women wishing to lead a religious life, motherhood was lifted up to the spiritual plane, now meaning the care for other people's souls instead of, primarily, for their bodies.[81] The role model for women striving for this kind of spiritual motherhood was Mary. As God's bride she was supposed to bring forth spiritual children to Christ. So it is important to consider how Mary's motherhood is expressed in Birgitta's writings and to what extent Birgitta identified with it.

To start with Mary's physical motherhood, Birgitta described Christ's birth in Bethlehem as no other. In fact, her version of the story was so convincing that it penetrated into the art of her times: Birgitta saw Mary giving birth on her knees (so that she could start worshipping her baby at once), and so it was depicted by artists.[82] Moreover, it happened on a Christmas Eve that Birgitta felt the divine baby move in her own womb. Even the people around her witnessed this miracle.[83]

With pride, Mary describes for Birgitta how beautiful Jesus was as a young man. And with endless sorrow, she repeatedly dwells upon the horrible details of his passion.[84] The character of these visions, with their special attention for Mary's compassion, her partaking in the pain of Christ by witnessing his torture, is typical of the fourteenth century. The Black Death and the raging wars made people painfully aware of their own sinfulness. Mary, who as the *Mater Dolorosa* (the Grieving Mother) shared the griefs of the common people and at the same time could intercede for them with Christ, offered both consolation and hope in hard times.[85] Undoubtedly, the mourning mother at the cross made a deep impression on Birgitta, having gone through the pain of losing two sons herself.

As to Mary's spiritual motherhood, we have already seen that Birgitta had enjoyed Mary's motherly support in her own personal life. In Birgitta's youth both Christ and Mary served as substitutes for her own mother. Later on she, who herself gave birth without pain, once saved Birgitta from a very difficult delivery. So Birgitta must have been acutely aware of the power of this spiritual mother. In her writings, too, she ascribed Mary a great deal of spiritual power. Quite unusually, she put Mary's role at the Passion at an almost equal footing to Christ's, for, as Christ says himself: "And so I can say, that my mother and I have saved humankind as it were with one heart, I by suffering in heart and flesh, she by the grief and love of her own heart."[86] It is a traditional medieval theme to see a parallel between the pairs Adam-

Eve and Christ-Mary. Just as Eve played a part in the Fall, so Mary lent her support to the Redemption.[87] In Birgitta's version, however, Mary's part is considered of such importance that Mary, in fact, is divinized, in the sense that she is allowed to share Christ's function as mediator between God and humanity.[88] Thus Mary can declare to Birgitta:

> I am God's mother, for so it pleased him. I am even the Mother of all, who are in celestial joy. . . . I am also the Mother of all, who are in purgatory, for all punishments, that have to be undergone for the cleansing of their sins, are mitigated in some way or another at some hour because of my prayers. . . . I am also the mother of all justice that is in the world, which justice my son cherished with the most complete attachment. And, as a maternal hand is always prepared to come to the defense of the heart of her son against danger, if someone is trying to hurt him, so I am always prepared to defend the just that are in the world and to free them of all spiritual danger.

> I am called by all Mother of Mercy, truly daughter, the mercy of my son made me merciful, and seeing his mercy made me compassionate.[89]

Apparently, Mary's earthly motherhood has been lifted up to a higher plane to embrace a divine motherhood over all humankind. Of Birgitta's identification with Mary many examples can be given.[90] On an earthly plane, she identified with Mary's motherhood by feeling pregnant with Jesus and through re-living the Passion. Secondly, on a moral level, encouraged by Mary herself, she tried to imitate her virtues, though painfully aware of her failure.[91] And lastly, on a spiritual level, the identification took shape in Birgitta's imitation of Mary as the universal, spiritual mother.

It is Christ who informs Birgitta about her new duties after she has said farewell to her former way of life, including her earthly motherhood:

> I command you to hate from now on all physical blending, for, if you want to live according to my will, you will from now on be mother of spiritual sons, as hitherto you have been mother of physical sons.

> In the first place you have to be prepared for the wedding with my divinity, in which is no fleshly desire, but the sweetest spiritual love, such as is becoming for God to have with a pure soul, so that not the love for your sons, nor even your possessions or parents keeps you away from my love.[92]

Striking is that Christ here calls Birgitta the bride "of his divinity" rather than the spouse of his human appearance, which was far more common among female mystics of her time. Elsewhere she is otherwise called Christ's bride. The title "God's bride" is in doctrine reserved for Mary.[93] Like Mary herself,[94] Birgitta moved between being Christ's mother and his bride. We seem to return here to the ancient concept of the bride-mother who achieves eternal life through continuous spiritual generation. That becomes even clearer through the fact that Birgitta put her revelations on an equal footing with those of prophets, evangelists and apostles. With other female mystics in Birgitta's times, the images of pregnancy and delivery are often used to express a devotional unity with Christ. But if Birgitta feels pregnant with Jesus, this means according to Mary, the coming of Jesus into her heart. Just as Mary once was pregnant with the human Christ, so Birgitta is now bearing his divine message.[95] All this is beautifully expressed in the *Vita*, where a monk receives the following message about Birgitta:

> This is the woman who, coming from the ends of the earth, shall give countless peoples wisdom to drink.[96]

Repeatedly, she is addressed as Christ's *canale*, the mouthpiece of the Holy Spirit, the Word, bearing him spiritual children. As such, she can also share in Mary's role of mediatrix and universal, spiritual mother:

> O my sweetest God, I pray to you for the sinners, in whose company I am, that you may deign to have mercy upon them.

And like Mary, her prayer will be answered:

> Then God the Father answered: "I hear and know your will, therefore what you ask for will be done because of your charity."[97]

CONCLUSION

Because of her religious breakthrough, Birgitta, heeding Christ's calling his disciples in the Bible, felt she had to give up her earthly love for her children. The examples of Karl and Katarina indicate that she was not always successful, that she could not banish her children completely from her heart. However, her involvement in motherhood, her maternal love, from then on sought other ways of expression. And found these, on the one hand, by frequently using the image of the mother to visualize spiritual relations, and, on the other hand, through special adoration for and identification with the Mother of mothers, Mary. In imitation of her, Birgitta aspired to a universal, spiritual motherhood, feeling responsible for the whole Christian community and even for the pagans outside, and interceding for them by Christ or God.

Thus in the religious world-view of Birgitta, a synthesis comes into being between an earthly female role and a religious way of life, the combination of which on a purely worldly plane could only lead to inward conflict.

NOTES

* I would like to express my gratitude to Ms. Dr. G. de Nie for her encouragement and her help and advice in getting through the final stages of this article. Her comments and suggestions proved to be very worthwhile. I am very grateful to Prof. Dr. A.P. Orbán for checking the translations of the Latin text of Birgitta's revelations.

1. In this article the Swedish name "Birgitta" will be used instead of the English form "Bridget" in order to avoid confusion with Saint Bridget of Ireland. The version of the *Vita* used here is: Prior Petrus et Magister Petrus, *Vita b. Brigide*, in *Acta et Processus Canonizacionis beate Birgitte*, ed. Isak Collijn (Uppsala: Almqvist & Wiksells Bokmijckeri AB, 1924–31), where 77: "viro juueni diuiti, militi nobili et prudenti." There is, however, an earlier and less elaborated version of the *Vita*, preserved at the University Library of Uppsala as MS C 15. For a short discussion of the differences between the two versions, see Tore Nyberg, "Introduction," in *Birgitta of Sweden: Life and Selected Revelations*, ed. and trans. Marguerite T. Harris et al. (The Classics of Western Spirituality) (New York: Paulist Press, 1990), 14ff.

2. See Petrus et Petrus, *Vita b. Brigide*, 77ff.; for a review of Birgitta's life, relatives and surroundings in Sweden, see Birgit Klockars, *Birgittas Svenska Värld* (Stockholm: Gebers, 1976).

3. To refer to the revelations, I follow the generally accepted method of first giving the number of the book in Roman numerals and then the number of the revelation within the book in Arabic numerals.

The following editions have been used:

Sancta Birgitta, *Revelaciones, Liber I*, ed. Carl-Gustaf Undhagen (Samlingar utgivna av Svenska Fornskriftsällskapet, 2d ser., Latinska skrifter 7, 1) (Stockholm: Almqvist & Wiksell International, 1977).

Revelationes Sanctae Brigittae, olim a Card. Turrecremata recognitae nunc a Consalvo durando a sancto Angelo in Vado Presb. et sacrae Theol. Profess. Notis illustratae (Antwerp: Petrus Bellerus, 1611) (here used for books II, III, VIII).

Sancta Birgitta, *Revelaciones, Liber IV*, ed. Hans Aili (Samlingar utgivna av Svenska Fornskriftsällskapet, 2d ser., Latinska skrifter 7, 4) (Stockholm: Almqvist & Wiksell International, 1992).

Sancta Birgitta, *Revelaciones, Liber V: Liber Questionum*, ed. Birger Bergh (Samlingar utgivna av Svenska Fornskriftsällskapet, 2d ser., Latinska skrifter 7, 5) (Uppsala: Almqvist & Wiksells Bokmijckeri AB, 1971).

Sancta Birgitta, *Revelaciones, Liber VI*, ed. Birger Bergh (Samlingar utgivna av Svenska Fornskriftsällskapet, 2d ser., Latinska skrifter 7, 6) (Stockholm: Almqvist & Wiksell International, 1991).

Sancta Birgitta, *Revelaciones, Liber VII*, ed. Birger Bergh (Samlingar utgivna av Svenska Fornskriftsällskapet, 2d ser., Latinska skrifter 7, 7) (Uppsala: Almqvist & Wiksells Bokmijckeri AB, 1967).

Sancta Birgitta, *Revelaciones Extrauagantes*, ed. Lennart Hollman (Samlingar utgivna av Svenska Fornskriftsällskapet, 2d ser., Latinska skrifter, 5) (Uppsala: Almqvist & Wiksells Bokmijckeri AB, 1956).

4. *Revelaciones*, VII.31; *Revelaciones Extrauagantes*, 49.

5. Birgit Klockars, *Birgitta och Böckerna: En Undersökning av den heliga Birgittas Källor* (Lund, 1966), 31. See also Nyberg, "Introduction," 40, who speaks of "a dialectical process between Birgitta and her confessors."

6. Sancta Birgitta, *Opera Minora, 1: Regula Salvatoris*, ed. Sten Eklund (Samlingar utgivna av Svenska Fornskriftsällskapet, 2d ser., Latinska skrifter, 8, 1) (Stockholm: Almqvist & Wiksell International, 1975); Sancta Birgitta, *Opera Minora, 2: Sermo Angelicus*, ed. Sten Eklund (Samlingar utgivna av Svenska Fornskriftsällskapet, 2d ser., Latinska skrifter 8, 2) (Uppsala: Almqvist & Wiksells Bokmijckeri AB, 1972). For the edition of the documents compiled for the canonization process, see n. 1.

7. The importance attached in this article to Birgitta's motherhood as a moving force in her life and work, is not an entirely original concept. Already in 1919, Emilia Fogelklou wrote a highly imaginative study of Birgitta, in which she stressed the meaning of Birgitta's motherhood: Emilia Fogelklou, *Birgitta* (Stockholm: Bonniers, 1919).

8. *Revelaciones*, V, *Interrogacio 3, Responsio Questionis Quarte*: "Item dedi semen commixtionis ea de causa, vt loco et modo germinaret debito et vt causa iusta et racionabili fructificaret." (Book V differs from the other books in that it relates only one, very long, revelation, which Birgitta received while riding on a horse. She saw a monk, standing on a ladder lifted towards the sky, posing questions to "the judge" in heaven. The book is divided into sixteen series of such questions (*interrogaciones*) and their answers, interspersed with shorter messages and revelations.) See also *Sermo Angelicvs, Feria 4, Leccio 1*: "Hec denique lex, qualiter Deus diligeretur et proximus et qualiter coniugium inter virum et mulierem honesto et diuino iure teneretur, edocebat, vt ex tali coniugio illi procrearentur, quos Deus vocare vellet suum populum."

9. The translations from the Latin original are by my own hand. For the *Vita*, as well as revelations from book V and VII, the translations by Albert Kezel in *Birgitta of Sweden*, have been of help. *Revelaciones*, V, *Interrogacio 6, Responsio Questionis Prime*: "Omnis quippe fortitudo corporis pueri de patris et matris semine sumitur, sed quia, quod conceptum est, propter aliquam patris vel matris infirmitatem non habet debitam fortitudinem, ideo cicius moritur."

10. Birgitta's view seems to be derived from Albertus Magnus, see Claudia Opitz, *Frauenalltag im Mittelalter: Biographien des 13. und 14. Jahrhunderts* (Ergebnisse der Frauenforschung, 5) (Weinheim [etc.]: Beltz, 1987), 195f.

11. Donald Weinstein and Rudolph M. Bell, *Saints and Society: The Two Worlds of Western Christendom, 1000–1700* (Chicago: University of Chicago Press, 1982), 20, 23; Opitz, *Frauenalltag*, 198.

12. *Revelaciones*, VIII.11: "et causa fugiendi dolores." *Revelaciones*, VII.27: "Ideo facitis sicut meretrices, diligentes voluptatem et delectacionem carnis, non autem prolem. Cum enim senciunt infantem viuum in vtero suo, statim procurant abortiuum herbis et aliis rebus, ne careant carnis voluptate et continua delectacione pessima, vt sic semper vacent luxurie et fetide commixtioni carnali."

13. *Sermo Angelicvs, Feria 5, Leccio 3, Capitulum 15*: "ipse idem in virgine tanto morabatur tempore, sicut aliis infantulis ante suum partum in maternis visceribus morari necesse est."

14. *Revelaciones*, IV.26; *Revelaciones*, I.47.

15. *Revelaciones*, I.43: "Numquid scis, quid est onus grauissimum de hiis, que crescunt? Certe hoc est infantis, qui venit ad partum et non potest nasci sed intra viscera matris moritur, et ex hoc eciam mater rumpitur et moritur, quam pater cum filio defert ad sepulchrum."

16. *Revelaciones*, V, *Interrogacio 6*: "Cur alius infans procedit de vtero matris viuus, . . . alius . . . intra viscera matris moritur?" *Revelaciones*, V, *Interrogacio 14*: "Item cur nascuntur omnia cum dolore?"

17. *Revelaciones*, VI.28: "'Tu,' inquit, 'fuisti michi quasi puer abortiuus matri sue. Que non minorem dolorem patitur pro eo quam pro illo, qui viuus procedit de vtero eius. . . . Verum sicut puer abortiuus non habet dulcedinem de vberibus maternis, non consolacionem de verbis, non calorem de pectore.'"

18. *Revelaciones*, VIII.47: "saepe enim contingit, quod infans in vtero matris ita fortiter cum matre ligatus est, quod nullo modo separare se potest ab eo. Quod obstetrix prudens perpendens, cogitat secum dicens: 'Si infans vlterius morabitur vtero matris, moriuntur ambo, si vero separabuntur ab inuicem mortua quidem matre, viuere potest infans' et sic obstetrix procedens, separat infantem a matre."

19. Opitz, *Frauenalltag*, 191–194. Although Birgitta mentions John the Baptist's mother Elizabeth, for instance in *Revelaciones*, VI.59, she does not present her as a saint helping at childbirth. Anne, however, in *Revelaciones*, VI.104, makes it clear to Birgitta that she is such a helper: "Ego sum Anna, domina omnium coniugatarum, que fuerunt ante legem. Ego eciam sum mater omnium coniugatarum fidelium, que sunt post legem." Then, she urges Birgitta to pray thus to Jesus: "Ideo propter preces Anne miserere omnibus, qui in coniugio sunt, vt fructificent Deo!" By far the most powerful support at childbirth in Birgitta's eyes was Mary herself, as will become evident from the next quotation in the text.

20. Petrus et Petrus, *Vita b. Brigide*, 79: "Igitur cum quodam tempore periclitaretur domina Brigida in partu et desperaretur de vita eius, nocte vigilantibus mulieribus et videntibus, que astabant ad custodiam eius, persona quedam serico albo induta subito visa est ingredi et stare ante lectum et pertractare singula membra domine Brigide jacentis, timentibus omnibus que aderant. Cum autem egressa esset persona illa, ita faciliter peperit domina Brigida, quod mirum erat et non dubium, quin beata virgo, que sine dolore peperit, erat persona illa, que illos labores, dolores et periculum sue ancille mitigauit."

21. *Revelaciones*, IV.51: *Declaratio*: "Hec mulier vouit virginitatem in manu sacerdotis et postea nupsit; que in partu postea periclitata moriebatur." This soul had, of course, also committed other sins to do penance for.

22. Opitz, *Frauenalltag*, 191–197.

23. *Revelaciones*, VI.19: "Numquid ego sicut mater fui eis? Que habens in vtero filium optat in hora partus, vt procedat infans viuus de vtero; si consequitur baptisma, non curat de morte sua." *Revelaciones*, II.21: "Eram enim sicut mulier pariens cuius omnia membra post partum tremula sunt, quae licet prae dolore vix respirare possit, tamen gaudet interius quantum potest eo quod scit filium suum natum, in eandem miseriam, de qua exiuit, nunquam rediturum."

24. Ulpho, *Vita de S. Catharina Suecica* in *AASS 9 Martii* (3rd ed. Paris, 1865), vol. 3, 503f.: "Quae eum adhuc in cunis mortalis hujus vitae ageret exordium, ejus futurae sanctitatis et puritatis indicia divina gratia demonstravit. Nam nutricis officio tradita, propter impudicam et lascivam vitam (ut probabili conjectura conjicitur) surgere mammas abhorrebat: mammillas vero matris suae sanctae, et quarumdam continentium mulierum, sine horrore bibebat: incontinentium lac sicut absynthium refugiens cum lacrymis et vagitu."

25. See the article by Renée Nip, "Godelieve of Gistel and Ida of Boulogne," in this book; Weinstein and Bell, *Saints and Society*, 25; Shulamith Shahar, "Infants, Infant Care, and Attitudes toward Infancy in the Medieval Lives of Saints," *The Journal of Psychohistory*, 10 (1983), 283–286, 295f.; Christian Krötzl, who studied parent-child relations in Scandinavian miracle stories, states that his sources do not indicate that the upper classes handed over their sucklings to a wet nurse. The general attitude towards breast-feeding by the mother seems to have been positive: Christian Krötzl, "Parent-child Relations in Medieval Scandinavia according to Scandinavian Miracle Collections," *Scandinavian Journal of History*, 14 (1989), 29; Clarissa W. Atkinson, *The Oldest Vocation: Christian Motherhood in the Middle Ages* (Ithaca, N.Y.: Cornell University Press, 1991), 76.

26. *Revelaciones*, IV.126.

27. Philippe Ariès, *Centuries of Childhood: A Social History of Family Life*, trans. Robart Baldick (New York: Vintage Books, 1962); Weinstein and Bell, *Saints and Society*, 19, 28ff., 46f.; Opitz, *Frauenalltag*, 46, 54, 107f., 200; Krötzl, "Parentchild Relations," 26, 28, 30, 36.

28. Petrus et Petrus, *Vita b. Brigide*, 78: "maxima materna caritate."

29. *Revelaciones*, V, *Interrogacio* 13: "Ego sum quasi mater, que videns in filiis spem vite aliis dat forciora, aliis leuiora. Hiis vero, de quibus non est spes, eciam compatitur et facit, quantumcumque potest."

30. *Revelaciones*, IV.139: "Sicut enim pia mater dilectum videns filium suum nudum et frigidum in terra iacentem et ad erigendum se vires corporis nullas habentem, set pre desiderio fauoris et lactis materni querulis vocibus cum vagitu plorantem, que tunc tenera dileccione compassa filio festine currit et, ne deficiat frigore, pia manu materna de terra eleuat ipsum, quem statim leniter fouet et materno calore sui pectoris mitissime calefacit eumque dulciter mamillarum suarum lacte cibat."

31. *Revelaciones*, IV.117 and VI.19.

32. For the Bible's influence on Birgitta's work, see Anders Piltz, "Uppenbarelserna och uppenbarelsen: Birgittas förhållande till bibeln," in *Birgitta: Hendes værk og hendes klostre i Norden*, ed. Tore Nyberg (Odense University Studies in History and Social Sciences, 150) (Odense: Odense Universitetsforlag, 1991), 447–469.

33. Caroline Walker Bynum, " '. . . And Woman His Humanity': Female Imagery in the Religious Writing of the Later Middle Ages" in her *Fragmentation and Redemption: Essays on Gender and the Human Body in Medieval Religion* (New York: Zone Books, 1991), 151–179.

34. In *Revelaciones*, VI.28, Christ compares a damned soul to an abortive child. He himself feels like the mother, who regrets that she will not be able to give the child her milk and warmth, despite her pain and labor (the Redemption). In *Revelaciones*, II.15, Christ rejoices like the mother of the lost son upon his return, when he welcomes the blessed. This example is the more striking, while the biblical story does only mention the father of the lost son, not the mother (Lk. 15:11–32). In *Revelaciones*, VI.42, Mary asks Christ to feed Birgitta with his body, for without that she would languish like a child without mothermilk. See also Atkinson, *The Oldest Vocation*, 182f.

35. *Revelaciones*, I.47.

36. Bynum, ". . . And Woman His Humanity," 157–164.

37. To Atkinson, *The Oldest Vocation*, 183, 193, however, power, sorrow and responsibility are the main characteristics of motherhood, as expressed by Birgitta and other mother-saints of the late Middle Ages. As I will argue below, in the section about Birgitta's own children, I think Birgitta's motherly love is the very essence, wherefrom all other attributes are derived.

38 *Revelaciones*, II.21; IV.139 and VI.20.

39. *Revelaciones*, VI.52; IV.126 and *Revelaciones*, V, *Interrogacio* 15.

40. *Revelaciones*, IV.126: "ut et suorum familiarium pater sit per diuinam auctoritatem et eorum mater et nutrix per informacionem benignam." Something similar is said in *Revelaciones*, III.1.

41. *Revelaciones*, I.43; see n. 15.

42. *Revelaciones*, VIII.47.

43. Compare for instance Kari E. Børresen, "Birgitta's Godlanguage: Exemplary Intention, Inapplicable Content," in *Birgitta*, ed. Nyberg, 63–66, with Sven Stolpe, *Birgitta i Sverige* (Stockholm: Askild & Kärnekull, 1973), 40f., and Atkinson, *The Oldest Vocation*, 171f.

44. *Acta et processus*, ed. Isak Collijn, 305: "quia ipsa pluries audiuit ab ipsa domina Brigida matre sua, quod, antequam contraheret matrimonium, in virginitate existens desiderabat tote corde seruire Deo omnipotenti totis temporibus vite sue in virginitate et statu virginitatis et non contrahere matrimonium, sed tamen parentes eius compulerunt, coegerunt et induxerunt eam ad contrahendum matrimonium, et dicebat

ipsa domina Brigida tunc, ut asseruit ipsa testis, quod tunc voluisset libencius mori quam contrahere."

45. This is the view of Klockars, *Svenska värld*, 42; see also Weinstein and Bell, *Saints and Society*, 44: "[M]otherhood with its disfigurement in pregnancy, screams of labour, filth of afterbirth, and early decay of beauty—offered no joy that could be compared with the ethereal serenity of the Madonna."

46. Hjalmar Sundén, *Den heliga Birgitta: Ormungens Moder som blev Kristi Brud* (Stockholm: Wahlström & Widstrand, 1973), 30, 205.

47. Ibid., 32f. For a comparison between Birgitta's view of marriage and the practice of her own life see Jeannette Nieuwland, "Birgitta's View of Marriage: Theory versus Practice," in *Birgitta*, ed. Nyberg, 83–91.

48. Here my view is divergent from Kari Børresen, "Birgitta's Godlanguage," 66, who concludes that "the hagiographical axiom of Birgitta's enforced marriage is unwarranted in historical research on her life and writings." That may be true, but does not, in my eyes, automatically erase all truth in Katarina's testimony and certainly does not mean that Birgitta could not wait to be married. To me Sundén's view that Birgitta at first felt uneasy with the idea of getting married both out of a wish to lead a religious life and out of a reluctance against sexuality, which she grew over during her marriage, seems closer to the truth: *Den heliga Birgitta*, 208f.

49. Ibid., 35f.

50. Petrus et Petrus, *Vita b. Brigide*, 79: "Sponsa igitur Christi cum magna sollicitudine et diligencia virtuose educauit et nutriuit filios suos et filias tradens eos magistris, a quibus instrebantur disciplina et bonis moribus; plorabat illa cotidie peccata filiorum timens, quod offenderent Deum suum." See Atkinson, *The Oldest Vocation*, 174.

51. See for instance *Revelaciones*, VI.52, where the daughter, speaking to her mother from purgatory and reproaching her for her bad example, has been identified with Birgitta's daughter Ingeborg. See also *Revelaciones Extrauagantes*, 98: "Sed ex hoc ploro, quia non instruxi eam secundum mandata tua."

52. Petrus et Petrus, *Vita b. Brigide*, 91f.: "Reversa igitur domina Brigida a rege Swecie ad monasterium Aluastri jnuenit quendam filium suum, quem infirmum diu reliquerat iam in extremis agentem, et plorans multum de tam longa infirmitate eius reputabat hoc accidere pro peccatis parentum. Tunc diabolus apparens ei dixit: 'Quid tibi mulier cum tantis lacrimarum aquis debilitas visum et jnuanum laboras? Numquid aque possent ascendere in celum?' Eadem hora Christus in forma humanitatis apparens sponse dixit: 'Huius pueri infirmitas non est ex constellacionibus stellarum, vt fatui dicunt, nec propter peccata eius, sed propter nature condicionem et maiorem eius coronam. Jdeo si vsque huc vocatus est proprio nomine Benedictus filius Vlfonis, jam de cetero vocabitur filius lacrimarum et oracionum, et faciam finem necessitati eius.' Post ista vero quinta die auditus est cantus suauissimus quasi auium inter lectum pueri et parietem, et ecce tunc anima pueri egressa est; et dixit spiritus sanctus eidem domine Brigide: 'Ecce quid faciunt lacrime, iam filius aquarum transiuit ad quietem. Jdeo diabolo odiose sunt lacrime bonorum, que procedunt ex caritate diuina.'" Of course, the example of Augustine's mother Monica, who also wept much over her son's sins, immediately springs to mind here. See Atkinson, *The Oldest Vocation*, 76.

53. *Revelaciones*, VI.32; Sundén, *Den heliga Birgitta*, 18–24.

54. *Revelaciones*, IV.52: "Ego sum una de illis," and: "Mater quoque nostra sedebat cum primis vestita nobiliter habensque seruitores plurimos et enutriens nos cum honore. Cur talia non debeam hereditare filie mee, que didici, scilicet gerere se nobiliter et viuere cum corporali gaudio, mori quoque cum grandi honore mundi?" Prove of Birgitta's former pride can also be found in *Revelaciones Extrauagantes*, 62, where the devil asks her why she does not love pride any more, like she did before.

55. Sundén, *Den heliga Birgitta*, 213f. A very striking example of this process is given in *Revelaciones Extrauagantes*, 53, where Birgitta receives a hard blow

on her head because she and Ulf had acquired a luxurious and comfortable bed. *Revelaciones Etrauagantes*, 75 is an example of how strongly Birgitta disapproves of her former lifestyle.

56. Sundén, *Den heliga Birgitta*, 34ff.

57. Ibid., 38, 214.

58. See for instance Lk. 14:26–27 and *Revelaciones*, I.1: "Tu autem, filia mea, . . . dilige me toto corde, non sicut filium et filiam seu parentes, sed plus quam aliquid in mundo! . . . Dilige ergo me solum."

59. *Revelaciones Etrauagantes*, 95: "Contigit semel in monasterio Aluastri, quod animus beate Birgitte, cum itura esset Romam, accendebatur ad amorem filiorum suorum, compaciens relinquere eos quasi orbatos consolacione materna, timens eciam, quod post eius recessum audacius offenderent Deum in aliquo, quia iuuenes erant, diuites et potentes. Et tunc vidit in visione vnam ollam positam super ignem et quendam puerum sufflantem prunas, vt olla accenderetur. Cui dixit beata Birgitta: 'Cur tantum inflare conaris, vt succendatur olla?' Respondit puer: 'Vt amor filiorum tuorum magis accendatur et inflammetur in te.' Beata Birgitta respondit: 'Quis,' inquit, 'tu es?' Cui ille: 'Ego,' inquit, 'sum negociator.' Tunc ipsa, intelligens amorem aliquem inordinatum in corde suo existere ad filios, statim correxit se, vt nichil preponeret amori Christi."

60. *Revelaciones Etrauagantes*, 63: Speaking about herself, Birgitta realizes: "Ipse denique nouit, quod Maria, filia Ioachim, est michi carior quam liberi Vlphonis et Birgitte. And Mary answers: Et eadem Maria, filia Ioachim, que est mater Dei, vult esse pro matre liberis Vlphonis et Birgitta."

61. See below, "Spiritual Motherhood." The quotation is from Giselle de Nie, "Consciousness Fecund through God," elsewhere in this volume.

62. *Revelaciones*, IV.71: "Iterum dixit Dominus: 'Tu michi dedisti filiam tuam, . . . Si vero unum sine alio defuerit, scilicet virginitas carnis et non virginitas mentis, deformata est virginitas. . . . Miraris quare virgo hec non peruenit ad coniugium eo modo, quo sperabas. . . . ipse magis adhesit inimicis meis et ideo non peruenit ad ea, que promittebam.'"

63 *Revelaciones*, VI.52. See n. 48.

64. *Revelaciones Etrauagantes*, 98. See Atkinson, *The Oldest Vocation*, 176.

65. *Revelaciones*, VI.118: "Aliquanto itaque tempore elapso, postquam beata Katherina vouisset cum matre sua Rome remanere, horrore inconsuete vite concussa memorque libertatis preterite multum anxia peciit a matre sua, vt ad Sueciam posset remeare. Matri vero eius pro hac temptacione in oracione existenti apparuit Christus dicens: 'Dic virgini illi filie tue, quod facta est vidua. Et consulo, vt tecum remaneat, quia ego ipse volo sibi prouidere.'" Ulpho, *Vita S. Catharinae Suecica*, 506: "Unde rogare benignam matrem suam coepit, ut si quod secundum Deum sciret remedium, ei sic affectae adhiberet. Venerabilis mater ejus, omnium talium tentationum jam triumphatrix, filiae sauciatae carnali affectione, remedium providit salutare, vocans magistrum Confessorem suum, rogando suppliciter et devote, ut caede virgarum mentis incommodum excutiat, ipsaqua Domina Catharina hoc idem remedium instanter efflagitabat."

66. Sven Stolpe, *Birgitta i Rom* (Stockholm: Askild & Kärnekull, 1973), 71ff.; See *Revelaciones*, IV.72 for Christ's advice to Katarina and Birgitta about how they should live.

67. Birger became "lagman" (highest juridical official in a certain district) and knight. He seems to have been a pious man. He visited his mother several times in Rome and accompanied her on the pilgrimage to the Holy Land. After her death, he assisted in practical matters with regards to the canonization process and the founding of the monastery. See Stolpe, *Birgitta i Sverige*, 42 and Klockars, *Svenska värld*, 153ff.

68. *Revelaciones*, II.13.

69. *Revelaciones*, IV.74: "Propter merita parentum."

70. *Revelaciones*, VII.13:

"In eadem igitur hora domina Birgitta in quoddam palacium magnum et pulchrum raptam se videbat et Dominum Ihesum Christum pro tribunali ibi sedentem quasi coronatum imperatorem cum infinito famulancium exercitu angelorum et sanctorum, et prope eum videbat suam dignissimam matrem stantem et ad iudicium diligenter auscultantem.

Videbatur eciam coram iudice quedam anima astare in magno timore et pauore et nuda sicut infans tunc natus et quasi totaliter ceca, ita quod nichil videbat; in consciencia tamen intelligebat, quid in palacio dicebatur et agebatur. Angelus autem quidam stabat ad dexteram partem iudicis prope animam et quidam dyabolus ad sinistram eius, sed neuter corum animam tangebat vel attractabat. . . . Post hec loquitur dyabolus ad iudicem dicens: 'Ego scio, quod tu es ipsa iusticia et potencia. Tu non magis iudicas iniusticiam dyabolo quam angelo. Adiudica ergo michi istam animam. In illa enim sapiencia, quam habui, quando me creasti, scripseram omnia peccata ipsius. . . . Nam quando primo anima ista ad illam etatem discrecionis peruenit, quod iam bene intelligebat esse peccatum illud, quod faciebat, tunc propria voluntas ipsum trahebat ad viuendum magis in mundana superbia et carnali delectacione quam talibus resistere.'

Respondit angelus: 'Quando primo eius mater intellexit ipsius voluntatem esse flexibilem ad peccatum, statim ipsa succurrebat ei misericordie operibus et precibus diuturnis, vt ei Deus misereri dignaretur, ne ab ipso se elongaret. Propter ista denique matris sue opera optinuit diuinum timorem, ita quod, quocienscumque cecidit in peccatum, confestim ad faciendum confessionem properauit.'

Respondit dyabolus: 'Me oportet peccata sua narrare.' Et statim volens incipere in eadem hora clamare cepit et plangere et in se ipso diligenter inquirere in capite et in membris cunctis, que videbatur habere, totusque videbatur tremere et ex turbacione magna clamauit: 'Ve michi misero, quomodo perdidi meum longum laborem, quia non solum oblitus est textus et abolitus, verum eciam materia tota combusta est in qua omnia fuerunt scripta.' . . .

Respondit angelus: 'Hoc fecerunt lacrime et longi labores multeque oraciones matris sue, ita quod Deum compaciens suis gemitibus dedit eius filio talem graciam, scilicet quod pro quolibet peccato, quod commisit, contricionem optinuit, humilem confessionem faciendo ex diuina caritate, et ideo illa peccata oblita et neglecta sunt in tua memoria.' . . .

Respondit angelus: 'Hoc fecit mater eius assiduis oracianibus et labore, quia animam eius dilexit toto corde. Ideo placuit Deo propter ipsius caritatem omnia peccata eius venialia indulgere, que ab infancia vsque ad mortem commisit . . . . Audi igitur tu, dyabole! Mater eius caritatiuis precibus et pietatis operibus ad portam misericordie perseueranter pulsauit pro eo, plus quam triginta annis fundendo milia multa lacrimarum, vt Deus cordi eius Sanctum Spiritum infundere dignaretur, ita quod bona sua corpusque et animam idem filius suus ad Dei seruicium libenti animo exhiberet. Sic eciam fecit Deus. . . . Virgo vero mater Dei dedit illi ex virtute sua, quidquid sibi deficit in armis spiritualibus et indumentis, que pertinent ad milites, qui debent intrare in regno celi ad summum imperatorem. . . . Scito, quod modo in celo vocatur 'filius lacrimarum.' Dyabolus vero clamans."

71. Examples of other judgment-revelations are: *Revelaciones*, I.28 (a nobleman is sent to hell; even Mary can't find a reason to defend him); IV.52 (a couple is damned, a.o. because they got married although they were relatives); IV.102 (a monk also goes to hell because of his lack of obedience, love of God and believe in God's

justice); IV.134 (same story again for a priest who did not live according to his vocation); IV.51 (a woman has to undergo severe punishment in purgatory and has only just escaped worse because she showed remorse on her deathbed); IV.144 (Birgitta witnesses the punishment of a deceased pope in purgatory: he had shown too much love for worldly things and he had not always given the good example he should have); IV.8 (the Italian nobleman Nicolaus Acciajuolis is sent to purgatory); VI.39 (a Swedish nobleman also goes to purgatory; he is saved from worse by Mary and his guardian angel); etc.

72. *Revelaciones*, VII.13: "Veni tu, o mi electe!"

73. Striking in this context is also that Birgitta in another vision sees someone ending up in purgatory because he had misled her by saying that Karl had been hung: *Revelaciones Etrauagantes*, 112: "Nullus homo credit, in quanto timore sedet hic anima ista. Et hoc ideo, quia existens in corpore inquietauit amicos Dei." Atkinson, *The Oldest Vocation*, 179, associates the tears with which Birgitta's belly is filled with the waters of spiritual birth.

74. Atkinson, *The Oldest Vocation*, 76, 177.

75. Ibid., 179; *Revelaciones*, VI.52.

76. Sundén, *Den heliga Birgitta*, 202–207.

77. In *Revelaciones* VI.52, the mother (Birgitta) amends her ways and from the vision about the judgment of Karl it becomes clear that she deeply regrets her former ways.

78. See n. 61.

79. Petrus et Petrus, *Vita b. Brigide*, 78: "cum tenera compassione et maxima materna caritate."

80. Atkinson, *The Oldest Vocation*, 167, seems to give the physical aspect priority: "Motherhood was comprehended in terms of physical suffering and service, and the mother-saints of the late Middle Ages extended maternal service to all those in need—with the exception, very often, of their own children."

81. Ibid., 64–100.

82. *Revelaciones*, VII.21: "tunc virgo genuflexa est cum magna reuerencia, ponens se ad oracionem, . . . Et sic ea in oracione stante vidi tunc ego mouere iacentem in vtero eius, et illico in momento et ictu oculi peperit filium." Mieke L. de Kreek, "Bene veneris deus meus, dominus meus. . . ," in *Birgitta van Zweden 1303–1373: 600 jaar kunst en cultuur van haar kloosterorde*, ed. Léon C.B.M. van Liebergen (Tentoonstellings-catalogus Museum voor Religieuze Kunst Uden, 22 maart–25 mei 1986) (Uden: Museum voor Religieuze Kunst, 1986), 36–41. See also Atkinson, *The Oldest Vocation*, 182.

83. *Revelaciones*, VI.88: "Nocte natalis Domini tam mirabilis et magna aduenit sponse Christi exultacio cordis, vt vix se pre leticia tenere posset, et in eodem momento sensit in corde motum sensibilem admirabilem, quasi si in corde esset puer viuus et voluens se et reuoluens. Cumque motus iste duraret, ostendit patri spirituali suo et aliquibus amicis spiritualibus suis, ne forte esset illusio. Qui visu et tactu probantes veritatem admirabantur."

84. *Revelaciones*, IV.70 and I.10; II.21; IV.70; VII.15.

85. See Marina Warner, *Alone of All Her Sex: The Myth and the Cult of the Virgin Mary* (London: Weidenfeld and Nicolson, 1976), 207–223.

86. *Revelaciones Extrauagantes*, 3: "Et ideo bene dicere possum, quod mater mea et ego quasi cum vno corde saluauimus hominem, ego paciendo corde et carne, ipsa cordis dolore et amore."

87. See Atkinson, *The Oldest Vocation*, 109.

88. For a more extensive treatment of Mary's role in the Redemption, see Børresen, "Birgitta's Godlanguage," 39–42. Cf. Ivetta of Huy's views in Anneke Mulder-Bakker's contribution to this volume, "Ivetta of Huy: *Mater et Magistra*."

89. *Revelaciones*, IV.138: "'Ego eciam sum Mater omnium, qui sunt in superno gaudio. . . . Sum eciam Mater omnium qui sunt in purgatorio, quia omnes pene,

que debentur purgandis pro peccatis suis, in qualibet hora propter preces meas quodammodo mitigantur. . . . Ego sum eciam Mater tocius iusticie que est in mundo, quam iusticiam filius meus dilexit dileccione perfectissima. Et sicut materna manus semper parata est ad opponendum se periculo in cordis filii sui defensionem, si aliquis niteretur in sui lesionem, ita ego sum parata iugiter iustos qui sunt in mundo defendere et de omni spirituali periculo liberare.' *Revelaciones*, II.23: 'Ego vocor ab omnibus Mater misericordiae, vere filia, misericordia filii mei fecit me misericordem, et misericordia eius visa compatientem.'"

90. According to Atkinson, *The Oldest Vocation*, 182, a certain development in Birgitta's relationship to and identification with Mary can be discerned: "The tone of Birgitta's account of her vision of the Nativity is less like that of a daughter-in-law than of another mother or a grandmother, taken into Mary's confidence about the birth of the wonderful child. As Birgitta grew older and more accustomed to heavenly conversation, her relationship with Mary grew stronger, deeper, and more intimate." See also Atkinson, 183.

91. For instance *Revelaciones*, II.24: "Ideo filia mea licet a multis oblita et neglecta sim, tu tamen non obliuiscaris me, vide dolorem meum, et imitare quantum potes." See also *Revelaciones*, II.23, where Mary urges Birgitta to obtain her cloak of humility, and *Revelaciones*, III.29, where Birgitta utters in frustration that her own temple is completely contrary to Mary's: "quia templum meum contrarium omnino tuo est," i.e. filled with sin.

92. *Revelaciones Extrauagantes*, 75: "Precipio tibi omnem carnis commixtionem in perpetuum odire, quia, si secundum voluntatem meam esse volueris, eris mater filiorum deinceps spiritualium, sicut hactenus fueras mater carnalium." *Revelaciones*, I.20: "Primo debes esse parata ad nuptias meae, in quibus nulla est libido carnalis sed spiritualis delectatio suauissima, qualem decet Deum habere cum anima casta, ita vt non amor filiorum tuorum, non etiam bonorum, vel parentum retrahat te ab amore meo. . . . et ego per te volo generare michi multos filios, non carnales sed sprituales."

93. The title "God's bride" is frequently used in the first version of the *Vita*, see n. 1. In the later version, written with the canonization process in mind, it has been adapted to doctrine and replaced by "Christ's bride." So only at a later stage the confessors seem to have removed the unusual title, which they must have heard Birgitta use many times. See Børresen, "Birgitta's Godlanguage," 24.

94. In *Revelaciones*, IV.11, this is confirmed by Saint Agnes. See Atkinson, *The Oldest Vocation*, 110f.

95. *Revelaciones*, VI.88: Mary says to Birgitta: "Ideo, filia, non timeas illusionem sed gratulare, quia motus iste, quem tu sentis, signum aduentus filii mei est in cor tuum." Compare Børresen, "Birgitta's Godlanguage," 24f., 38f., with "Consciousness Fecund through God," by Giselle de Nie in this book. By stressing the unusualness of Birgitta's claim as compared to other female mystics of her time, Børresen seems to pass by the fact that Birgitta is in fact reverting to a very old concept, expressed already by Origen. See also Atkinson, *The Oldest Vocation*, 162f.; although she mentions Hadewych as being pregnant with "religious truth," she emphasizes the growth of the more usual form of spiritual motherhood, i.e. mystical union with the infant God. Speaking about Birgitta herself on 179f. she does not mention the deeper meaning of Birgitta's being pregnant with Christ.

96. Petrus et Petrus, *Vita b. Brigide*, 82: Hec est mulier, que a finibus terre veniens propinabit innumerabilibus gentibus sapienciam.

97. *Revelaciones*, III.23: "O mi dulcissime Deus, rogo te pro peccatoribus, in quorum consortio ego sum, vt eius misereri digneris. Respondit Deus Pater. Audio et scio voluntatem tuam, ideo perficietur oratio charitatis tuae."

Figure 10.1. Anonymous, Spes Nostra, *a commemorative painting, c. 1508 (Rijksmuseum, Amsterdam)*

10. *Sancta Mater versus Sanctus Doctus?*

Saint Anne and the Humanists

Karin Tilmans

The starting point for my story is an early-sixteenth-century painting which carries the title *Spes Nostra*. This painting is presently in the possession of the Rijksmuseum and certainly merits a place in a book on sanctity and motherhood (fig. 10.1). The name of the painter is unknown—he is referred to simply as the Master of the *Spes Nostra*.[1] The words *spes nostra*, "our hope," refer to the pregnant woman in the background: it is the young Mary, visited here by Elizabeth who is seen touching her belly. The words also refer to the well-known medieval song "*Salve Regina*" about the Virgin Mary: she is the hope of mankind at the hour of death, because through her son Jesus Christ she realized the redemption of mankind. As Marbod of Rennes describes her in his poem "*Stella Maria*" from the beginning of the twelfth century:

> After the Lord, you are the hope of men whom the mind conscious of sin consumes—the mind which is contaminated through contact with Venus.[2]

Apart from the visitation scene with the two women, there are two other images of interest in this painting: one with the children playing in a monastic court, in the background of the painting, and then, at the front, one with the six men and a corpse. The background scene can be interpreted as an episode from Christ's youth. It is the scene at the front which poses more problems of interpretation, however, because it is telling us something about the purpose and commission of this painting. Unmistakably we see the two Church Fathers, Jerome, standing to the left, and Augustine, in similar position to the right, and four Augustinian canons, kneeling down. The corpse is half-covered with a stone, carrying the inscription *Requiescant in pace*, "Rest in peace."

There are two opinions about the intended site of this painting. The first, posed by Schulte Nordholt in 1962,[3] associates this panel with the Augustinian (male) monastery of Sion near the city of Delft, and interprets its meaning as an early allegory on transitoriness. A second possibility was proposed in 1979 by Jeremy D. Bangs,[4] who saw a connection between the painting and the (female) Augustinian monastery of Marienpoel, near the city of Leiden. There the painting may have appeared on the High Altar as a commemoration panel for four deceased male rectors. Mary, Jerome and Augustine were the saints to whom the High Altar must have been dedicated, according to Bangs. Although both opinions remain hypothetical as far as the original monastery is concerned, Bangs's hypothesis of a commemoration piece is more convincing than Schulte Nordholt's idea of an allegory. The four kneeling canons are clearly portraits of the commissioners or the commemorated rectors, and there is no sign of an allegorical figure in the whole.[5]

In this paper, however, we are not so much interested in the exact original location of this painting—without further information we can only speculate on that—but more in the internal story of the painting, that is, in the combination of the three layers presented here: the child Jesus Christ, the future mother Mary, and the reflecting, pensive men in the foreground. If we ask ourselves about the relationship between the three layers, in other words, about what these learned men contributed to the sanctity of Mary and the child Jesus, then we come very close to the problem posed in the title of this paper: *sancta mater versus sanctus doctus*. The answer to the question on the relationship between material saintliness, of Mary and especially Anne, and humanism can be a straightforward one: there is in fact no opposition between the two but rather a causal relationship. *Sancta mater causa sanctorum doctorum*: Holy Mother Mary, but even more so Holy Mother Anne, owed her undisputed holiness in large part to the writings and propaganda of Northern humanism.

As Brandenbarg points out in his contribution, "Saint Anne: A Holy Grandmother and her Children,"[6] the cult of Saint Anne knew a real boom in the fifteenth century. She became the patron of mothers, pregnant women and of those longing to become mothers. At the same time Anne is venerated as the patron of marriage, family and widows. Everything to do with the household fell under her protection. For a time the (grand)mother Anne overshadowed the virgin-mother Mary and she pushed the male actors in this family history, Saint Joseph and Saint Joachim, very much out of the picture. Saint Anne seems to defy what Demyttenaere recently stated as: "In the holiness of the women we find an implicit underestimation of the woman and a reinforcing ambivalence: the weaker the woman, the greater God's grace. Female as well as male saints were preferably virgins. When they were married, they preferred to live in chastity. When a mother, their holiness mainly appeared in their chaste and devout life as a widow. The female saint above all was Mary, virgin and mother at the same time."[7] The relationship between Anne's holiness and motherhood was of a different intensity and nature than we have seen in the cases of the holy virgin/mothers, discussed elsewhere in this book. The historical dimension of her relationships and of her three marriages is one thing which sets Saint Anne apart.[8] Her role as teacher and educator of the mother of Jesus Christ is another. For both of these aspects, the writings of the Northern humanists were the major authorities in spreading and integrating her cult in late-medieval, religious consciousness.

SAINT ANNE AND THE CARMELITES

In considering the cult of Saint Anne, the Northern humanists confronted an old theological problem, the freedom of original sin of Jesus and the nature of his conception.[9] That Jesus Christ had been miraculously conceived by a virgin was a problem which wracked the brains of theologians. But a complicating question was whether the *ovum* which Mary had produced before the conception was also free of original sin. To insure that this was the case, we can see that very early on in theological writing efforts are made to argue in favor of an Immaculate Conception of Mary herself and thus to give her a supernatural position.[10] There was nothing in the Bible which indicated that the Virgin was free from original sin. The Church Fathers therefore did not dare to claim Mary's freedom of original sin openly, whereas they praised her miraculous virginity whenever they could. Augustine was the source of a lot of discussion among Mariologists by saying that all people were born in sin, but that he wanted to make an exception for Mary, "of whom out of honor to the Lord I wish no question to be made where sins are treated of—for how do we know what mode of grace wholly to conquer sin may have been bestowed on her?"[11] The point as to whether freedom of sin was valid for Mary from the moment of her birth, is not touched upon by Augustine, and it is through his silence that the problem which occupied theologians for centuries to come came into existence.

In the later Middle Ages the discussions over the Immaculate Conception of Mary gained new momentum under the influence of two movements, which actually interconnect at the end of the fifteenth century, carmelitism and humanism. The Carmelites, who claimed their descent from the prophet Elijah and his disciples, the eremites on Mount Carmel, developed a new type of Immaculate Virgin, giving her an allegorical and historical dimension. First of all, they saw an allegory of Mary in the rain-carrying cloud which appeared miraculously on top of Mount Carmel at the end of a great drought, following the sacrifice of Elijah to Jahweh (1 Kings 18:44), according to which Mary appeared as the harbinger of the end of the great drought before the arrival of the Messiah. The conception of Mary, therefore, became closely linked to the origin of the Carmelite order, and it is little wonder that they dedicated an extensive cult to the worship of Mary and her Immaculate Conception. In this context, the Carmelites developed the historical component of her conception. The virginal birth of Christ was expanded to include similar births among his and Mary's ancestors. The parents of Anne, so the Carmelites claimed, named Stollanus and Emerentiana, were already elected by divine signs. The story was that Emerentiana had joined the Carmelites, but that, after a vision, her colleagues realized that she was elected to be the ancestor of the Saviour and encouraged her to leave the monastic life and to marry. After six different husbands, each of them killed by a jealous and threatened Satan, Emerentiana succeeded finally with Stollanus and became pregnant with Anne. The cult of the bizarre ancestry of Mary was spread not only by the Carmelites, but also by the Poor Clares, the female branch of the Franciscans, who took an active part in this propaganda.

The debate on the role of Mary's and Anne's ancestry took place against the background of a renewed minute analysis of the Bible. Renaissance humanists used refined linguistic techniques to trace forgeries, apocryphal elements and mistakes in the previously inviolable Latin Vulgate-translation by Jerome. Their philological method immensely stimulated Bible study and in the period between 1457 and 1500 more than one hundred Latin editions of the Bible were printed. Paradoxically, under the influence of this new biblical criticism, Catholic apologists held on to the old statement of the Immaculate Conception and it is then that humanists, in disagreement, looked for further literary and more historical arguments, other than those already used by the Carmelites.

The most important passage used by these apologists to define the Immaculate Conception of Mary was the so-called *Protevangelium*.[12] In this text God's curse on the serpent in the Garden of Eden was interpreted as the first promise of a Redeemer, the first beam of light into the shadows of Adam and Eve going into exile. In Jerome's Vulgate, God's words to the serpent are as follows: "I will create enmity between you and the woman, and between your children and her children: *she* will crush your head, and you will stare at her heel" (Genesis 3:15; emphasis added). In the "she" the

Figure 10.2. *The Immaculate Conception. Panel of the Retable of the Brotherhood of Saint Anne in Frankfurt, c. 1500 (Historisches Museum, Frankfurt am Main)*

apologists saw a prophecy of the Virgin Mary, and the promised victory over the serpent was used to develop the image of the second Eve who triumphs where the first one failed. With the discussion of original sin in full swing, this victory over the devil was used as an argument for the fact that Mary, from the very beginning of creation, was destined to escape the power of Evil. According to these Catholic apologists, a total victory of the devil must imply a total absence of sin, and hence Immaculate Conception.

But the humanists questioned the translation of Jerome. In the modern authorized version they produced a more accurate translation of the Hebrew: "And I will place enmity between you and the woman, and between your seed and her seed: *it* will crush your head, and you will repel its heel" (emphasis added). The seed of the woman, not the woman herself, attacks the serpent; and whatever this attack entails, the serpent strikes back. So God did not prophesy a decisive victory over Satan by a woman, but an indecisive battle between the serpent and her offspring. Although the humanists pointed elaborately and repeatedly to this problem, the Council of Trent continued to follow the Vulgate-version.

Saint Anne and the Humanists

The humanists also looked beyond theology for solutions to the question of Mary's original sin. They found help in the cult of Saint Anne, mother of Mary. At first sight it seems strange that a saint like Anne, more typical of the "Earthmother"-saint, became the object of humanist hagiography and devotion. As has been stressed in recent literature, humanists working in hagiography had been mainly interested in erudite and well-educated saints who could preach up to rhetorical standards, who had literary aspirations, and who did not excel in fantastic miracles.[13] But while Saint Anne seems hardly able to measure up to these conditions of erudition and eloquence, the most common visual representation of Saint Anne as the teacher or *praeceptor* of her daughter Mary, must have been of great appeal to the Dutch humanists for whom teaching was the prime goal of their intellectual ambitions.[14] It was thus that the prominent figures in Dutch humanism, namely Rudolf Agricola, Arnold Bostius, Cornelius Aurelius, and Desiderius Erasmus, dedicated work to her. Rudolf Agricola, the founding father of humanism in the Netherlands from the Northern city of Groningen, wrote a poem *Anna mater*, 310 verses long, which was published in 1483–85 by Richard Paffraet in Deventer. The Carmelite Arnold Bostius, active in Ghent, was the initiator of the *Fraternitas Joachimi* and, as such, organized a poetic competition to promote the cult of Saint Anne and her husband, Saint Joachim. In the nineties the Augustinian canon from Leiden,

Cornelius Aurelius, wrote a huge epos entitled *Marias*, of which the remaining first part includes no less than 5,000 verses, and begins with a *Life* of Saint Anne. Finally Erasmus, in the year 1500–01, sent the poem "*Rhythmus Iambicus in Laudem Annae, Aviae Iesu Christi*," accompanied with a letter, to his patron Anne of Borssele, Lady of Veere.

What is immediately striking, is that all of these writings are similar in form. They are all more or less ingenious long poems in classical meters. The most popular metrical form for religious poetry was the elegiac distich, followed by iambic verse. The language forms were new at the time and were characteristic of Northern humanism. Inspired by the classic poet Virgil and by the Italian humanist Baptista Mantuanus, these Northern humanists dressed their religious themes in an aesthetic jacket of classical Latin. Depending on their literary talent, the individual poets succeeded in this aim. It might be worthwhile to have a look at the form and content of each of their works and see what sort of (mother-) saint they depict in Saint Anne.

Agricola had written other religious poems before he ventured on a poem dedicated to Saint Anne. He wrote on Saint Judocus, Saint Anthony and, as the only female, Saint Catherine, but never before did he make any effort to publish any of these.[15] His poem on Saint Anne proved to be different. At this stage of his life—Agricola was nearly forty years of age—and at a time when all of his humanist colleagues were publishing their poetry, religious or not, he felt the need to prove his own capacity in the field. If his poetry had to be printed, then the best example would be a poem on a fashionable subject of the time. However, Agricola introduced the edition of his poem with the greatest possible modesty. When he mentioned it in 1484 in a letter to his friend Antonius Liber he wrote: "I got the poem '*Anna Mater*' printed, to—in Cicero's words by singing my own praises—collect even more witnesses of my own folly. But why shouldn't I? I don't want to deprive myself and don't feel like letting go of the freedom to let something be heard which is either permitted to everyone or which everyone demands and claims."[16] Written in 1483, this poem was the most voluminous of all, with 310 verses in elegiac distichs. He gave it the simple title "*Anna Mater*," because "it is to her of all who carry the name Anne, we give with the uttermost justice the reverent epithet of Mother."[17]

At this stage, however, every poet or writer who took on the task to write on this female saint was confronted with the problem that hardly anything was known about her. True, a full-fledged life story was provided by the *Evangelia apocrypha*, also summarized in James of Voragine's *Legenda Aurea*; but neither of these could be serious sources for a humanistic poet.

Agricola set to work in another way. According to him, Anne deserved her fame and glory first and foremost thanks to Mary. The opening verses can illustrate this point of departure:

> Anne, mother of the Highest, to be revered procreator of the mother
> Who is the first road to the Salvation for the lost people.[18]

In the forty-five introductory verses which follow, the triad Anne, Mary, and Jesus are hailed. In the narrative part of the poem a few essential facts taken from the *Legenda Aurea* are given which introduce Anne, such as the appearance of Gabriel who prophesies the miraculous late birth of a daughter to the old couple Anne and Joachim. There is no direct mention of Mary's conception. The longest part of the poem is subsequently dedicated to alternating praises of Anne and Mary, in ever different and varied phrases, making 150 verses in total. In the case of Anne, the poet mainly stresses her learnedness; in the case of Mary her virginity. The physical motherhood of both saints was not of interest to the humanist. The view advanced by Brandenbarg in his important book on the late-medieval cult of Saint Anne in the Netherlands and the Rhineland that "the humanist from the North put the accent more on the scholastic-realistic than on the formalistic-aesthetic aspects," is certainly not confirmed by Agricola's poem on Saint Anne.[19] Agricola concludes the poem with a lyrical praise of the healing power of Anne. Here the poet also describes his own recent illness and his ardent invocation of Saint Anne, when he promises her a poem if she helps to promote a quick recovery. The proof of Anne's fortunate intercession is in our hands.

In a vocabulary which is inspired entirely on the classical poet Prudentius and in its masterly verbosity, Agricola's *"Anna Mater"* has little to do with the Saint Anne who was the subject of scholastic and theological disputes about the Immaculate Conception of the Virgin Mary. This theme remains as vague in Agricola's poem as it had been since Augustine. Agricola's Saint Anne is an aesthetic Anne, a sort of unreachable *Magna Mater* to whom the poet declares his platonic love. Any religious or theological inspiration is hidden far under a cover of Latin verbosity. Agricola's poem certainly was not intended to figure in the theological dispute about the Immaculate Conception. Rather; it seems more a proof of his capacity to write humanist religious poetry. His invocation of Anna to heal his illness and the subsequent dedication of his *"Anna Mater"* is in the spirit of classical, Prudentian writing and is not necessarily compatible with Anne's contemporary role as a female saint.

To contrast with the language virtuoso Agricola we can best pose the other great "light" of Dutch humanism, Erasmus, with his poem on Saint Anne. In January 1500–01 Erasmus sent the poem *"Rhythmus Iambicus in Laudem Annae, Aviae Iesu Christi"* to his patron, Lady Anne of Borssele. In the accompanying letter of dedication he wrote:

> Three Annas there were, on whom ancient literature conferred enduring fame: first, Anna who bore the cognomen Perenna and in ancient days was held to have been allowed to join the heavenly hosts for her extraordinary devotion to her sister Dido; next, Hannah the wife of Elkanah, for whose glory it is enough that in her old age, with the blessing of God, she bore Samuel, yet bore him not for herself only, but that he might be a faithful priest to God and serve the people as an upright judge; and lastly Anna, parent to the Virgin Mother and grandmother to Jesus, who was God and Man, so that she at least has no need of further eulogies. The first is immortalized by the poetic muses of Rome. The second receives high praise in Hebrew annals. The third is an object of adoration to pious Christians, celebrated in the eloquent words of Rodolphus Agricola and Baptista Mantuanus. And I would that now my pen too might find skill enough to make posterity aware how devout, how pure, how chaste your soul is, for then it would add you a fourth Anna, to the former three; which will surely come to pass, if my poor talent should but prove equal to your goodness.[20]

With this introduction of an alternative Anna-triad, Erasmus sketched the outlines of his humanistic program, running from classical antiquity, via Old-Testamentary wisdom, to Modern Devotion religiosity. For it was under the influence of the religious teaching of the Brethren in Deventer and his poetry teacher Cornelius Aurelius that he had written the poem on Saint Anne some ten years before. Erasmus wrote his poem probably in 1490–91, after Agricola's poem had appeared. Erasmus's other cited source of inspiration, the *Parthenice Mariana* of Baptista Mantuanus, appeared for the first time in Bologna in 1481 and was reprinted frequently, including in the Netherlands.[21] The exact date of Erasmus's poem is a point of academic discussion, not in the least brought on by Erasmus's own words in the same letter to Anne of Borssele: "I am sending you a version of yourself—another *Anna*—in the shape of a poem, or rather a set of verses which I threw off when I was a mere boy; for ever since my earliest years I have burned with eager devotion to that saint."[22] Although Erasmus pretends he was merely a boy, while writing it, the literary quality of the poem and the religious theme mean that he probably did not write it before 1489. Reedijk, the editor of Erasmus's poems, dates it c. 1489.[23] Vredeveld, who first published corrections on Reedijk's edition and later annotated the English translation of the poems, pleads in the end for a dating in winter 1490–91.[24]

Erasmus, under the influence of his older *praeceptor* ("teacher"), turned to religious themes for his poetry from 1489 onwards, and intended to send these to his former Friar school in Deventer.[25] Whatever caused this thematical turn, it is certainly clear that from a very young age, Erasmus was a most talented Neolatin poet, and that he applied Horatian meter to Christian themes seemingly without any effort. It is equally clear that he had a good feeling for the coming trend and that he was the first in the small circle of learned men in the county of Holland to write a poem on Saint Anne. The work circulated internationally in a collection of poems of different humanists, among them Robert Gaguin and Fausto Andrelini, and was printed by Froben in an edition of Erasmus's *Epigrammata* of 1518. It was also included in other later editions.

It seems that Erasmus himself never sought publicity with this poem, apart from the dedication to his patron lady. This is an exceptional fact in the light of Lisa Jardine's latest picture of the over-publicity-minded Erasmus.[26] Nor did he try with the poem to take a stand in the theological disputes about the Immaculate Conception. The text-critical theologian who translated the New Testament from the Greek in 1515 is not evident in the poem. What is more, he seems a long way from the humanist hagiographer, critically searching his sources, as we know him from his *Vita Hieronymi*, published by Froben in Basel in 1516.[27] Erasmus's sources for his Anna poem were all *Apocrypha*: the *Protevangelium Jacobi Minoris*, the *Evangelium de Nativitate S. Mariae* and the *Historia de Nativitate Mariae et de Infantia Salvatoris*.[28] The issue of Mary's conception, therefore, remains as vague as ever in the poem. Anne and Joachim remained childless and never stopped praying to God to lift this stigma of childlessness. Then an angel appeared who predicted to Anne the birth of a child and Anne became the mother of a daughter, not just any daughter, but a daughter who would bear as a virgin the Redeemer of mankind. For Erasmus the greatest merit of Anne, if we may put it that way, is the fact that she is the grandmother of Jesus Christ and as such an essential building stone in the redemption of men. The opening lines make this clear from the onset:

Salve, parens sanctissima,
Sacra beata coniuge,
Sacratiore filia,
Nepote sacratissimo.

[Hail, most saintly mother,
Blessed in having a holy spouse
An even more holy daughter
A most holy grandchild.][29]

This is a beautiful literary image of the well-known fifteenth-century sculptural image of the Saint Anne Trinity. Thus, for Erasmus, the essence of Saint Anne is not her motherhood and is not the *Anna Magna Mater*, nor the theological problems of original sin and Immaculate Conception, but the relationship between grandmother and grandson. As the title of the poem already suggests: "*Rhythmus Iambicus in Laudem Annae, Aviae Iesu Christi.*" The alternative, humanistic Anna-triad in the letter to Lady Anne of Borssele of 1500–01 had been preceded by a very religious Saint Anne-triad in Erasmus's poem of the late eighties, breathing a simple but thorough and individual religiosity which was clearly inspired by the *Imitatio Christi*-thought of the Brethren of the Modern Devotion. The (grand)motherhood, propagated in this spirit, was one of intimacy and wisdom, both aspects of great importance for the success of the Modern Devotion movement itself.

Arnold Bostius and Cornelius Aurelius

For Agricola, Saint Anne was very much the classical mother-goddess, and for Erasmus, the holy grandmother. With the writings of the remaining couple, however, those of Arnold Bostius and Cornelius Aurelius, we enter a wholly different humanistic program, but nevertheless one which is more familiar in theological terms. In form the poems are, once again, in classical meter. In content, however, the theological question of the Immaculate Conception emerges. Arnold Bostius somewhat combined the two movements, carmelitism and humanism, and was the most important initiator of propaganda for Saint Anne in the Netherlands.[30] In his own writings, however, he took the plea for the Immaculate Conception of Saint Anne a step further and concentrated mainly on the male part in this, Anne's husband, Saint Joachim. On his behalf Bostius organized a poetic competition within the so-called *Fraternitas Joachimi*.[31] Joachim deserved a very high saintly status, according to Bostius, because he fulfilled a role predestined by God and did not interfere at the conception of Mary. In this sense he was very close and directly linked to Jesus Christ. Between Joachim and Christ there was no intermediate; between Anne and Christ there was always Mary. Poor Saint Joseph was completely ignored in this propaganda, but Bostius did succeed in his efforts to award a special position to Joachim within the Carmelite order; from 1498 onwards his feast was officially celebrated within the order.

Finally we come to Aurelius and his great epic *Marias* on Anne, Joachim, Mary and her kinship, written in the years 1495–98. This work was intended for the pupils of the Brethren in Deventer. It is here that humanism and theological education are linked, and that we descend from the literary heights of Agricola and Erasmus to a poetic level that could be followed and emulated by young students. In the prologue to the poem the author exclaims: "Let the learned school of the region of the Almere select me for her teaching!"[32] Aurelius set himself four pedagogical aims: to enforce stylistic imitation, to spread the Immaculate Conception idea, to give a historical dimension to this century-old problem by outlining Mary's ancestry, and, finally, to set a religious example for the boys to live in devotion *and* wisdom.

The complete work of the *Marias* consisted of three decades, or thirty books in elegiac meter, but only the first decade, consisting of roughly 5,000 verses, survives in a manuscript in the Athenaeum Library in Deventer.[33] In a prefatory letter to Jacobus Faber of the Deventer Latin school, Aurelius stated that his poem should be a kind of alternative to the classical profane poetry that was popular at that time with the Deventer schoolboys. At the same time he pretended not to know the most important modern source of his inspiration, namely the *Parthenice Mariana* of Baptista Mantuanus. In this same letter of dedication we read: "At the moment I was writing this letter after having completed the first decade, I got offered the work of an Italian, who under Mary's inspiration, treats the same subject matter as I do. But under the influence of poetic passion he let himself be carried away so far as to become totally oblivious to evangelical simplicity."[34] As has been pointed out clearly by IJsewijn, Aurelius knew the poem of the *quidam Italicus* from the very moment he started writing, and he exploited his model thoroughly in a great number of literal or almost literal borrowings.[35] Some examples can make this dependency clear. Both poets include in their work Mary's genealogy and a description of wall tapestries with some scenes of the Bible story. This is an obvious Christianization and modernization of the description of a shield in classical epics, and similar passages in other poems, such as the description of the bedspread in a major poem of Catullus.

Mary's genealogy is given by Mantuanus at the end of Book I when Mary refuses to marry, in spite of her mother's fervent insistence. Aurelius introduces it at a much earlier stage, immediately after the birth of Mary, and his elaboration has a stronger medieval flavor. Mantuanus inserts the description of the tapestries at the beginning of his poem. They adorn the walls of the house in which Mary is born, and there the visitors admire the Creation, Adam's sin, the Flood and so on. Aurelius in his turn also places the tapestries in the house of Joachim and Anne, but he does not describe them until the moment of the betrothal of Mary and Joseph, thus making a link between her anticipated mother-role and the stories of the Old Testament told on the tapestries. The interdependence of both texts already becomes clear in the opening lines where Anne deplores her childlessness. Mantuanus begins with the lines:

> Anna diu vanos secum ploraverat usus
> Conubi sterilemque torum tristemque Hymenaeum.

> [Anne had long deplored for herself the idle use /
> of her marriage and the sterile bed and the sad union.]

Aurelius condenses these into one line:

> Anna diu vacuos fructu peragens Hymenaeos.

> [For long Anne fulfilled her married life without offspring.]

Despite the obvious influence of the Italian on the Dutch humanist, the latter tried at the same time to make something of his own. It is this intention which can explain his reluctance to admit his debt to his "model." In the introductory letter to Jacobus Faber, mentioned above, Aurelius tries to establish his own position as a humanist, but nevertheless Christian poet: "But let me confess to you and tell it in the most clear way: although there is a great abundance of rhetoric and poetry reaching me, flowing through the broadest veins possible of Minerva, nevertheless I would always prefer to express this history of divine things in clear and commonly used words."[36] This view on the task of the Christian poet is not new; we know the discussion all too well from his correspondence with Erasmus in the year 1489.

There is an interesting set of letters exchanged between the two, the one living in Steyn near Gouda and the other in Lopsen near Leiden. These letters are interesting precisely because they are the first proof that humanism has reached the northern Netherlands.[37] They are also interesting because the young Erasmus acts as an "angry young man" who despises anything on offer in the monastic environment and who adores the writings of Lorenzo Valla. Aurelius acts as the more prudent and the more conservative of the two. He admires the Italian Christian poet, Girolamo Balbi, whom he may have heard as professor in Paris in 1485. According to Aurelius a good poem—he called it *poesis* or *fictio*—had not only external form, that is literal sense, but also content, that is metaphorical sense. A *poeta doctus*, a good poet, must be able to compose a harmonious poem, in which form and content, literal and metaphorical meaning, are clear and in harmony.[38] Otherwise a poet is only a *versificator*, an outrage for one who considered himself a humanist poet. Aurelius stressed the didactic usefulness of the metaphor by referring to the classical writers Strabo and Virgil who "invented fables for the public good."[39] In his answer to Aurelius, Erasmus acknowledges that good poetry should have a profound significance. But for him a *poeta doctus* had to follow the principles of rhetoric and poetics found in the writings of Cicero, Quintilian and Horace.[40] Although Aurelius mitigated his view on classical rhetoric in the course of the 1490s, he stuck to his opinion on the didactic usefulness of poetry for the rest of his life, and we find similar thoughts in the collection of poems called *Psalterium Davidicum*, completed after 1520.[41] All in all, therefore, when he set out with his long epos *Marias* in the nineties, he was likely to have been driven by didactic zeal and pedagogic intentions.

It is in the context of his later poetry that Aurelius expresses his by then infinite admiration for the work of the Italian poet Baptista Mantuanus: "Truly nobody except Baptista Mantuanus can imitate Virgil, Ovid, Horace, and Valerius Flaccus."[42] So his earlier worry in the *Marias* that the Deventer pupils might be set on the wrong path made way for his admittance of a spiritual debt to his Italian contemporary. In fact, theologically, they stood at the same side, although Aurelius seems to be the more polemical in proclaiming Anne's Immaculate Conception of Mary. Joachim is portrayed as a very old man, "bent with years," and although they had wanted children for a long time, they remained childless. "At last the appearance of an angel brought them relief and Saint Anne was fertilized by God's grace."[43] An angel appeared to Joachim and Anne to announce God's gift and to prophesy the great role their child was to play. And indeed, while they slept separately, Anne became pregnant and "that which nature had refused was attained by the childless couple through the prayers of immovable faith."[44]

Aurelius tries to give this theological issue more ground and body by elaborating widely on Mary's genealogy. He is in fact the only Dutch humanist to do so and he seeks a closer connection with the more popular tradition in art and literature on the theme of Mary's kinship. In fact, we could state that in Aurelius' *Marias* Saint Anne comes closest to the type of *Mater familias*, so familiar in late-fifteenth century painting and vernacular literature (fig. 10.3). The difference is that the last category, the vernacular literature, was produced in Dutch cities, among others as an example for families and could have a widespread audience.[45] Aurelius, however, was never successful in publishing his long Latin epic and apart from the pupils in Deventer and Arnold Bostius, to whom he gave a copy, the work was not well known.

In a way, the *Marias* of Aurelius marks an endpoint in the literary relation between the *sancta mater* and the *poetae docti*, the learned humanists of the Netherlands, and Saint Anne does not recur as a theme in Neo-Latin poetry later on. The reason for this is that their campaign had been successful. Anne and Joachim were firmly established as saints in the minds of the Latin elite, the theological issue of the Immaculate Conception had gained new aesthetic, literary, and historical dimensions, and these were to be carried on and elaborated in art.

CONCLUSION

The Neo-Latin poems on Saint Anne had little to say about marriage and family-life, intended as they were for religious, Latin-trained schoolboys and humanists, who preferred to avoid an overly demanding married life.[46] Within the total oeuvre of these Northern humanists the elaborate attention given to a Mother Saint is exceptional and striking. As noted above, Saint Anne did not fall under the criteria for humanist hagiography. Even in the case of a more prolific hagiographer, Cornelius Aurelius, Saint Anne is the exception among his other, shorter poems on virginal martyrs and male learned saints, culminating in a long, elaborate prose *Life* on Saint Jerome.[47] What attracted these humanists to Saint Anne was her stature as a classical *Magna Mater*, and her wisdom. They see her as the first teacher of her daughter Mary, who through her learns to read and at the same time learns of her destiny. The function of the mother as the first and most important teacher and educator of her offspring is a new theme in the humanistic writing of the fifteenth century.[48]

The humanist propaganda on Saint Anne and Saint Joachim was very powerful and had an immediate impact. Saint Anne is pictured and portrayed invariably as a wise woman, reading a book (fig. 10.4). In some respects we can even claim that their propaganda was carried a bit too far with the image of Anne as the type of a classical goddess and of Joachim as a saint near

Figure 10.4. Albrecht Dürer, The Holy Family *with Saint Anne reading a book. Woodcut 1531*

to Christ. In reaction, in vernacular writing the two were brought back to their more human dimensions of Christ's grandparents. It was in the context of the early-sixteenth century secular urban society that the nuclear family became of more interest and that here a different type of Anne and Joachim were cultivated. No wonder, then, that Saint Joseph was also allowed back on the stage (fig. 10.5).[49]

In the sixteenth century, Anne gradually returned to her most original function in medieval devotion, as the patron saint of infertile women. From the early eighth century onwards she was prayed to in Mass by women

---

Figure 10.3 (facing page). Lucas Cranach the Elder, The Holy Kinship. *Central panel: Anne, Mary and Jesus with a sleeping Joseph and the three husbands of Anne in the background; left: Mary Cleophas with Alpheus and their children; right: Mary Salomas with Zebedeus and their offspring. Torgauer Altarpiece, c. 1509 (Frankfurt am Main, Städelsches Museum)*

347

Figure 10.5. Sculpture group of the Holy Family: Mary with a playing child Jesus, Anne teaching from a book and their husbands Joachim and Joseph. Antwerp, c. 1520 (Private collection)

who longed to become mothers and who did not succeed: "Almighty God, Who changed the ceaseless sighing of Anna after she had prayed to you, into happiness, when you made her fertile: have mercy and fulfil the longing of your servant and lift the shame of infertility."[50] This prayer from the collection *Orationes ad Missam pro Sterilitate Mulierum* was one of many, all directed to Holy Mothers. The prayer to Anne is followed by one to Elizabeth, mother of John the Baptist, and one to the Virgin Mother Mary.

The theological discussion on the Immaculate Conception and the humanist poetry on Saint Anne overshadowed this function of the spiritual mother Anne for those who longed to become physical mothers. But infertility is a feature of all times, and in daily religious practice prayers to Saint Anne to lift the shame of infertility never ceased.

When, finally, we return to the panel *Spes Nostra* with which we began this analysis of the holiness of Anne in humanist hagiography, we have a better idea of the relationship and depth of the three scenes. The central scene of the pregnant Mary, visited by Elizabeth, stands for spiritual motherhood, which inspires in the faithful belief and trust. The background scene, where Mary plays with her child in an enclosed garden, stands for the happiness and joy of physical motherhood. Both spiritual and physical motherhood are connected and "translated" into the destiny and salvation of mankind by the foreground scene, where the Church Fathers and regular canons represent the theological knowledge of the Immaculate Conception, and where the corpse can then "rest in peace."

NOTES

1. On this painting: Henk Schulte Nordholt, "Meester van Spes Nostra: Allegorie op de vergankelijkheid," *Openbaar Kunstbezit* (1962), 35; Jeremy D. Bangs, *Cornelis Engebrechtsz.'s Leiden: Studies in Cultural History (ca 1450–ca 1500)* (Assen: van Gorcum, 1979), 23f., 197.

2. "Post dominum tu spes hominum, quos conscia mordet Mens sceleris, quae per Veneris contagia sordet," in Marbod de Rennes (d. 1123), "Stella Maris," in *The Penguin Book of Latin Verse*, ed. Frederick Brittain (London: Penguin, 1961), 189f.

3. Schulte Nordholt, "Meester van Spes Nostra," 35.

4. Bangs, *Engebrechtsz.'s Leiden*, 23f.

5. On the portraits see: Karin Tilmans, *Historiography and Humanism in Holland in the Age of Erasmus: Aurelius and the Divisiekroniek of 1517* (Nieuwkoop: De Graaf Publishers, 1992), 1f.

6. See Ton Brandenbarg, "Saint Anne: A Holy Grandmother and her Children," in this volume.

7. Bert Demyttenaere, "Wat weet men over vrouwen? De vrouw in de duistere Middeleeuwen," in *Vrouw, familie en macht: Bronnen over vrouwen in de Middeleeuwen*, ed. Marco Mostert et al. (Hilversum: Verloren, 1990), 11–47, quoted passage on 40.

8. For a summary of Saint Anne's life see Brandenbarg's contribution on "Saint Anne" in this volume.

9. See Brandenbarg's contribution in this volume.

10. Marina Warner, *Alone of All Her Sex: The Myth and Cult of the Virgin Mary* (London: Weidenfeld & Nicholson, 1976), 238.

11. Augustine, *De Natura et Gratia*, 16, in Augustine, *Opera Omnia*, vol. 7 (Basel, 1543), 731f.

12. M.R. James, *The Apocryphal New Testament* (Oxford: Oxford University Press, 1953), 38–49.

13. Donald Webb, "Eloquence and Education: A Humanist Approach to Hagiography," *Journal of Ecclesiastical History*, 31 (1980), 10–39; Karin Tilmans, "L'hagiographie humaniste aux Pays Bas, 1450–1550," in *Hagiographies: Histoire*

internationale de la littérature hagiographique, latine et vernaculaire, en Occident, des origines à 1550, ed. Guy Philippart (series Corpus Christianorum) (Turnhout: Brepols, to appear).

14. On the representation of Saint Anne in late-medieval art: Pamela Sheingorn, "'The wise mother': the image of St. Anne teaching the virgin Mary," *Gesta*, 32 (1993), 69–80. On the pedagogical character of Dutch humanism see the classical, but unfortunately untranslated study of Pieter Bot, *Humanisme en onderwijs in Nederland* (Utrecht, 1955).

15. Hendrik E.J.M. van der Velden, *Rodolphus Agricola (Roelof Huusman): Een Nederlandsch Humanist der vijftiende eeuw* (Leiden: Sijthoff, s.a. [1911]), 216–220; Pieter Schoonbeeg, "Agricola alter Maro," in *Rodolphus Agricola Phrisius (1444–1485): Proceedings of the International Conference at the University of Groningen 28–30 October 1985*, ed. Fokko Akkerman and Arjo J. Vanderjagt (Leiden: Brill, 1988), 189–200.

16. Letter to Antonius Liber, written Deventer, April 7, 1484 in *Rodolphi Agricolae Phrisii Lucubrationes aliquot . . . per Alardum Aemstelredamum* (Cologne: J. Gymnich, [1539]), 176f.; the quotation is based on Van der Velden, *Rodolphus Agricola*, 217.

17. In a letter to Adolph Rusch, written Heidelberg, October 1, 1484 in Karl Hartfelder, "Unedierte Briefe von Rudolf Agricola: Ein Beitrag zur Geschichte des Humanismus," *Festschrift der badischen Gymnasien, gewidmet der Universität Heidelberg zur Feier ihres 500-jährigen Jubiläums* (Karlsruhe, 1886), 30.

18. "Anna parens summae genetrix veneranda parentis/ Quae pandis populis prima salutis iter," text cited in Schoonbeeg, "Agricola alter Maro," 198.

19. Ton Brandenbarg, *Heilig familieleven: Verspreiding en waardering van de Historie van Sint-Anna in de stedelijke cultuur in de Nederlanden en het Rijnland aan het begin van de moderne tijd (15de /16de eeuw)* (Nijmegen: SUN, 1990), 110.

20. P. S. Allen, *Opus epistolarum Des. Erasmi Roterodami*, vol. 1 (Oxford, 1906), letter 145, 342.

21. Karin Tilmans, *Historiography and Humanism*, 26, n. 66.

22. Allen, *Opus epistolarum*, 1, 345.

23. Cees Reedijk, *The Poems of Desiderius Erasmus* (Leiden: Brill, 1956), 201–205.

24. Harry Vredeveld, "Towards a Definitive Edition of Erasmus' Poetry," *Humanistica Lovaniensia: Journal of Neo-Latin Studies*, 37 (1988), 143f. and *Collected Works of Erasmus: Poems*, 86, annotated by Harry Vredeveld (Toronto: University of Toronto Press, 1993), 407–410.

25. Josef IJsewijn, "Erasmus ex poeta theologus, sive de litterarum instauratarum apud Hollandos incunabulis" in *Scrinium Erasmianum*, vol. 1, ed. J. Coppens (Leiden: Brill, 1969), 375–389; Karin Tilmans, "Cornelius Aurelius (c. 1460–1531), Praeceptor Erasmi?" in *Rodolphus Agricola*, ed. Akkerman and Vanderjagt, 200–211.

26. Lisa Jardine, *Erasmus, Man of Letters: the Construction of Charisma in Print* (Princeton: Princeton University Press, 1993).

27. Cf. Karin Tilmans, "Erasmus and Aurelius and their Lives of Jerome: a Study of Cooperation and Dependence," in *Acta Conventus Neo-Latini Torontonensis: Proceedings of the Seventh International Congress of Neo-Latin Studies* (Medieval and Renaissance Texts and Studies) (New York: Binghamton, 1991), 755f.

28. Reedijk, *Poems of Erasmus*, 202.

29. Ibid., 202f.; *Collected Works of Erasmus: Poems*, 85, trans. Clarence H. Miller, ed. and annotated by Harry Vredeveld (Toronto: University of Toronto Press, 1993), 8f.

30. Brandenbarg, *Heilig familieleven*, 118–122 and *Heilige Anna, Grote Moeder: De cultus van de Heilige Moeder-Anna en haar familie* (Nijmegen: SUN, 1992), 54ff. as well as his contribution to this volume.

31. The poems of this "concours poétique" can be found in Bibliothèque Sainte

Geneviève, Paris, MS 618, fols. 486–497 and MS 1149–1150, fols. 82–86 and fols. 92–93. Cf Tilmans, *Historiography and Humanism*, 27, and Ioan P. Culianu, *Éros et magie à la Renaissance* (Paris, 1984), 83ff.

32. Tilmans, *Historiography and Humanism*, 26, n. 66.

33. Athenaeum Library, Deventer, MS I.31. On this work: IJsewijn, "Erasmus ex poeta theologus;" Tilmans, *Historiography and Humanism*, 25–30; Jozef IJsewijn, "Imitation of Italian Models by Neo-Latin Authors from the Netherlands in the Age of Erasmus," in *Renaissance Culture in Context: Theory and Practice*, ed. Jean R. Brink and William F. Gentrup (Aldershot: Scolar Press, 1993), 157ff.

34. IJsewijn, "Erasmus ex poeta theologus," 384–389. The quoted passage is on 388, par. 23.

35. IJsewijn, "Imitation of Italian Models," 157f; and paper read by Karin Tilmans, "Aurelius, un Mantuanus Olandese?" *XI Congresso Internazionale di Studi Umanistici Piceni* (Sassoferrato, 1990).

36. IJsewijn, "Erasmus ex poeta theologus," 387.

37. Tilmans, "Praeceptor Erasmi," 204f.

38. Allen, *Opus epistolarum*, 1, letter 25, lines 13–48.

39. Ibid., letter 25, lines 37ff.

40. Ibid., letter 27.

41. University Library, Leiden, MS Vulcanius 99, fols. 1–4.

42. Ibid, fol. 2r.

43. Athenaeum Library, Deventer, MS I.31, fol. 10v.

44. Ibid., fol. 12v.

45. See Brandenbarg's contribution in this volume.

46. Cf Eugene F. Rice Jr., "Erasmus and the Religious Tradition, 1495–1499," in *Renaissance Essays*, ed. Paul Oskar Kristeller and Philip P. Wiener (Library of the History of Ideas, 9) (New York, Rochester Press, 1968, rpt 1992), 162–186 and Catrien G. Santing, "Femme fatale, femme savante, femme absente, wie is de ideale vrouw voor de geleerde in de renaissance?" in *Utopische voorstellingen van het sekseverschil*, ed. Wendy Schutte et al. (Vrouw'n, letter'n, Groning'n, 3) (Groningen: Athena, 1989), 132–140.

47. A good impression of Aurelius' hagiographic interest we find in University Library, Leiden, MS Vulcanius 66, fols. 73–126 with poems on six female and seven male saints: Mary, saintly personifications of *Natura* and *Gratia* (Nature and Grace), Hieronymus, Livinus, Bernardus of Clairvaux, Maria Magdalena, Agnes, Adelardus, Dimpna of Geel, Alexius, Reinerus and Franciscus. On his *Vita Gloriosi Jheronimi*, kept in Deventer, Athenaeum Library, MS I.32 see: Tilmans, "Erasmus and Aurelius," 755–765.

48. See also in general: *A History of Women in the West 2: Silences of the Middle Ages*, ed. Christiane Klapisch-Zuber (Cambridge Mass: Belknap Press, 1992) 123ff, 297f, 399f. From an art-historical point of view: Sheingorn, "The Wise Mother," 69–80.

49. See Brandenbarg's contribution in this book.

50. Cited by Edvard O. van Hartingsveldt, "De schande van onvruchtbaarheid," in Mostert et al., *Vrouw, familie en macht*, 72f.

EPILOGUE

Epilogue

Clarissa W. Atkinson

Over 2,000 years of Christian history, motherhood has been regarded as both holy and profane, at once a sacred calling and a role and status inferior to virginity. The complex and ambiguous relationship of motherhood to holiness is shaped in part by the models of sanctity available in particular geographical and chronological contexts. The editor and authors of this volume of essays identify and interpret certain specific intersections of holiness and motherhood in northern Europe in medieval times, deepening our appreciation of the religious and cultural ideals and realities of both maternity and sanctity in that place and time.

In her thoughtful introduction, Anneke Mulder-Bakker makes a useful distinction between "mother saints"—notably the Virgin Mary and Saint Anne, but also certain legendary women—and "holy mothers," those female parents whose faith and deeds were noted, remembered and recorded in *vitae*. Saint Anne and the Virgin obviously have had enormous influence on Christian motherhood: their central roles in the history of salvation make these towering figures unique. Their well-documented cults and rich life-stories—"essentially phantasms," according to Mulder-Bakker—require special investigation. Their history is entirely relevant to but distinct from that of the "holy mothers" whose image and experience we attempt to tease out of recalcitrant sources—for the most part, *vitae* composed by men who did not necessarily value human motherhood or take it seriously.

In the early Middle Ages, married women were not often counted among the saints. Among the small number of wives whose holiness achieved recognition was an even smaller number of mothers, "honored . . . despite rather than because of their children." In that period the preeminent Christian mother, Mary, served as a model not only or especially for mothers, but for all women—notably, in fact, for consecrated virgins who bore the spiritual fruit so highly valued by St. Jerome and other Fathers. Motherhood, in its ordinary form too closely associated with the material world of sex and property, was frequently demeaned or spiritualized. Essays by De Nie and Van't Spijker illustrate the prejudice in favor of virgins, considered "better" than wives and mothers by influential Christian clergy and theologians. The holy motherhood of the later Middle Ages was a *new* phenomenon: after about the thirteenth century, for certain women of the upper classes, marital and maternal status not only did not preclude holiness, but actually provided a public stage for saintly behavior. The diachronic range of this volume allows us to see very clearly that neither motherhood nor sanctity is fixed or "natural": definitions of good mothers as well as of saints are no more static than the social, economic, political and intellectual environments in which they exist and are continually remade.

Historical work on motherhood requires careful examination and analysis of broad issues of family, sexuality and marriage. The essays illustrate significant change as well as continuity in the social, economic and religious meanings of "family" over the medieval period. In the early Middle Ages, at least in the aristocratic world, "family" included many kinds of relationships through blood and marriage, established and maintained by women as well as men. In the early period, too, distinctions between family and church were not as sharp as they became in the wake of the Gregorian Reform in the eleventh and twelfth centuries. Ineke van't Spijker points out that as founders and members of monastic institutions, noble families dominated cloisters and convents that tended to become "part of the family;" children raised within such institutions held their places among temporal as well as spiritual kin. We discover in these essays a narrowing of the meanings of "family" from wide and varied ties of kinship to households headed by a married pair.

Mulder-Bakker argues that social and religious changes after the twelfth century involved not only the appearance of "holy mothers," but the increasing influence of lay people in Christian ideologies and institutions. With the growth of cities and an urban middle class, the lives and interests of lay people, more and more of whom were now literate, were reflected in texts that purveyed models of sanctity. The essays illustrate laicization in various religious phenomena, including the Beguine movement and the late medieval cult of Saint Anne as well as a broader respect for and attention to marriage and parenthood on the part of preachers and theologians.

Despite that increased respect, tension between the roles of saint and wife persisted in the later Middle Ages. Saintly women still were not expected to be *happily* married: the ancient prejudice against sexual passion and physical ease mitigated against too much enjoyment of married life. The strict obligations of the married state, upheld by Church and clergy, tended to limit the options for holiness of both partners, but especially of women; most of the holy mothers were widows, or arranged with difficulty to live apart from their husbands. (Sanctity, or in any case the recognition of sanctity, among single mothers was and is extremely rare. With a very few exceptions such as Margaret of Cortona, an unmarried woman with a child was much more likely to be designated a "harlot" than a saint.) Some married women became holy *in spite of* their status as wives and mothers; suffering of many kinds could be transformed into sanctity. Nip's discussion of Godelieve of Gistel tells an extraordinary story of the construction of martyrdom through domestic violence. We are reminded by Mulder-Bakker, Petrakopoulos and Nieuwland that even for more fortunate women such as Ivetta of Huy, Elizabeth of Thuringia and Birgitta of Sweden, the loss of virginity could cause great unhappiness; conflict and ambivalence did not vanish with holy motherhood. Birgitta's care for and Christian instruction of her children were represented as exemplary, but such virtuous behavior did not make her a saint; that status was derived from her relationship with Christ and Mary, not with husband and children. Only exceptional qualities and circumstances allowed some extraordinary mothers to overcome the many obstacles to sanctity.

It is appropriate that this volume begins and ends with Saint Anne, whose cult flourished in art and devotion in the later Middle Ages. For many reasons, explored along different lines by Brandenbarg and Tilmans, the stature of Christ's grandmother kept rising in northern Europe during late medieval times. Anne was a prominent figure in the discourse of moralists and humanists who promoted her cult along with their special domestic and educational agendas. The new bourgeois family of late medieval and early modern Europe held a respected place for the wise old grandmother—anti-type of the horrifying, family-destroying witch of the same era. Anne was the sponsor of married people, helper of infertile women, model teacher of the young. In her analysis of the sixteenth-century painting *Spes Nostra*, Karin Tilmans presents Saint Anne as the focal figure of an iconographic resolution of physical and spiritual motherhood. The saint and her cult hold more than one key to difficult, persistent questions about the relationship of holiness and motherhood in the Christian Middle Ages.

The central role and omnipresent image of Christ's mother, unlike that of his grandmother, is not thoroughly examined (although frequently invoked) in these essays: the *lacuna* may indicate a promising direction for further research and analysis. The lives, legends, and aspirations of all Christian women were shaped in significant ways by the image and adoration of Christ's virgin mother, but her cultural and devotional role is not yet well understood or fully explicated in feminist scholarship. Our increasingly extensive and nuanced appreciation of the holy mothers, and especially of the cult of Saint Anne, ought to provide a solid basis for investigation of the complex and difficult history of the figure and cult of the Virgin Mary.

For readers in the United States, one of the intriguing questions raised by this volume concerns the relationship of historical work to gender analysis as a broad theoretical category. Unlike many American historians of women, these authors do not work *primarily* with gender as a theoretical analytical tool. In the tradition of European historical scholarship, they begin with texts—with hagiographic, literary and artistic representations of female sanctity—and with text criticism. Their findings and interpretations make important contributions to discussions of gender, but the writers do not necessarily pursue all the theoretical implications of their work. There are exceptions: the papers by Samplonius and De Nie, for example, explicitly address not only the status of women, but the cultural construction of the "feminine" in ancient Germanic and Latin societies. Their material lends itself to, or even demands, such interrogation; Samplonius is concerned with explicitly "female" powers of divination as represented in pre-Christian Germanic texts, while De Nie examines transformations of Christian symbols "from male fighter to spiritual bride-mother." I do not wish to exaggerate the contrast with American feminist scholarship. There is substantial overlap and an important common bibliography; these authors make excellent use of the work of Caroline Walker Bynum, among others, on religion and gender. (Bynum, of course, is herself a medievalist, and we should not be surprised that the writings of Joan Scott and other feminist theorists of historical deconstruction outside the medieval field have been less influential.) However, even minor differences in assumptions and starting-points will enrich the discussion on both sides of the Atlantic.

This volume is a significant entry in a dialogue arising out of our increasingly sophisticated attempts to discover the history of women, to take motherhood seriously as a historical phenomenon and construct, and to enrich both the history of religion and the history of the family by examining their intimate and important connections over time. Those who work in these areas welcome these essays with enthusiasm and look forward with interest and excitement to the continuation of the dialogue.

Contributors

CLARISSA W. ATKINSON is associate dean for academic affairs and senior lecturer in the history of Christianity at the Harvard Divinity School. Her publications include *The Oldest Vocation: Christian Motherhood in the Middle Ages* (1991) and *Mystic and Pilgrim: The* Book *and the World of Margery Kempe* (1983).

TON BRANDENBARG is director of the Rijksmuseum Meermanno-Westreenianum/ Museum of the Book in The Hague. His publications on Saint Anne include *Heilig Familieleven: Verspreiding en waardering van de Historie van Sint-Anna in de stedelijke cultuur in de Nederlanden en het Rijnland aan het begin van de moderne tijd* (1990).

ANNEKE B. MULDER-BAKKER is senior lecturer at the University of Groningen. Her thesis *Vorstenschool: Vier Geschiedschrijvers over Alexander en hun visie op het keizerschap* (1983) and several articles focused on medieval historiography. She is preparing a book on hermits and anchorites in the Low Countries.

GISELLE DE NIE is senior lecturer at the University of Utrecht. Her publications on Gregory of Tours and the Merovingian period include *Views from a Many-Windowed Tower: Studies of Imagination in the Works of Gregory of Tours* (1987).

RENÉE NIP teaches at the University of Groningen. She focuses on the hagiography of the High Middle Ages and just completed her Ph.D. on the Flemish Saint Arnulf of Soissons.

JEANNETTE NIEUWLAND studied history and Swedish at the University of Utrecht. She published "Birgitta's View on Marriage: Theory versus Practice," in *Birgitta, hendes vaerk og hendes klostre i Norden*, ed. Tore Nyberg (1991).

ANJA PETRAKOPOULOS studied at Smith (B.A.) and at the University of Amsterdam (doctoraal geschiedenis). She is now a history teacher at the International School Eerden and prepares a Ph.D. on Dutch Saints' Lives of the Early Renaissance.

KEES SAMPLONIUS studied old Germanic and Scandinavian languages at the University of Amsterdam and graduate courses in Icelandic Literature and Linguistics at the University of Iceland at Reykjavik. He published on Eddic poetry.

INEKE VAN'T SPIJKER lectures at the Universities of Groningen and Utrecht. Her publications include *Als door een speciaal Stempel: Traditie en vernieuwing in heiligenlevens uit Noordwest-Frankrijk (1050–1150)* (1990).

KARIN TILMANS lectures at the University of Amsterdam. She published on late-medieval historiography and hagiography, among which *Historiography and Humanism in Holland in the Age of Erasmus: Aurelius and the Divisiekroniek of 1517* (1992).

DATE DUE

			Printed in USA